from Continuum

Contemporary Culture, edited by Rachel Carroll

: A Reader's Guide, Gregg A. Hecimovich

ub & Armchair Companion to Jane Austen, Douglas Buchanan, Kelly
arol J. Adams

of Jane Austen in Europe, edited by Anthony Mandal and Brian

Nigel Boonham, *Jane Austen in Heaven*, 2010. Plaster, 0.67 m. © 2011 Artists Rights Society (ARS), New York/DACS, London. Sculpture displayed at Winchester Cathedral June–August 2010 as part of "In This Sacred Place," an exhibition of works by the Society of Portrait Sculptors.

Everyb

Everybody's Jane
Austen in the Popular Imagination

Juliette Wells

continuum

Continuum International Publishing Group

The Tower Building   80 Maiden Lane, Suite 704
11 York Road   New York
London SE1 7NX   NY 10038

www.continuumbooks.com

British Library Cataloguing-in-Publication Data
A catalogue record for this book is available from the British Library.

ISBN: 9781441145543 (paperback)
        9781441176547 (hardcover)

Library of Congress Cataloging-in-Publication Data
Wells, Juliette, 1974-
  Everybody's Jane : Austen in the popular imagination / Juliette Wells.
     p. cm.
  Includes bibliographical references and index.
  ISBN 978-1-4411-7654-7 (hardcover) – ISBN 978-1-4411-4554-3 (pbk.)   1.   Austen, Jane, 1775-1817–Appreciation. 2.   Austen, Jane, 1775-1817–Influence. 3.   Austen, Jane, 1775-1817–Adaptations. 4.   Austen, Jane, 1775-1817–In mass media. I. Title. II. Title: Austen in the popular imagination.
  PR4037.W457 2011
  823'.7–dc23

              2011025052

Typeset by Fakenham Prepress Solutions, Fakenham, Norfolk NR21 8NN
Printed and bound in India

Dedicated with love to Rodney, Lucy, and Eric
and in memory of Frederick A. Klemm

I *have* lost a treasure, such a Sister, such a friend as never can have been surpassed,—She was the sun of my life, the gilder of every pleasure, the soother of every sorrow, I had not a thought concealed from her, & it is as if I had lost a part of myself. I loved her only too well …

Cassandra Austen to Fanny Knight, July 20, 1817

A good reader also creates.

Sheenagh Pugh, *The Democratic Genre: Fan Fiction in a Literary Context* (2005)

Contents

Acknowledgments

My heartfelt gratitude to all those who contributed to this book:

First and foremost, my husband, Rodney Yoder, and our delightful children, Lucy Yoder-Wells and Eric Yoder-Wells, who assisted especially in my literary tourism research. Thanks to my parents, Virginia and William Wells, to my late grandfather Frederick A. Klemm, and to all the Wells, Wells-Dang, Yoder, and Yoder/Leupen families for their support.

My students and colleagues at Manhattanville, where my ideas about Austen and popular culture have had the chance to grow. Special thanks to the English department and the Office of the Provost for course development, research, and publication support.

The visitors to Jane Austen's House Museum in Chawton during July 2009 who thoughtfully answered my questions about the experience of their visit and what Austen means to them. At the museum, special thanks to Louise West, Ann Channon, Madelaine Smith, and Tom Carpenter, and to all the staff and volunteers who generously shared their impressions with me.

At Goucher College, Nancy Magnuson, Tara Olivero, Sandy Ungar, Kate Dannals, and Cassie Brand. I gratefully acknowledge Goucher's Jane Austen Scholar-in-Residence Program, which made possible my research in the Burke Collection and JASNA archives.

The many members of JASNA who have listened, encouraged, and offered ideas, including Susan Allen Ford, Marsha Huff, and Alice Villaseñor; in the New York metropolitan region, Joyce Melito, Nili Olay, Elsa Solender, Kerri Spennicchia, and Jerry Vetowich; in Rochester, NY, Celia Easton and Edith Lank; in the Ohio North Coast region, Amy Patterson and Jennifer Weinbrecht; in Ottawa, Emily Arrowsmith. I gratefully acknowledge JASNA's Traveling Lecturer program, which made possible my presentations at several regional meetings, as well as the International Visitor Program fellowship, which supported my research in Chawton,

Colleagues in the world of Austen studies who have offered encouragement and feedback on work in progress, and who have generously shared their own work, especially Rachel Brownstein, Gillian Dow, Marilyn Francus, Katie Halsey, Clare Hanson, Felicity James, Deidre Lynch, Mary Ann O'Farrell, and Kathryn Sutherland; as well as participants in the "Jane Austen and Contemporary

Culture" study day and "New Directions in Austen Studies" conference at Chawton House Library, and attendees at meetings of the Northeast Modern Language Association and British Women Writers Association.

All those who have shared with me their expertise with Austen and the Austen industry, as well as stories of being inspired by her, including Nigel Boonham, David Baldock, Andrew Honey, Perri Klass, Sheila Solomon Klass, Catherine Medeot, Philip Nathan, Jason Rekulak, Lori Smith, Dom Nicholas Seymour, and Ben H. Winters.

Friends who have kept me in touch with Austen manifestations, especially Eva Geertz, Daniel Fogg, Rachel Lewis, Matt Pearson, and Edie Stern; and Bliss Temple, with whom I first visited Chawton.

For opportunities to speak and write about Austen for a popular audience, Elda Rotor of Penguin Classics, the staff of Masterpiece, the Morgan Library & Museum, and the White Plains Public Library.

The teachers and professors with whom I had the good fortune to study Austen: Erica Jacobs, Mary Poovey, Frances Ferguson, Avrom Fleishman, Sandra Macpherson, and Jill Campbell. Special thanks to Linda Peterson for her mentorship and to Ruth Bernard Yeazell for first pointing me towards JASNA and popular culture.

Hearty thanks to this book's editorial and production team: Colleen Coalter, Anna Fleming, Rachel Eisenhauer, David Avital, Kim Storry, and Sandra Stafford.

Finally, I gratefully acknowledge that some of the material included in this book appeared in earlier form as the following:

"Austen's Adventures in American Popular Fiction, 1996–2006." In "New Directions in Austen Studies," edited by Susan Allen Ford and Gillian Dow, special issue, *Persuasions On-Line* 30.2 (2010). http://www.jasna.org/persua sions/on-line/vol30no2/wells.html.

"The Closeness of Sisters: Imagining Cassandra and Jane." *Persuasions On-Line* 30.1 (2009). http://www.jasna.org/persuasions/on-line/vol30no1/ wells.html.

"From Schlockspeare to Austenpop." In "Shakespeare and Austen," edited by Lisa Hopkins, special issue, *Shakespeare* 6:4 (2010): 446–62.

"Jane Austen in Mollywood: Mainstreaming Mormonism in Andrew Black's *Pride & Prejudice* (2003)." In *Peculiar Portrayals: Mormons on the Page, Stage, and Screen*, edited by Mark T. Decker and Michael Austin, 163–82. Utah State University Press, 2010.

"Seeking Austen, from Abroad: Lori Smith's Memoir *A Walk with Jane Austen* (2007)." In "Austen Abroad," special issue, *Transnational Literature* 1.2 (2009). http://dspace.flinders.edu.au/dspace/bitstream/2328/3412/1/Seeking%20 Austen.pdf

"Shades of Austen in Ian McEwan's *Atonement*." *Persuasions* 30 (2008): 101–11.

"True Love Waits: Austen and the Christian Romance in the Contemporary U.S." In "The Global Jane Austen," edited by Susan Allen Ford and Inger Sigrun Brody, special issue, *Persuasions On-Line* 28.2 (2008). http://www.jasna. org/persuasions/on-line/vol28no2/wells.htm.

Chapter 1

Introduction: Approaching Austen in the Popular Imagination

What does Jane Austen mean to you?

Visitors to Jane Austen's House Museum in Chawton, Hampshire, offered these replies.

Probably one of the greatest female novelists.

Woman, 40s, from New Zealand

A fantastic author who wrote one of my favourite books: *Pride and Prejudice*!

Woman, 18–24, from Australia

Jane Austen represents the ideal woman. Unusual of the time, she was able to create a life without a husband and felt no obligation to perform the expected female duties. I find her very inspiring.

Girl, under 18, from the US

Someone with whom I feel I have a lot in common! I appreciate her humour in her novels.

Woman, 40s, from the UK

She was a great writer—teaches me/us about being a human being.

Woman, 50s, from Denmark

I love her work, although I have never read her novels, the dramatisations are fantastic. This encourages me to read them.

Girl, under 18, from the UK.[1]

Do any of these answers sound like one you would give? Would you think, as did the first person I quoted, about Austen's place in literary history as a woman writer? Or would you concentrate, like many of the other respondents, on the personal significance that Austen has for you? Is your knowledge of Austen based on reading, or, like that of the last person I quoted, based on your familiarity with adaptations of her works?

How you answer that simple question—"What does Jane Austen mean to you?"—can reveal a great deal about you, including why you read, how you think about the importance of your reading, and why you would choose to spend time with the works (or adaptations of the works) of an English author who died in 1817. Your answer is likely to be affected by your age. If you are school or college age, your most recent encounter with Austen may well have taken place in the classroom, and hence may not have been of your choosing. (Or, perhaps equally likely, your most recent encounter with Austen may have taken place online, as would be comparatively less common for your elders.) Your answer is also likely to be affected by your gender, since women more than men tend to gravitate towards novels, and adaptations of novels, by women. Did you notice that everyone I quoted was a woman or girl? So were 75% of the visitors I surveyed at Jane Austen's House.

None of the visitors I quoted is a literary scholar. If you are a literary scholar, would you answer or avoid a question about what Jane Austen means to you? You might answer such a question, but only off the record, lest your colleagues hear you speaking in a way that seems unprofessional. In order to maintain the status of literature as a subject worthy of university-level study and research, professors tend to be very invested in emphasizing theoretical, historical, and cultural approaches to literature, rather than the kinds of personal reactions offered by the visitors I surveyed. After all, a literary scholar might well think, anyone can be "inspired" by Jane Austen, but how many people can undertake really groundbreaking research on her writings?

The "Everybody" in *Everybody's Jane*

Austen's popularity began to surge in 1995, thanks to the release of several screen adaptations of her novels. In that year, I was a college student majoring in English who had had only moderate exposure to Austen's writings. I had read *Emma* in high school, thanks to a very forward-looking AP English teacher, and had read *Northanger Abbey* for a college course on the history of the English novel. Since my housemates and I didn't have cable television, I missed the broadcasts of the enormously popular miniseries version of *Pride and Prejudice* that starred Colin Firth;[2] I caught up with that adaptation years later. Instead, I encountered the feature film *Sense and Sensibility*, starring Emma Thompson, Hugh Grant, and Kate Winslet.[3] *Sense and Sensibility* the novel was unknown to me at the time. Indeed, while I would later study *Persuasion* in college and *Mansfield Park* in both college and graduate school, and while I would write a dissertation chapter on Austen, I never studied *Sense and Sensibility* or *Pride and Prejudice* in the classroom. Nor, unlike so many Austen fans, did I pick up *Pride and Prejudice* on my own or at the urging of a friend or relation. Instead, I read that novel when I was studying for my doctoral qualifying exams—which, I have to say, did not lead to a rapturous experience with what is certainly Austen's most enduringly popular work. ·

The *Sense and Sensibility* film, on the other hand, made a deep impression on me. I loved it. I couldn't tell you now just why that was so. I might not have been able to articulate a reason even at the time, since I don't remember having a good answer when my college boyfriend teased me about walking miles to the discount cinema to see the film again and again. I enjoyed other 1990s Austen films, particularly *Clueless* with Alicia Silverstone and *Persuasion* with Amanda Root and Ciaran Hinds, but *Sense and Sensibility* was the one that really did it for me.[4]

I mention the appeal to my younger self of the *Sense and Sensibility* film as a way of including myself in the "everybody" embraced by this book's title. I participated in Austen's popularity long before I thought of studying it. Having been an enthusiast myself, I treat with sympathy and respect those whose encounters with Austen take place outside of the classroom, and whose activities inspired by her writings take forms other than academic work. The experiences and ideas of those everyday readers, not mine, are the subject of this book.[5]

I have taken my title, *Everybody's Jane*, from a much-quoted derogatory comment by Henry James. Decrying the commercialization of Jane Austen in 1905, James criticized "the body of publishers, editors, illustrators, [and] producers of the pleasant twaddle of magazines[,] who have found their 'dear, our dear, everybody's dear, Jane so infinitely to their material purpose, so amenable to pretty reproduction in every variety of what is called tasteful, and in what seemingly proves to be saleable, form."[6] From James's phrase, I have dropped the "dear," which no longer universally pertains in an era when Jane Austen and her heroines are imagined as having been alternately vivacious, fierce, lusty, and weary. The space between "Jane" in my title and "Austen" in my subtitle plays with the ways in which this author is referred to today. Fans generally use her first name, as if she is a friend or even a family member, while scholars use her last name, as would be the case with any author, regardless of gender. For the sake of clarity, I will refer to her as "Austen" except when differentiating among members of the Austen family; I will refer to fictional and cinematic depictions of her as "Jane."[7]

Today, the commercialization of Austen and the market value of her name far exceed what Henry James found so objectionable.[8] Of course writers, publishers, film producers, and tourist industry professionals seek outlets for their ambitions in the Austen brand and attempt to trade on its value. How could they not? Such trading only works, however, if readers, audiences, and visitors are willing to give their attention, and their money, to Austen-related material—as has proved true repeatedly since 1995. Austen's ever-growing popularity and market share encourage writers, dramatists, and composers to create new versions of her novels; publishers to release new books; producers to green-light new screen and stage adaptations; museums and cultural destinations to inaugurate new exhibits; and tour operators to design new trips. These opportunities to interact with Austen both feed the interest of existing fans and attract the attention of new audiences, who—if hooked—will in turn seek out information and experiences that enhance their appreciation of Austen's works. Participating in the world of commerce is one way for fans to perpetuate, and deepen, their sense of connection to Austen and to each other.

My aim in *Everybody's Jane* is to look beyond the best known, most highly promoted elements of the "Austen industry" to investigate how ordinary people think about Austen today, and why they find it rewarding to do so. For every sensationally hyped new work derived from an Austen novel, plenty of low-key Austen-oriented occasions take place, and countless readers have thought-provoking, meaningful, or inspiring experiences that relate to Austen in some way. The "everybody" I have in mind includes people who read Jane Austen's writings and books about her, as well as people who only watch films or consume fiction based on her novels or on accounts of her life. I have in mind people who read on their own and people who seek out communities of fellow enthusiasts, either online or in author societies. People who travel only in their imaginations, and people who are literary tourists to Austen-related sites. People who enjoy collecting rare editions of Austen, and people who collect modern sequels to her writings. People who write introductions to Austen's novels designed for novices, advice literature derived from Austen, and romance or horror that takes off from Austen— and who then post these materials online, self-publish them, publish them with small presses, or publish them with major houses. Actively engaging with and responding to Austen's writings in different modes—modes that include but are not limited to the literary—each of these readers is the "good reader [who] also creates," to adapt the declaration by Sheenagh Pugh that stands as the second epigraph to this book.[9] These readers' thoughts about and perceptions of Austen, collectively, comprise what I mean by "the popular imagination."[10]

Everybody's Jane even deals, albeit to a lesser degree, with people who don't particularly like Austen, or who come to her with initial reluctance. Such is Austen's prominence in today's popular culture that people can sometimes feel embarrassed about not having read her, or by having read her (or viewed a screen adaptation) and not seen what the point was. Jane Austen is not, in fact, for absolutely everybody. Men in particular are underrepresented among today's lovers of Austen, a fact that is especially striking given what vocal male partisans she has had in the past.[11]

My phrase "everybody's Jane" recalls, and deliberately departs from, Rudyard Kipling's well-known 1926 description of Austen as "England's Jane."[12] Popular audiences around the globe certainly associate Austen strongly with ideas of Englishness. Her achievement as an English stylist and her importance to the English novel tradition are emphasized in literature and language classrooms worldwide. For those who do not encounter Austen in school, the impression of her as an English writer is reinforced by screen versions of her novels that saturate the viewer in English accents, period costumes, landscapes, architecture, décor, and manners.[13] Austen's English identity is underscored, too, for those literary tourists of international origins who visit sites related to her life and works. Seeking Austen, in a geographical sense, requires traveling to (or within) England. Yet Austen's subject matter resonates well beyond her nation and period. Audiences around the world respond appreciatively to her depictions of such topics as difficult family relationships, journeys of self-discovery, and cultural imperatives to marry. Austen's own life story as an unmarried woman author also holds broad appeal.

A major focus of mine in this book is Austen appreciation in the US, which is exceptionally wide and varied—and has yet to be investigated in depth.[14] In Chapter 2, I explore the writings and collection of Alberta H. Burke, which shed light on the extraordinarily personal significance of Austen's writings to a woman whose own identity—twentieth-century, American, Jewish, married, wealthy, university-educated—distinguishes her considerably from the author to whom she was devoted. My sixth chapter examines the exceptionally inventive hybrid versions of Austen's works created by Americans, most famous of which is *Pride and Prejudice and Zombies* (2009);[15] much less well known are the approaches to Austen's novels by American evangelical Christians, which I also treat. While the original UK Jane Austen Society, founded in 1940, has been much studied, the same is not true of the Jane Austen Society of North America, the founding (in 1979) and early years of which I consider in my last chapter. How American Austen fans compare with their counterparts from other nations emerges from my other chapters, which integrate material from the US, UK, and beyond. My survey at Jane Austen's House Museum, in particular, offers insight into international visitors' impressions of Austen, as expressed in their own words.

Even with a primarily American focus, it would be impossible to offer a fully comprehensive, up to date account of popular responses to Austen's writings and behavior inspired by them. Such is the extent of interest in Austen that coverage of fan fiction sequels to *Pride and Prejudice* alone would require volumes. Austen-inspired books and films continue to be released at ever-decreasing intervals, and of course Austen-related blog and YouTube postings accrue daily. I have chosen to analyze representative sources that illuminate the behavior of everyday readers. Since each popular evocation of Austen and her world reworks earlier depictions, I devote particular attention to very recent sources that respond to the successful feature film *Pride & Prejudice* (2005), the biographical film *Becoming Jane* (2007), and *Pride and Prejudice and Zombies* (2009).[16] Treatments of Austen's world in the late 2000s and early 2010s are growing ever more ingenious—and sometimes gleefully outrageous—as creators attempt to stake original claims on imaginative territory that is already quite crowded.

Austen's popularity did not begin in 1995, of course. The first sequel to Austen's novels authored by a devotee, Sybil G. Brinton's *Old Friends and New Fancies*, appeared in 1914.[17] The first feature film Austen adaptation, *Pride and Prejudice* with Laurence Olivier and Greer Garson, was released in 1940;[18] as a result, Austen books aimed at popular audiences flourished in the following decade. As I have mentioned, the UK Jane Austen Society was founded in 1940, and Jane Austen's House was opened to the public in 1949. My second chapter, on the American Austen collector Alberta H. Burke, offers a vantage point on Austen-love in the mid-twentieth century, as practiced by a woman whose omnivorous enthusiasm for Austen anticipated that of today's fans. The early years of the Jane Austen Society of North America, which I consider in my final chapter, also shed light on relations between Austen scholars and amateurs in the decades prior to 1995.[19]

My first epigraph to this book, an excerpt from Cassandra Austen's letter in which she describes her sister's death and articulates her own grief, points to the connections that exist between Austen's earliest devotees and those today. Cassandra's eloquent expression of her love for her sister mattered deeply to Alberta Burke, who, as I discuss in Chapter 2, bought and treasured this very letter in the mid-twentieth century. Present-day audiences encounter Cassandra's moving sentiments in biographical fiction and films that depict the Austen sisters (which I treat in Chapter 5) as well as in exhibits that allow a direct encounter with the letter or a facsimile.[20]

The question "Why Jane Austen?" has been insightfully addressed by a variety of thinkers in recent years, most recently Rachel M. Brownstein.[21] Reasons for Austen's enduring popularity will emerge in this book through the voices of her devotees. Overall, however, the "why" question concerns me less than *how* Austen has been put to use by her present-day readers. Asking why Austen interests readers today leads to a limited number of answers: e.g. romance plots, strong women characters, humor, morality. In contrast, asking how Austen matters brings into view a seemingly limitless inventiveness.

In another sense, the question "Why Jane Austen?" could be taken to mean, "Why pay attention to Austen's popularity in particular?" After all, we are in the midst of a vogue for re-imagining the inner lives, as well as the literary creations, of our canonical authors, from Shakespeare to the Brontës to Dickens and beyond. As has often been said, our postmodern age revels in reinvention and mash-up, generic hybridity and boundary crossing.[22] What's special about Austen? Can we prove that her popularity exceeds that of any other author of "classic" literary works? Of course not. What we can do is attend to the astonishingly extensive and varied landscape of her influence, which demonstrates the fecundity of the popular imagination as well as the peculiar, and apparently unstoppable, pull of Austen upon that imagination.

Austen's presence in contemporary popular culture has often been remarked upon and occasionally surveyed, but not, until now, fully explored.[23] *Everybody's Jane* is the first book to take into account, and take seriously, the great variety of ways through which people engage with Austen today. Scholars, of course, value reading Austen's writings as the most direct form of engagement with her; the study of adaptations of her writings, especially on screen, is also well developed. Yet to be considered in depth and without disparagement, however, are other ways that those outside the academic or literary world might encounter Austen, such as by watching a biographical film, reading a book of advice drawn from her novels, visiting a tourist site, or participating in a Jane Austen society. By applying theories and methods from both within and outside the discipline of literary criticism, we can study the attitudes and behaviors of these everyday readers—as well as the texts and places through which they encounter Austen—without veering into ridicule on the one hand or uncritical celebration on the other.

When a non-academic reader does sit down with a work by Austen, that person's experience of reading may have little in common with the interpretation performed by a scholar. Rather than pointing out "misreadings" or denigrating personally applied (as opposed to analytical) responses, it is essential that we take each reader's account *on its own terms*, asking what she or he seeks through contact with Austen, and what she or he finds. If we evaluate non-academic approaches according to scholarly standards, or if we dismiss those whose literary knowledge is less than or different from our own, we will not appreciate fully what Austen means to readers today.[24] For literary scholars like myself, adopting this non-judgmental vantage point requires a conscious, and sometimes considerable, effort. Austen as she variously appears in the popular imagination may resemble not at all the Austen whose writings we know. We must set aside our professional assumptions and adopt new paradigms and methods of inquiry that allow the voices of amateur readers to be heard, rather than solely our own voices—or even Austen's voice, as we experience it in her fiction and letters.

Non-academic readers are not only the subject of *Everybody's Jane* but, I hope, a large part of this book's audience as well. By writing about the reading experiences and behaviors of ordinary people in an accessible way, I aim to bridge the gap between amateur and scholarly readers. These two groups are often mutually dismissive, suspicious, even hostile, and the differences between them have been exacerbated by the anxieties of each. It is hardly surprising that traditional scholars find much to mock and even to find offensive in popular approaches to canonical texts, which revel in the freedom to be irreverent, selective, and anachronistic. Nor is it an accident that amateur readers can feel intimidated and alienated by the discussions of academics. Using jargon, theory, insider references, and a critical tone that can sound disparaging enables literary scholars to bolster the institutional prestige of their own profession and to set a clear boundary between the initiated and the uninitiated.

I have done my best in *Everybody's Jane* to steer clear of these professional tactics, while still treating my subject matter in a manner that makes a substantial contribution to our understanding of the popular Austen today.

To help meet the expectations of different groups of readers, I have adopted the following strategies. I will err on the side of quoting liberally from sources, out of courtesy to those who are interested in but not well acquainted with the academic disciplines that converge in a study of literature and popular culture, as well as those less familiar with popular Austen material. For the sake of those who are not at all interested in academic sources, I will make clear, near the beginning of each chapter, which section or sections will deal primarily with such material; I will also include publication dates in the text proper, out of courtesy to those who are curious about what came when, but who do not relish footnotes. With non-academic readers in mind, too, I have been somewhat more selective in references to previously published scholarship than I would have been if writing solely for an audience of fellow academics.

In the next section of this chapter, I show how my approach to Austen in the popular imagination both builds on and departs from the work of earlier scholars in this recently established, fast-growing field. I then introduce critical tools from related areas of literary and cultural study that help us investigate Austen's presence in the popular imagination. I consider first what the long established field of Shakespeare and popular culture has to offer Austen scholars. Next, I present theories from the disciplines of literary criticism, sociology, and cultural studies that illuminate the behaviors and activities of today's everyday readers in general, and Austen enthusiasts in particular. I conclude with an overview of the specific topics I treat in the chapters that follow.

As long as Jane Austen's novels have existed, they have been read and appreciated by a wide variety of people, from supposedly "uneducated" women—like Austen herself[25]—to distinguished literary men, and everyone in between. Yet, as Judy Simons argued in her influential 1998 article "Classics and Trash: Reading Austen in the 1990s," "in distinguishing between reading communities, the history of Austen criticism has created a tension in reading practices between the academy and the amateur or casual reader. Universities professionalize reading strategies and determine ownership of critical skills, which tends to demote the 'common' reader to the margins as an uninitiated amateur. One of the most pertinent debates in Austen studies today relates to the construction of these reading communities and the mantle of privilege they assume."[26] Thinking about what Austen means to people today helps us look beyond the differences between those inside and outside the academy, to remember that literature belongs to every curious reader, and to appreciate how all kinds of imaginations find inspiration in Austen's works. By investigating with open minds how ordinary people encounter Austen, we gain an unprecedented view of the significance of reading and of "classic" literature in our own era.

Establishing a Field of Study in Austen and Popular Culture

Everybody's Jane joins a growing area of scholarship on Austen that concerns the study of adaptations, and more broadly the reception of Austen by her readers from her own lifetime till today. This field of study gained credence and momentum in the 1990s, just as—and in part because—Austen's popularity crested during those years. As literary scholars use the term, "reception" incorporates reactions ranging from privately recorded responses to public appraisals, and from the very personal to the self-consciously critical.[27] Reception history encompasses all readers, regardless of age, educational level, status, or motive for reading. Moreover, the idea of reception is flexible enough to address, in addition to reading itself, actions taken as a result of reading (such as conversing, corresponding with, or meeting in groups of fellow appreciators) as well as activities inspired by one's reading (such as travel or creative writing). Reception, in other words, includes not only the process of taking in one's reading but also the process of responding to that reading. Related to reception studies is "reader-response criticism," an area of literary criticism that, as its name suggests, investigates how and why readers respond to texts as they do.[28] In the last section of this chapter, I will identify concepts from reader-response criticism that are especially helpful to us as we approach Austen's popular appeal today.

The first scholar to devote attention to Austen adaptations was Andrew Wright, whose "Jane Austen Adapted" appeared in a special issue of the academic journal *Nineteenth-Century Fiction* published to commemorate the bicentennial of Austen's birth in 1975. While Wright's "annotated list of adaptations, school editions, and performances" is valuable,[29] his critical approach to those sources demonstrates the disdain that, for decades, had caused scholars to ignore popular material. Not surprisingly, Wright prizes fidelity to Austen's text: "The closer the rendering to the words of Jane Austen the better," he declares, since "no one writes Jane Austen so well as Jane Austen. Any tinkering means a change for the worse."[30] And though Wright does single out representative quotations and elements of many adaptations, overall he asserts that "protracted analysis of each adaptation would be tedious and is, in my opinion, unnecessary, since the problems of abridgment and simplification remain stubbornly similar from novel to novel and year to year."[31]

That knowledge of Austen ought to include awareness of reworkings was reinforced in 1982 by David Gilson, whose monumental *Bibliography of Jane Austen* included sections on "dramatisations" and "continuations and completions" as well as more standard bibliographical lists of original and subsequent editions of Austen's actual novels.[32] Like Wright, Gilson manifests obvious distaste for popular treatments: he asserts the "virtual impossibility of catching or imitating the style of the classic novelist" and comments that "having never seen a stage performance of any of these plays, I cannot judge of their dramatic qualities; but the texts read uniformly badly. The authors generally feel compelled to meddle with what dialogue JA provides and to make additions of their own in quite uncharacteristic vein, besides doing frequent violence to the plots."[33] In Chapter 2, I will have more to say about Gilson and his friendship with the American collector Alberta H. Burke.

Roger Sales's *Jane Austen and Representations of Regency England,* published in 1994 with a new edition in 1996, was the first critical study to include substantial discussion of Austen adaptations.[34] We can see from Sales's two publication dates that he both anticipated and quickly responded to the boom in Austen films that took place in 1995. The new afterword, subtitled "Austenmania," that Sales wrote for his 1996 edition offers a detailed and thoughtful consideration of the international fervor ignited by the 1995 miniseries version of *Pride and Prejudice.*[35] Prophetically, Sales ventures that "it is quite possible that this already extremely intense level of interest in [Austen's] life and works will actually increase."[36] Sales's most important contribution, however, was to begin his study by considering how others, post-Jane Austen, have represented her. "The origins, growth and remarkable survival of the Austen industry are complex cultural developments," he claims.[37] In his usage, though he never defines the term precisely, "the Austen industry" encompasses all efforts to comment on and interpret Jane Austen, including everything from her family members' reminiscences in the nineteenth century to popular-audience books and television serials in our own era, as well as the work of scholarly critics. In this capacious sense, rather than the narrower commercial context in which the phrase is often used, "the Austen industry" today is the subject of *Everybody's Jane.*

Sales further distinguishes himself from his predecessors (and certain of his successors) in Austen studies by offering a resounding defense of the study of Austen in popular culture. In contrast to Wright and Gilson, who disparaged Austen-related popular texts even as they collated bibliographical references to them, Sales asserts that "popular modern texts are relevant to the academic study of Austen since readers construct an idea of the author, and therefore of her works and their historical period, from the materials that are readily available within a particular culture at a particular time. It would be very arrogant indeed to assume that all those who teach or study Austen are necessarily exempt from, rather than implicated in, this cultural process."[38] In *Everybody's Jane,* I follow Sales in focusing on materials (including activities) that are popular in the sense he uses the term, of "readily available," rather than popular in the more limited sense of being widely known. I accept, too, his contention that those who study and teach about Austen participate crucially in the cultural process by which readers form their conceptions of her; throughout this book, I will call attention to the involvement of scholars in the promulgation of popular ideas about Austen.

That Austen herself took a keen interest in the views about her work expressed by her family and close friends is evident from her letters and especially from two lists, in her own handwriting, of opinions that she solicited about *Mansfield*

Park (1814) and *Emma* (1815). These private opinions of Austen's first readers were included by Brian Southam in his two-volume collection of criticism, *Jane Austen: The Critical Heritage*,[39] and are often reprinted in classroom editions of *Mansfield Park* and *Emma* alongside extracts from more highbrow criticism. Until recently, scholars considered these lists essentially an amusing index of how Austen's intimates judged her work. (For instance, Austen recorded that her mother did not like *Mansfield Park* "so well as P. & P.—Thought Fanny insipid.—Enjoyed Mrs. Norris."[40])

A turning point came in Laura Fairchild Brodie's 1995 article "Jane Austen and the Common Reader: 'Opinions of *Mansfield Park*,' 'Opinions of *Emma*,' and the Janeite Phenomenon." Brodie argues that these private opinions, when viewed through the lens of reader-response theory, "offer a rare glimpse into the reading habits of Austen's popular audience—'popular' not in the sense of a mass, working-class readership but referring to those 'everyday' enthusiasts, primarily women, who were central to the novel's success as a genre."[41] In addition to "reclaim[ing] the voice of the female amateur in Austen's early reception," Brodie persuasively connects to the behaviors of Austen fans today what she calls the "family-circle model of response" evident among Austen's original readers.[42]

I pick up from Brodie in focusing centrally on today's amateur readers, who—like those who shared their thoughts with their friend and relation, Jane Austen—are "everyday enthusiasts," without professional training or credentials, and who remain predominantly women. To minimize repetition, I will refer interchangeably to those who read for pleasure as "amateur readers" and "everyday readers"; if I am placing emphasis on forms of interpretation that take place outside scholarly norms, I will refer to "non-academic readers." To avoid potentially misleading connotations as well as vagueness, I will steer clear of several terms frequently employed by literary critics: "common reader," "lay reader," "general reader," and "middlebrow reader."[43] I will refer to "Austen fans" or "Austen lovers" when I wish to include, as well as readers, those who are interested in films and popular works derived from Austen's novels.[44]

The term "amateur" is especially valuable for several reasons. As opposed to terms like "non-academic" and "non-professional," which define a reader by what he or she is not, "amateur" is a positive term: "one who loves or is fond of; one who has a taste for anything," according to the word's first definition in the *Oxford English Dictionary*. Of course, the word "amateur" carries an additional, potentially pejorative, meaning: as the *OED*'s second definition runs, an amateur is "one who cultivates anything as a pastime, as distinguished from one who prosecutes it professionally; hence, sometimes used disparagingly, as = dabbler, or superficial student or worker."[45] When I refer to an "amateur reader" or an "Austen amateur," I intend no disparagement; I mean someone who loves books, or who loves Austen, and who cultivates that love as a pastime rather than a scholarly profession. Of course, a reader can simultaneously be a literary amateur—as distinct from a literary scholar—and also a published writer or creator.[46]

In 1996 and 1997, even as Austen film adaptations continued to accrue and popular attention directed towards Austen became ever more intense, two groundbreaking, complementary treatments of Austen and popular culture were published: Deidre Lynch's "At Home with Jane Austen" and, in the *Cambridge Companion to Jane Austen*, Claudia L. Johnson's "Austen Cults and Cultures."[47] In "At Home with Jane Austen," Lynch contributes to reception history by considering in depth Austen's cultural and literary status in England between the two world wars, or, as she phrases it, "the ideological work of Janeisms in interwar England."[48] Lynch treats such varied material as the formation of the Jane Austen Society in 1940; the conversion of Austen's last home, Chawton Cottage, into a tourist destination; the Regency romances of Georgette Heyer; detective fiction, including that of Dorothy Sayers; critical appraisals by eminent writers and scholars; and the place of novels, including Austen's, in university curricula. I take Lynch's study as a model for my own investigation of comparable topics in the post-1995 period. I will discuss the kinds of scholarship and fellowship fostered by author societies, principally the Jane Austen Society of North America, in Chapter 7. Austen-oriented literary tourism, which is no longer limited to Chawton Cottage, is my subject in Chapter 4. Chapter 6 deals with reworkings of Austen material into popular genres, including Christian romance and horror.

In her enormously influential essay "Austen Cults and Cultures," Johnson turns critical attention to Austen as a cultural icon, both in historical terms and in the present day. Approaching Austen as "a commercial phenomenon and a cultural figure," Johnson considers "not Austen's works *per se*, but our reception of them, the ideas about culture Austen has been thought to represent, and the uses to which we have put her and her achievements."[49] In addition to articulating the rationale for studying Austen's traces in popular culture, Johnson offers acute, appreciative attention to amateur reading practices. "So short [is] our institutional memory about the history of novel criticism itself," declares Johnson, "that we have forgotten that there are other ways to read." "The very different reading traditions of the Janeites" (Austen fans) are not only, claims Johnson, worthy of scholars' study but "can accordingly now enrich our own."[50]

Having, with Johnson, collectively set the agenda for the emerging field of Austen reception studies, Lynch firmly established that new field with her edited volume *Janeites: Austen's Disciples and Devotees* (2000), which includes essays on aspects of Austen's popular and scholarly reception from her lifetime till the 1990s films.[51] *Janeites* places particular emphasis on the formation and defense of Austen's literary reputation in the nineteenth and early to mid-twentieth centuries. In the view of many of Austen's scholarly supporters, this process of canonization was complicated by her gender, the genre in which she wrote (with the novel having a much shorter and less elevated literary pedigree than drama or poetry), and the tendency of her works to be beloved by popular readers. As Lynch asserts in her introduction to *Janeites*, "the worry that Austen has been afflicted by the wrong sort of popularity seems a backhanded acknowledgment of the tenuousness of the boundaries between elite and popular culture, and between the canonical and the noncanonical."[52] Thus the history of Austen's reputation casts light not only on her status today, both among academics and amateur readers, but on the history of the division between those two groups.

According to Lynch, the term "Janeite" does not straightforwardly identify lovers of Austen's writings. Instead, she argues, "this is the term that Austen's audiences have learned to press into service whenever they need to designate the Other Reader in his or her multiple guises, or rather, and more precisely, whenever they need to personify and distance themselves from particular ways of reading, ones they might well indulge in themselves. 'Janeite' can conjure up the reader as hobbyist—someone at once overzealous and undersophisticated, who cannot be trusted to discriminate between the true excellence of *Emma* and the ersatz pleasures of *Bridget Jones's Diary*."[53] Calling someone else a Janeite, in other words, says as much about you as about the person you're discussing. In *Everybody's Jane*, I will avoid the term "Janeite" altogether, except when referring to readers—such as Alberta H. Burke, in Chapter 2—who embrace the term themselves. Throughout, I will pay close attention to how lovers of Austen choose to identify themselves, as well as how they speak about those with whom they feel they share, and lack, common ground.[54]

The 1990s wave of Austen screen adaptations, which received attention in portions of *Janeites* and in Sales's *Rewriting the Regency*, fully came into their own as material for scholarly consideration in several essay collections published at the turn of the millennium. Leading the way was *Jane Austen in Hollywood* (1998; second edition in 2001), edited by Linda Troost and Sayre Greenfield, which was followed by John Wiltshire's *Recreating Jane Austen* (2001); *Jane Austen on Screen* (2003), edited by Gina Macdonald and Andrew F. Macdonald; and *Jane Austen and Co.: Remaking the Past in Contemporary Culture* (2003), edited by Suzanne R. Pucci and James Thompson.[55]

Jane Austen in Hollywood set the standard for subsequent analysis of the 1990s Austen-based films by investigating what it took for those adaptations to be, as Troost and Greenfield put it, "culturally successful."[56] "What," ask Troost and Greenfield, "in Jane Austen's novels has made them so readily adaptable to film in the 1990s and exactly what changes have they required to be successful in this period?"[57] Rather than faulting the adaptations for failure to live up to Austen's novels, as many critics and reviewers have done, the contributors to *Jane Austen in Hollywood* approach adaptations with an understanding that, as Troost and Greenfield put it, "translations too faithful to the books cannot achieve broad enough appeal for the movie industry, even if we could agree what 'faithfulness' to Austen might mean."[58] In other words, an adaptation created to appeal to a wide audience must, by definition, rework Austen's texts; the useful questions to be asked are how and with what effects the adaptation does so.

Troost and Greenfield emphasize as well the importance of examining how each new version of Austen reflects the desires of viewers, as those desires are imagined, if not necessarily shared, by the version's creators. "These adapta-tions," conclude Troost and Greenfield, "have more to tell us about our own moment in time than about Austen's writing. In watching them, we watch ourselves."[59] As we will see, this fundamental insight holds true for popular interpretations of Austen's novels beyond the screen medium. In every genre, representations of Austen's characters—and especially representations of Austen herself as a character, my subject in Chapter 5—hold up a mirror to readers' own wishes.

In several senses, and in different ways, *Recreating Jane Austen, Jane Austen on Screen*, and *Jane Austen and Co.* take a broader approach than does *Jane Austen in Hollywood* to the phenomenon of Austen's popularity on screen in the 1990s. Many of the essays collected in *Recreating Jane Austen* and *Jane Austen on Screen* analyze the 1990s versions in relation to the history of Austen adaptation—a history that, in the absence of significant prior critical work, these scholars also actively fill in. *Recreating Jane Austen*, while primarily focused on films, takes up other instances of what Wiltshire calls the "remaking, rewriting, 'adaptation', reworking, 'appropriation', conversion, mimicking" of Austen's works;[60] a particularly thought-provoking chapter, titled "Imagining Jane Austen's life," treats biography as a form of adaptation. Nearly half of the *Jane Austen and Co.* essays, too, range beyond Austen and film to other examples of the reinvention of the past for contemporary audiences. All three of these books shed new light on Austen's popularity by bringing in disciplinary perspectives beyond literary criticism. In *Recreating Jane Austen*, Wiltshire applies the psychological theories of D. W. Winnicott, while both *Jane Austen on Screen* and *Jane Austen and Co.* include the work of scholars who are specialists in French literature, film studies, cultural studies, or geography.

My approach in *Everybody's Jane* is influenced by all four of these turn-of-the-millennium studies of Austen's popularity. I am not, however, chiefly concerned with analyzing screen adaptations in relation to their source texts. Rather, I will consider how popular adaptations have contributed to ideas about Austen and have inspired fans' activities, behaviors, and creations.

Kathryn Sutherland's *Jane Austen's Textual Lives: From Aeschylus to Bollywood* (2005) has had a profound impact within Austen studies, including but not limited to reception history and the study of popular culture. *Jane Austen's Textual Lives* centers on, in Sutherland's words, "the ways in which Jane Austen is transmitted and transformed through texts: her manuscripts, the early published volumes, modern editions, biographies, continuations and film versions."[61] In Sutherland's groundbreaking investigation of the historical and cultural context surrounding biographies of Austen and editions of Austen's novels, she exposes more fully than has any prior scholar the roles Austen's family members played in propagating (and suppressing) ideas about her life in the nineteenth century, as well as the role of Austen's first scholarly editor, R. W. Chapman, in promulgating ideas about her writings as texts. Reworkings of Austen's writings in our own era are, comparatively, a more minor preoccupation for Sutherland. Indeed, in *Everybody's Jane* I take up where Sutherland leaves off, by considering how popular texts, and behaviors, in our own day continue to "transmit and transform" Jane Austen. I follow Sutherland, too, in taking as my primary focus "the role of interpretation in the production of meaning and the survival of culture."[62] Indeed, I will approach all versions and responses to Austen's novels as forms of interpretation.

The steadily growing importance accorded by Austen scholars to reception history and popular culture is evident from the tables of contents of two recent compendia that survey the landscape of Austen studies.[63] *Jane Austen in Context* (2005), edited by Janet Todd for the nine-volume *Cambridge Edition of the Works of Jane Austen*,[64] includes essays by Deidre Lynch on the "Cult of Jane Austen" and on "Sequels";[65] the latter is especially noteworthy as a scholarly, comparative treatment of fiction based on Austen's novels. Most recently, *A Companion to Jane Austen* (2009), edited by Claudia L. Johnson and Clara Tuite, devotes its substantial final section to the topic of "Reception and Reinvention," an umbrella that includes both historical and contemporary treatments of Austen's influence.[66] Of particular note within that section are essays by Judy Simons and Mary Ann O'Farrell. In "Jane Austen and Popular Culture," Simons focuses on what she calls "Austen's assimilation into the popular imagination" and her status as a "cultural icon."[67] In Chapter 6, when I treat versions of Austen's novels that are infused with unexpected elements such as horror, I will build on Simons' claim that the "cultural hybridity" of works that update Austen's material to our own day acts as "both their subject and their tribute to Austen."[68]

In her essay "Austenian Subcultures," O'Farrell argues that "a set of readily identifiable Austenian subcultures, in the presentation of their public faces, may be mappable along a continuum from a barely broken isolation to companionship on full display."[69] The concept of the continuum is helpful as well for approaching the broader topic of Austen's appeal to readers today. A continuum allows us to think in terms of degrees of difference and overlap among groups of readers, as well as in terms of movement from one identity to another. The concept of the continuum is especially crucial to my final chapter, in which I examine recent fictional depictions of Austen fans and consider the importance of the Jane Austen Society of North America as an organization hospitable to both amateurs and scholars.

Before Jane, There Was William

When, in 1994, Roger Sales urged Austen scholars to pay serious attention to popular sources, he followed in the footsteps of Shakespearean scholars, who had for several years asserted the importance of studying popular responses to and recreations of their own author. Shakespeare's influence on and appearances in popular culture continue to be the most widely studied and most thoroughly theorized of any canonical author's.[70] The field of Shakespeare and popular culture thus has much to offer Austen scholars who seek tools for approaching the ever increasing and highly varied material inspired by her.[71]

It is crucial to acknowledge upfront some of the significant differences between Shakespeare and Austen, both as authors generally and in terms of their traces in popular culture more specifically. At the risk of stating the very obvious, Shakespeare and Austen differ principally in terms of their gender; the centuries in which they lived; the amount that is known about their lives and, in Shakespeare's case, the existence of controversy over his identity; the literary genres to which each made a major contribution; and the nature of their authorship, given those genres.

In particular, present-day responses to Austen are affected very differently by gender than are present-day responses to Shakespeare. Consider Julie Sanders's argument about how contemporary women writers of literary fiction interact with Shakespeare's works: "Women writers frequently 'talk back' to Shakespeare, to use [Margaret] Atwood's phrase, questioning the silence or marginalization of female characters, according voices or rewriting endings, and even providing explanatory prequels to events. The act of engagement is rarely passive; Shakespeare is not invoked simply as an authenticating male canonical presence in these works but, rather, as a topos to be explored, dissected, and reconfigured as much as any other."[72] Austen's present-day admirers certainly explore, dissect, and reconfigure her life and fiction, and it is common for such rewriters of Austen to elevate her minor characters to starring roles and to experiment with both sequels and prequels. Because the majority of present-day lovers of Austen are women, and because their appreciation of her novels stems in part from her depictions of women's lives, however, these writers inspired by Austen do not "talk back" to her so much as converse with her.

As with gender, genre has consequences for how popular rewriters frame their works in relation to those of their beloved author. Issues arise when respondents to Shakespeare's plays choose to write in prose that do not arise in the same way in the Austen context. Indeed, Austen, best known for her prose, inspires primarily prose:[73] novels, predominantly, as well as variants of the prose forms—advice writing and memoir—that are evident in Austen's letters. The three prayers attributed to Austen have also been crucial to contemporary Christian readers' representations of her, as I will discuss in Chapter 6. As in the case of Shakespeare, however, those who seek either to parody Austen's fiction or to raise eyebrows by infusing it with horror face the challenge that Austen has already made use of such genres, most obviously in her juvenilia and *Northanger Abbey*.[74] I will address the recent spate of Austen/horror hybrids in Chapter 6.

A crucial difference between Shakespeare and Austen lies in how their audiences encounter their works. In our era, unlike earlier ones, young people do not typically elect to read Shakespeare on their own. Gary Taylor asserts that "Shakespeare is now usually read 'without any other reason than the desire' for a passing grade . .... And that very imposition of a text itself creates resistance to it. As a result, even when Shakespeare is taught, he doesn't stick. People don't internalize him, the way they used to."[75] Marjorie Garber contends that the choice is still made to read Shakespeare, but for purposes often quite distinct from academic literary study: "Shakespeare's plays are probably read and studied more, these days, *before* and *after* college—in high school and in reading groups, extension courses, lifelong learning and leadership institutes, and in the preparation of audiences attending play productions—than during the four years of traditional undergraduate college education."[76] In contrast, while Austen's novels certainly continue to be taught at all levels around the world, many fans and authors of Austen-inspired books remember first encounters with her works that took place outside the classroom, and Austen continues to be extracurricular reading for many of these fans into adulthood. Unlike the involuntary study of Shakespeare depicted by Taylor or the voluntary but non-academic forms of reading described by Garber, Austen's novels continue to be enjoyed, remembered, and shared by a wide variety of individual readers. If Austen is indeed "everybody's Jane," she is so because her texts have been embraced, not imposed upon, the masses. Her novels *do* "stick," to use Taylor's word, and both her characters and language—particularly from her most popular novel, *Pride and Prejudice*—certainly continue to be internalized by her readers.

Shakespeare scholars have offered several valuable general guidelines for approaching popular sources based on canonical literary works. Richard Burt has coined the term "Schlockspeare" to encompass what he calls "mass media as trash, kitsch, obsolete, trivial, obscure, unknown, forgotten, unarchived, beyond the usual academic purview."[77] While Burt defends the importance of taking seriously sources that are often irreverent and can be ill-informed, he cautions scholars that "total coverage" of this popular material is "impossible to achieve," and he further warns against "sheer description of the material."[78] I have taken Burt's warnings to heart in focusing *Everybody's Jane* on representative examples of Austen's presence in popular culture rather than attempting to be comprehensive. I follow Burt, too, in stressing analysis rather than description of popular sources.

Within the broad category of "Schlockspeare," Laurie Osborne points out that "there is trash Shakespeare and there is trash Shakespeare that attempts to distinguish itself from trash Shakespeare."[79] As Osborne reminds us, it is crucial to consider, in every case, how a popular source presents itself in relation to other popular sources, as well as in relation to the source text or texts. Such presentation involves the content of the work proper as well as efforts to position it by its creator and its distributor or publisher. In the case of printed books, such efforts are visible in prefatory or appended author's notes or acknowledgments, as well as in the book's cover, title, and publicity, including blurbs found on the back cover or first few pages.

Osborne calls attention too to a common failing manifested by Shakespearean scholars who turn to popular culture, a failing that is certainly evident among Austen scholars as well. Scholars tend, declares Osborne, to intervene in popular culture more selectively, and with less academic rigor, than when conducting more traditional forms of research—even though many questions about popular culture lend themselves very well to investigation along traditional lines. "When we explore the appearance of Shakespearean plots, language, or artifacts in mass culture," Osborne contends, "we risk letting our investment in Shakespeare supersede the very concerns of context, production, and reception on which we would insist if we were analyzing a particular Shakespearean production or edition. ... Pervasive Shakespearean allusion in a specific text always exists within the interaction of genres, publishers, and readers."[80] Osborne's reminders are decidedly applicable to the realm of present-day popular works derived from Austen; I will pay especial attention to the matrix of genre, publishing, and reception when considering Austen hybrids in Chapter 6. Important too is Osborne's call for comparative study: "If we consider Shakespearean allusions in isolation or only in the context of the current abundance," she warns, "we risk missing how very differently Shakespeare can function even in mass cultural forms that seem highly conventional and similar."[81] New versions of Austen's writings have too often been addressed in isolation, or in relation to one or two similar versions. A broader frame of reference yields deeper insights.

Douglas Lanier cautions that popular sources must be taken on their own terms, with reference to popular rather than scholarly expectations and conventions. "One of the foundational axioms of the popular aesthetic," Lanier argues, is "the continuity of biography and art. It is beside the point, then, to chastise popular representations of Shakespeare for their myriad and often willful factual inaccuracies, for they are less concerned with historical fidelity than with the ideological work of servicing, extending, reorienting, and at the same time drawing upon Shakespeare's inherited cultural authority, one of pop culture's most valuable resources."[82] That popular creators make different uses of canonical texts than do scholars, claims Lanier, results not from those creators' ignorance but from their deliberate choices, choices that moreover lead to distinctive effects: "Refusing the academic imperative to 'read closely' is often the point, a source of anarchic pleasure. ... Popular citations, with their concern to make Shakespeare speak to some aspect of everyday life, reject the fidelity and decorum that govern 'proper' Shakespearian interpretation. Their impertinence is the source of the fun."[83]

Lanier argues in particular against scholars' tendency, when dealing with popular sources, to use as "a stubbornly powerful evaluative criterion" the idea of fidelity to the source text.[84] Lanier urges us to widen our gaze: "given its deeply ambivalent relationship to Shakespearian language, Shakespop typically aims for fidelity elsewhere, in Shakespearian motifs, plot structures, characters, thematics, even atmosphere. Holding Shakespop to a standard of textual fidelity may blind us to other principles of fidelity at work, as well as productive relations other than fidelity."[85] The criterion of fidelity can lead, as well, to defenses and debates that make little contribution to the wider field, as scholars choose their own favorite examples of popular texts that, in their view, achieve a greater degree of fidelity than others and thus merit more attention. To move beyond "the complaint (or delight) that popular appro-priations aren't really Shakespeare or distort the true meaning of the text" is, according to Lanier, to appreciate that "these works open the question of what is 'really Shakespeare' and who gets to determine it."[86] Throughout *Everybody's Jane*, accordingly, my attention will remain on how, why, and with what effects present-day readers reconceive of Austen and her works. Levels, and percep-tions, of faithfulness and accuracy will concern me only insofar as they concern those who create, promote, and consume versions of Austen.

Diana Henderson offers a caution against another possible scholarly approach, one that veers too far away from analysis towards appreciation or enjoyment of popular sources. "To simply celebrate Schlockspeare," argues Henderson, can "serve as a form of scholarly evasion, a refusal to address the difficult question of value in a world where the sheer quantity of Shakeschlock as well as Bardolatry could fill (or waste) a lifetime."[87] While I will steer clear of making explicit value judgments about Austen-based works, the extent of attention that I give each source will indicate my sense of its importance to the field. In accordance with my intention of avoiding the mockery in which scholars often take refuge, I will stress what is original and thought provoking about each popular source, rather than seeking material to criticize. I bear in mind too the caution of cultural studies scholar Matt Hills against what he calls "scholarly 'distant reading' ... as academics write in a cursory, nondetailed, and dismissive manner about ... [media] they feel an aesthetic distaste for."[88]

Pertinent to the Austen realm, and to my project in *Everybody's Jane* especially, are the efforts of Shakespearean scholars to bridge gaps between groups with differing claims on Shakespeare. As in the case of Austen, these gaps result from the gradual professionalization of literary study (although the Austen world has no counterpart to the controversy about Shakespeare's identity, a controversy that draws particular energy from amateur readers). According to Lanier,

> In the last century, custodianship of the historical Shakespeare has become the province of professional scholars. ... Largely displaced has been the popular scholarship of the nineteenth century with its close ties to journalism and amateur antiquarianism. ... Contemporary Shakespeare studies have been progressively cordoned off from the public and reshaped into a disci-plinary expertise that wields considerable institutional authority. Part of the attraction of anti-Stratfordianism, then, is that it provides an avenue of resistance to the authority of a certain professional class, a resistance focused on Shakespeare because there remains the residual sense that of all writers

Shakespeare ought to be common cultural property rather than the domain of specialists.[89]

Those outside the institutional authority of Austen studies have indeed found ways, if not to "resist" that authority, then to counter it with endeavors of their own. Participants in author societies and other gatherings of Austen aficionados grapple with, and in some cases act out their commitment to, the idea that Austen too "ought to be common cultural property rather than the domain of specialists." The tensions that result from such competing claims on behalf of Austen, and the self-definitions of those who speak on her behalf, are crucial to analyze. As Graham Holderness, a founder of the field of Shakespeare and popular culture, has asked, "Is it possible for one Shakespeare to be everybody's? Or are some Shakespeares actually impossible to reconcile with those of others?"[90]

Referring to a particular rift that does not exist in the Austen context, Diana Henderson calls on "those currently on opposite ends of the academic/theater divide" to recognize the common ground between their endeavors as well with the work performed by tourist sites such as Shakespeare's Globe.[91] Austen scholars too share more than some might like to admit with museum professionals and tourist-site operators who present Austen to a popular audience. I will bear Henderson's admonition in mind when analyzing Austen tourism in Chapter 4.

Reading "Like a Woman," Reading for Self-Improvement, Reading Like a Fan

Rita Felski has recently urged literary critics to "engage seriously with ordinary motives for reading—such as the desire for knowledge or the longing for escape—that are either overlooked or undervalued in literary scholarship."[92] *Everybody's Jane* answers Felski's call. This final section of my introduction highlights some important recent work from both within and outside literary criticism that helps us examine the motives and activities of Austen's amateur readers. Just as valuable as the content of this research are the methods employed by the scholars, which go beyond traditional textual analysis and archival research, as well as the attitudes these scholars take towards popular culture, everyday readers, and fans.

Within literary criticism, the subdiscipline of reader-response criticism offers several helpful models for studying the behavior of amateur readers. Here is how one reader-response critic, Anne G. Berggren, describes her own approach to reading:

A passionate reader, a reader constantly immersed in novels, I've never been able to separate reading from life. I've identified—and wept over—characters in fiction. ... I've turned to fiction for clues on dealing with sex, raising children, and other important aspects of life. I've reread novels obsessively and longed for sequels to tell me how the characters turned out and what happened next. When I entered a doctoral program in English and education at the age of fifty-two, I noticed immediately that my lifelong reading practices—personal, accepting, emotional, addictive—contrasted sharply with the critical, cognitive approaches to novels that my more recently trained fellow students employed.[93]

As Berggren learned more about the history of reading, and in particular the tradition of disparaging attitudes towards women's reading habits, she came to think of her own reading style as being representative of her gender. Hence she adopted the phrase "reading like a woman" to cover the "personal, accepting, emotional, addictive" consumption of novels she engaged in herself. And, having herself found such an approach to be "positive, indeed life-sustaining," Berggren challenged herself to learn more about how ordinary women readers make use of their reading.

In our era, it is often assumed, to read "like a woman" means to favor women authors, whether producers of "classics" or what has come to be called "chick lit."[94] Berggren, however, is concerned not with what kind of fiction women choose but instead with how they read. In the course of interviewing three lifelong readers, all women, Berggren identifies further motives for reading that contrast with those valued by scholars. One of Berggren's interview subjects, for instance, states that she is "looking for books that make sense to me, that tell me something about myself."[95] Another declares that she was "struggling to find meaning, and somehow [had] a sense that there were answers" in novels[96]—answers not to scholarly questions but to personal ones having to do with growing up. Berggren notes of all her subjects that "to achieve the personal results they expected from reading, these women treated novels not as self-contained texts or as historical artifacts but as extensions of their own lives. Therefore academic literary practices ... worked against their purposes."[97] As we will see, many of Austen's amateur readers—especially, but not exclusively, women—approach her novels with very similar goals: to find meaning and to understand themselves. Like Berggren, we will discover those goals by listening to the stories of ordinary amateur readers, as ascertained in surveys and interviews and as revealed in personal writings, such as memoirs, blog postings, and letters.[98]

In the United States, the personal benefits of reading literature have been advocated assiduously by the enormously influential talk-show host Oprah Winfrey. (Oprah's Book Club initially featured new and recent books; after a hiatus, the club returned with a mixture of classic and contemporary titles—though never a work by Austen.) Winfrey has consistently encouraged her viewers, who are overwhelmingly women, to seek connections between their lives and those of fictional characters. As Kate Douglas has argued, "In opening up and even claiming literary fiction for the everyday reader: the popular-culture fan, the housewife, the occasional reader, and the television viewer, Oprah's Book Club celebrates the everyday reader and everyday reading practices."[99] Furthermore, Oprah encourages her viewers to transform themselves as a result of their reading—or to feel as if literature is transforming them. In the words of reader-response critic Rona Kaufman, Winfrey emphasizes reading as a "transformative—and by all means relevant—act" and promotes the "reading process as one that facilitates healing."[100] Douglas explains that in Oprah's handling, "the fictional texts, without being overtly 'self-help' books, were nevertheless established as books that readers could form a therapeutic bond with."[101]

Moving now outside the realm of literary criticism, our perspective on reading as a therapeutic practice can benefit from two recent scholarly investigations of self-help texts. Near the end of *Self-Help, Inc.: Makeover Culture in American Life*, sociologist Micki McGee steps back from the traditional definition of self-help books to question "whether 'self-help' ought to be a category defined by the reader's use of a text or the particular characteristics of the text itself. If one defines self-help literature as a mode of reading, rather than a genre, then nearly any publication—fiction, poetry, autobiography, philosophy, history, or social science—could fall within the category."[102] What McGee terms the self-help "mode of reading" has received a comparable but more thorough definition from the folklorist Sandra K. Dolby. Dolby contends that "people use contemporary self-help books in their own learning projects, much as people have used classical philosophers and the Bible in the past."[103] In a phrase reminiscent of Anne Berggren's discussion of the reading goals of her interview subjects, Dolby describes a reader's employment of self-help books as "the creative use of cultural resources towards a goal of self-education."[104] Dolby argues too that creativity is exercised not only in the reading and personal application of self-help books but also in their preparation: "the writers of these books," she declares, "perform as authors intent on expressing their own creativity as well as serving as teachers for their readers."[105] In Chapter 3, we will see that Austen-inspired advice guides and introductions to Austen geared for non-academic readers demonstrate the authorial creativity that Dolby has identified, even as such guides contribute to their readers' own imaginative use of Austen for a goal of self-improvement.[106]

I mentioned earlier in this chapter that I will use the term "fan" to encompass readers as well as lovers of Austen whose devotion attaches to reworkings of her novels and allied activities, without necessarily extending to her writings themselves. In this sense, "Austen fans" align with the kinds of media fans whose consumption of television, popular films, and other forms of mass culture has been examined by scholars in the area of cultural studies. As Jonathan Gray, Cornel Sandvoss, and C. Lee Harrington have pointed out—in terms very close to those used by reader-response critics like Berggren—fans engage with "texts not in a rationally detached but in an emotionally involved and invested way."[107] Fandom, claims Sandvoss, is essentially "a mode of reading," one that seeks "familiarity and the fulfillment of expectations."[108] Matt Hills reminds us, crucially, that fans can be scholars and scholars fans: "The literary scholar," he reminds us, "is an 'ordinary' reader as well as a scholar."[109]

Cultural studies scholars have only recently, and to a limited extent, begun to pay attention to high-culture texts, including literary ones.[110] "High-culture texts tap more directly and profoundly into my emotions than popular texts," declares Roberta Pearson, who has called on fan-studies researchers to pay more attention to the responses of fans to such neglected (in fan-studies terms) high-culture works as the music of Bach.[111] In addition to describing what listening to Bach's music does for her, Pearson attends to the comments posted by Bach fans online, which—at least as quoted by her—bear a striking similarity to the language employed by devotees of Austen.[112] Another fan-studies researcher, John Tulloch, has investigated theater fandom by asking attendees of Chekhov productions open-ended questions about "what going to this particular theater event *meant* to [them] in the context of their everyday life."[113] In Chapter 4, I will analyze responses to comparable kinds of open-ended questions I have asked of Austen-inspired literary tourists, in light of theories of fan pilgrimage.

Given the large number of Austen lovers who act out their enthusiasm for her by composing works inspired by hers, studies of fan fiction are especially pertinent to the behavior of today's Austen fans.[114] Scholars of fan fiction offer us several means by which to conceive of the relationship between texts inspired by Austen and those authored by her. Cornel Sandvoss has advanced the idea that "the object of fandom corresponds with a textual field of gravity rather than a text in its classical sense."[115] Sandvoss's concept is especially useful in the Austen context by helping make sense of what would otherwise seem to be the disproportionate cultural influence of lesser-known Austen works. *Sense and Sensibility*, in particular, exerts a very strong "textual field of gravity" because of the popularity of the 1995 film version, rather than (as in the case of *Pride and Prejudice*) because of the enduring appeal of the novel itself to amateur readers.

Two further, and more theoretical, approaches to fan fiction are important to consider for their new perspective on the value of what has often been called "derivative" writing. Focusing on how fan fiction is generated, Daria Pimenova contends that "the relationship between fan fiction and its source text is far from clear-cut. The only dependency that can be stated for sure is that of origin. Born out of affection for a particular text, fan fiction borrows its characters and settings and expands its already existent universe without wanting to achieve independency in the sense of breaking free from the source and its characters. Instead, what it wants is to be a tribute to the source and to belong, but belong on its own terms."[116] Pimenova's explanation rings true for a great number of Austen-derived books, whose authors proclaim (in introductions or notes on the text) their devotion to Austen's writings, and who cast their efforts explicitly as "tributes" to Austen. Given the market value of the Austen brand, however, Austen-based popular texts challenge Pimenova's definition of fan fiction as "non-profitable, non-commercial texts based on other fictional texts (series, movies, and books) and written by their fans."[117]

The final theoretical construct from fan studies that I wish to introduce is Abigail Derecho's concept of "archontic literature." As Derecho contends, "archontic texts are not delimited properties with definite borders that can be transgressed. So all texts that build on a previously existing text are not lesser than the source text, and they do not violate the boundaries of the source text; rather, they only add to that text's archive, becoming a part of the archive and expanding it. An archontic text allows, or even invites, writers to enter it, select specific items they find useful, make new artifacts using those found objects, and deposit the newly made work back into the source text's archive."[118] Derecho brings this concept home to Austen studies by describing the "*P&P* archive, which contains such usable artifacts as Elizabeth Bennet [and] Fitzwilliam Darcy"; writers of popular sequels have, in Derecho's words, "made withdrawals from the *P&P* archive, used their selections to make new texts, and deposited their new creations back into the *P&P* archive."[119] This way of thinking is especially useful when approaching sources that rework not Austen's writings themselves but other, earlier reworkings: for example, books that reinterpret Austen-based films. Conceiving of a second-generation reworking as partici-pating in an Austen "archive" helps us attend to that new work's contribution to Austen's status in popular culture, rather than disparage the work because of its attenuated relationship to the "original" text. Derecho calls our attention, too, to the particular appeal of archontic literature to "writers who belong to 'cultures of the subordinate,' including women, colonial subjects, and ethnic minorities"[120]—a claim that has significant implications as we consider not only the preponderance of women writing in response to Austen but also the influence of Austen globally.

Throughout this introductory chapter, I have glanced ahead in order to indicate the relevance of particular ideas and theories to upcoming topics. Let me now offer a more sustained preview of the chapters to follow.

In Chapter 2, I present a historical portrait of an "Austen omnivore": someone who enthusiastically consumes all manner of material related to Austen, from her writings themselves through films and other popular treat-ments. Alberta H. Burke devoted her life to collecting everything, from the priceless to the ephemeral, that she felt brought her closer to Austen. The archives of Alberta Burke's correspondence offer a matchless view of the personal importance of Austen to an everyday reader, albeit one with excep-tional means, in mid-twentieth-century America.

How amateur readers engage with Austen's writings today is my subject in Chapter 3. After an overview of literary critics' approaches to everyday readers, I examine reports of individual encounters with Austen's works as well as accounts of reading groups' engagement with her novels. I survey editions of and handbooks to Austen's novels that are aimed at enhancing amateur readers' understanding of Austen—and of themselves. Finally, I consider arguments made on behalf of an increasingly popular form of readerly engagement with Austen's text: the writing of sequels.

A particular kind of amateur-reader behavior, literary tourism, is the focus of Chapter 4. I first identify how scholars both within and outside literary criticism have illuminated travel that is inspired by reading. Next, I explain what awaits visitors in the places most closely associated with Austen's life and career. I pay special attention to the two central, and very distinct, sites of Austen tourism: Jane Austen's House Museum in Chawton and the Jane Austen Centre in Bath, which opened in 1999. To gain insight into the meaning of Austen places to today's literary tourists, I first analyze two recently published travelogues focused on Austen and then present responses to my surveys of visitors, as well as of staff and volunteers, at Jane Austen's House.

Chapter 5 continues my examination of how readers and viewers conceive of Austen's life, this time in the realm of imagination rather than geography. I sum up scholarly approaches to myths about Austen's appearance, experiences, and attitudes before examining new portraits of Austen as well as portrayals of her in fiction and film. I compare recent depictions of Austen's loves, her attitudes towards authorship and fame, and her experiences of freedom and adventure. Finally, I examine depictions of intimate relationships with Austen that invest readers and viewers in thinking of her as a close friend, even a sister.

In Chapter 6, I treat recent American reworkings of Austen's novels that move unabashedly in directions she herself avoided: erotica, horror, and the supernatural on the one hand and explicitly Christian content on the other. I first consider how recent theories of fan fiction can be fruitfully applied to published writings that play with Austen sources. Next, I trace the evolution and reception of works that infuse Austen's novels with sex; those that incorporate horror/paranormal elements into her novels and life; and those that approach her life and works from the perspective of evangelical Christian faith.

My final chapter concerns how Austen enthusiasts themselves have imagined and negotiated the continuum of identities that includes scholars and amateurs. I first analyze recent novels that depict Austen readers who move along this continuum and who also encounter societies of Austen fans. Next, I look back to the origins of the Jane Austen Society of North America, whose archives reveal the dedication of the organization's founders to fostering conversation among all of Austen's readers. I conclude with a call to all lovers of Austen, scholars and everyday readers alike, to come together to explore her writings, her influence, and the significance of literature today.

Notes

1 Survey of visitors to Jane Austen's House Museum, July 13–23, 2009. All surveys were conducted in confidentiality and are transcribed exactly as written.

2 *Pride and Prejudice: The Special Edition*, directed by Simon Langton, screenplay by Andrew Davies (1995; New York: New Video, 2001), DVD.

3 *Sense and Sensibility*, directed by Ang Lee, screenplay by Emma Thompson (1995; Culver City, CA: Columbia TriStar Home Video, 1999), DVD.

4 *Clueless*, written and directed by Amy Heckerling (1995; Hollywood: Paramount Pictures, 2005), DVD. *Jane Austen's Persuasion*, directed by Roger Michell, screenplay by Nick Dear (1995; Culver City, CA: Columbia TriStar Home Video, 1999), DVD.

5 Several recent books on Austen by distinguished scholars incorporate elements of memoir. Reading Austen as a young boy, according to D. A. Miller, was like having been "put in a dress." *Jane Austen: Or The Secret of Style* (Princeton: Princeton University Press, 2003). Rachel M. Brownstein weaves strands of memoir of her student and teaching years into *Why Jane Austen?* (New York: Columbia University Press, 2011) as a way of tracking Austen's changing cultural meanings and exploring literary influences both personal and generational. In *A Jane Austen Education: How Six Novels Taught Me about Love, Friendship, and the Things that Really Matter* (New York: Penguin Press, 2011), William Deresiewicz maps onto Austen's novels episodes of his development during his years of graduate study.

6 Henry James, "The Lesson of Balzac," reprinted in B. C. Southam, ed., *Jane Austen: The Critical Heritage*, 2 vols (London: Routledge & Kegan Paul, 1968, 1987), 2:230.

7 Many present-day writers, both academic and popular, on Jane Austen worry at the question of how most appropriately to refer to her. Using her whole name—"Jane Austen"—is a common solution; her initials ("JA") also appeal to some. Others, as Emily Auerbach has pointed out, continue the long tradition of referring to her familiarly—and sometimes with a whiff of disparagement—as "Jane." *Searching for Jane Austen* (Madison: University of Wisconsin Press, 2004), 30–32.

8 Harriet Margolis investigates the "Austen brand" through the early years of the new millennium in "Janeite Culture: What Does the Name 'Jane Austen' Authorize?," in *Jane Austen on Screen*, ed. Gina Macdonald and Andrew F. Macdonald (Cambridge: Cambridge University Press, 2003), 22–43.

9 Sheenagh Pugh, *The Democratic Genre: Fan Fiction in a Literary Context* (Bridgend, Wales: Seren, 2005), 218.

10 For a comprehensive introduction to popular culture as an idea and an influential assertion of why scholars should pay attention to it, see John Fiske, *Understanding Popular Culture*, 2nd ed. (London: Routledge, 2010).

11 On the history of Austen appreciation by men readers, see Claudia L. Johnson, "The Divine Miss Jane: Jane Austen, Janeites, and the Discipline of Novel Studies," in *Janeites: Austen's Disciples and Devotees*, ed. Deidre Lynch (Princeton: Princeton University Press), 25–44. Previously published in *boundary 2* 23.3 (1996): 143–63.

12 Rudyard Kipling's story "The Janeites," first published in 1924, was preceded by the following verse when it appeared in the 1926 collection *Debits and Credits*: "Jane lies in Winchester—blessed be her shade! / Praise the Lord for making her, and her for all she made! / And while the stones of Winchester, or Milsom Street, remain, / Glory, love, and honour unto England's Jane!" "The Janeites," in *Debits and Credits* (Garden City, NJ: Doubleday, Page & Company, 1926), 124.

13 Unlike period versions, updated screen adaptations of Austen often take advantage of the opportunity to explore her plot and characters in international settings: see Amy Heckerling's *Clueless*, which transposes *Emma* to 1990s Beverly Hills, CA. Set in India, England, and California, *Bride & Prejudice*, directed by Gurinder Chadha, introduces cultural prejudice—and Bollywood musical elements—to Austen's most popular novel (2004; Burbank, CA: Buena Vista Home Entertainment, 2005), DVD.

14 Appreciation of Austen by Americans in the nineteenth and early twentieth centuries has been well studied: see in particular Mary A. Favret, "Free and Happy: Jane Austen in America," in *Janeites: Austen's Disciples and Devotees*, ed. Deidre Lynch (Princeton: Princeton University Press, 2000), 166–87.

15 Jane Austen and Seth Grahame-Smith, *Pride and Prejudice and Zombies* (Philadelphia: Quirk Books, 2009).

16 *Pride & Prejudice*, directed by Joe Wright, screenplay by Deborah Moggach (2005; Universal City, CA: Universal Studios, 2006), DVD; *Becoming Jane*, directed by Julian Jarrold, screenplay by Sarah Williams and Kevin Hood (2007; Burbank, CA: Buena Vista Home Entertainment, 2008), DVD. It remains to be seen what, if any, influence on the popular imagination will result from the most recent (at the time of writing) period screen adaptation of an Austen novel: *Emma*, directed by Jim O'Hanlon, screenplay by Sandy Welch (2009; Burbank, CA: Warner Home Video, 2010), DVD.

17 Sybil G. Brinton, *Old Friends and New Fancies: An Imaginary Sequel to the Novels of Jane Austen* (1914; Naperville, IL: Sourcebooks Landmark, 2007). Austen's novels were translated into European languages during her lifetime, with her plots as well as her prose often freely reworked. In 1815, two years before Austen's death, the novelist Isabelle de Montolieu rendered *Sense and Sensibility* in French with many noteworthy changes from the original, including a new ending in which Willoughby repents. Isabelle Bour, "The Reception of Jane Austen's Novels in France and Switzerland: The Early Years, 1813–1828," in *The Reception of Jane Austen in Europe*, ed. Anthony Mandal and Brian Southam (London: Continuum, 2007), 21–25. One of Austen's nieces, Catherine Anne Hubback, jump-started her own writing career in 1850 by reworking an unpublished Austen manuscript, *The Watsons*, into *The Younger Sister*, which Hubback dedicated—without any acknowledgment of her source material—to "the Memory of her Aunt, the Late Jane Austen." Kathryn Sutherland, *Jane Austen's Textual Lives: From Aeschylus to Bollywood* (Cambridge: Cambridge University Press, 2005), 72. For an in-depth consideration of Hubback's rewriting of *The Watsons*, see Alice Marie Villaseñor, "Women Readers and the Victorian Jane Austen" (PhD diss., University of Southern California, 2009), *Dissertations & Theses: Full Text* (AAT 3389576), accessed October 6, 2010.

18 *Pride and Prejudice*, directed by Robert Z. Leonard (1940; Burbank, CA: Warner Home Video, 2006), DVD.

19 Claudia L. Johnson's *Jane Austen Cults and Cultures* (Chicago: University of Chicago Press, forthcoming), the first full history of the views and activities of those devoted to Austen, will allow unprecedented consideration of how Austen lovers today reenact, or depart from, the behavior and attitudes of their predecessors.

20 Cassandra's letter was a centerpiece of the 2009–2010 exhibit "A Woman's Wit: Jane Austen's Life and Legacy" at the Pierpont Morgan Library in New York, to which Alberta bequeathed the document. A facsimile of the letter is permanently displayed at Jane Austen's House Museum in Chawton.

21 Brownstein, *Why Jane Austen?*. See also Susannah Carson, introduction to *A Truth Universally Acknowledged: 33 Great Writers on Why We Read Jane Austen*, ed. Susannah Carson (New York: Random House, 2009), xi–xx; Joanna Trollope, "Homecoming," *Persuasions* 25 (2003): 21–25; and John Wiltshire, "Jane Austen's England, Jane Austen's World," in *Jane Austen: Introductions and Interventions* (2003; repr., London: Palgrave Macmillan, 2006), 108–20.

22 One of the best introductions to postmodernism remains Linda Hutcheon, *A Poetics of Postmodernism: History, Theory, Fiction* (London: Routledge, 1988).

23 Claire Harman offers an overview of Austen's presence in popular culture in the final chapter of *Jane's Fame: How Jane Austen Conquered the World* (Edinburgh: Canongate, 2009).

24 It is commonplace among scholars to disparage self-proclaimed fans for their lack of actual knowledge about the supposed object of their enthusiasm. The eminent Austen critic John Wiltshire, for example, has recently commented that, "to be frank, some people who think of themselves as fans of Jane Austen have not read her novels, or have read one or two of them so long ago that it hardly counts." "Why Do We *Read* Jane Austen?," in *A Truth Universally Acknowledged*, ed. Carson, 163. The impulse to define who is and who isn't a "real" Austen fan exists as well among fans themselves. See for instance the survey of Janeites conducted in 2008 by Jeanne Kieffer, who asked would-be participants to certify that they had "read all six major Austen novels." In her analysis of results, Kieffer explained her stipulation as follows: "I did not wish to set the

bar overly high. I felt any reader who had persevered all the way through *Mansfield Park* and *Northanger Abbey* (as well as the four more accessible novels) had met some sort of minimum requirement." "Anatomy of a Janeite: Results from *The Jane Austen Survey 2008*," *Persuasions On-Line* 29.1 (2008), http://www.jasna.org/persuasions/on-line/vol29no1/kiefer.html.

25 Every Austen biographer comments on the fact that Jane Austen received approximately two years of formal schooling, with the rest of her education coming from her reading (which was encouraged by her father, who allowed both Jane and her sister Cassandra free rein in his comparatively extensive library) and her exposure to her highly literate family. See for instance Jan Fergus, *Jane Austen: A Literary Life* (Houndmills, Basingstoke: Macmillan, 1991), 34–43.

26 Judy Simons, "Classics and Trash: Reading Austen in the 1990s," *Women's Writing* 5 (1998): 32.

27 See Robert C. Holub, *Reception Theory: A Critical Introduction* (London: Routledge, 2002) and James L. Machor and Philip Goldstein, eds, *Reception Study: From Literary Theory to Cultural Studies* (London: Routledge, 2000).

28 The founding texts of reader-response criticism are Wolfgang Iser, *The Act of Reading: A Theory of Aesthetic Response* (Baltimore: Johns Hopkins University Press, 1978) and Stanley Fish, *Is There a Text in This Class?: The Authority of Interpretive Communities* (Cambridge, MA: Harvard University Press, 1982). For a history and overview of reader-response criticism, see Patrocinio P. Schweickart and Elizabeth A. Flynn, introduction to *Reading Sites: Social Difference and Reader Response*, ed. Patrocinio P. Schweickart and Elizabeth A. Flynn (New York: Modern Language Association of America, 2004), 3–18. Schweickart and Flynn sum up the tenets of reader-response criticism as follows: "All critics are readers and all criticism is someone's response to a text. ... Second, the reader is a producer of meaning. ... And third, readings are necessarily various" (1–2).

29 Andrew Wright, "Jane Austen Adapted," *Nineteenth-Century Fiction* 30.3 (1975): 423.

30 Ibid., 439, 423.

31 Ibid., 424.

32 David Gilson points out that the prior standard bibliography of Austen, that of Geoffrey Keynes (1929), did include "three dramatic adaptations" but describes these as "trifling attempts, meant only for amateur reading or performance." *A Bibliography of Jane Austen*, new ed. (Winchester: St. Paul's, 1997), 405.

33 Ibid., 421, 405.

34 For a brief comparative treatment of Austen sequels through the mid-1980s, see Marilyn Sachs, "Sequels to Jane Austen," in *The Jane Austen Handbook*, ed. J. David Grey with Brian Southam and A. Walton Litz (London: Athlone Press, 1986), 374–76.

35 Roger Sales, "Afterword: Austenmania," in *Jane Austen and Representations of Regency England*, new ed. (London: Routledge, 1996), 227–39. The term "Austenmania," or "Austen-mania," has often been used to refer to the wave of Austen's popularity that began in 1995: see for example Simons, "Classics and Trash." A commercial example is Penguin Books' "Austen-mania!," a webpage devoted to Austen-related merchandise: http://us.penguingroup.com/static/html/features/austenmania/austenmania.html, accessed October 5, 2010.

36 Sales, *Jane Austen and Representations of Regency England*, 229.

37 Ibid., 25.

38 Ibid., 26.

39 Austen's first scholarly editor, R. W. Chapman, included the two sets of "Opinions" in 1954 in the final volume of his collected edition of Austen's works; thus the "Opinions" appear in collections both of Austen's writings and of criticism about her writings. See *The Works of Jane Austen: Minor Works*, ed. R. W. Chapman, rev. ed. (Oxford: Oxford University Press, 1988).

40 "Opinions of *Mansfield Park*," in Southam, *Jane Austen: The Critical Tradition*, 1:49.

41 Laura Fairchild Brodie, "Jane Austen and the Common Reader: 'Opinions of *Mansfield Park*,' 'Opinions of *Emma*,' and the Janeite Phenomenon," *Texas Studies in Literature and Language* 37.1 (1995): 56.

42 Ibid., 69. For a full treatment of the reactions of Austen's readers from her lifetime

through the Second World War, see Katie Halsey, *Jane Austen and Her Readers, 1786–1945* (London: Anthem, 2011).

43 Virginia Woolf inaugurated her series of essays titled "The Common Reader" by quoting Samuel Johnson's praise of "the common sense of readers, uncorrupted by literary prejudices"; she added, in her own words, that "the common reader … differs from the critic in the scholar" in being "worse educated" and someone who "reads for his own pleasure rather than to impart knowledge or correct the opinions of others." "The Common Reader," in *The Common Reader* (1925; repr., New York: Harcourt, 1984), 1. On the term "general reader," see Janice A. Radway's remark that "the very term 'general reader' had perhaps evolved historically precisely as a rejection and critique of some other reader, presumably a reader not general but focused, professional, technical, and specialized. The general reader was most obviously *not* the academic reader." *A Feeling for Books: The Book-of-the-Month Club, Literary Taste, and Middle-Class Desire* (Chapel Hill, NC: University of North Carolina Press, 1997), 10. Radway points out, too, how publishers and scholars use the terms "academic" and "middlebrow" to disparage each other: "The academic, it gradually became clear, was something the people at the Book-of-the-Month Club defined themselves against. They used the word 'academic' to dismiss books they did not like in much the same way my academic colleagues and I had used the word 'middlebrow' to dispense with texts we judged inadequate." Ibid., 9.

44 According to the *OED*, a fan is "a fanatic; … a keen and regular spectator of a (profes-sional) sport, orig. of baseball; a regular supporter of a (professional) sports team; hence, a keen follower of a specified hobby or amusement, and *gen.* an enthusiast for a particular person or thing." *Oxford English Dictionary Online*, accessed October 12, 2010.

45 *Oxford English Dictionary Online*, accessed October 6, 2010.

46 For a very different take than mine on the cultural significance of amateurs' contribu-tions to present-day discourse, see Andrew Keen, *The Cult of the Amateur: How Blogs, MySpace, YouTube, and the Rest of Today's User-Generated Media Are Destroying Our Economy, Our Culture, and Our Values* (New York: Doubleday, 2008).

47 Deidre Lynch, "At Home with Jane Austen," in *Cultural Institutions of the Novel*, ed. Deidre Lynch and William B. Warner (Durham, NC: Duke University Press, 1996), 159–92. Claudia L. Johnson, "Austen Cults and Cultures," in *The Cambridge Companion to Jane Austen*, ed. Edward Copeland and Juliet McMaster (Cambridge: Cambridge University Press, 1997), 211–26. See also Johnson's influential 1996 article "The Divine Miss Jane."

48 Lynch, "At Home with Jane Austen," 159.

49 Johnson, "Austen Cults and Cultures," 211–12.

50 Ibid., 222.

51 *The Reception of Jane Austen in Europe*, ed. Mandal and Southam, complements and extends *Janeites* by contributing accounts of the historical and contemporary reception of Austen from France all the way to Russia; the volume's timeline of European reception of Jane Austen, which was prepared by Anthony Mandal and Paul Barnaby, is especially valuable. For more scholarship on global responses to Jane Austen, see You-me Park and Rajeswari Sunder Rajan, eds, *The Postcolonial Jane Austen* (London: Routledge, 2000) as well as two special issues of *Persuasions On-Line*: Susan Allen Ford and Inger Sigrun Brodey, eds, "The Global Jane Austen," 28.2 (2008), http://www.jasna. org/persuasions/on-line/vol28no2/index.html; and Susan Allen Ford and Gillian Dow, eds, "New Directions in Austen Studies," 30.2 (2010), http://www.jasna.org/persua sions/on-line/vol30no2/index.html.

52 Deidre Lynch, "Introduction: Sharing with Our Neighbors," in *Janeites*, 8.

53 Ibid., 12.

54 I asked those respondents to my survey at Jane Austen's House Museum who identified Austen as their favorite, or a favorite, author to select one or more terms they would use to describe themselves. "Janeite" was decidedly less popular (chosen by 6 out of 50 respondents) than "an Austen enthusiast" (20), "a fan of Austen" (16), "a lover of Austen" (11), and "an Austen fanatic" (9).

55 Linda Troost and Sayre Greenfield, eds, *Jane Austen in Hollywood*, 2nd ed. (Lexington: University Press of Kentucky, 2001); John Wiltshire, *Recreating Jane Austen* (Cambridge: Cambridge University Press, 2001); Suzanne R. Pucci and James Thompson, eds, *Jane*

Austen and Co.: Remaking the Past in Contemporary Culture (Albany: State University of Albany Press, 2003); Gina Macdonald and Andrew F. Macdonald, eds, *Jane Austen on Screen* (Cambridge: Cambridge University Press, 2003). In addition, *Persuasions* and *Persuasions On-Line*, the journals of the Jane Austen Society of North America, have steadily published articles devoted to Austen-based films, beginning with Patrice Hannon, "Austen Novels and Austen Films: Incompatible Worlds?," *Persuasions* 18 (1996): 24–32. Of especial note are two issues of *Persuasions On-Line* devoted to films of individual novels: Laurie Kaplan, ed., "*Emma* on Film," "Occasional Papers No. 3" (1999), http://www.jasna.org/persuasions/on-line/opno3/index.html; and Jen Camden and Susan Allen Ford, eds, "Joe Wright's *Pride & Prejudice* (2005)," special issue 27.2 (2007), http://www.jasna.org/persuasions/on-line/vol27no2/index.html. Two less widely influential, yet still valuable, studies of Austen and film adaptation from this period are Sue Parrill, *Jane Austen on Film and Television: A Critical Study of the Adaptations* (Jefferson, NC: McFarland, 2002) and Eckhart Voights-Virckow, ed., *Janespotting and Beyond: English Heritage Retrovisions Since the Mid-1990s* (Tübingen: GunterNarrVerlag, 2004). Most recently, see David Monaghan, Ariane Hudelet, and John Wiltshire, *The Cinematic Jane Austen: Essays on the Filmic Sensibility of the Novels* (Jefferson, NC: McFarland, 2009).

56 Linda Troost and Sayre Greenfield, "Introduction: Watching Ourselves Watching," in *Jane Austen in Hollywood*, ed. Troost and Greenfield, 3.

57 Ibid.

58 Ibid., 6.

59 Ibid., 11.

60 Wiltshire, *Recreating Jane Austen*, 2.

61 Sutherland, *Jane Austen's Textual Lives*, v. A few years after its publication, Sutherland's monograph became embroiled in a controversy that vividly and uncomfortably highlights tensions involving perceptions of professionalism in the Austen arena. In the spring of 2009, Sutherland alleged that *Jane's Fame: How Jane Austen Conquered the World*, a new book by the award-winning biographer Claire Harman, borrowed heavily from *Jane Austen's Textual Lives*. Harman counter-accused Sutherland of manifesting "professional jealousy of a patent and most unattractive sort." Vanessa Thorpe, "Jane Austen Scholars Clash in Textbook Research Row," *Observer* (London), March 15, 2009, http://www.guardian.co.uk/books/2009/mar/15/jane-austen-research-row.

62 Sutherland, *Jane Austen's Textual Lives*, 22.

63 See also Gillian Dow and Clare Hanson, eds, *Uses of Jane Austen: Twentieth-Century Afterlives* (Houndmills, Basingstoke: Palgrave Macmillan, forthcoming).

64 Published from 2005 to 2009, the Cambridge Edition is a landmark in Austen scholarship; the previous, and only, comprehensive scholarly edition of Austen's novels was prepared for Oxford University Press by R. W. Chapman in the 1920s and revised in subsequent decades. Also noteworthy is the free-access online digital edition of Jane Austen's fiction manuscripts, a project led by Kathryn Sutherland and launched in 2010. "Jane Austen's Fiction Manuscripts Digital Edition," http://www.janeausten.ac.uk/index.html.

65 Deidre Shauna Lynch, "Cult of Jane Austen," in *Jane Austen in Context*, ed. Janet Todd (Cambridge: Cambridge University Press, 2005), 111–20; Lynch, "Sequels," in *Jane Austen in Context*, ed. Todd, 160–68. Lynch is preparing further research on author-love: see Deidre Lynch, *At Home in English: A Cultural History of the Love of Literature* (Chicago: University of Chicago Press, forthcoming).

66 Claudia L. Johnson and Clara Tuite, eds, *A Companion to Jane Austen* (Oxford: Wiley-Blackwell, 2009).

67 Judy Simons, "Jane Austen and Popular Culture," in *A Companion to Jane Austen*, ed. Johnson and Tuite, 473, 476.

68 Ibid., 475.

69 Mary Ann O'Farrell, "Austenian Subcultures," in *A Companion to Jane Austen*, ed. Johnson and Tuite, 481.

70 While of all canonical authors Shakespeare is by far the most fully studied in terms of his popular influence, he is of course not alone. Will Brooker's *Alice's Adventures: Lewis Carroll in Popular Culture* (London: Continuum, 2004) is a model example of a

participant-observer's investigation of an author society, tourist sites, and other manifestations of present-day popular interest.

71 In this section, I highlight recent work on Shakespeare that is especially pertinent to the topics I will address in *Everybody's Jane*. For a more comprehensive introduction, for non-specialists, to scholarship on Shakespeare and popular culture, including discussion of Marjorie Garber's influential essay "The Jane Austen Syndrome," in *Quotation Marks* (New York: Routledge, 2002), as well as earlier acknowledgments by Austen scholars of parallels in the Shakespeare realm, see my article "From Schlockspeare to Austenpop," in "Shakespeare and Austen," ed. Lisa Hopkins, special issue, *Shakespeare* 6.4 (2010): 446–62.

72 Julie Sanders, *Novel Shakespeares: Twentieth-Century Women Novelists and Appropriation* (Manchester: Manchester University Press, 2001), 13.

73 Jane Austen, like other members of her family, did write poetry, particularly to celebrate family occasions; see *The Poetry of Jane Austen and the Austen Family*, ed. David Selwyn (Iowa City: University of Iowa Press, 1996). The three Austen prayers are reprinted in *Minor Works*, ed. Chapman, 453–57.

74 See Terry Eagleton's assertion that "what we call 'unique' or 'authentic' in Shakespeare, the genuine article, is really no more than his extraordinary ability to parody himself. Shakespeare is continually serving up uncannily accurate Shakespearean parodies, many so lifelike as to be positively startling." "Afterword," in *The Shakespeare Myth*, ed. Graham Holderness (Manchester: Manchester University Press, 1988), 205.

75 Gary Taylor, "Afterword: The Incredible Shrinking Bard," in *Shakespeare and Appropriation*, ed. Christy Desmet and Robert Sawyer (London: Routledge, 1999), 202.

76 Marjorie Garber, *Shakespeare and Modern Culture* (New York: Pantheon, 2008), xviii. Among other popular sources, Garber attends to Shakespeare-based leadership guides written for and by businesspeople, which she argues are "not useful in illuminating, analyzing, or interpreting Shakespeare." Ibid., 197.

77 Richard Burt, "To E- or Not to E-?: Disposing of Schlockspeare in the Age of Digital Media," in *Shakespeare after Mass Media*, ed. Richard Burt (New York: Palgrave Macmillan, 2002), 8.

78 Ibid.

79 Laurie Osborne, "Harlequin Presents: That '70s Shakespeare and Beyond," in *Shakespeare after Mass Media*, ed. Burt, 130.

80 Ibid., 144–45.

81 Ibid., 146.

82 Douglas Lanier, "Shakespeare™: Myth and Biographical Fiction," in *The Cambridge Companion to Shakespeare and Popular Culture*, ed. Robert Shaughnessy (Cambridge: Cambridge University Press, 2007), 112.

83 Douglas Lanier, *Shakespeare and Modern Popular Culture* (Oxford: Oxford University Press, 2002), 52–53.

84 Ibid., 98.

85 Ibid., 99.

86 Ibid., 19. For a recent reconsideration of the concept of fidelity with respect to popular Austen sources, see John Wiltshire, "Afterword: On Fidelity," in Monaghan, Hudelet, and Wiltshire, *The Cinematic Jane Austen*, 160–70.

87 Diana Henderson, "Shakespeare: The Theme Park," in *Shakespeare after Mass Media*, ed. Burt, 107.

88 Matt Hills, "Media Academics as Media Audiences: Aesthetic Judgments in Media and Cultural Studies," in *Fandom: Identities and Communities in a Mediated World*, ed. Jonathan Gray, Cornel Sandvoss, and C. Lee Harrington (New York: New York University Press, 2007), 41.

89 Lanier, *Shakespeare and Modern Popular Culture*, 140.

90 Graham Holderness, *Cultural Shakespeare: Essays in the Shakespeare Myth* (Hatfield, Hertfordshire: University of Hertfordshire Press, 2001), 177.

91 Henderson, "Shakespeare: The Theme Park," 124.

92 Rita Felski, *Uses of Literature* (Malden, MA: Blackwell, 2008), 14.

93 Anne G. Berggren, "Reading like a Woman," in *Reading Sites*, ed. Schweickart and Flynn, 167. Berggren mentions in particular a memory, from twenty years earlier, of being immersed almost helplessly in *Pride and Prejudice*: "I can't stop reading, starting the

novel again every time I finish. After five or six readings, over a period of a week, the obsession runs its course, and I am again able to function." Ibid., 166.

94 Writers of so-called chick lit have often claimed Austen as a source of inspiration: see my article "Mothers of Chick Lit?: Women Writers, Readers, and Literary History," in *Chick Lit: The New Woman's Fiction*, ed. Suzanne Ferriss and Mallory Young (New York: Routledge, 2006), 47–70.

95 Berggren, "Reading like a Woman," 176.

96 Ibid., 177.

97 Ibid., 184.

98 Compilations of readers' opinions about Jane Austen have tended to feature exclusively the views of prominent people. See in particular Carson, ed., *A Truth Universally Acknowledged*, which includes essays by renowned writers of the past and present.

99 Kate Douglas, "Your Book Changed My Life: Everyday Literary Criticism and Oprah's Book Club," in *The Oprah Affect: Critical Essays on Oprah's Book Club*, ed. Cecilia Konchar Farr and Jaime Harker (Albany: State University of Albany Press, 2008), 236.

100 Rona Kaufman, "'That, My Dear, Is Called Reading': Oprah's Book Club and the Construction of a Readership," in *Reading Sites*, ed. Schweickart and Flynn, 224. According to Kaufman, Oprah's message that fiction reading can be therapeutic has appealed especially to those viewers who "can read" literary fiction "but have chosen not to," those who have experienced "the failure of a kind of academic reading." Ibid., 225. Kaufman places her discussion of Oprah's Book Club in the context of debates about "middlebrow" reading; as Kaufman paraphrases the arguments of Janice Radway, the middlebrow reader "values use over aesthetic." Ibid., 242.

101 Douglas, "Your Book Changed My Life," 246.

102 Micki McGee, *Self-Help, Inc.: Makeover Culture in American Life* (Oxford: Oxford University Press, 2005), 193.

103 Sandra K. Dolby, *Self-Help Books: Why Americans Keep Reading Them* (Urbana: University of Illinois Press, 2005), xi.

104 Ibid., 17. Dolby notes that many undergraduate students view their education as a kind of self-development project: "the practice of selecting and reading a self-help book," she claims, "is a procedure not so very different from that undertaken by the average undergraduate in signing up for a variety of courses in a modern university." Ibid., 78–79.

105 Ibid., 14.

106 Advice guides derived from Austen fall in what Dolby terms the "*textual interpretation subtype*" of self-help books, in which "the author selects one text to serve as a basis for discussion throughout the entire book." Ibid., 43; emphasis original.

107 Jonathan Gray, Cornel Sandvoss, and C. Lee Harrington, "Introduction: Why Study Fans?," in *Fandom*, ed. Gray, Sandvoss, and Harrington, 10.

108 Cornel Sandvoss, "The Death of the Reader?: Literary Theory and the Study of Texts in Popular Culture," in *Fandom*, ed. Gray, Sandvoss, and Harrington, 31, 30.

109 Matt Hills, "Media Academics," 46. See also Matt Hills, "Introduction: Who's Who? Academics, fans, scholar-fans and fan-scholars," in *Fan Cultures* (New York: Routledge, 2002). See too Kristina Busse and Karen Hellekson's embrace, as academics, of what they identify as "the strengths of fan culture": "self-reflection, collective production, and acceptance of conflict." "Introduction: Work in Progress," in *Fan Fiction and Fan Communities in the Age of the Internet*, ed. Karen Hellekson and Kristina Busse (Jefferson, NC: McFarland, 2006), 9. "Rather than privileging a particular interpretation as accurate," Busse and Hellekson explain, "we have learned from fandom that alternative and competing readings can and must coexist. We thus use fannish practice as a model for academic practice." Ibid., 8.

110 For an overview of the reasons for the longtime neglect of high-culture texts in cultural studies, see Roberta Pearson, "Bachies, Bardies, Trekkies, and Sherlockians," in *Fandom*, ed. Gray, Sandvoss, and Harrington, 99–100. As a model for how cultural studies can be brought to bear on literary fandom, see Brooker, *Alice's Adventures*.

111 Pearson, "Bachies, Bardies," 107.

112 "What would life be without JSB," posted one Bach enthusiast, while another described feeling "slightly addicted" by Bach's music and "dreading the impending withdrawal phase." Ibid.

113 John Tulloch, "Fans of Chekhov: Re-Approaching 'High Culture,'" in *Fandom*, ed. Gray, Sandvoss, and Harrington, 112; emphasis original.

114 For studies of Austen-based online fan fiction, see Pugh, *Democratic Genre* and Roberta Grandi, "Web Side Stories: Janeites, Fanfictions, and Never Ending Romances," in *Internet Fictions*, ed. Ingrid Hotz-Davies, Anton Kirchhofer, and Sirpa Leppänen (Cambridge: Cambridge Scholars Publishing, 2009).

115 Sandvoss, "The Death of the Reader?," 29.

116 Daria Pimenova, "Fan Fiction: Between Text, Conversation, and Genre," in *Internet Fictions*, ed. Hotz-Davies, Kirchhofer, and Leppänen, 48.

117 Ibid., 44.

118 Abigail Derecho, "Archontic Literature: A Definition, a History, and Several Theories of Fan Fiction," in *Fan Fiction and Fan Communities*, ed. Hellekson and Busse, 64–65. Derecho has coined and derived this term from what the theorist Jacques Derrida called the "archontic principle," which she summarizes as "that drive within an archive that seeks to always produce more archive, to enlarge itself. The archontic principle never allows the archive to remain stable or still, but wills it to add to its own stores." Ibid., 64. Derecho asserts the advantages of thinking in terms of "archontic literature" rather than describing works as "derivative," "appropriative," or "intertextual." Ibid., 64–65. For an alternate interpretation of Derrida's concept of the archive and an appreciative critique of Derecho's application of it to fan fiction, see Pimenova, "Fan Fiction," 50–52.

119 Derecho, "Archontic Literature," 65.

120 Ibid., 71. For a related argument that "the question and concept of the [literary] classic is perhaps always that of the outsider," see Ankhi Mukerjee, "'What is a Classic?: International Literary Criticism and the Classic Question," *PMLA* 125.4 (2010): 1040.

Figure 2.1: Portrait of Alberta Burke, [194?]. Henry and Alberta Hirshheimer Burke Collection, Goucher College Library.

Chapter 2

Alberta H. Burke, Austen Omnivore

I am always enchanted by any little scrap of knowledge which has anything
to do with Jane Austen.

Alberta Burke, letter to Eleanor Falley, April 14, 1941

In this chapter, we meet an American woman from an earlier generation who
dedicated her adult life to her amateur passions, central among them Jane
Austen. Alberta Hirshheimer Burke (1907–1975) was, in her own words, "a
most ardent 'Janeite' and a collector of all things pertaining to Jane Austen."[1]
Indeed, Alberta did everything that lovers of Austen do today—except publish
her own books inspired by her favorite author. Together with her husband,
Alberta read all of Austen's novels aloud every year.[2] A bibliophile, she acquired
manuscripts and first editions, some exceptionally rare, amassing what was
called the "finest privately owned" collection outside the Austen family.[3] Trained
in English literature through the master's degree level, Alberta bought and
read new scholarly books and articles about Austen, though she neither taught
nor undertook traditional research. She was equally committed to pursuing
popular material pertaining to Austen. She sought out radio programs, films,
and theatrical performances with an Austen connection; delighted in owning
translations of Austen even into languages she did not know; devoured every
new general-audience book that dealt with Austen; corresponded tirelessly
with fellow Austen enthusiasts; and traveled regularly to Chawton to visit Jane
Austen's House (then known as Chawton Cottage) and to attend meetings of
the Jane Austen Society, which she joined as a life member in 1947.

Getting to know Alberta—and her partner in collecting, her husband Henry
G. Burke (1902–1989)—is possible because Alberta not only did everything,
she documented everything, saved everything, and gave it all to her alma
mater, Goucher College in Baltimore, Maryland, which now proudly houses
the Alberta H. and Henry G. Burke Collection.[4] (All, that is, with the exception
of the Austen manuscripts; as we will see, Alberta chose the Pierpont Morgan
Library in New York, now known as the Morgan Library & Museum, as the
beneficiary of those documents.) Alberta's card files, annotated scrapbooks,
and above all her letters bring us closer to the woman who described herself
as "a whole-hearted admirer of Jane Austen."[5] These personal writings, never

intended for publication, have much to tell us about how a dedication to Austen can shape an individual life, as well as how one person's passion for Austen can affect the broader landscape of Austen appreciation and Austen studies.

Collecting in Order to Connect with Jane

No origin tale has been preserved for Alberta Burke's love of Austen. According to her husband Henry, she was "a natural and avid reader [who] from the days of her earliest recollection had the run of the La Crosse [Wisconsin] Library in the town where she was born."[6] None of Alberta's application materials for Goucher, however, indicates a deep interest in literature. Her high school principal described her as "very conscientious, and trustworthy," someone who "should take more interest in athletics and recreation" and "should be directed into activities of the school outside of class work."[7] A family friend praised Alberta as "a very interesting and clever girl with an unusual amount of imagination and considerable artistic talent."[8] Alberta's mother, Joanna (Mrs. Louis C.) Hirshheimer, who wrote several anxious-sounding letters to the Dean and President of Goucher in the year and a half leading up to Alberta's matriculation, did mention that her daughter "may specialize to teach English and history."[9] (Alberta did not need to work for a salary, and indeed never did, thanks to an inheritance from a grandfather who was a successful businessman.)[10] Most of Joanna's energy, however, went towards inquiring about Goucher's policies of religious tolerance; she made clear that Alberta was "of the Jewish race," though "ignorant of all the religious forms."[11] She also requested that Alberta be housed in a single room, since "she has never shared a room with anyone, & we would much prefer, that she have one to herself."[12] The composite portrait of the young Alberta that emerges from these sources is of a rather shy and protected young woman with considerable imaginative depths.

Though we do not know how Alberta first encountered Austen's writings, we do, thanks to Henry, have an account of how her Austen collection began. (Alberta and Henry—who was known as Harry to his family and friends—met through his sister, a Goucher classmate of Alberta's, and married in 1930. By that time, Alberta had received her MA in English from the University of Wisconsin. Henry, the son of Eastern European immigrants, was completing a PhD in political science at Johns Hopkins University while working as an accountant and a lawyer.[13]) "I think all collections, particularly book collections, are necessarily love stories," Henry told a gathering of the Baltimore Bibliophiles in 1976, the year after Alberta's death.

We had both been intensely interested in Jane Austen but my interest was decidedly lower in the scale. As the Chapman edition of [Austen's] novels and of the letters appeared [in 1923 and 1932, respectively], they were promptly acquired and sat beside Geoffrey Keynes' *Bibliography* [*of Jane Austen*, 1929].[14] We were not too sure at the time what purpose the *Bibliography* would serve but somehow or other felt it was appropriate that this interesting work with facsimiles of title pages of first editions, references to early translations, periodicals and critical works be available to us as a guide. This work which is now in the Goucher Library has almost doubled in size as my wife continued to update the entries by interleaving the pages.

I used the year 1935 because in that year we made our first trip abroad together. When we emerged from the boat train at Waterloo Station in London and drifted toward the W. H. Smith book kiosk, our eyes naturally fell upon Lord David Cecil's attractive paperback edition of his *Jane Austen* [1935]. The acquisition of the David Cecil essay marked the dividing line between just owning Jane Austen books and embarking on some sort of collection. We had no idea at that moment how extensive the collection would become•or the ground that it would eventually cover.

While in London, we wandered up and down Charing Cross Road, gazing into the book shop windows and handling the contents of the attractive stands. ... On our first walk, we discovered Marks & Co. at 84 Charing Cross Road. We walked in and began asking about some of the Jane Austen bibliographical items we carried in our heads. We were also attracted to the beautiful color plate books and topographical items published in the Jane Austen period.[15]

Henry's account makes it clear that the collection originated as a joint effort: the only work that he specifically ascribes to Alberta alone is that of annotating Keynes's *Bibliography*. To what extent Alberta's purchases were funded by her own family's money, as opposed to Henry's earnings, is unknown. I will continue to refer to the collection as having been Alberta's, since both the Burkes attributed it to her throughout her lifetime and it was bequeathed at her death, not Henry's.[16]

Yet it is worth remembering Henry's significant role, which did not go unnoticed by the couple's friends in spite of his tendency to downplay his contribution. As one correspondent astutely noted to Henry, "I am impressed with your part in the collections even though you have been modest enough to step into the background and lay all the praise at Alberta's door. This is a great tribute to your love and respect for your wife. In her letters to me Alberta often spoke of your part in the Austen collection."[17] Henry himself described his involvement to the director of the Morgan Library by means of a wry reference to a busybody character from Austen's novel *Mansfield Park*: "Like Mrs. Norris, I did write many of the letters concerning our acquisitions, and I am sure that, if the telephone had been invented, Mrs. Norris would have made the calls."[18]

At least in his decades-later recollection for the Baltimore Bibliophiles, Henry presents the couple's interest in Austen as developing serendipitously,

Figure 2.2: Alberta and Henry Burke, photographed about to board the RMS *Queen Mary*, [1958]. Goucher College Library.

rather than as a result of definite intention. Further insight into the couple's possible motivations emerges from Keynes's *Bibliography*, which Henry had described in the Baltimore Bibliophiles talk as an "interesting work" and a "guide." (Indeed, the Burkes' copy of Keynes itself obliquely indicates the couple's eagerness to be up to date with work on Austen: the last page of the volume contains the notation, "THIS EDITION CONSISTS OF 875 COPIES, OF WHICH 200 ARE FOR THE UNITED STATES OF AMERICA … THIS IS NUMBER 24.")[19] Keynes's "Preface" offered his readers an enthusiastic, personal account of the rewards of collecting Austen. Keynes's own devotion to book collecting and the practice of bibliography, in which he was self-taught, accompanied his highly distinguished professional career as a surgeon.[20] "The field of bibliography," states Keynes, is "where I happen to find my special pleasure, and through which I can best express my homage to the genius of Miss Austen."[21] In Keynes's view, collecting and keeping track of early editions of an admired author is not work but "pleasure," not dry scholarship but "homage." So too would Alberta's practices of collecting and record-keeping become for her.

Keynes believed, furthermore, that the fundamental purpose of collecting rare books was to deepen the enjoyment of reading one's favorite works. Reading Austen's novels in their first editions, he declares, affords a special kind of access to the author and her era:

> No one who is at all sensitive to the right relations between the outsides of the early editions of so many famous books and their contents can fail to appreciate the special propriety of these issues of Jane Austen's novels. The format, typography and binding, whether the original boards or contemporary half-calf, all seem somehow to be full of the spirit of the period, and to read any of them in this shape gives a definite addition to the reader's pleasure. … To read any of these [six novels] now in the original boards is a satisfaction which only the very opulent could enjoy, even were the state of the paper joints of the covers usually not too delicate for it to be bibliophilically permissible; but anyone may be allowed to enjoy a bound copy, which at its best may be an even more delicate repast, some of the binders of the period having been able to invest the volumes with a demure neatness which is most comforting.[22]

In the Burkes' copy of Keynes's *Bibliography*, a penciled "!" appears in the margin opposite the last sentence. We are left to wonder whether Alberta objected to or appreciated Keynes's description of the bound first editions of Austen's novels as conveying, in their very physical shape, a "demure neatness." Aside from the somewhat strained analogy between feminine ("delicate") books and a female author, what comes across very clearly in this passage is Keynes's readerly rationale for collecting. Value and rarity for their own sake are not at issue here. Instead, Keynes focuses on the capacity of a historical volume to convey "the spirit of the period," and to contribute "a definite addition to the reader's pleasure." A true lover of Austen, he implies, would wish to take in her words in just the same form as was available to her original readers. To collect first editions of Austen, in other words, is to make possible for yourself a reading experience that is as close as possible to the one shared by Austen's earliest appreciators.

From Alberta's correspondence, we discover that her desire to feel closer, as a reader, to her favorite author extended beyond first editions to manuscripts: pages that were actually touched and inscribed by the beloved writer's hand. Alberta's reasons for seeking Austen manuscripts emerge most clearly from an exceptionally revealing letter she wrote on May 21, 1948 to one of her longtime dealers, Percy H. Muir of Elkin Matthews, Ltd.[23] In order to understand the circumstances that Alberta discusses in this letter, we need to look at the series of letters that concern the purchase and its aftermath. In addition to uncovering Alberta's very personal reasons for wishing to own Austen material, these letters establish the knowledge and care that she brought to her collecting endeavor, as well as the exceptional opportunities afforded her by the auction market in the years following the Second World War.

As was typical of her purchases at auction, Alberta began by studying the catalogues prepared by the auction houses and making strategic choices of items to pursue, including maximum bid amounts for each. On April 15, 1948, Alberta wrote to Percy Muir to say that she was "very excited" to see the catalogue for an upcoming sale at Sotheby's of Jane Austen manuscripts, and to give him instructions on how to bid. "I would be very pleased," she told Muir, "to have almost anything on the list (items 255 to 266)[.] I am willing to spend up to two hundred pounds (£200) at the sale." She stated which items she would prefer and how much she would be willing to spend for each: "I will be very pleased with anything which you can get for me within these prescribed limits. ... I am most anxious to secure so many items from this Jane Austen collection as is possible for a total of two hundred pounds."[24] It is worth noting the firmness with which Alberta emphasizes her budget here. Though she and Henry certainly invested a considerable amount of money in their collection, their means were by no means infinite, and they evidently prided themselves on paying what they felt to be fair prices.[25] Percy Muir's letter to Alberta a few days after the sale, in which he reports what he had obtained on her behalf, indicates the delicate position of a dealer who aims to satisfy both the desires and budget of his client: he apologized profusely for exceeding her overall limit by £20 in order to purchase, for £80, a particular item that he thought she would very much want.[26]

Alberta assured Muir in return that she was far happier to exceed her planned bid "by a moderate amount" than to "lose out on Lot 266, which will form a sentimental companion piece to the CEA letter which you bought for me last year."[27] The item Alberta hoped to secure was an unsigned set of verses on the subject of the Winchester Races, dated a few days before Austen's death in the cathedral city of Winchester; according to the Sotheby's auction comfortably, indeed during the last eight & forty hours she was more asleep than awake. Her looks altered & she fell away, but I perceived no material diminution of strength & tho' I was then hopeless of a recovery, I had no suspicion how rapidly my loss was approaching. — I have lost a treasure, such a Sister, such a friend as never can have been surpassed, — She was the sun of my life, the gilder of every pleasure, the soother of every sorrow, I had not a thought concealed from her, & it is as if I had lost a part of myself. I loved her only too well, not better than she deserved, but I am conscious that my affection for her made me sometimes unjust to & negligent of others, & I can acknowledge, more than as a general principle, the justice of the hand which has struck this blow. You know me too well to be at all afraid that I should suffer materially from my feelings;

time, with rest & change of air will remove. I thank God that I was enabled to attend her to the last & amongst my many causes of self-reproach I have not to add any wilfull neglect of her comfort. She felt herself to be dying about half an hour before she became tranquil & apparently unconscious. During that half hour was her struggle, poor Soul! she said she could not tell us what she suffered, tho' she complained of little fixed pain. When I asked her if there was any thing she wanted, her answer was she wanted nothing but death & some of her words were "God grant me patience, Pray for me Oh Pray for me". Her voice was affected but as long as she spoke she was intelligible. I hope I do not break your heart my dearest Fanny by these particulars, I mean to afford you gratification whilst I am relieving my own feelings. I could not write so to any body else, indeed you are the only person I have written to at all excepting your Grandmama, it was to her not your

Figure 2.3: Cassandra Austen, autograph letter to Fanny Knight, July 20, 1817, pages 2 and 3. The Pierpont Morgan Library, New York. Bequest of Alberta H. Burke, 1975. MA 2911.10. Photographic credit: The Pierpont Morgan Library, New York. Visible near the top of the left-hand page is Cassandra's heartfelt statement, written two days after Jane's death, that she has "lost a treasure, such a Sister, such a friend as never can have been surpassed ..."

catalogue, the verses were in Jane Austen's hand. In order to appreciate fully Alberta's desire for this poem, we must pause for a moment to identify the "CEA letter" to which she intended this new purchase would become "a sentimental companion piece." The letter in question is a long, grief-stricken account penned by Jane's sister Cassandra Elizabeth Austen that describes Jane's death, in Cassandra's arms, in July 1817. (My first epigraph for this book is drawn from this letter of Cassandra's.) "She was the sun of my life, the gilder of every pleasure, the soother of every sorrow," Cassandra wrote to her niece, Fanny Knight, whom she called "doubly dear to me now for her dear sake whom we have lost."[28]

By owning this document—which is by far the most emotionally moving of any letters written by or about Austen that remain in existence[29]—Alberta could connect herself as directly as possible to those who had originally, and most intimately, loved Jane Austen. In a letter following Alberta's successful bid for this document, Muir confirmed what we might imagine about what Cassandra's letter meant to Alberta, as an ardent admirer of Austen: "It caused a little heartburning in these quarters," Muir reported, "that the letter should be leaving England but it is a considerable consolation to know that it has gone to someone who appreciates it so deeply and warmly as you do."[30]

We can now see that to own this letter of Cassandra's as well as a piece of writing penned by Jane Austen shortly before her death would have afforded Alberta the maximum possible sense of access to Austen's final days. When Alberta received her purchases from the 1948 auction, however, she discovered to her dismay that the verses from Lot 266 did not appear to be in the same handwriting as other Jane Austen manuscripts she owned. Even before Alberta wrote to Percy Muir to explain her misgivings, she sent off a letter to R. W. Chapman, the eminent editor of Austen, at Oxford to request his expert view on the handwriting. "I have been very disturbed," Alberta informed Chapman,

> by a question which arose in my mind concerning Lot 266 (the verses on the Winchester Races.) The document was described as "M.S." in Sotheby's catalogue ... [yet] my doubts as to the writing are great. My own knowledge of Jane Austen's handwriting is limited to the specimens which I own and the collotype facsimiles in your books, so that I hesitate to pronounce any judgement on my own authority. Since I have bought the verses, I am not unhappy to have them. However for my own satisfaction, I would very much like to have your opinion ... [PS] After all, who am I to question the accuracy of Sotheby's cataloguer, but I still do doubt.[31]

In this letter to Chapman, Alberta's incomplete confidence in her own expertise is obvious. Her knowledge, as she states, comes from her own collection—her "specimens"—and from her personal familiarity with facsimiles published by Chapman; she lacks the training and authority of an editor like Chapman or an auction house cataloguer. "Great" as are her doubts, she cannot, on her own, be certain.

While Alberta represented herself to Chapman as an experienced collector who sought the "satisfaction" of a professional opinion, the letter she wrote to Percy Muir the next day reveals a much more personal and visceral reaction to the verses in question. Unlike Alberta's usual very neatly written pages, this letter is full of crossings-out and crammed-in additions, suggesting that she was working exceptionally hard to fix her ideas on paper. In the following transcription, I have noted which sentences she crossed out and which she inserted.

> The packet arrived yesterday and I spent an exciting and delightful day collating the letters and looking over my new treasures. [The following sentence is crossed out.] I am ~~delighted~~ so pleased with <u>everything</u> and I have had a wonderful time just handling and ~~petting~~ gloating over my new acquisitions. … It certainly was my impression, from the catalogue, that the verses were in Jane Austen's own hand-writing or I should not have been interested in them because they are insignificant in their own right. … Of course, I am not a hand-writing expert, nor even a student of the matter, but the question really does bother me. I have written to Mr. Chapman. … Naturally, I am very pleased to have the verses, but I would be much more pleased, were I certain that they were in Jane Austen's own autograph. Of course, that question would also affect their value.
>
> I have never bought anything for my Jane Austen collection because it was "valuable" or because I thought that someday it would be worth more than at the present. That question has never ~~entered my thoughts~~ come up. [The following sentence is inserted.] The J.A. collection is the perpetual pleasure of my life. I have bought each thing because I felt I could not live without it, and because Jane Austen is "St. Jane" in my private hagiology. [The following sentence is inserted.] However neither my adoration nor my purse extends to relics of her family. But I do feel rather unhappy about the question of the hand in which these verses are written. They do not have enough merit in themselves [the next eighteen words are crossed out] to merit a place in my limited shelves unless they are what I imagined them to have been—one of the last bits of writing which literally came from her hand. … You can see why the question of the verses is of concern to me in my idolatry.[32]

Nowhere else in her correspondence does Alberta describe in such a heartfelt and thorough manner her impulse to collect. Indeed, according to Henry, Alberta typically evaded direct questions about her love of Austen. "Alberta was frequently asked how she came to be interested in Jane Austen," recalls Henry, "but the expression on her face in response to that question was very much the kind of expression that you would see on the face of someone sitting over a filet mignon and being asked how he came to like steak."[33] Thus this letter to Muir is exceptionally valuable in affording us a unique window onto Alberta's most private motivations and feelings.

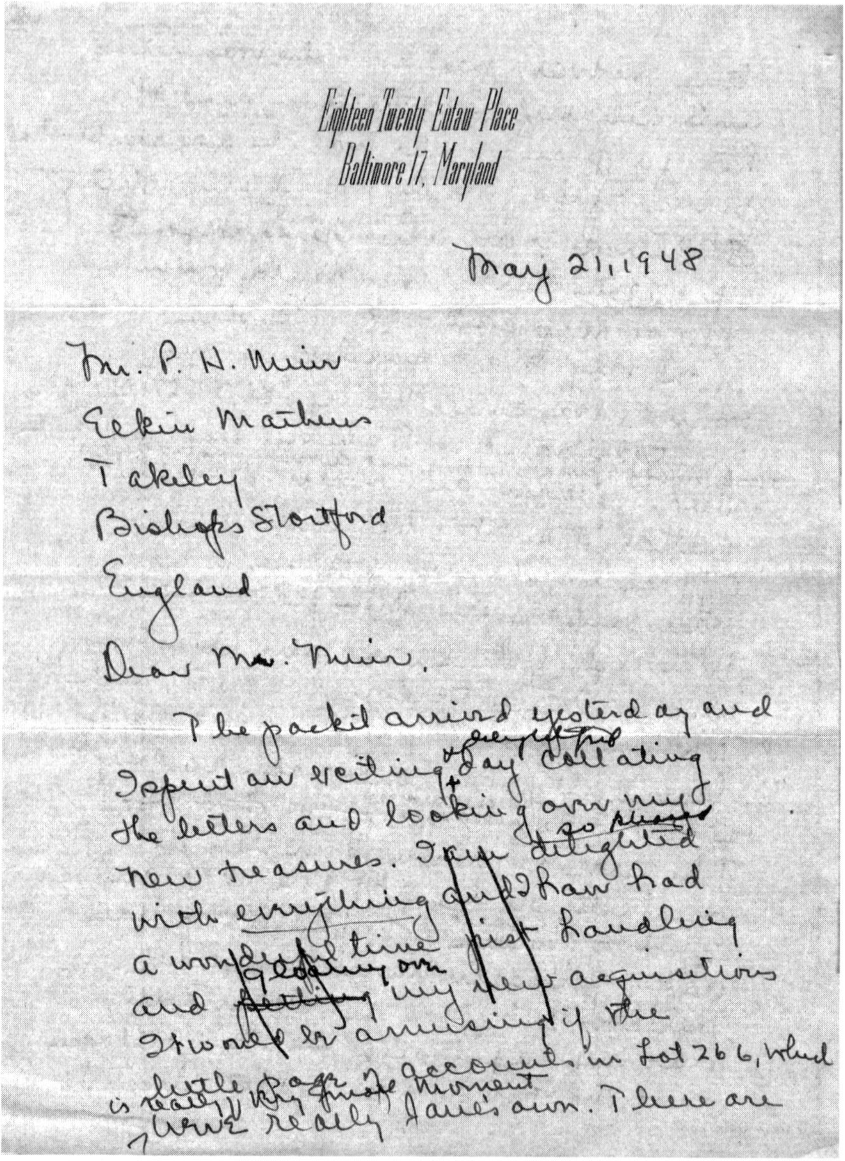

Figure 2.4: Alberta Burke, letter to Percy H. Muir, May 21, 1948, page 1. Goucher College Library. Note the crossings-out, which show Alberta's effort to choose words that precisely convey her experience of beholding new items for her collection.

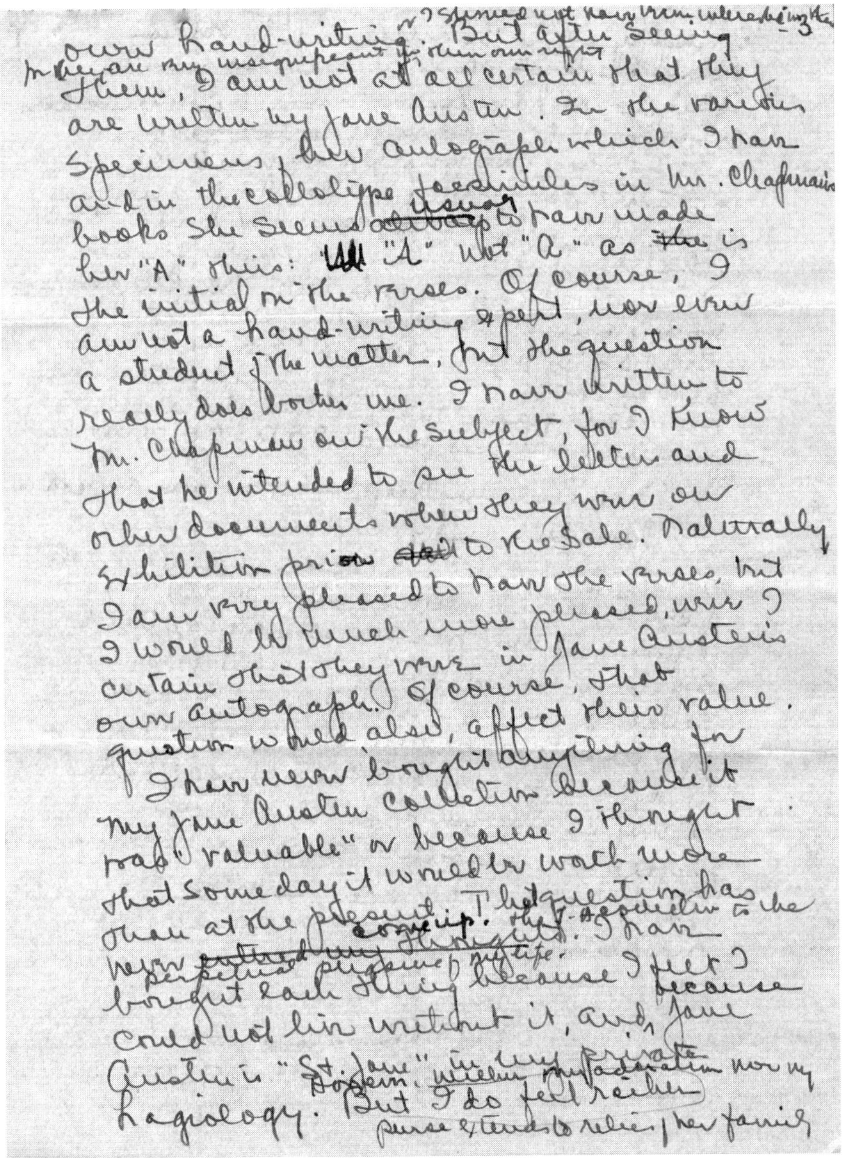

[illegible] –3
own hand-writing. But after seeing
[illegible]
them, I am not at all certain that they
are written by Jane Austen. In the various
specimens of her autograph which I have
and in the collotype facsimiles in Mr. Chapman's
books she seems ~~always~~ usually to have made
her "A" thus: "A" not "a" as ~~the~~ is
the initial on the verses. Of course, I
am not a hand-writing expert, nor even
a student of the matter, but the question
really does bother me. I have written to
Mr. Chapman on the subject, for I know
that he intended to see the letter and
other documents when they were on
exhibition prior ~~to~~ to the sale. Naturally
I am very pleased to have the verses, but
I would be much more pleased, were I
certain that they were in Jane Austen's
own autograph. Of course, that
question would also affect their value.
I have never bought anything for
my Jane Austen collection because it
was "valuable" or because I thought
that someday it would be worth more
than at the present. That question has
never ~~entered my thoughts~~. I have [illegible] the J.A. collection to be the perpetual pleasure of my life.
bought each thing because I feel I
could not live without it, and, because Jane
Austen is "St. Jane" in my private
hagiology. But I do feel rather [illegible]
purse extends to relics of her family

Figure 2.5: Alberta Burke, letter to Percy H. Muir, May 21, 1948, page 3. Goucher College Library. On this page Alberta refers with exceptional intimacy to her "J.A. collection" as the "perpetual pleasure" of her life.

Alberta makes clear, furthermore, that her devotion is strictly to Jane, not to the Austen family, and that she shapes her collection around what brings her closer to her beloved author. Especially given her own Jewish identity, Alberta's choice of overtly religious language—"St. Jane," "hagiology," "relics," "idolatry"—is striking, and also revealing. Just as a relic or icon is thought, in orthodox Christianity, to make possible direct contact from a believer, to a saint, to God, so too does Alberta seem to have felt that she was coming as close as possible to Austen herself by owning, touching, and reading works that, as she said, "literally came from her [Austen's] hand." Alberta evidently cherished manuscript items that convey intimate glimpses of Austen. In addition to Cassandra's letter after Jane's death, Alberta purchased two of the only manuscript items in existence that shed light on Austen's literary ambitions and successes: one tiny page fragment in Austen's handwriting tracks the profits of her novels, while another in Cassandra's handwriting records the composition dates of Austen's novels.[34]

Indeed, Alberta's letter to Muir confirms that she collected Austen material chiefly for personal reasons, rather than as investments. Like Keynes, who emphasized the delight rather than the value of owning first editions, she describes her "J.A. collection" as the "perpetual pleasure" of her life. Yet her statement "I have bought each thing because I felt I could not live without it" presents her collecting as less a delight than a necessity. Alberta's Austen collection was her life's work in two senses: she devoted her life to it, and it, in a way, sustained her.

In spite of Alberta's declaration to Muir that she was "very pleased to have" the verses regardless of the handwriting, once R. W. Chapman confirmed her judgment, she was eager to be rid of them. (Chapman guessed that the handwriting was that of Austen's brother James.)[35] Since too much time had elapsed for Sotheby's to accept a return of the purchase, Percy Muir arranged, with evident relief, a resale of the document. We will meet T. Edward Carpenter, the man to whom Muir disposed of the verses, in the next section of this chapter.

How perceptive *was* Alberta in identifying the handwriting as not belonging to Jane Austen? I wondered when I read this series of letters at the Goucher College Library in February, 2010. My curiosity was satisfied in July, 2010, at Winchester Cathedral, where Austen is buried and which at the time of my visit had mounted an exhibit titled "The Jane Austen Story." (I will discuss Winchester Cathedral as an Austen tourist site in Chapter 4.) On one level of the exhibit case were the Winchester Races verses—now generally referred to as the "Venta" verses, after their title on the manuscript page—and on other levels of the case were several items signed by Austen. The differences in handwriting were very obvious, with the verses featuring much wider spaces between words and lines, and many differently shaped letters, than were to be seen on the pages signed by Austen. Anyone comparing the manuscripts would agree with Alberta; she demonstrated neither exceptional knowledge nor instinct in making her judgment. We have the sloppiness of Sotheby's cataloguer to thank for the occasion on which Alberta wrote most revealingly about how collecting brought her closer to Austen.

The Omnivore's Reach

I call Alberta an Austen omnivore because her enthusiasm kindled in response to anything associated with her favorite author: not only manuscripts and rare editions, but any new book (popular or scholarly), radio broadcast, newspaper article, or product that could claim an Austen connection, however small or tenuous. As Alberta wrote to Eleanor Falley, Goucher's librarian in the 1930s and a fellow enthusiast, "I am always enchanted by any little scrap of knowledge which has anything to do with Jane Austen."[36] Whether taking in a new adaptation of an Austen novel or reading a new work of scholarship, however, Alberta's eager expectation often gave way to a feeling of letdown. Referring to a new version of *Emma*, she told the same correspondent, "I always anticipate these attempts most eagerly, and hope that *this* one will be the perfect adap[ta]tion, then I end with pursed lips and disappointment."[37] To the bibliographer David J. Gilson, she gave the following report on her reading of a new scholarly treatise, Karl Kroeber's 1971 *Styles in Fictional Structure*: "I did not enjoy the book nor did it make me pause to think about J.A. in any new way."[38] Yet Alberta persevered, always seeking out new works and always giving them a chance. "I am most eager to see the new book on Jane Austen," she wrote to R. W. Chapman in 1939, in a manner typical of her lifelong attitude. "When is it to be published, and what is its title? A new work on Jane is always a most exciting pleasure for me."[39] Having focused so far on the items in the Burke Collection that are valuable in a conventional sense—the manuscripts and rare editions—it is time to widen our gaze to take in the full extent of the material pertaining to Austen that Alberta enthusiastically acquired and carefully preserved.

In 1936, Alberta began the first of a series of ten scrapbooks: bound notebooks into which she pasted newspaper clippings, theater programs, print advertisements, crossword puzzles and other ephemera with an Austen connection, as well as some of her own correspondence about Austen. As Henry put it in his 1976 address to the Baltimore Bibliophiles, Alberta "maintained careful notes of all references to Jane Austen and her works no matter how insignificant or trivial the comments."[40] Alberta dated each new addition and often recorded her opinions, especially of new adaptations: she noted that a 1941 radio broadcast based on *Pride and Prejudice*, for instance, struck her as a "thoroughly unsatisfactory and bastardized version!"[41] Indeed, Alberta did her best to capture as much material as possible relating to new dramatic or cinematic versions of an Austen novel. As Henry pointed out when describing the scrapbooks to the director of the Morgan Library, "the three big events which almost filled a notebook apiece were the production of Helen Jerome's [play] *Pride and Prejudice* [1935], the movie with Lawrence Olivier and Greer Garson [1940], and the musical *First Impressions* [1959]. Records and stills were also added."[42] Several of Alberta's correspondents who knew of or shared her admiration of Austen supplied her with material to include as well, sometimes newspaper clippings, sometimes more elaborate contributions. "I have found time to do one little thing for you, dear," Alberta's friend Averil G. Hassall wrote in 1966, "which was to go to see a performance of PRIDE and PREJUDICE, by proxy for you. And I intend to write you an account of it—a sort of essay—to tuck in the programme & add to your J.A. collection."[43]

Far from focusing only on the most publicized adaptations of her day, Alberta cast her net as widely as possible. The carbon-copy letters that she included in her scrapbook reveal how tirelessly she sought out new material. Consider, for instance, the following request she made in 1940 for the script of a radio program that had starred Helen Hayes, to which Alberta had apparently just finished listening:

> The broadcast version of Jane Austen's *Pride and Prejudice* which Miss Hayes gave this evening was a very charming glimpse into the highlights of one of my favorite novels. Miss Hayes' "Elizabeth" was an interesting version of one of the "most delightful creatures who has appeared in print." To one who is a whole-hearted admirer of Jane Austen, her appearance in a new medium is a most thrilling and interesting event.
>
> I am hoping that it will be possible for me to purchase a copy of the script of the broadcast version which you gave tonight. I have a collection of several hundred items of material by and related to Jane Austen, including several autograph letters, first editions of all her novels, biographical and critical works, magazine material, and the script which was used in a broadcast version of Jane Austen's life (her first appearance on the air.) My collection is my own private diversion, and is not connected with any sort of institution, public or private. I can therefore promise that if you do permit me to purchase a copy of the *Pride and Prejudice* script no commercial or any other use will be made of it. It would be merely a private possession of which I should be extremely proud. Anything which is in any way related to Jane Austen is of intense interest to me, and an item in which her name is associated with that of the actress for whom I have a most unbounded admiration, would be indeed a highly prized part of my collection.
>
> I realize, of course, that the scripts of broadcasts are not generally available to the public, but I am hoping that you will be able to make an exception for me.[44]

As this letter makes clear, Alberta exerted herself as a collector with equal energy whether she was pursuing a radio script or a manuscript. Moreover, she took equal pride in all her rarities, even those—like a radio script pertaining to Austen's "first appearance on the air"—that would not necessarily be "highly prized" by more conventional collectors. (We can see, too, that Alberta quoted from Austen's writings habitually, if sometimes loosely, regardless of whether her recipient could reasonably be expected to understand her references.)[45]

The omnivorous nature of Alberta's collecting, to which the contents of her scrapbooks attest, is strikingly evident too in her handwritten indices to the volumes. At the back of the first scrapbook appears a list, in minuscule handwriting, of numbered entries headed "References and Allusions to Jane Austen (Not Exhaustive) (Begun September 22, 1936)," which includes titles of works with an Austen connection, including scholarly articles, of which Alberta wished to keep track. Continued in each of the subsequent volumes, her list of "References and Allusions" had reached #2805 at the time of her death.

Alberta's ten scrapbooks challenge the notion that she, shying away from publishing herself, sought to contribute to Austen scholarship only by forming a collection for the benefit of others.[46] Her scrapbooks are, in their idiosyncratic way, manuscript works of amateur scholarship. She numbered the pages, cross-referenced her entries, and prepared handwritten title pages, with volume numbers, for each book. Alberta's imitation of the form of a published book, especially in her title pages, is strongly reminiscent of the efforts of the teenage Austen, in her own manuscript notebooks of stories, to mimic the appearance of professionally printed books.[47]

Paging through Alberta's scrapbooks is an almost overwhelming experience. She included so much more than a researcher could recover today, even with the web searches and databases now at our disposal: literary quizzes, plays on words, print advertisements, letters to the editor of various publications, as well as programs from live performances. Not only the range of material but its physical presence in the scrapbooks—tiny clippings squeezed in, envelopes bulging from the pages—conveys a very powerful sense of Alberta's fascination, perhaps even obsession, with Austen.[48] Alberta's ten scrapbooks resemble the creation of a visionary artist: intricate, time-intensive, and the product of a most unusual mind.

Not surprisingly, the Baltimore rare-books dealer who was hired to appraise Alberta's collection after her death was uncertain what to make of her scrapbooks. "Although they would have little value on their own," William Filby concluded of the scrapbooks, "they represent years of collecting, and with the other works they have a considerable value. $100 a volume, at least."[49] A more effusive assessment of the scrapbooks came from J. David Grey, who was to become, along with Henry Burke, one of the founders of the Jane Austen Society of North America in 1979. Grey praised the Burkes for having "performed consummately well on behalf of Miss Jane Austen" and confessed to that he "hope[d] someday to be able to accomplish as much. If I do, it will only be with the assistance of those precious notebooks at Goucher. Anyone who purports to evoke 'her' shade and do it justice is compelled to make the

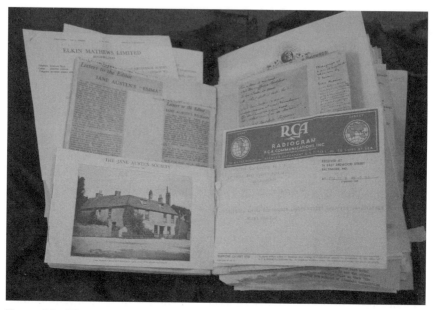

Figure 2.6: Alberta Burke's first scrapbook, covering the years 1936–1944. Goucher College Library. In her scrapbooks, Alberta preserved and annotated articles, ephemera, and correspondence pertaining to Austen. These pages include a photograph of Jane Austen's House in Chawton from a Jane Austen Society report as well as Alberta's correspondence with her principal dealer, Elkin Matthews.

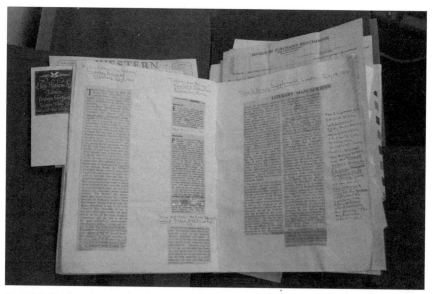

Figure 2.7: Alberta Burke's fifth scrapbook, covering the years 1952–1956. Goucher College Library. Visible on these pages is Alberta's careful annotation of the excerpts she chose to include: note, on the right-hand page, her list of Austen materials in the collection of the Pierpont Morgan Library, the eventual beneficiary of her own Austen manuscripts.

pilgrimage from this day forward."[50] As both Filby's and Grey's remarks make clear, the importance of Alberta's scrapbooks lies to a considerable degree in the eye of the beholder. To Filby, the appraiser, the scrapbooks gain worth chiefly from their association with the more conventionally valuable contents of Alberta's collection. To Grey, who shared Alberta's ardent admiration of Austen, the scrapbooks seem "precious" and as worthy of attention as other sites of Austen "pilgrimage."

Among the many items with fleeting references to Austen that Alberta preserved in her scrapbooks is a newspaper article that invites more sustained consideration: an anonymously published *New York Times* article from 1965 titled "True Devotion to an Author." "Readers of particular authors, those who have known that absurdly one-sided love for writers who make their own lives interesting, show their devotion by their downward glance," asserts the article's author; a subheadline identifies such devotees as "unrequited readers."[51] "When there are no more stories to wait for … they read the biographies, the literary essays, the letters, travel articles, early poems, diaries, and finally the memoirs of all who knew them. There are those who publish books about their authors. … And there are those nonwriters who publish bibliographies as their contribution. Or they start literary groups for readers of Jane Austen or the Brontës …"[52] In particular, argues the journalist, reading works admired by your own beloved author can bring you closer to understanding him or her: "The devoted and unpedantic reader of an author has probably found, by enjoying his author's bookish interests, as much of the secret as anyone is ever likely to know."[53]

As I read this clipping in Alberta's scrapbook, I wondered what she thought of it. She underlined, as was her habit, the reference to Jane Austen, but surely more than the mention of literary groups alone would have held meaning for her. Perhaps she appreciated some descriptive phrases more than others; perhaps she would have preferred to think of herself as a "devoted and unpedantic reader" rather than as someone possessed of (possessed by?) an "absurdly one-sided love" for a writer who made "her own life interesting." Having given form to her devotion in an extensive collection, and having arranged to deposit that collection at institutions for the enjoyment and use of others after her death, perhaps she felt that her love, if "one-sided," was not without purpose. A "nonwriter" she might have been, but a productive and influential amateur nonetheless.

Sharing with Other Janeites

Alberta's description of herself to Percy Muir as "gloating over [her] new acquisitions"[54] might encourage the impression that her Austen possessions provided her with pleasure that was purely selfish, or shared only with her husband. On the contrary, Alberta sought to make her collection accessible to fellow enthusiasts both during her lifetime and, through bequests, after her death. Her letters amply demonstrate her interest in sharing her knowledge of and passion for Austen. So too does her participation in the Jane Austen Society, which she joined as a life member in 1947 and whose Annual General Meetings in Chawton she and Henry frequently attended. As we will see, Alberta's most public act on behalf of fellow Austen lovers was her sensational announcement, at the 1949 meeting of the Jane Austen Society, that she would donate an especially prized Austen relic to Jane Austen's House, which had just opened to visitors for the first time. Throughout her lifetime, furthermore, Alberta influenced the world of Austen appreciation and Austen studies much more steadily, by sharing information with individual Austen lovers and scholars, as well as with the reading public more generally. Her careful, if somewhat unconventional, planning for the disposition of her Austen collection was in keeping with her lifelong impulse to spread the word about her favorite author.

Alberta's desire to celebrate Jane Austen with fellow devotees was manifest years before any Jane Austen Society existed to bring together those passionate amateur readers for whom Rudyard Kipling, in a 1926 short story, had popularized the name of "Janeites."[55] The original, UK Jane Austen Society was founded in 1940. Five years earlier, Alberta wrote to one of her favorite periodicals, the *Saturday Review of Literature*, to note the significance of December 16, 1935 as the 160th anniversary of Austen's birth and to urge Janeites to recognize the occasion appropriately. "Since there are no clubs which bear her name, no Jane Austen Society to issue learned treatises," Alberta reasoned, "Jane Austen's admirers ought to commemorate her birth with some fitting exercise." Quoting from the poem that accompanied Kipling's story "The Janeites," Alberta continued, "we cannot drink a toast of 'Glory, love, and honor unto England's Jane' in old Constantia wine these days. However, we can all manage to celebrate with, at least, a baked apple (baked three times according to Mr. Woodhouse)"—a reference to Austen's *Emma*—"or some dried cherries, and honor at one time 'England's Jane' and the man who gave our cult its most appropriate name."[56]

Alberta's efforts to build connections among Janeites, and, indeed, to recruit new enthusiasts to what she herself termed a "cult" of admirers, continued unabated in subsequent decades. One of her tactics was to urge the editors of periodicals to which she subscribed to review new books about Austen—and, sometimes, to berate those editors for not having already published reviews of the books in question. To the *Saturday Review of Literature*, she complained in 1949 that

> it is high time that you paid some attention to the tastes and desires of your readers who do not spend all their time brooding about the problems of the Atomic Age. There have been published this year five books about Jane Austen, none of which you have noticed in any way. ... For the admirers of

Jane Austen, and for any others who might become such, why not devote a column or two to a review of *Jane Austen: Facts and Problems* by R. W. Chapman, *More About Jane Austen* by Sheila Kaye-Smith and G. B. Stern, *Jane Austen* by Elizabeth Jenkins, *Parson Austen's Daughter* by Helen Ashton and *Pemberley Shades* by D. A. Bonavia-Hunt? Or, if this is contrary to your present policy, why not change the name of the magazine to *Saturday Review* and drop the very misleading words "Of Literature?"[57]

Alberta's aim here is evidently to proselytize. Already well aware herself of the new Austen-related publications she lists, she hopes to have these titles brought to the attention of others who already are or "might become" admirers of Austen. A staff member at the *Saturday Review* thanked Alberta rather dryly for her "friendly interest" and assured her that plans had been made to review the books in question "long before" her letter was received.[58]

Alberta contributed with equal force, though with a somewhat moderated tone, to debates about Austen that took place in a more highbrow venue, the letters column of the *Times Literary Supplement*. In pre-Internet days, the *TLS* functioned as the premier forum for scholars and amateurs of literature to compare notes and resolve controversies. Intervening in a 1962 discussion concerning the date of composition of *Northanger Abbey*, Alberta announced to the readers of the *TLS* that she owned "the scrap of notes on the composition of Jane Austen's novels written by Cassandra," and she proceeded to knowledgeably discuss both sides of the dating question.[59] In a 1963 letter to the *TLS*, she recounted the story of the misattributed "Venta" verses, which had caused her such anguish in 1948, and offered her own well-informed opinion on whether a second copy of those verses could be in Cassandra's handwriting.[60]

In addition to writing letters for publication, Alberta generously shared the resources of her collection with fellow knowledgeable enthusiasts, and scholars, who corresponded with her. In May 1975, just before her death, she answered enquiries from Andrew Wright, whom I mentioned in Chapter 1 as the first scholar to survey adaptations of Austen. Most significantly, Alberta offered both encouragement and practical support to David J. Gilson, whose project of expanding Keynes's *Bibliography* culminated in the 1982 publication of his own *Bibliography of Jane Austen*. Like Keynes, who was by profession a surgeon, Gilson approached his Austen scholarship from something of an outsider's perspective. As he explained when introducing himself (by letter) to Alberta, he was a staff member of Oxford University's modern languages library, the Taylor Institution Library; modern languages had been his own subject of study at Oxford. Collecting material related to Austen, Gilson explained, was one of his "chief private interests."[61]

Until Alberta's death, she and Gilson corresponded regularly, exchanging news of new Austen publications and sometimes the books themselves. Alberta and Gilson also met several times when the Burkes traveled to England, as well as in Baltimore a few months before Alberta's death, when Gilson came to study the Burkes' collection. Each evidently found in the other a true kindred spirit: a lover of Austen who found fullest expression for that devotion through collecting and bibliography.[62] Each served as the ideal audience, too, for the other's effusions. Alberta, for instance, thanked Gilson for mailing her a new essay about Austen by telling him that possessing it left her "so thrilled and excited" that she could "scarcely write."[63] For his part, the more reticent Gilson wrote with evident pain to Henry after Alberta's death, saying that he found it "difficult to put into words how much I have valued our correspondence and friendship for the past almost eight years."[64]

Alberta's confident, determined advocacy in her letters for lovers of Austen belies her personality: she was exceptionally introverted and averse to fame. Henry described her after her death as having been "a very, very retiring person."[65] Certainly she did not seek to broadcast the existence of her collection outside of the comparatively narrow world of Austen studies.[66] She did, we know, welcome a Goucher literature class to her apartment on at least one occasion to show the students her collection. According to the college newspaper's account of the field trip, Alberta impressed the class not only with her possessions but with her "tremendous store of knowledge about her subject: she is able to tell immediately the precise chapter in the exact Austen novel which mentions any place or happening, and she knows all about the customs and manners of Jane's day."[67] In public, however, Alberta acknowledged her Austen collection only once: at the meeting of the Jane Austen Society (JAS) on July 23, 1949. On that day, Jane Austen's House (also known as Chawton Cottage) was officially opened to visitors for the first time. Purchased in 1947 by T. Edward Carpenter with the intent that it serve as a memorial to his son (recently killed in the Second World War), the building was repaired with funds generated by a JAS appeal and was administered by the newly formed Jane Austen Memorial Trust.[68]

Several distinct sources give us access to the events, and emotions, of that July day. The JAS's official minutes, after recapitulating the history of the house, offer a dry account of the proceedings: "Mr. Carpenter ... referred to the danger of relics leaving the country, and said that he himself had acquired a collection of relics, valued at £1116, which could be passed on to the Trustees at the value paid for them as and when funds were available. After his speech, Mrs. Henry G. Burke, of Baltimore, U.S.A., rose and amid applause offered to give to the society certain souvenirs, including locks of the hair of Jane Austen and her father, which she had bought in London in 1948. (The locks of hair have already been received)."[69] More of the emotional temperature of the occasion comes across in Henry's recollections:

> When we attended the Jane Austen Society meeting on July 23, 1949, Mr. Edward Carpenter, who had recently acquired Chawton Cottage as a memorial to his son killed in the war, complained bitterly that because of a shortage of funds valuable relics were leaving England and noted with

particular sadness that a lock of Jane Austen's hair had been purchased at Sotheby's by an American. Alberta muttered under her breath, "I will give them the damned hair." She then rose and said very simply, "I am the American who bought Jane's hair and if the Society would like to have it, I shall be glad to make a contribution of the hair." At that point, the tent in which the meeting was being held almost collapsed.[70]

Alberta preserved her own memories of the day in red-pencil marginal annotations to her copy of the JAS's meeting minutes. "It was *not* Mr. Carpenter's appeal," she wrote, "but his very bad manners which made me so angry that I gave the Society the hair on the spot rather than waiting to make it a posthumus gift!"[71] Evidently, Alberta felt offended first by Carpenter's pointed complaint and subsequently by the implication, in the JAS minutes, that her response to him resulted from generosity rather than a sense of having been insulted.

Those in attendance at that day's meeting attested to the high drama of the occasion. One JAS member, Katharine Kenyon, wrote to Alberta to thank her profusely for her gift, declaring that she would "never forget the delicious thrill of hearing you say so surprisingly, so delightfully, that the 2 locks of hair mentioned by Mr Carpenter wd come back to England. It was a sudden twist of simple drama that Jane herself wd have loved & oh how astonished *she* wd have been—Tho' I fancy Cassandra wd have been far more so."[72] Dorothy Darnell, the founder of the JAS, gave warm thanks on behalf of the Society and added, "There was such a flutter of excitement as you know, which is an indication of what pleasure the possession of anything so precious will be to so many in the future."[73] Kenyon and Darnell convey vividly the affect of these mid-twentieth-century English enthusiasts of Austen, particularly their attachment to relics such as the hair and their tendency to imagine what Jane and Cassandra would have felt.

As Henry's account in particular makes clear, Alberta's gift of the hair held special significance because of her own identity as an American. Indeed, a second letter from Dorothy Darnell underscores, apparently unintentionally, the sense of distance and difference felt by English lovers of Austen towards their American counterparts. "The whole feeling about your generosity and your unique gift has touched us all most deeply," wrote Darnell to Alberta and Henry, "and it is with the warmest gratitude that we hope that you will not think of yourselves as American strangers, but as one of us, if you will."[74] By returning the lock of hair to Chawton, in other words, Alberta did more than restore to Chawton Cottage a piece of Austen's very body so that Austen lovers could visit and venerate it. Alberta's gift ensured her admission, despite her nationality, to the tight circle of English lovers of Austen.

Characteristically, Alberta declined to capitalize on the international notoriety that could have attended her donation. In one of her scrapbooks, she pasted in a request for a radio interview from a journalist named Miss Alwyn and annotated it thus: "I refused all requests for an interview on the air or at home, or a discussion of my collection or my gift of the hair. However Miss

Alwyn ... used the English article as a jumping off place for a discussion of the hair ... a 5 minute talk in which she identified J.A. 'as a prolific writer of light novels, much admired in England'! How right I was not to get embroiled with such a one from the outer darkness!"[75] As often with Alberta's private writings, it is hard to discern just how flippant she is being here; at any rate, her relief at having remained silent is apparent.

Despite thoughts to the contrary, Alberta did not make further donations or plan bequests to Chawton Cottage. Even before the momentous 1949 JAS meeting, Alberta was aware, thanks to her dealer Percy Muir, that she was competing with Carpenter to purchase Austen relics. As Muir informed Alberta in 1948, following the auction that yielded the lock of hair as well as the problematic "Venta" verses,

> You will be interested to know that after the sale I had some correspondence with a gentleman who has bought Jane's house at Chawton and who is proposing, in co-operation with the Jane Austen Society, to put it into suitable repair and make it into a Jane Austen Museum. The purpose of his writing to me was to say that he had been the buyer of all the other lots at Sotheby's and would like to acquire the three that I had bought. I explained, of course, that this was impossible, and it may perhaps add just a little to your enthusiasm in possessing them that they were wanted for this purpose.[76]

Alberta reacted just as Muir predicted, replying that she was "now doubly glad that so much of the things fell to my share. I feel very selfishly in the matter, even though I know that Mr. Carpenter's purchases will give pleasure to so many more people than my solitary gloatings."[77] How *did* Alberta justify to herself owning, and "gloating" over, items that could have been seen and appreciated by many more people, if she had allowed Carpenter to acquire them? In large part, I would argue, because only a few years after beginning her collection she laid plans to ensure that it would reach a wider audience, in America, after her death.

In 1939, only four years (according to Henry's account) after the couple started purchasing Austen material in earnest, Alberta sounded out Goucher's president, David Allan Robertson, about leaving her collection to her alma mater. "During the past few years," she wrote to Robertson, "I have gathered together a small library of about two hundred books and magazines by, or concerning, Jane Austen. ... The collection contains a few rare and valuable items, as well as many merely interesting ones. The most important features are a set of the first editions of the six novels in contemporary bindings, one first edition (*Emma*) in original boards, and two holograph signed letters of Jane Austen."[78] Robertson responded the next day, with evident eagerness: "As a Jane Austen enthusiast, as a former professor of English literature, as the executive of Goucher College, as one interested in securing an increasing emphasis in Goucher College on the achievement of distinguished women like Jane Austen, I am enthusiastic in appreciation of your generosity."[79] He offered, furthermore, to show Alberta architectural plans for the college's new campus in Towson, Maryland, so that she could see what he called the "future home of the 'Alberta H. Burke collection of Austeniana.'"[80]

In November 1954, spurred by a quite explicit appeal from Carpenter that she sell him what he called the "relics" in her possession,[81] Alberta renewed contact with Goucher to offer an update as to the extent of her collection and to ensure that the library would still welcome it. Goucher's librarian at the time, Sarah D. Jones, subsequently visited Alberta and viewed the collection. Jones's follow-up letter reveals that she and Alberta discussed the possibility (which Alberta had not mentioned in writing) that a different institution would receive the Austen manuscripts.[82] In reply, Alberta expressed her relief at settling the question of her collection's future: "From the time when my Jane Austen material first began to overflow the one-shelf bounds assigned to it, I have always intended that Goucher should be the ultimate recipient of the Jane Austen books, and I have hoped that, sometime in the future, others would partake of the very great pleasure which they have given to me for many years. Now, after receiving your assurances, I do not feel that it will be necessary for me to reconsider the matter again. Goucher College Library will have the Jane Austen collection, minus only the letters."[83] Alberta indicated, too, that she might have Chawton Cottage in mind to receive whatever Goucher did not: "Since 1949, when the Jane Austen Society acquired a permanent home, I have thought of it," she told Jones, "as an alternative beneficiary to Goucher College Library. I shall continue to remember it in that capacity."[84]

It was not the Jane Austen Memorial Trust or the JAS, however, but the Pierpont Morgan Library to which Alberta announced that she would donate her Austen manuscripts. Though Alberta was familiar with the Morgan's extensive holdings of Austen manuscripts from previous visits to the library, she had not given the institution any earlier indication that she was considering it as a prospective beneficiary.[85] Alberta's bequest, according to Charles Ryskamp, the Morgan's director at the time of her death, "came as a complete surprise to the Library; it was in keeping with her modesty and reticence."[86]

Carpenter, who remained unaware of Alberta's arrangements with the Morgan, did not give up on his rather transparent efforts to persuade her to give her manuscripts to the Jane Austen Memorial Trust. "So many people are generous after death by will but why not scatter benefits whilst one is alive and see the welcome fruits[?]" he urged her in July 1955. In the same letter, he attempted to appeal to Alberta's nationality, implying that American lovers of Austen appreciate Chawton Cottage more than the English do. "I count myself very fortunate in having so many good American friends," he wrote, pointedly. "I constantly meet them at Chawton and receive much valuable commendation from them as to the House and its arrangement, a generous tribute I do not have from many English visitors."[87] Alberta, however, evidently held quite a different idea of what it meant to be an "American friend" of Austen. By bequeathing her Austen materials to Goucher and the Morgan Library, Alberta made it possible for other American Janeites to share a sense of closeness with Austen without having to cross the Atlantic.

Alberta's decision to keep her collection, with the exception of the famous lock of hair, at such a distance from Jane Austen's House is especially surprising given her own attachment to English places associated with Austen's life. Not only did Alberta visit Chawton frequently for JAS meetings, but she chose an image of Winchester Cathedral—Austen's burial site—as the centerpiece of the bookplate she designed for herself. We might, then, expect Alberta to have agreed with Carpenter's declaration, in a 1954 letter, that "the House at Chawton is the sanctuary where her relics should rest."[89] Perhaps Alberta felt offended, as she had at the 1949 AGM, by being importuned by Carpenter. Perhaps the request would have been more persuasive had it come from another source. Or perhaps Alberta took exception more generally to the notion that American hands were unworthy of English treasures.

Figure 2.8: Alberta Burke's bookplate. Goucher College Library. The image is of the front of Winchester Cathedral, where Austen is buried. The quotation is from the poem Rudyard Kipling composed to accompany the 1926 publication of his story "The Janeites."[88]

Though Alberta did not bequeath her Austen manuscripts to Goucher, her gift of the other rare materials in her collection to an undergraduate college makes a strong statement about the purpose she intended her lovingly acquired books to fulfill after her death. Alberta wished her materials to be available not solely to trained researchers but to everyone with an interest in literature. In her earliest letter to Goucher about her prospective donation, she stipulated that, if the library accepted her materials, "all of the items must be available for use at all times."[90] Sarah Jones, the librarian in the 1950s with whom Alberta negotiated the definite terms of her bequest, expressed particular sympathy for Alberta's views on access to the collection, as well as with her approach to literature more generally. Jones noted in a letter that "we wish to expose the students to books, not only as tools in the acquisition of knowledge, but also as literature which needs no other excuse for being, a means in itself of enriching life."[91] Alberta's decision to make her materials available in an undergraduate library is fully in keeping with her efforts, throughout her life, to share with others the great pleasure she found as an amateur in reading, discussing, and collecting Austen.

The landscape of Austen appreciation has altered considerably since Alberta's lifetime. Austen-inspired collecting now usually means acquiring newly published books, DVDs, and tchotchkes, not manuscripts and rare editions. Thanks to the efforts of many creators (and, arguably, some opportunists), much more Austen-related material is available to consume. Instead of a few film and stage adaptations of Austen's novels, we now have dozens. Sequels to and updates of Austen novels have proliferated even more, with some including content—from erotica to horror—that Alberta could never have imagined. Not only the materials but also the activities available to Austen enthusiasts have changed. Rather than making private scrapbooks, Austen devotees keep track of new publications and events on blogs. Possibilities for Austen tourism now extend well beyond Chawton Cottage. Admirers of Austen are much more numerous, and they can join together not only at JAS meetings in Chawton but in Jane Austen societies around the globe—and, of course, online.

While Alberta was a Janeite of another era, as an Austen omnivore she was ahead of her time. She approached with enthusiasm and without prejudice each new manifestation of Austen in her world, and she oriented her life around her love of Austen. With her ever-renewed appetite for "scraps" of Austen, Alberta was the direct forerunner of post-1995 Austen fans. The spirit of Alberta's ardent, omnivorous, and proudly American appreciation of Austen is especially evident in the Jane Austen Society of North America, of which Henry Burke was one of three co-founders in 1979, as I will discuss in Chapter 7. But all those who read Austen as amateurs today, and especially those who share their thoughts with other enthusiasts, are following in Alberta's footsteps, whether they know it or not.

Notes

1   Alberta Burke to Columbia Broadcasting System, Script Library Department, June 14, 1944, Alberta H. and Henry G. Burke Papers and Jane Austen Research Collection, MS 0020, container 8, folder 7, Special Collections and Archives, Goucher College Library (hereafter cited as Burke Collection). In transcribing Alberta and Henry's letters, I have preserved their occasionally idiosyncratic spelling, emending only where necessary for clarity.
2   Nancy Magnuson, Goucher College's Librarian, included the anecdote about the Burkes reading Austen every year in her address "A Collectors' Love Story: The Henry and Alberta Burke Collection at Goucher College," podcast audio, December 13, 2008, http://www.omahapubliclibrary.org/whats-hot/podcasts. I am very grateful to Nancy for sharing with me her research into the Burkes and her impressions of Henry Burke, whom she met in the last years of his life.
3   Charles Ryskamp, preface to *Jane Austen: Letters & Manuscripts in the Pierpont Morgan Library* (New York: Stinehour Press, 1975), 7. The greatest rarities in Alberta's collection of Austen editions are two copies of *Emma*: the first English edition in the original boards (that is, in the form issued by the printer, without having been rebound by the purchaser), and the first American edition of *Emma*, one of three copies known to exist. See Laurie Kaplan et al., *"Such a lovely display of what imagination does": A Guide to the Jane Austen Collection of the Julia Rogers Library, Goucher College*, 4th edn. (Baltimore: Goucher College Library, 1996), 2, 4.
4   When Alberta attended, from 1924 to 1928, Goucher was a women's college located in the city of Baltimore; it is now a coeducational institution in suburban Baltimore.
5   Alberta Burke to Helen Hayes Theatre, Columbia Broadcasting System, November 24, 1940, Burke Collection, container 7, folder 4.
6   Henry Burke to Charles Ryskamp, July 1, 1975, Burke Collection, container 2, folder 13.
7   Recommendation by G. M. Wiley, June 25, 1924, alumna folder for Alberta Hirshheimer Burke, Special Collections and Archives, Goucher Library (hereafter cited as AHB alumna folder).
8   G. van Steenwyck to the President of Goucher College, October 22, 1923, AHB alumna folder.
9   Joanna Hirshheimer to the Dean of Goucher College, May 19, 1923, AHB alumna folder.
10 Magnuson, "A Collectors' Love Story."
11 Joanna Hirshheimer to the Dean of Goucher College, May 19, 1923, AHB alumna folder.
12 Joanna Hirshheimer to the President of Goucher College, October 22, 1923, AHB alumna folder.
13 Kaplan et al., *"Such a lovely display,"* 9, 18.
14 In another reminiscence, penned to the director of the Morgan Library, Henry specified that "the large paper edition of the novels and the Keynes *Bibliography* [see note 19 for details] ... were sitting on the Austen shelf shortly after our marriage on December 26, 1930. The letters appearing in 1932 were added to the shelf as a birthday gift." Henry Burke to Charles Ryskamp, July 1, 1975, Burke Collection, container 2, folder 13.
15 Henry Burke, "Books, Burkes, and Bibliophiles," Accessions 1975.001: Henry and Alberta Hirshheimer Burke Collection, Special Collections and Archives, Goucher Library (hereafter cited as Accessions 1975.001).
16 Though the Burkes are best known now for their interest in Austen, they also built noteworthy collections in the areas of ballet, costume, visual art, literature, and history. In addition to Goucher, the Burkes bequeathed material to the Moore College of Art in Philadelphia; the Enoch Pratt Free Library and Walters Art Gallery in Baltimore; and the Baltimore Hebrew University. Kaplan et al., *"Such a lovely display,"* 19.
17 Myer Katz to Henry Burke, February 22, 1976, Burke Collection, container 4, folder 22.
18 Henry Burke to Charles Ryskamp, July 1, 1975, Burke Collection, container 2, folder 13.
19 Geoffrey Keynes, *A Bibliography of Jane Austen* (London: Nonesuch Press, 1929), n.p.
20 Sir Geoffrey Langdon Keynes (1887–1982) is a fascinating example of a passionate literary amateur. Knighted for his work on a new method of blood transfusion during

the First World War, he pioneered lumpectomy as a surgical treatment for breast cancer. Over many decades, he compiled bibliographies, somewhat idiosyncratic in both style and format, of numerous major English authors, based on his own extensive book collections; he also edited the works of William Blake and Rupert Brooke. See Stephen Tabor, "Sir Geoffrey Langdon Keynes," in *Twentieth-Century British Book Collectors and Bibliographers: First Series*, edited by William Baker and Kenneth Womack (Detroit: Gale Research, 1999), accessed November 3, 2010, http://go.galegroup.com.librda.mville.edu:2048/.

21 Keynes, *A Bibliography*, vii.

22 Keynes, *A Bibliography*, viii–ix.

23 As a book dealer, an author of works about book collecting, and a leader in associations of antiquarian booksellers, Percy Muir is credited with having "promote[d] wider interest in book collecting as a humanistic pursuit rather than as a way of investing money." Yvonne Schofer, "Percival H(orace) Muir," in *Twentieth-Century British Book Collectors and Bibliographers: First Series*, edited by William Baker and Kenneth Womack (Detroit: Gale Research, 1999), accessed November 3, 2010, http://go.galegroup.com. librda.mville.edu:2048/. Muir's interactions with Alberta are indicative of what Schofer calls Muir's firm belief "in the partnership of collectors and booksellers." Ibid.

24 Alberta Burke to Percy H. Muir, April 15, 1948, Burke Collection, container 1, folder 4.

25 Henry, too, had had to assert the couple's budgetary limits several years before, when an especially persistent dealer urged him to purchase an exceptional set of association volumes (first editions of Austen's novels owned by Cassandra and other family members). To the dealer, who had offered a payment plan, Henry wrote, "I am sorry not to be able to take up your offer on the association copies. There is no doubt they are reasonably priced, but way beyond our scope." Henry Burke to W. G. Worthington, August 14, 1939, Burke Collection, container 7, folder 2.

26 Percy H. Muir to Alberta Burke, May 7, 1948, Burke Collection, container 8, folder 7.

27 Alberta Burke to Percy H. Muir, May 10, 1948, Burke Collection, container 8, folder 7.

28 Cassandra Austen to Fanny Knight, July 20, 1817, in *Jane Austen's Letters*, ed. Deirdre Le Faye, new edn. (1995; repr., Oxford University Press, 1997), 344, 343.

29 Le Faye's edition prints 161 letters attributed to Jane Austen. In Chapter 5, I will discuss Cassandra's role in guarding her sister's legacy through the destruction and disposition of manuscripts, including letters.

30 Percy H. Muir to Alberta Burke, July 23, 1947, Burke Collection, container 8, folder 7. Bequeathed by Alberta to the Morgan Library, this letter of Cassandra's was exhibited in the Morgan's 2009–2010 exhibit "A Woman's Wit: Jane Austen's Life and Legacy"; a two-sided display case allowed visitors to read Cassandra's very legible handwriting on both sides of the page. A facsimile of Cassandra's letter is on display upstairs at Jane Austen's House Museum in Chawton. For further discussion of the Morgan Library exhibit on Austen and Jane Austen's House Museum, see Chapter 4.

31 Alberta Burke to R. W. Chapman, May 20, 1948, Burke Collection, container 8, folder 9.

32 Alberta Burke to Percy H. Muir, May 21, 1948, Burke Collection, container 8, folder 7.

33 Henry Burke to Charles Ryskamp, July 1, 1975, Burke Collection, container 2, folder 13.

34 The Morgan Library now owns both these manuscripts; one, catalogued as "Autograph note concerning the 'Profits of my Novels, over and above the £600 in the Navy Fives' ca. March 1817," is on view in an online exhibition at http://www.themorgan.org/exhibitions/exhibitionList.asp?page=1&exhibition=Austen.

35 R. W. Chapman to Alberta Burke, May 25, 1948, Burke Collection, container 1, folder 4.

36 Alberta Burke to Eleanor Falley, April 14, 1941, Accessions 1975.001.

37 Alberta Burke to Eleanor Falley, n.d. [1941?], Accessions 1975.001.

38 Alberta Burke to David J. Gilson, September 29, 1971, Burke Collection, container 1, folder 5.

39 Alberta Burke to R. W. Chapman, n.d. [1939], Burke Collection, container 7, folder 2.

40 Henry Burke, "Books, Burkes, and Bibliophiles," Accessions 1975.001.

41 Alberta H. Burke, "'Pride and Prejudice' and Other Material Relating to Jane Austen," 1:28.

42 Henry Burke to Charles Ryskamp, July 1, 1975, Burke Collection, container 2, folder 13.

43 Averil G. Hassall to Alberta Burke, n.d., Burke Collection, container 1, folder 5. The production that Hassall describes is a stage adaptation of *Pride and Prejudice* by James Liggatt and Robert Sheat, performed in Oxford from May to June, 1966.

44 Alberta Burke to Helen Hayes Theatre, Columbia Broadcasting System, November 24, 1940, Burke Collection, container 7, folder 4.

45 "As delightful a creature as ever appeared in print" is Austen's own estimation of Elizabeth Bennet. To Cassandra Austen, January 29, 1813, *Jane Austen's Letters*, 201.

46 David Gilson, for instance, stated that "Mrs. Burke at no time felt impelled to publish on Jane Austen, but devoted herself rather to a more selfless service to scholarship: the formation of a collection of material on which others may work." This declaration appears in Gilson's undated typescript draft of what appears to be an obituary, in Burke Collection, container 1, folder 2.

47 See Jan Fergus's influential argument that Jane Austen recopied her works into manuscript notebooks "as a way to 'publish' them privately"; Fergus points out that Austen "follows as many of the contemporary conventions of printing as she can." *Jane Austen: A Literary Life* (Houndmills, Basingstoke: Macmillan, 1991), 51.

48 A similar experience results from opening Alberta's copy of Keynes's *Bibliography*, which she accurately described to David Gilson as "a working bible for over 35 years [that] is full on almost every page of penciled notes, inserted slips, variants of various editions described in book catalogues, lists of translations. ... Any bibliographical knowledge which I possess about J.A. is all written *somewhere* in Keynes if I can only find it!" Alberta Burke to David J. Gilson, February 7, 1969, Burke Collection, container 1, folder 5.

49 P. W. Filby, "Alberta H. Burke's Austen Collection and Association Collection," July 1, 1975, Accessions 1975.001.

50 J. David Grey to Henry Burke, November 15, 1975, Burke Collection, container 2, folder 12.

51 "Topics: True Devotion to an Author," *New York Times*, February 6, 1965, in Alberta H. Burke, "'Pride and Prejudice' and Other Material Relating to Jane Austen," 8:49.

52 Ibid.

53 Ibid.

54 Alberta Burke to Percy H. Muir, May 21, 1948, Burke Collection, container 8, folder 7.

55 On the publication history and influence of Kipling's story "The Janeites," see Kathryn Sutherland, *Jane Austen's Textual Lives: From Aeschylus to Bollywood* (Cambridge: Cambridge University Press, 2005), 16–23 and Claudia L. Johnson, "The Divine Miss Jane: Jane Austen, Janeites, and the Discipline of Novel Studies," in *Janeites: Austen's Disciples and Devotees*, ed. Deidre Lynch (Princeton: Princeton University Press, 2000), 25–44.

56 Alberta Burke to the Editor of the *Saturday Review of Literature*, December 14, 1935, Burke Collection, container 1, folder 4.

57 Alberta Burke to the Editor of the *Saturday Review of Literature*, October 29, 1949, Burke Collection, container 1, folder 4.

58 Roland Gellatt to Alberta Burke, November 30, 1949, Burke Collection, container 1, folder 4.

59 Alberta Burke to the Editor of the *Times Literary Supplement*, November 9, 1962, Burke Collection, container 1, folder 1.

60 Alberta Burke to the Editor of the *Times Literary Supplement*, February 8, 1963, Burke Collection, container 1, folder 1.

61 David J. Gilson to Alberta Burke, August 10, 1967, Burke Collection, container 1, folder 5.

62 For their help illuminating the relationship between Gilson and Alberta Burke, I gratefully acknowledge Nancy Magnuson, Goucher College Librarian, and Kate Dannals, Goucher class of 2009, who analyzed the Gilson-Burke correspondence for her senior project in psychology.

63 Alberta Burke to David J. Gilson, January 31, 1970, Burke Collection, container 1, folder 5.

64 David J. Gilson to Alberta Burke, June 2, 1970, Burke Collection, container 2, folder 8.

65 Earl Arnett, "Group will honor Austen, Mrs. Burke," *Baltimore Sun*, April 23, 1976, Burke Collection, container 1, folder 2.

66 After Alberta's death, columnist James H. Bready of the *Baltimore Sun* marveled that she had amassed her treasures so quietly, literally across the street from Johns Hopkins University: "Down to Mrs. Burke's death last May, no newspaper here or abroad had

reported the presence in Baltimore of the … finest privately owned Jane Austen collection anywhere, outside the Austen family. … Across University Parkway from the Burkes, who were original Broadview [apartment building] occupants from 1952 on, successive Johns Hopkins scholars, Avrom Fleishman and Alistair Duckworth, meantime expanded Ph.D. dissertations into Jane Austen books, in mutual unawareness." James H. Bready, "The Austen Link," *Baltimore Sun,* January 25, 1976, Burke Collection, container 1, folder 2. While the Burkes were certainly unknown to the Hopkins scholars, the reverse was not true: Alberta mentioned to Gilson in August 1967 that she had "just received a new book from the University of Minnesota Press, *A Reading of Mansfield Park: An Essay in Critical Synthesis* by Avrom Fleishman" and that she was "longing to settle down to reading it." Alberta Burke to David J. Gilson, August 15, 1967, Burke Collection, container 1, folder 5.

67 Edna Golomb, "Goucher Alumna Collects Jane Austen Material," *Goucher College Weekly,* November 22, 1946, Burke Collection, container 1, folder 1.

68 *The Jane Austen Society: Report for the Period October, 1946 to September, 1949* (Alton: C. Mills & Co., 1949), 3–4. Carpenter contributed "A Note on the Jane Austen Memorial Trust" to the same *Report,* explaining how he had purchased the house and why he had decided to place it in the hands of a trust.

69 Ibid., 4.

70 Henry Burke to Charles Ryskamp, July 1, 1975, Burke Collection, container 2, folder 13.

71 *The Jane Austen Society: Report 1946–1949,* 4. Burke Collection, container 8, folder 9.

72 Katharine Kenyon to Alberta Burke, July 26, 1949, Burke Collection, container 8, folder 9.

73 Dorothy Darnell to Alberta Burke, July 26, 1949, Burke Collection, container 8, folder 9.

74 Dorothy Darnell to Alberta Burke, September 1, 1949, Burke Collection, container 8, folder 9.

75 Alberta H. Burke, "'Pride and Prejudice' and Other Material Relating to Jane Austen," 3:56.

76 Percy H. Muir to Alberta Burke, May 27, 1948, Burke Collection, container 8, folder 7.

77 Alberta Burke to Percy H. Muir, June 2, 1948, Burke Collection, container 8, folder 7.

78 Alberta Burke to David Allan Robertson, January 19, 1939, Accessions 1975.001.

79 David A. Robertson to Alberta Burke, January 20, 1939, Accessions 1975.001.

80 Ibid.

81 T. Edward Carpenter to Alberta Burke, April 22, 1954, Burke Collection, container 9, folder 12.

82 "A word," wrote Jones, "about the manuscripts: hard common sense tells me that you are right." Sarah D. Jones to Alberta Burke, December 8, 1954, Accessions 1975.001.

83 Alberta Burke to Sarah D. Jones, December 12, 1954, Accessions 1975.001.

84 Ibid.

85 The Morgan's director, thanking Alberta for the "very pleasant surprise" of her announcement of her intended donation, mentioned that he remembered having met her "at the time of Dr. Chapman's visit a couple of years ago." F. B. Adams, Jr. to Alberta Burke, December 14, 1954, Burke Collection, container 9, folder 12.

86 Ryskamp, preface to *Jane Austen,* 8.

87 T. Edward Carpenter to Alberta Burke, July 25, 1955, Burke Collection, container 9, folder 12.

88 "During 1935," Henry recalled decades later, "we thought it appropriate to design a bookplate for the Jane Austen books. As the principal feature of the bookplate, we chose the view of the west front of Winchester Cathedral with the bare wintry trees on each side of the road. Below this drawing, we added the first line of the quatrain which precedes Kipling's story, *The Janeites,* "Jane lies in Winchester—blessed be her shade." Henry Burke, "Books, Burkes, and Bibliophiles," Accessions 1975.001. While Henry remembers Kipling's epigraph correctly, the bookplate renders "in" as "at." For the text of Kipling's quatrain, see Chapter 1, footnote 12.

89 T. Edward Carpenter to Alberta Burke, April 22, 1954, Burke Collection, container 9, folder 12.

90 Alberta Burke to David Allan Robertson, January 19, 1939, Accessions 1975.001.

91 Sarah D. Jones to Alberta Burke, December 8, 1954, Accessions 1975.001.

Chapter 3

Reading Like an Amateur

Perhaps there is no perfect word for the kind of people I have raised my children to be: a word that encompasses obsessive scholarship, passionate curiosity, curatorial tenderness, and an irrepressible desire to join in the game, to inhabit in some manner—through writing, drawing, dressing up, or endless conversational riffing and Talmudic debate—the world of the endlessly inviting, endlessly inhabitable work of popular art. The closest I have ever come for myself is *amateur*, in all the original best sense of the word: a lover; a devotee; a person driven by passion and obsession to do it—to explore the imaginary world—oneself.

Michael Chabon, "The Amateur Family," in *Manhood for Amateurs* (2010)[1]

Like the works of "popular art" (chiefly comic books and television series) to which the American novelist Michael Chabon refers in my epigraph, Austen's novels attract amateurs who take delight in engaging their imaginations with her fictional worlds. Different readers explore Austen's works in different ways, and for different reasons. Some readers enjoy solitary contact with Austen's writings, while others prefer to share their thoughts with fellow readers, or to fortify their own interpretations with the aid of accessibly written guidebooks. Some opt to read Austen's original text without commentary, while others enrich their understanding by consulting footnotes or more knowledgeable fans. Some readers seek a greater understanding of Austen's art as a novelist, or of the social world she depicts; others seek greater insight into themselves. Whether reading for pure pleasure, edification, or self-enrichment, all of these amateurs choose the methods and means that suit themselves, rather than ones sanctioned by literary scholars.

This chapter begins with an overview of how amateur reading has been described, defended, and advocated both by those with academic literary training and by those who are themselves amateur readers. The next two sections concern the direct testimony of those who value Austen for personal, rather than professional, reasons. First, we will hear from a wide range of everyday readers, in their own words, why they find Austen's works to be personally meaningful, and how they choose to read and interpret those works. Next, we will eavesdrop on two discussions of Austen novels conducted for and by amateurs. In the light of sociological studies of reading groups, I will consider how, and for what purposes, these readers discuss Austen's works. The next section, which treats reading guides and editions aimed at amateurs, is subdivided according to those books' goals of increasing a reader's understanding of Austen, enjoyment of Austen, or understanding of her/himself. Finally, I will examine claims made by writers of sequels on behalf of the benefits, for both themselves and their readers, of participating creatively in the worlds invented by Austen.

Literary Criticism and the Experience of the Amateur Reader

Any investigation of personal motives for and methods of reading is indebted to Janice A. Radway's groundbreaking book *Reading the Romance: Women, Patriarchy, and Popular Literature* (1984), which explored the devotion of a group of housewives in a Midwestern American town to their preferred form of fiction, romance novels. Asked why they sought out this particular leisure activity, the women of Smithton, Illinois overwhelmingly cited the pleasure of escaping the daily monotony of their lives: a bookstore owner whom Radway interviewed "explained that romance novels provide escape just as Darvon [a narcotic] and alcohol do for other women."[2] Radway, who is unfailingly attentive to and respectful of her subjects' views, notes that "reading to escape the present is neither a new behavior nor one peculiar to women who read romances" and acknowledges too that "the women themselves vehemently maintain that their reading has transformed them in important ways."[3] While Radway focuses only on contemporary romance fiction and a small group of female readers, her study remains significant for its investigation of the importance of reading to people far outside academic and literary circles.

Radway's second book, *A Feeling for Books: The Book-of-the-Month Club, Literary Taste, and Middle-Class Desire* (1997), delved even more deeply into the experience of reading for pleasure. As Radway shadowed editors at the Book-of-the-Month Club, she noticed and pondered how those editors, and the readers who reported on new titles, evaluated a book according to what each of them felt like while reading it. The reading experience prized at the Book-of-the-Month Club, Radway explains, "was, above all, characterized by the pleasure it gave. The particular pleasure referred to again and again in reader's reports was always bound to a certain extent with a feeling of immersion, a sense of boundaries dissolved."[4] Radway describes this reading experience more fully as involving some of the sense of "escape" cited by the romance readers in her earlier book, while at the same time engaging more extensively both the feelings and thoughts of the reader:

What gave the editors the greatest pleasure, I thought, was a feeling of transport and betweenness, a feeling of being suspended between the self and the world, a state where the one flowed imperceptibly into the other, a place where clear boundaries and limits were obscured. Good reading, as they described it, produced an awareness of the self expanded, a sense that the self was absorbed into something larger, not dissolved exactly, but quivering in solution, both other and not. ...

The modality of reading privileged at the Book-of-the-Month Club emphasized both sense and sensibility, both affect and cognition. It mobilized the body and the brain, the heart and the soul. It was a mode of reading that stressed immersion and connection, communication and response.[5]

The "mode of reading" Radway describes here operates independently of the genre of book being read. Either fiction or non-fiction, if written in a way that the Book-of-the-Month Club editors found effective, could elicit this complete readerly absorption and sense of connection to a book, and beyond that book to "something larger" still.

As Radway endeavors to understand the kind of reading experience the Book-of-the-Month Club seeks to provide its subscribers, she recalls the immersive reading in which she herself engaged as a child, long before she was trained in literary analysis. In her childhood, as at the Book-of-the-Month Club, she states, "reading seemed to exist as an uncanny pleasure, an act that was weirdly private but deeply social as well. I felt intense satisfaction at encountering this view of reading again."[6] With evident discomfort, Radway begins to question the assumptions about reading, interpretation, and critical writing that she has internalized through her professional training: "Why was professional academic writing about books presented virtually without anecdote and affect? Why was so much of it so tedious to read? Why did academic literary critics show no interest in relating their own concrete experience of a text or in appealing to the emotional responses of their readers? Why was it so clear to everyone else that 'authentic literature' and 'real art' were necessarily challenging and difficult to read, characterized always by complexity, intricacy, ambiguity, and irony?"[7] As we will see, Austen's novels are prime examples of books that can, depending on their reader, be taken as "challenging" or enjoyable, complex or straightforward, intellectually stimulating or emotionally gratifying. Rarely does an individual reader of Austen admit to experiencing her novels on both levels. And guides designed to assist Austen readers are invariably pitched to one side (intellectual understanding or analysis) or the other (enjoyment or personal application).

One of the very few literary critics to promote a kind of reading that incorporates what Radway calls "both sense and sensibility, both affect and cognition"[8] is Harold Bloom. The fundamental goal of reading "as a solitary praxis, rather than as an educational enterprise," Bloom argues in *How to Read and Why* (2000), is the development of the self.[9] If reading is, as he contends, "the most healing of pleasures," this effect comes about because the mind is expanded, not anesthetized.[10] "Ultimately we read," Bloom asserts, "in order to strengthen the self, and to learn its authentic interests. We experience such augmentation as pleasure."[11] Even more strongly than Radway, Bloom openly mourns the losses that result, in his view, from literary-critical training, especially (though this remains implicit in the following passage) from an investment in literary theory:

> The sorrow of professional reading is that you recapture only rarely the pleasure of reading you knew in youth, when books were a Hazlittian gusto. The way we read now partly depends upon our distance, inner or outer, from the universities, where reading is scarcely taught as a pleasure, in any of the deeper senses of the aesthetics of pleasure. ... There are still solitary readers, young and old, everywhere, even in the universities. If there is a function of criticism at the present time, it must be to address itself to the solitary reader, who reads for herself, and not for the interests that supposedly transcend the self.[12]

The lovers of Austen from whom we will shortly hear attest to the existence of plenty of "solitary readers" of all ages, nationalities, and genders. And the pleasures these amateur readers find in Austen do indeed range from youthful "gusto" to more mature appreciation of the aesthetic, and indeed the moral, effects of fiction reading.

Unlike Bloom and Radway, who stress (albeit with regret) the distance between professional and amateur readers, Rita Felski has recently urged her fellow literary theorists to recognize that their own methods of reading are more varied, and have more in common with popular reading practices, than is commonly admitted. In *Uses of Literature* (2008), Felski notes that

> the use of the term "reading" in literary studies to encompass quite disparate activities, from turning the pages of a paperback novel to elaborate exegeses published in *PMLA*, glosses over their many differences. The latter reading constitutes a writing, a public performance subject to a host of gate-keeping practices and professional norms: a premium on novelty and deft displays of counter-intuitive interpretive ingenuity, the obligation to reference key scholars in the field, rapidly changing critical vocabularies, and the tacit prohibition of certain stylistic registers. This practice often has little in common with the commentary a teacher carries out in the classroom, or with what goes through her mind when she reads a book in an armchair, at home. Published academic criticism, in other words, is not an especially reliable or comprehensive guide to the ways in which academics read. We are less theoretically pure than we think ourselves to be; hard-edged poses of suspicion and skepticism jostle against more mundane yet more variegated responses.[13]

In Felski's conception, every scholarly reader is also an "armchair" reader and, if a teacher, a classroom popularizer as well; no literary critic is "theoretically pure." According to Felski, a scholar need not reach out to her own lost personal history as a reader for pleasure, as did Radway. Instead, that scholar need only take a hard look at the actual "reading"—in all the senses of that word—in which she continues to participate.

Felski's overall aim in *Uses of Literature* is to demonstrate that high literary theory, far from being alien to the concerns and interests of everyday readers, in fact offers potent tools for exploring those readers' experiences. "There is no compelling reason," she argues, "why the practice of theory requires us to go behind the backs of ordinary persons in order to expose their beliefs as deluded or delinquent."[14] Yet with one exception, which I will discuss shortly, Felski's own discussion remains in the realm of theory. While she does not "go behind the backs of ordinary persons," neither does she talk *to* those persons. She does not, she states quite firmly, intend to make "a populist defense of folk reading over scholarly interpretation"[15]—an accusation that could be leveled at my own approach to amateur readers. (I would reply that I am pursuing, much more fully than does Felski herself, her declaration that literary theory "has manifest difficulty in recognizing that literature may be valued for different, even incommensurable reasons.")[16]

The only account of the experience of a non-academic reader that appears in *Uses of Literature* comes from Felski herself. At times depicting the experience as her own, at times attributing it to an imagined "you," Felski analyzes the thought process and feelings of the engaged reader:

> What does it mean to recognize oneself in a book? The experience seems at once utterly mundane yet singularly mysterious. While turning a page I am arrested by a compelling description, a constellation of events, a conversation between characters, an interior monologue. Suddenly and without warning, a flash of connection leaps across the gap between text and reader; an affinity or an attunement is brought to light. I may be looking for such a moment, or I may stumble on it haphazardly, startled by the prescience of a certain combination of words. In either case, I feel myself addressed, summoned, called to account: I cannot help seeing traces of myself in the pages I am reading. Indisputably, something has changed; my perspective has shifted; I see something that I did not see before.[17]

In this passage, Felski treats with respect a reaction that is common among amateur readers, and is equally commonly disparaged by academic professionals: feeling personally connected to, or personally affected by, the work you are reading. Felski's word choices—"I feel myself addressed, summoned, called to account"—suggest that recognition, while it can be pleasurable, can also involve a sense of being judged. As we will see from the accounts of Austen lovers as well as in guides designed to help readers apply lessons from her novels, Austen's fiction lends itself particularly well to being read for self-improvement.[18]

Not only does Felski honor the tendency of amateur readers to recognize aspects of themselves in a book, but she also, in a passage of extraordinary vividness and intensity, conveys the experience of being immersed in a literary work:

> Enchantment is characterized by a state of intense involvement, a sense of being so entirely caught up in an aesthetic object that nothing else seems to matter. ... This sense of immersion seems self-enclosed and self-sustaining, demarcated by a distinct boundary; the transition back to the everyday world feels unwelcome, even intrusive. ...
>
> Enchantment is soaked through with an unusual intensity of perception and affect; it is often compared to the condition of being intoxicated, drugged, or dreaming. ... The analytical part of your mind recedes into the background; your inner censor and critic are nowhere to be found. Instead of examining a text with a sober and clinical eye, you are pulled irresistibly into its orbit. There is no longer a sharp line between self and text but a confused and inchoate intermingling. ... You feel oblivious to your surroundings, your past, your everyday life; you exist only in the present and the numinous presence of a text.
>
> Not only your autonomy but your sense of agency is under siege. You have little control over your response; you turn the pages compulsively. ... Rather than having a sense of mastery over the text, you are at its mercy. You are sucked in, swept up, spirited away, you feel yourself enfolded in a blissful embrace. You are mesmerized, hypnotized, possessed. You strain to reassert yourself, but finally you give in, you stop struggling, you yield without a murmur.[19]

The idea of "escape" seems pallid and simplistic next to Felski's visceral, poetic description of enchantment by a text. According to her, it is the power of the text, not the weakness of the reader, that creates the effect of oblivion or possession; however well developed is the "analytical part of your mind," it can be extinguished by a book that sucks you in. As in her earlier depiction of a scholar who adopts different modes for the professional arena, the classroom, and as a private "armchair" reader, Felski encourages her fellow academics to recognize themselves in the "you" who is vulnerable to being at the mercy of a text. Following Felski, I will ask those among my own readers who are scholars to hold back from making assumptions about amateur readers of Austen, and from casting aspersions on the kinds of sources that yield insights into those readers' experiences.

Turning now to reading practices advocated by amateurs themselves, let us look more closely at the influential model I cited in Chapter 1: the on-air book club hosted by the hugely popular American talk-show host Oprah Winfrey. As Kelley Penfield Lewis has argued, "Most of Oprah's literacy work is accomplished by promoting the 'usefulness' of reading. She focuses on the experiential aspects of reading and frames it as an activity that can be both enjoyable and therapeutic."[20] Indeed, Winfrey invests novels with a transformative power that exceeds that of other, more conventional modes of self-reinvention. "It is just remarkable to me," she told her audience in 2000, "how a work of fiction can touch, and, really, begin to help heal the lives of readers in ways that a lot of self-help and therapy and conversations cannot."[21] Such healing, according to Lewis, results from a particular kind of applied reading, one that is rehearsed and reinforced through televised discussions: "The televised book discussion tends to focus primarily on the experience of reading and how the messages in the book can be applied to readers' personal lives. Attention is paid to subjective emotions and accessible, uplifting messages that can be extracted from the book."[22] As a result, other elements of the novels and modes of reading are de-emphasized. "Especially during the early Book Club episodes," notes Lewis, "little or no attention was paid to style, language, or other formal elements."[23]

Examining an episode of Oprah's Book Club devoted to Joyce Carol Oates's novel *We Were the Mulvaneys*, Kate Douglas found too that "the dominant motivation for reading inherent within this reading community is personal development."[24] Douglas points out that the personal application of literature has long been a feature of community book clubs: "The reasons for the existence of these clubs varies from a shared love of reading, social and intellectual stimulation, fashion, friendship, support, self-help, or therapy."[25] Furthermore, Douglas argues that all book clubs demonstrate a "belief in the value of everyday literary criticism, an assertion of the value of critical discussion on books by persons who may have no formal skills or knowledge of literature."[26] Douglas attributes to Oprah's Book Club "an integral role in a more general cultural departure from professional literary criticism," as evident for instance in the influence of Amazon.com's customer reviews, in which purchasers post opinions of books read.[27] Elizabeth Long, whose sociological study of book clubs I will discuss in greater depth later in this chapter, emphasizes in particular how the "experiential" purpose of reading modeled by Winfrey departs from the "analytic" mode promoted by academics: in Winfrey's handling, argues Long, "books offered moral instruction" as well as "the potential for seeing oneself anew. ... Winfrey offered an alternative to more academic literary canons and analyses, and that might have opened up some cultural space for readers—spaces for them to forge their own ways of relating to the books they read."[28]

Oprah Winfrey's message of empowerment through fiction reading continues to be spread by writers who practice what Douglas calls "everyday literary criticism." A recent example is Erin Blakemore's book of short essays, *The Heroine's Bookshelf: Life Lessons, from Jane Austen to Laura Ingalls Wilder* (2010), which presents chatty commentary on works by twelve women authors. Blakemore, who claims no authority other than that of a devoted reader, advocates returning to familiar classics when life gets tough. "When the line between duty and sanity blurs," she writes, "you can usually find me curled up with a battered book, reading as if my mental health depended on it. And it does, for inside the books I love I find food, respite, escape, and perspective."[29] The heroines of her favorite novels, Blakemore declares, have "been there for me through everything adolescence and adulthood have lobbed my way. They're there for you, too, should you choose to acknowledge them."[30] Both literary classics like *Pride and Prejudice* and children's classics like *The Secret Garden* hold the power, contends Blakemore, "to comfort us when we're lonely" as well as to impart "lessons" valuable to the modern-day woman.[31] "A moment with a book," she declares, "is basic self-care"; a "bit of literary intervention can give your inner heroine the guts she needs" to tackle daily tasks.[32]

While a few of the books Blakemore includes could also appear on a reading list for school or college, her recommendations, like those of Oprah Winfrey, are based not on literary value but on personal meaningfulness. Blakemore offers resources for women, not items of cultural capital: "Time travel, redemption, escape, and self-knowledge are all neatly bound and sewn into the modest covers of the books we pass from hand to hand, library to purse, mother to daughter."[33] While Blakemore's writing style, appropriately for her audience, has little in common with that of Radway, Bloom, or Felski, she shares with those scholars a commitment to reading for reasons, and in ways, that are outside the bounds of traditional literary criticism.

Why and How Amateurs Read Austen Today

In her introduction to *A Truth Universally Acknowledged: 33 Great Writers on Why We Read Jane Austen* (2009), a collection to which Harold Bloom contributed a brief foreword, Susannah Carson sums up as follows her view of why present-day readers turn to Austen: "We read her novels to identify and improve, to laugh and to sympathize, to enjoy the present and revisit the past, and at times to escape our own muddled lives for a bit and find the clarity that only the best fiction can provide."[34] The power of Austen's novels, according to Carson, derives in large part from *how* readers experience them:

When we come upon a passage that hits us with more than ordinary force, we feel unnerved but somehow comforted. There seems to be no distance at all between Austen's world and our own. … Such passages seize us, draw us into the novels, and in some mysterious way transform us. By reciting time and again the familiar lines, we not only come to know the characters intimately, but we often arrive at a greater understanding of ourselves. … When we pass from the fictional world back into the real, we hear her turns of phrase, see her characters, and overlay her scenes onto the experiences of our everyday lives.[35]

As Carson describes it, the process of reading and reflecting on an Austen novel has the capacity to change readers' perceptions both of the world around them and of themselves. Significantly, Carson attributes this effect to a selective kind of reading, through which particular passages—or even just "familiar lines"—lodge in the reader's mind and affect her or him. In other words, the transformative potential of Austen's writing, as Carson sees it, results less from the reader's beginning-to-end investment in a novel than from the reader's meditation on aspects of that novel that seem to speak directly to her.

Carson's discussion of how "we" read Austen aside, *A Truth Universally Acknowledged* contains very few accounts of what actual readers, whether amateurs or literary critics, seek and find in Austen. (On the whole, the essays Carson has assembled and, in some cases, commissioned, tend much more towards a conventional kind of literary discussion, albeit one accessible to non-professionals.) More insight into why and how encounters with Austen matter to people today can be gained by consulting personal writings—in the form of published essays or memoirs, paratextual materials such as forewords, and blog posts—as well as through questioning people who have demonstrated an interest in Austen, as I did when surveying visitors to Jane Austen's House Museum in July 2009.[36]

Many readers attest to the capacity of encounters with Austen to afford healing, self-repair, and self-development. Jill Pitkeathley, the English author of two novels based on Austen's life, recalls how she recovered from critical illness with the help of her favorite novels: "For the last fifty years, I have re-read two or three of [Austen's] novels each year and never go on holiday without at least one in my luggage. ... As, eventually, I began to recover, my levels of physical and mental energy did not allow me to concentrate on reading new books at all, however many were supplied to me by family and friends. It was familiar books that I needed, ones which I already knew well and I needed none more so than those of Jane Austen."[37] In an interview with *Jane Austen's Regency World* magazine, British actress Angela Barlow comments that "one element to enjoy and pass on in Jane Austen, it seems to me, is her sane orderliness and balance. I love to read her when I'm confused, angry, tired, or ill."[38] Sociologist Elizabeth Long articulates how she found Austen's novels personally beneficial in the past, in response to fellow members of her book group who found it hard to relate to Austen's leisured characters: "I used to read Austen as a way of coping with going back to the college town I grew up in. She had made me understand the ways a small, insular community remains the same in nature despite vast historical changes. ... I spoke at length about the way Austen's precision in accounting for subtle emotional transformations had helped me understand my own intense and private feelings about people in my life."[39]

Achieving therapeutic benefits from reading Austen does not, according to readers, necessarily require approaching one of her works with sustained attention or reading it fully from beginning to end. The Man Booker

Prize-winning English novelist Hilary Mantel has commented acerbically that "no one who read it closely was ever comforted by an Austen novel."[40] Perhaps so; we could also say that those who are unapologetic about finding comfort in Austen know how to read in order to achieve that goal. A UK resident in his 70s who spoke to me at Jane Austen's House Museum described as follows how his wife makes use of her favorite Austen novel: "If she's ever feeling poorly, she takes *Pride and Prejudice* to bed with her and reads the parts she likes. She *has* read the whole book, but she doesn't read it *as* a book—but in parts. She knows it by memory."[41] An even more vivid account of recourse to Austen during physical illness comes from American memoirist Lori Smith. "To me," writes Smith,

> Jane Austen's books (and the movies based on them) have become the entertainment equivalent of comfort food, what I return to over and over again when I need a break from the real world, when I need to retreat. Once, flat on my back with a four-month-long exhaustion that my doctors could only describe as a "mono-like virus," I pulled out my VHS copy of the BBC version of *Pride and Prejudice*, only to find that I had worn out the pictures and was left only with sound. I watched five hours of gray static that time, listening to the voices and music, imagining the scenes in my head.[42]

A strikingly comparable testament to the soothing power of auditory Austen is reported by the daughter of Barbara Winn Adams, an American collector of early Austen editions and other rare books: "Toward the end of her life," writes Susanna Adams, "she recorded the novels on tape and played them to herself at night to help her sleep."[43] According to Frankie Brewer, an Australian high school student, Austen's prose can actually forestall low spirits, not just repair them: "Every night, before I went to bed, I would read my favourite scenes from *Pride and Prejudice*, so I would have sweet dreams and wake up in a good mood the next day."[44] In none of these four cases is an Austen (or Austen-based) work being experienced in a conventional way. Selective reading, listening, or watching fulfills these readers' purposes. Indeed, we can understand these readers as adapting Austen's writings in very personal ways to address their own needs.

For a wide variety of readers, Austen's novels relieve the stresses of daily life by affording mental escape. "Relaxing reading after the 10:00 news, which is often rather upsetting," comments a UK man in his 80s, who studied literature at secondary level.[45] "My happiest memories of holiday reading come from nearly 30 years ago," recalls the English biographer and journalist Humphrey Carpenter, "when I was about to get married, and we read the whole of Jane Austen aloud. It was a life-saver whenever we got stuck somewhere on holiday; I remember an entire morning in a remote railway junction in Normandy during a train strike, reading *Mansfield Park*, thanks to which the time passed incredibly swiftly and unstressfully."[46] Elizabeth Shek, a 13-year-old Australian high school student, testifies to a comparable effect on a much younger, and more contemporary, reader: "In Jane Austen's books, in particular *Pride and Prejudice*, I could escape from reality and life. It was a place where I felt safe, and where I didn't carry my fears or worries with me. They all seemed to just fade away, and I felt as if I was really alive, happy, intrigued, and excited all at the same time when reading her books."[47] The more distant Austen's world from your own, the better, according to New Zealander Joe Bennett, a teacher, who identifies "a novel by Jane Austen" as essential packing for an outdoor camping trip with schoolchildren:

> In the bush Jane Austen kept me sane. Every night when the day's horrors were done and the kids had finally retired to their wet tents and lay together grumbling with excitement and I realized with relief that I was twenty-four hours closer to an innersprung mattress, I would check the ridge of my tent, murder the mosquitoes that dangled there, then get into bed with Miss Austen. With a rucksack beneath my head and a torch beneath my chin and Jane Austen on my chest I would withdraw into the early nineteenth century where delight was a handsome curate and horror a twisted ankle. And as the rain beat its little hammers on the canvas and the creatures of the night made moan, Jane Austen made me happy.[48]

For all these readers, regardless of their gender, age, or nationality, imaginatively entering Austen's fictional worlds means leaving behind, and even forgetting, discomfort, worry, and chaos.

A significant number of my Jane Austen's House Museum survey respondents described themselves as having been personally inspired by Austen. This reaction, which was expressed to me only by women, was especially common among younger age groups. "Jane Austen is my role model in many ways," declared an Australian teenage girl, who was studying literature at the secondary level.[49] "She's a heroine of mine," stated a woman in her 50s from the UK who had studied literature through the secondary level. "As a woman," elaborated a UK woman in her late 20s who had studied literature as an undergraduate, "Jane Austen's intellect, talent, wit, and writing are an inspiration to my life." An American woman in her late 20s, who had studied literature at the undergraduate level, recalled having been especially influenced by Austen when younger: "She was an inspiration for me as a teenager. Her insight into society and people formed my worldview from an early age. I respect her and look up to her." Another American woman also in her late 20s, who did not specify the level of her literary study, described Austen as being a "role model somewhat—to evaluate life & reflect on it. Gives me, as a woman, passion & ambition to look forward to." Brief as they are, these responses attest to the significance that Austen holds, as both writer and woman, for women readers today.

Judging by the survey responses I collected, men readers are unlikely to identify Austen as a source of inspiration per se. Indeed, some men respondents had difficulty articulating any answer to my open-ended question "What does Jane Austen mean to you?" One UK man in his 30s spoke for many with his reply, "Cannot really phrase easily."[50] Both in this survey and in published accounts, men readers tend to articulate appreciatively what they have learned from Austen rather than what they feel about her. For example, one American man in his 30s responded, "I find her to be very interesting and enjoy learning about relationships through her eyes."[51] The American novelist James Collins calls Jane Austen his "moral guide" and states, "I find that reading Jane Austen helps me clarify ethical choices, helps me figure out a way to live with integrity in the corrupt world, even helps me adopt the proper tone and manner in dealing with others."[52] In the memoir *A Jane Austen Education: How Six Novels Taught Me about Love, Friendship, and the Things that Really Matter* (2011), William Deresiewicz, an American former professor, likewise credits Austen's novels with having opened his eyes to "a new kind of moral seriousness" that transformed him from a jerk into a sensitive, self-aware man.[53] Benjamin Nugent, author of a book about the nerd in American culture, advocates a more particular application of Austen for a subgroup of readers: "Young nerds should read Austen because she'll force them to hear dissonant notes in their own speech they might otherwise miss, and open their eyes to defeats and victories they otherwise wouldn't even have noticed."[54]

All of these sources attest to the interest of today's readers in putting Austen's novels to important personal purposes. Of course, not all encounters with Austen involve particular motivations beyond enjoyment or appreciation. Exactly what appeal do Austen's novels hold for present-day readers? Or, as memoirist Lori Smith puts it, "People ask, 'Why? Is it the romance?' The truth is, I don't know exactly. There are all kinds of reasons. And yes, it is the romance (*but only partly*, she says with great pride). Poor, intelligent women. Rich, full-charactered men. Happy endings."[55] One version of my survey at Jane Austen's House Museum aimed to quantify what interests present-day audiences about Austen. On the advice of museum staff members, who cautioned me that many visitors are familiar primarily with screen versions of Austen's novels, my survey first asked respondents to specify whether they would like to think about what interested them in Austen's novels, in films inspired by Austen, or in both Austen's novels and films inspired by them. Out of 50 respondents to this version of the survey, 12 said that they would focus on the novels, 7 on the films, and 18 on both (3 did not specify). Respondents were then asked to identify, from a twelve-item list, all the elements of Austen's writing that interested them, as well as the single aspect that most interested them. (The option to write in an element not mentioned by me was available as well.) Table 3.1 shows how popular each aspect was with the 50 respondents to this version of the survey, as well as which aspects earned votes of "most interesting" from the 33 respondents who designated one such.

Table 3.1: Readers' Interest in Aspects of Austen's Novels

Aspect of Austen's novels	# of respondents interested	# _most_ interested
Her insight into the human experience	38	9
Her wit and humor	38	6
Her style of writing	36	6
Her depictions of life in Regency England	34	3
Her irony	31	0
Her perspective as a woman writer	31	4
Her heroines	29	1
Her heroes	28	0
Her comic characters	26	0
Her depictions of love and romance	26	3
Her morality	23	1
Her happy endings	22	0

Source: JAHM survey.

We must bear in mind the small number of participants in this version of the survey, as well as the self-selected nature of the respondents, who opted first to visit Jane Austen's House, then to complete a lengthy survey. Nevertheless, these findings offer an intriguing challenge to common assumptions about Austen's popularity today. In particular, love and romance and happy endings, elements often strongly associated with screen versions of Austen's novels, are close to the bottom of the list. Interest in Austen's characters—the aspect of a novel often thought to hold the greatest pull for amateur readers[56]—is present but decidedly less prominent than appreciation of literary elements including irony and style of writing.

Amateur Reading in Action

Survey responses and the statements of individual readers offer us glimpses of what draws ordinary people to Austen today. Greater insight into how amateurs approach Austen and derive meaning from her works emerges from listening in on sustained discussions by groups of readers.

The cultural importance of reading groups, also called book clubs, has recently been explored by the UK literary scholar Jenny Hartley and the American sociologist Elizabeth Long. Both Hartley and Long call attention to how the motives and methods of amateur readers differ from those of scholars. In *Reading Groups* (2001), Hartley points out that "reading groups are about reading in the community rather than in the academy. Indeed, being non-academic may be part of their self-definition. Their sort of reading is what French scholars call poaching; groups take over and appropriate their books to read in the ways that best suit them."[57] In *Book Clubs: Women and the Uses of Reading in Everyday Life* (2003), Long attends in particular to the ways in which amateur readers approach so-called "classic" works of literature:

> Even if intellectuals and reading group members categorize the same book as a classic, they may expect something different from the book and subject it to somewhat different standards of judgment, because the "ordinary reader" is working with an existential or psychological definition of greatness that subsumes it to the criterion of personal enhancement. Even those readers who automatically defer to cultural authority may stand at some distance from it because they are amateurs who look to books for the pleasures of deep emotional involvement, meaningfulness, or illumination of their experience rather than for the more rationalist pleasures that come with analytic distance.[58]

Because amateur readers pursue essentially personal goals, notes Long, such readers are free to discuss a text in ways that would not be considered appropriate in the classroom: "One reason these groups can be playful is that they are not held accountable for their interpretations in the way that 'professional readers' and their students are. Group members do not have to assert their interpretations in a serious way or defend them with tightly reasoned arguments from the text. Indeed, women often expand on an opinion by discussing their personal reasons for making a certain interpretation, using the book for self-understanding and revelation of the self to other participants rather than for discovery of meaning within the book."[59]

Long's participant-observation of women's book groups in Houston, Texas reminds us that not all amateur readers find Austen's works appealing, or even accessible. Long reports on the "merciless criticism" that one group wielded against *Mansfield Park*: "Boring, boring, boring. It's a seminar about right and wrong," complained one participant, while another commented disparagingly that "it was like reading one Miss Manners column after another Miss Manners column."[60] Overall, Long concludes that Austen's works

> proved difficult for three groups I observed because of both the formality and the elegance of the language and because of the very different ways people are portrayed as living in her novels. Both stylistically and substantively, these books were so different from what these book group members were used to that the books proved inaccessible even to willing readers. Substantively, readers found it hard to relate to a social world in which the protagonists were not gainfully employed, where the people who did the work (such as servants) were invisible, and where parents seemed to have only a limited involvement with their children.[61]

The resistance to Austen shown by the members of Long's book groups is important to bear in mind. Austen may speak to many present-day readers, but she does not resonate with everyone.

A rich resource concerning the engagement of amateur readers with Austen's works can be found at the Austen fans' website The Republic of Pemberley. Since 1996, the website's registered members have regularly taken part in "Group Reads," which are discussions paced according to a preset reading schedule, with approximately six weeks typically allotted per novel. Works by Austen have been read by Republic of Pemberley groups more than forty times; the group occasionally varies its diet with other classics and works about Austen. Recent "Group Read" discussions, which are archived by discussion thread, have averaged between 1500 and 2500 postings over the course of the scheduled weeks.

In keeping with the overall culture of the members-only Republic of Pemberley,[62] the site's "Group Reads" are structured, more so than many a face-to-face book club might be. Participants are cautioned, in "General Group Read Guidelines," to avoid spoilers (mentions of plot events in upcoming chapters); to keep their attention on the novel at hand and contribute thoughts on other matters to other forums; and to "agree to disagree and move on" if things get heated.[63] One guideline does distinguish a Pemberley "Group Read" from an ordinary book club: "Quote directly from the text to support your opinion instead of making a general allusion or summarizing."[64] In this respect, the Pemberley participants share common ground with academic readers, for whom accurate references to a text and close readings of it remain of paramount importance (but who would speak of "arguments" rather than "opinions").

Indeed, because of Pemberleyans' avowed interest in Austen, and because of the extended time they devote to a single novel in a "Group Read," they create a discussion that in some ways resembles a slow paced, collectively led college class rather than a typical book group.[65] Participants comment on and debate the meanings of individual lines of text, compare views on characters (e.g. "Is Wickham a compulsive liar?"), and float more extensive interpretations of themes (e.g. an allegorical interpretation of Elizabeth Bennet as representing nature and Darcy as art).[66] As befits a group of fans rather than students or literary critics, discussions sometimes take up what-if scenarios, for example what would have happened in *Mansfield Park* had Fanny Price agreed to marry Henry Crawford.[67] And participants do sometimes support their interpretation of characters or events with references to their own lives: one reader of *Pride and Prejudice* compared Darcy's lack of self-awareness to an episode of her own history in which, as she explained, "it wasn't until some social fallout that I realized how I appeared to others."[68]

The overall goal of the participants in a "Group Read" is enrichment of their reading experience, rather than learning in a conventional academic sense, or literary therapy in the sense promoted by Oprah's Book Club.

The greatest compliment these participants can bestow is that reading, or re-reading, an Austen novel in the online company of fellow fans has brought them greater understanding and appreciation of the novel under scrutiny, and of Austen as author, with as much pleasure in the process as possible. "I've enjoyed the Group Read so much," posted a participant in the fall 2010 discussion of *Mansfield Park*. "It's been a joy reading and conversing as we go along. Your shared knowledge has deepened my enjoyment of the novel."[69] Another contributor to the same *Mansfield Park* discussion called it "a wonderfully enriching experience for me. So many thoughtful posts, so many insights, and some splendidly juicy L&T [life and times] offerings to chew on. I'm in awe at the complexity and the subtlety of JA's writing, and my brain cells have enjoyed a really invigorating work-out. Above all, I feel that I have been among friends."[70] One participant in the spring 2010 discussion of *Pride and Prejudice* declared that he "so much appreciate[s] the opportunity to share from the 'fellowship of the unashamed:' Men who also love Jane Austen."[71]

While the "Group Reads" give a picture of collective effort to support amateur reading of Austen, the participants' postings offer little access to the thought processes of readers who are not already committed Austen fans. And the Group Read participants, thanks to the guidelines and moderation of the forum, do not tend to dilate on their personal responses. We can surmise that these readers are experiencing versions of the "enchantment" and "recognition" anatomized by Rita Felski, but we must turn elsewhere for confirmation of Austen's power to suck in present-day readers and affect their understanding of their own worlds.

The opportunity to hear at length, and in their own words, ordinary readers' reactions to Austen emerges in Steve Chandler and Terrence N. Hill's *Two Guys Read Jane Austen* (2008), a collaborative account by two long-time friends in their 60s, both Americans. During the course of reading *Pride and Prejudice* and *Mansfield Park*, one of the "guys" overcomes his preconceptions about Austen—and, indeed, is converted to an ardent admirer—while the other rediscovers what he has always enjoyed about Austen's writings.[72]

Chandler and Hill's title, as well as their epistolary style and overall just-folks approach, follow the precedent set by their two previous co-authored books, *Two Guys Read the Obituaries* and *Two Guys Read Moby-Dick*. As Hill writes in his introduction to *Two Guys Read Moby-Dick*, "there was never any intention that this be serious literary criticism. It couldn't have been even if we had intended it. For though we are both reasonably well read, we are amateurs. We had no interest in faking it. No part of the 'text' would be 'deconstructed.' And not a single element of the novel would 'resonate' with anything. We were just two guys reading *Moby Dick*."[73] But reading Austen, as Chandler makes clear in his introduction to *Two Guys Read Jane Austen*, was a different kind of endeavor than riffing on the "manly adventure" of Herman

Melville's novel: "I'd made it through sixty some years without reading Austen at all and so I thought I was pretty much home free. What guy, really, wants to read Jane Austen?"[74] Encouraged by his and Hill's wives, and heartened by his own appreciation of Austen film adaptations—"Such good movies!"[75]—Chandler embarks, still reluctantly, on the project. As Chandler states, "I had no desire whatsoever to read what I assumed was chick lit that had simply translated entertainingly into chick flicks."[76] Hill, in contrast, has already read *Pride and Prejudice* three times but is new to *Mansfield Park*; he teases Chandler for being "virtually a Jane Austen virgin" but says, more seriously, that he envies his friend "the chance to discover her for the first time."[77]

Chandler, the initially reluctant reader, soon finds himself converted to the pleasures of reading Austen. "I hate to say it," he writes after reading eleven chapters of *Pride and Prejudice*, "but this is just pure fun reading this book."[78] "I find the books always amusing and often just laugh-aloud funny," agrees Hill.[79] Indeed, Hill identifies Austen's humor as the element that originally hooked him as a reader: when he was 23, his father read him a line of *Pride and Prejudice* that was so funny that it prompted him to read the whole novel.[80] While delighted by Austen's wit, the Two Guys need not laugh in order to remain engrossed. *Mansfield Park*, the novel that Elizabeth Long's Houston book club judged thoroughly boring, captivates Hill and Chandler thanks to Austen's ability to invest even the quotidian with meaning. "This is where Jane is fabulous," Hill remarks appreciatively in the midst of reading *Mansfield Park*, "in these unexceptional events of country life. ... Jane makes the incidents crackle with scheming and intrigue."[81]

As such comments make clear, gender is no barrier to Chandler and Hill's enjoyment of Austen. If anything, the Two Guys find Austen more interesting, not less, because of her focus on the experiences of women. Chandler remarks near the end of the book that he values how "Jane Austen allows male readers a secret look into the minds of brilliant, creative, virtuous women."[82] Furthermore, gender makes less of a difference to the Two Guys' appreciation of Austen than Chandler, at least, anticipated. The authors occasionally draw analogies that are in keeping with their personae as "guys"—and, more seriously, that are in keeping with their lives and reading experiences as men. After reading Elizabeth Bennet's climactic defiance of Lady Catherine de Bourgh, Chandler declares that he "challenge[s] any military or spy novel to have such a scene where the hero is so airtight and eloquent in arguing her principles. So unstoppable."[83] And, in response to an Austen–football analogy drawn by Chandler, Hill jokes, "I know that this has been a question that has been debated for years, but I *do* believe Jane would have made a great football coach. Not a blocking-and-tackling type, but a speed-and-deception coach. Her books are all about X's and O's."[84]

Both Chandler, the one who is new to Austen, and Hill, the one who already appreciates her writings, vividly convey the immersion they feel as they read.

Darcy's letter after his first marriage proposal "took my breath away," Chandler exclaims, and his "jaw dropped in the next chapter when Elizabeth reads and re-reads the letter. ... Her tears and hatred and remorse are so real."[85] For his part, Hill attests to "the intense enjoyment and participation I experienced in the reading. I am consciously pulling for Darcy and Elizabeth to find each other; I am hating Mr. Collins and I never intend to speak to that cad Wickham again. It is really quite amazing to me that Austen can get me this involved in the story ... again. It's not as if I don't know how it all ends; I mean I *have* read the book three times before. And yet here I am again absolutely wrapped up in the fates of the characters and thrilling to the sentences."[86] In these passages, each man emphasizes a separate aspect of the reading experience, with Chandler focusing on the capacity of *Pride and Prejudice* to evoke physiological reactions (taking his breath away, making his jaw drop) while Hill concentrates on his emotional investment in the characters and unfolding plot. In their different ways, both men are experiencing a recognizable form of the readerly "enchantment" memorably described by Rita Felski.[87]

By crediting their reading of Austen with bringing them new perspective on their lives, Chandler and Hill demonstrate versions of Felski's concept of "recognition" as well.[88] Chandler comments in general terms that the pleasure of reading *Pride and Prejudice*, far from being merely escapist, is in fact "the opposite. I see it as traveling deep within, deeper still, down, down to your true potential."[89] Hill offers two more specific examples of the influence of his Austen reading on his view of his own world. In the first, he observes that, on a family visit, he has been "paying a lot of attention to the relationship between" his wife and her sister, and he declares that "this is entirely due to spending so much time noting the relationship between Elizabeth and Jane in the book."[90] In the second, written in the course of musings about *Mansfield Park*, Hill recounts an experience that is very similar to Felski's characterization of a reader as "addressed, summoned, called to account" by a moment of recognition:

> One of the effects Jane's books have on me is regret. Her better characters' standards of morality, kindness and manners make me look back on some of the events in my life and feel pangs of sharp disappointment with myself. Supposing the standards held by the best of her characters were Jane's own, she makes me wish I could somehow show her my life and be given her seal of approval. And I feel I'd fall short in her eyes.
>
> This is, naturally, beyond ridiculous and I feel vaguely foolish even writing about these feelings, but they are nonetheless there. Nor do I mean this as some kind of major confession; because the truth is that I see myself as basically a good, and occasionally even admirable, person. ... It's just that reading Jane makes me wish I'd lived to a higher standard.
>
> Amazingly, Jane creates this feeling in me without ever seeming sententious, preachy, or holier-than-thou. And I can think of no other writer who

makes me feel this way, including (perhaps *especially* including) any number of far more overtly "moral" writers.[91]

Chandler agrees that Austen "shows us there is a beauty to morality. ... There's beauty in integrity! It's Jane's message if she has a message."[92] Clearly, the moral nature of Austen's writing strikes these two men very differently than it did the women of Elizabeth Long's book clubs, who complained that *Mansfield Park* felt like reading one advice column after another. As we will see later in this chapter, secular advice guides based on Austen capitalize on her capacity, to which Hill attests so personally, to cause readers to take closer looks at themselves and reevaluate their standards of behavior. In Chapter 6, we will see how Austen's morality has been placed in the context of evangelical Christianity.

Throughout their book, Chandler and Hill demonstrate the "playfulness" and lack of academic constraint that Long identifies as characteristic of book groups.[93] The two men are evidently delighted to be free to move easily back and forth between their reading and their lives, as well as between the Austen they are reading and other Austen-related works with which they are familiar, whether film adaptations or criticism. As avowedly amateur readers, the Two Guys are free to direct their attention where they choose and to add to their experience of Austen's texts whatever other materials they find illuminating. With respect to *Mansfield Park*, Chandler calls attention to the profound difference between reading for school and reading for yourself: "If I'd had to read this in college my attitude would be that it was merely hard work," he comments, whereas now he finds that "it's fun reading Nabokov's lecture on *Mansfield Park* right along with the book."[94] Early on in the reading project, Chandler discovers that he strongly prefers reading an unannotated edition of *Pride and Prejudice*: "My reading is much swifter and happier now. Amazing how notations can cause you to lose the whole rhythm of Jane Austen's wit."[95] Chandler's reservations about annotations are important to bear in mind as we turn, in the next section of this chapter, to guides to Austen and editions of Austen's novels aimed at amateur readers.

Guiding the Amateur Reader

As we have seen from the examples of the Two Guys and the Pemberley "Group Reads," reading Austen in the company of others affords many benefits, regardless of the group's size and whether the conversations take place face-to-face, through correspondence, or through online postings. Group members can check their interpretations against each other's, point out nuances that might have escaped each other's notice, heighten each other's enthusiasm, celebrate the author's importance to them, and, if necessary, hearten each other through the reading process. While the solitary reader sitting down with Austen has none of these outlets or forms of support, that reader does have, thanks to the efforts of both Austen fans and Austen scholars, a wide choice of books that aim to enrich her or his reading experience. A solitary reader can read an Austen novel in an edition designed to offer information, assist with interpretation, or simply enhance pleasure. She or he can read introductions and guides to Austen novels that place the author in historical and cultural context, clarify issues that tend to confuse present-day readers, or aid those whose main goal in reading fiction is to improve their own lives.

These ancillary texts vary considerably in tone, presentation, and approach, and few—to the dismay of some scholars—adhere to academic standards of writing. Taken together, however, all these books attest to the commitment of Austen lovers to reaching others who want some help, or at least some fellowship, as they read. As Elizabeth Long has pointed out, "scholars do not often think that the reception of legitimate culture is so difficult, because they think of it as 'our' culture, which tends to erase its distance from present-day lived reality. Such difficulty, coupled with readers' efforts to reframe and render the distant aspects of the classics on more familiar terms, shows the cultural labor that audiences as well as educators must perform to keep the classics alive."[96] Keeping Austen alive, and making Austen more familiar, is the common goal of all these guides to her writings.

Separating guides and editions according to whether they increase a reader's understanding or enjoyment of Austen requires making something of an artificial distinction. The claim has often been made that to understand Austen more deeply is to enjoy her works more fully, and many readers may well agree. "This book will add depth to all readers' enjoyment of Jane Austen," proclaims the back cover blurb of the American paperback edition of Josephine Ross's *Jane Austen: A Companion* (2002).[97] "Of course, one can enjoy the novel without knowing the precise definition of a gentleman," asserts the back cover blurb of David Shapard's edition of *Pride and Prejudice* (2004), "but readers of *The Annotated Pride and Prejudice* will find that these kinds of details add immeasurably to understanding and enjoying the intricate psychological interplay of Austen's immortal characters."[98] While all these books contain information about Austen, her works, and her world—in some cases, the very same facts again and again in different guises—the ways in which the books present that information vary considerably. In the next subsection, I will consider guides and editions that, in their tone and presentation, aim chiefly to edify. I will begin with the most accessible resource and end with the one that, if read fully, offers an experience most comparable to that of an academic edition. The middle subsection considers books that are designed chiefly to entertain and amuse lovers of Austen. The final subsection treats resources that apply Austen's writings to the reader's project of self-improvement.

(I) Towards Greater Understanding of Austen

In keeping with the conventions of the "Dummies®" series, *Jane Austen for Dummies®*" (2006) presents facts about Austen's life and times in an easy-to-follow format and with a level of explanation aimed at the novice. As the book's author, former Jane Austen Society of North America president Joan Klingel Ray, asserts in her introduction, "You don't need a degree in English to enjoy, or even love, Austen's novels. And you don't ever have to read any academic literary criticism to understand Austen's work."[99] The reader Ray anticipates is one who "want[s] to know more about Austen but want[s] to find a lot of information in one reasonably priced and readable book." (At the time of publishing, the list price of *Jane Austen for Dummies®* is $19.95.) Indeed, *Jane Austen for Dummies®* is fundamentally, as Ray calls it in her introduction, a "reference tool"[100]: a well-organized, well-indexed one-volume resource for readers who appreciate the forthright style and you-can-understand-this ethos of the "Dummies®" series. In addition to edifying readers, Ray guides those who wish to pursue further their interest in Austen: she includes topics and questions for discussion of each of Austen's novels as well as a list of ideas of how to "enjoy her once you've read and re-read the books and seen the films and television series."[101]

Unlike *Jane Austen for Dummies®*, which contains quite a bit of coverage of Austen's role in popular culture, Josephine Ross's *Jane Austen: A Companion* focuses entirely on Austen's writings, life, and times. Readers, not viewers, of Austen are Ross's target audience, and she addresses them accordingly not with reference-style brief entries but with continuous, engagingly written prose. Ross is particularly concerned, she explains in her preface, with illuminating "aspects of Jane Austen's world and work [that] are, inevitably, unfamiliar to many modern readers."[102] Offering cultural context without the scholarly feel of footnotes, Ross's book addresses an amateur reader who welcomes a wide range of information and references, and who has an attention span sufficient to carry him or her through chapter-long discussions of topics related to Austen.

Readers who prefer their supplemental information to be keyed directly to the points of the text that have caused them confusion are the target audience of David Shapard's series of annotated versions of Austen's novels, which began with *The Annotated Pride and Prejudice*. In their very heft and design, Shapard's editions convey a sense of comprehensiveness. The back cover blurb of *The Annotated Pride and Prejudice* promises "more than 2,300 annotations on facing pages" (as opposed to mere "hundreds" for *The Annotated Persuasion*).[103] To open either of these editions at random is to confront the sheer volume of material that Shapard has added to Austen's original prose. His annotations are printed in a slightly smaller font than the text of the Austen novel, and in many cases he has found so much to say about a page of Austen's prose that his word count exceeds hers. That Shapard's editions of Austen appeal to readers can be judged by his success in parlaying his original hardcover edition of *The Annotated Pride and Prejudice*, published by the tiny press Pheasant Books of Delmar, NY, into an arrangement to annotate all six novels for Anchor Books, a subsidiary of Random House.

The quantity of material that Shapard has assembled, together with the footnote format, might mislead a purchaser to think that this edition is a scholarly one, rather than an exceptionally detailed one aimed at amateur readers with an appetite for information. Shapard's author bio, which prominently mentions his "Ph.D. in European History from the University of California at Berkeley," contributes to his air of authority (though actual scholars would immediately notice that he is a historian rather than a literary critic). In a lengthy, critical review posted on Amazon.com, Joan Klingel Ray—author of *Jane Austen for Dummies®*, and herself an English professor—faulted Shapard for his failure to credit his sources and tendency to indulge in his own opinions. "I remind students and teachers to be wary of the editor's cavalier practice of citation omission," she cautioned, and recommended that readers instead consult "Cambridge University Press's excellent 2006 scholarly edition of *Pride and Prejudice*, edited by Dr. Pat Rogers."[104] Responses to Ray's review by fellow Amazon.com customers offer evidence—if any more were needed—that the concerns and capacities of amateur readers do not necessarily align with those of academics. "I bought this book hoping to find information explaining the story," declared John F. Pepple. "I didn't want to slog through a lot of citations that I have no real interest in. As for the failure to introduce scholarly opinions from the last decade, I have no interest in those, either."[105] "Good heavens! 157.99 for the Cambridge University Press 2006 P&P?" wrote a reader named Jay Sax.[106] "This an interest, not an all-consuming passion for me and my family, and we are not perhaps in the proper economic stratum to be able to part with so much for a single volume!" (At the time of this book going to press, Shapard's annotated editions are priced at $16.95, roughly twice as much as other paperback editions with footnotes that are designed for classroom use.)

The most scholarly of the popular books aimed at edifying amateur readers of Austen is also, thanks to its lavish design, the most appealing as a physical object. Indeed, so beautifully presented is Patricia Meyer Spacks's annotated edition of *Pride and Prejudice* (2010) that it would seem to fall decisively into my category of books that, in their very packaging, stress the authors' desire to promote readers' enjoyment. Spacks's edition looks for all the world like a coffee-table book: it is exceptionally large (nine inches square), heavy, and printed with an appealing degree of clarity. (Her notes to the text take up approximately the outer third of each page.) Illustrations, many in full color, add to the overall effect of lushness.

The impression that this handsome edition of *Pride and Prejudice* exists to be marveled over and dipped into, rather than read attentively or consulted for purposes of serious reference, is underscored by the book's lack of

an index. Yet in her introduction and annotations, Spacks strongly resists
the notion that this edition, or *Pride and Prejudice* as a text, ought to be
approached purely as a means to enjoyment—and it is for this reason that I
treat her edition here.

Indeed, Spacks makes the case that a novel like *Pride and Prejudice*, which has
so often been read with delight in the absence of any apparatus of annotation
or other contextual information, has especial need of just such material.
"Generations of teenage girls—indeed, generations of men and women of
every age—have happily read *Pride and Prejudice* without benefit of notes,"
Spacks acknowledges in her introduction. "They may not know the difference
between a curricle and a gig or have more than a vague notion just what the
nineteenth-century English militia did, but such bits of ignorance hardly
impede enjoyment of this novel about wishes fulfilled."[107] What concerns
Spacks, it emerges, is not the "bits of ignorance" per se, nor the capacity of
Austen's novel to continue to delight readers who, in taking "imaginative
possession" of it, let some details slide.[108] Rather, Spacks contends that interpretations that are wholly personal are by their nature partial, and even potentially
misguided. In her view, to read *Pride and Prejudice* as a wish-fulfilling fantasy
is to fail to do justice either to it as a work of literature or to Austen's artistry.
"Although one can happily read *Pride and Prejudice* in the absence of notes,"
Spacks concludes, "their presence introduces us to a richer, more provocative
book."[109]

Spacks's goal is to make visible the aspects of Austen's novel that are
more than merely delightful, and thereby to help all willing readers have "a
complex response to the words on the page."[110] She candidly and disarmingly
uses herself—a distinguished American literary scholar—as an example of a
reader who discovered more than she thought she could about a very familiar
text: "The process of writing notes taught me not only how much I didn't
know but also the importance of what I learned. ... I became aware of dark
suggestions in *Pride and Prejudice*, suggestions that various delightful films have
ignored. Writing notes revealed that more than fantasy operates in Austen's
construction of plot and showed how complicated an apparently straightforward novel can be. Most important, the process uncovered, or as Austen
herself would say, *unfolded*—the need to understand a historical moment in
order to understand the fiction written in it."[111] Spacks offers readers information, certainly, but she goes beyond mere annotation to promote a mode
of reading that emphasizes curiosity and a willingness to entertain alternative
interpretations.

Spacks stresses the capacity of *Pride and Prejudice* to deepen under an
attentive reader's gaze, rather than suggesting that the reader's life can
improve as a result of an encounter with Austen. Spacks does claim, however,
that *Pride and Prejudice* "urges its readers, too, to open their minds: to realize
the gap between plausibility and exactitude in making human judgments, to
grasp the urgency of such judgments as well as the difficulty of making them,

to acknowledge that wishes can come true, while understanding that many lives are lived in disappointment."[112] In this sense, Spacks shares common ground with those authors who, in very different modes, assert the potential of Austen's writings to enrich, or even change, a reader's life.

(II) Towards Greater Enjoyment of Austen

For the sake of comparison, let us begin with a very different kind of annotated edition of Austen's novels than those prepared by Spacks and Shapard: the "Insight Editions" of *Pride and Prejudice* (2007) and *Sense and Sensibility* (2010) published by the Christian press Bethany House. Certainly these are editions aimed at Christian readers, for whom one appropriate discussion question, included in each novel, is "Who in the novel lives the most authentic Christian faith?"[113] And the editors do make an effort, as they put it, to "pay special attention to the book's quiet but resonant faith themes," although compara- tively few annotations focus on those themes.[114] What is most striking about these "Insight Editions," and why I have decided to discuss them here rather than alongside other Christian reworkings of Austen in Chapter 6, is that these editions are explicitly and proudly prepared by Austen fans for the benefit of other amateur readers of Austen. These editors claim only the authority of loving Austen, and their professed goal is simply to share their enthusiasm with other non-academic readers. Their "Editors' Note" to *Pride and Prejudice* begins with the following "confession":

> There's not a Regency historian, Austen scholar, or doctoral literary critic among those of us who tackled this project.
> Instead, we're fans who deeply love this book and truly admire Jane Austen. And more than anything, we wanted a chance to share our admiration for this wonderful novel with others who cherish it. Or, if you've never read Austen, we want to come alongside ... not with dry analysis but with hints and helps that hopefully will enhance your experience.
> The notes and facts and thoughts that fill the margins of this book aren't designed to be comprehensive. Instead they're meant to highlight, inform, and sometimes just entertain. Some will reveal parallels with Austen's own life or highlight important historical information or show Austen's impact in our world today. Others will comment on the book itself, or offer romance advice, or simply point out our favorite funny bits. ...
> Our goal is simple: we want you to enjoy yourself. This isn't an eleventh grade homework assignment. It's a sparkling love story with a whip-smart heroine who may be too witty for her own good.[115]

The editors' chatty, often humorous comments are much more sparing than those of Shapard or Spacks; just one or two annotations appear per page, on

average. Rather than presenting Austen's text as in need of extensive explanation for present-day audiences, the "Insight Editions" implicitly suggest that
even first-time readers need only light assistance in order to derive pleasure
from Austen's writings. And the editors, in keeping with their non-academic
approach, encourage personally applied interpretations of each novel, asking
readers to compare their own beliefs and behaviors to those of Austen's
characters.[116] In this sense, the "Insight Editions" overlap with the books I will
consider in the next subsection, which promote reading Austen for the sake of
self-improvement.

That enjoyment of Austen requires little academic knowledge—and,
furthermore, that an academic approach might inhibit appreciation of Austen's
writings—is strongly asserted by Natalie Tyler in her preface to *The Friendly Jane
Austen: A Well-Mannered Introduction to a Lady of Sense & Sensibility* (1999; 2001).
Tyler recalls enrolling in a graduate class on Austen in the hopes of enhancing
her "love for Austen's novels," only to be "thwarted" by the professor's
insistence on "the arcane metalanguage of academic theory."[117] Tyler's aim in
her own miscellany is to support a very different kind of reading experience,
one that she herself subsequently enjoyed with a bedridden aunt: "It became
easier to see how we could cope with our boorish brothers, crude cousins,
indecorous in-laws, and surly sons after the tonic effect of Jane Austen's wit.
... In reading Jane Austen, we had in fact become better people. We had
learned how to read the characters of others."[118] Unlike those writers who
apply precepts from Austen's novels directly to dilemmas of present-day life,
Tyler works more obliquely to empower readers to operate without scholarly
language and outside interpretive constraints. Through offering a mixture of
anecdotes, interviews, questions, and vignettes both historical and personal,
Tyler reassures readers that it is acceptable, and even admirable, to approach
Austen as an enthusiast.[119]

In design as well as content, three recently published guidebooks to Austen
encourage an even more self-indulgent form of imaginative communion with
Austen's world. Margaret C. Sullivan, in her introduction to *The Jane Austen
Handbook: A Sensible Yet Elegant Guide to Her World* (2007), promises "step-by-
step instructions that will allow one to conduct one's fantasy life with perfect
aplomb. ... This book is for the Janeite who, while relatively content living in the
modern world, indulges in the occasional unashamed wallow in Austenland."[120]
Both the high level of design and the compact size of Sullivan's book announce
its difference from more sober, academic volumes. Even more appealing to
the eye and hand is *Jane Austen's Guide to Good Manners: Compliments Charades
& Horrible Blunders* (2006), with text by Josephine Ross and watercolor illustrations by Henrietta Webb. "Perhaps the following Rules of social behaviour may
provide some guidance as to how to behave in 'Polite Society,'" Ross suggests.[121]
She leaves it to the reader to decide whether to compare the mores of Austen's
day to those of the contemporary world or to delight in the fantasy of being
instructed in etiquette by their favorite "Authoress."

Those who find props helpful for their flights of fancy can take advantage of Rebecca Dickson's *Jane Austen: An Illustrated Treasury* (2008), which includes facsimiles of Austen letters (which can be removed from their envelopes) as well as a facsimile of Austen's "The History of England," a facsimile page from Austen's canceled chapter of *Persuasion*, and even life-size reproductions of Cassandra's two portraits of Jane. "These special features," according to the back cover blurb, "make *Jane Austen: An Illustrated Treasury* an intimate and unique experience for anyone who appreciates the timeless significance of her work."[122] Handling these reproductions, you can indulge in any of several fantasies. You can imagine that you are the recipient of letters from Jane Austen, or a member of her inner circle who would potentially have had access to her manuscript fiction. You can imagine that you, like Alberta H. Burke, my subject in Chapter 2, are a collector of Austeniana who through possessing such items attains special closeness to your favorite author. Or you can imagine that you are the kind of person—a scholar, perhaps, or curator—whom the British Library or the National Portrait Gallery would allow to handle original manuscripts and portraits.[123]

(III) Towards Greater Self-Actualization

Throughout this chapter, we have heard many lovers of Austen's writings attest to the personal insights and assistance, even benefits to physical and mental health, that they have derived from their favorite books. Those attracted to the idea of reading Austen in the self-help mode need not tackle the novels alone—or even at all, thanks to several recent publications that mine Austen's writings (and, in one case, an Austen-based film) for inspirational content.[124] Readers can choose to passively ingest lessons that others have already drawn from Austen's novels or to follow the lead of writers who offer models, and in some cases practical tools, for obtaining guidance from Austen.

The most unapologetically didactic resource for those who seek self-improvement through Austen is Lauren Henderson's *Jane Austen's Guide to Dating* (2005). Henderson's goal, as she explains in her introduction, is to counter the byzantine stipulations of existing dating guides with "a good injection of common sense," and Austen, she says, "is exactly the person who will give it to us."[125] Henderson takes for granted both that Austen's novels contain guidelines for conduct and that those "rules are as relevant today as they always were—maybe even more so."[126] Indeed, Henderson characterizes Austen's novels as being virtually a dating guide in themselves: "besides being wonderful stories ... they are also manuals for anyone who wants to learn about finding someone to spend the rest of your life with, someone with whom you share values and similar qualities, someone trustworthy and true."[127] Henderson describes herself as having made just this use of Austen's novels. "After several bad experiences in the New York dating scene," she declares, "I did what I often do in a crisis: I turned to Jane Austen, whose books I've been reading since I was twelve years old."[128]

Yet Henderson does not require that readers in search of advice pick up, or return to, Austen's novels themselves. Indeed, the blurb on the back jacket flap of *Jane Austen's Guide to Dating* reassures readers that no direct acquaintance with Austen's writing is necessary: "No need to have read Jane Austen. ... *Jane Austen's Guide to Dating* summarizes all the love stories in the books so you can dive right into the benefits of her great advice."[129] (The character summaries provided by Henderson have titles such as "Charlotte: The Settler" and "Miss Bingley: The Bitch."[130]) Following the conventional form of a self-help book, Henderson extracts ten fundamental "principles that Jane Austen lays out in her novels," from "If You Like Someone, Make It Clear That You Do" to "If Your Lover Needs a Reprimand, Let Him Have It."[131] After explaining, often in a series of examples, how each principle operates in its source novel, Henderson pauses on a "lesson to be learned"—for instance, "Enjoy the Moment"—before adding a pair of anecdotes about contemporary characters, the first demonstrating "what not to do" and the second "what to do instead." Henderson's addition of these anecdotes seems to belie her claim that Austen's "rules" are as relevant today as ever; she justifies the inclusion of these tips on the grounds that they "bring Jane Austen's expertise directly into the modern world, as an extra point of reference and help."[132]

Bringing enlightenment from Austen to those with more concerns than dating alone is life coach Cheryl Richardson, who was asked by the American public television show *Masterpiece* (formerly *Masterpiece Theatre*) to comment on the miniseries version of *Sense and Sensibility* that was originally broadcast in the US in spring 2008.[133] *Masterpiece*'s introduction to Richardson's remarks reaches out directly to the anticipated difficulties of present-day viewers: "Is Jane Austen trying to tell you something about your life? Are you hungry for a simpler way of life? Is there something missing from your significant relationships? Do you have trouble speaking up for yourself? If you answered yes to any of these questions, Jane Austen's *Sense and Sensibility* may have some unexpected insights for your life. ... Cheryl Richardson examines how modern day challenges can be addressed with wisdom from the Austen classic."[134] Richardson's commentary locates in this screen version of *Sense and Sensibility* (she does not refer to the novel) many truisms of present-day popular psychology, including "the power of a simple life," the need to "focus on connection and relationships," and the danger of "fall[ing] in love with the dream of what could be instead of the reality of what is."[135]

Richardson advocates a form of interpretation that is focused overwhelmingly on the viewer's personal reactions to characters, with the goal of obtaining insight into oneself, rather than into the *Sense and Sensibility* miniseries as a work of art, or as a version of Austen. Using her own interpretive process as a model, Richardson encourages viewers to begin their interpretations by paying attention to their gut responses:

And one of the things that I always like to do when I'm watching a character driven film, and Austen's work is all about character driven story lines, is I like to look at who are the characters that I identify with the most.

Who are the ones that stand out to me who I long to be like, that express the kinds of things that I wish I could express[?] Who are the characters that drive me crazy, that make me want to scream? All of those characters that allow us to have any kind of strong reactions are characters that are trying to tell us something about ourselves. So I invite you as you look at part two of the film to ask yourself the same question. Who do you identify with and why? Who do you wish you were more like?[136]

Of course, Richardson's questions are far from specific to Austen—and they are far from unique to her. I mentioned earlier that the "Questions for Conversation" printed at the end of the "Insight Editions" of *Pride and Prejudice* and *Sense and Sensibility* likewise encourage readers to compare Austen's characters' predicaments with their own. And, as I have noted, personally driven, therapeutically aimed interpretation is central to the "everyday literary criticism" promoted by Oprah Winfrey.[137]

Unlike Richardson's and Henderson's approaches, which require no particular knowledge of Austen on the part of the advice-seeker, Patrice Hannon's *Dear Jane Austen: A Heroine's Guide to Life and Love* (2005; 2007) tantalizes the Austen lover with insider references, while at the same time offering an inviting introduction to Austen's novels. Like Henderson, Hannon applies examples from Austen's novels to the predicaments of twenty-first-century women. While love problems are central to *Dear Jane Austen*, however, Hannon treats issues of character and family relationships as well. Inventively, she structures her book as a series of letters written by Jane Austen in response to made-up queries. Thus the advice-giving voice in *Dear Jane Austen* is that of Jane Austen herself, whom Hannon imagines as capable of commenting knowledgeably about events that occurred after her death as well as on topics related to her novels and life.[138]

To this hybrid of advice guide plus fictional depiction of Austen, Hannon adds two other elements as well. The first is a very approachable form of literary commentary, similar to that offered in Ross's *Jane Austen: A Companion* or Ray's *Jane Austen for Dummies®*. Hannon's author bio—the first text inside the front cover to meet the eye of the book buyer or reader—announces the author's scholarly credentials: she "holds a Ph.D. in English literature from Rutgers University" and has both taught and published extensively on Austen.[139] In her "Author's Note," Hannon explains she was "inspired to write a 'self-help' book about Austen's writings" because "hundreds of [her] students have found aspects of their own experience mirrored in Austen's novels."[140] We are immediately aware that we are in the hands of a teacher, not a mere reader or fan of Austen, as is the case with Henderson and Richardson. Hannon makes clear, too, that she has given herself—and, by extension, her readers—permission to think in a personal, as opposed to a scholarly or academic, way about Austen's novels and biography. In this respect, Hannon's book joins other titles—including her own book of literary-critical and biographical miniatures, *101 Things You Didn't Know about Jane Austen: The Truth about the World's Most Intriguing Romantic Literary Heroine* (2007)—that aim to shed light, for the non-academic reader, on the content and influence of Austen's novels. Yet even as Hannon sidesteps literary terms and theories and has Jane Austen herself mock scholarly interpretations of her fiction, both author and narrator stress a different kind of "proper" reading.[141] Unlike the attentive, analytical form of reading promoted in Spacks' edition of *Pride and Prejudice*, the reading advocated in *Dear Jane Austen* is focused on character improvement. "Read my novels, learn about the world, and cultivate your own judgment," Hannon's Austen advises her readers, much as Austen's heroines, through their experiences and reflections, cultivate their own.[142]

The second element Hannon adds is evident in the end of her "Acknowledgments," where she writes that she "can only hope [her] humble appreciation of Jane Austen's great art is evident in every word of this tribute."[143] By casting her work as a "tribute," Hannon distances herself further from scholarly criticism, placing herself in the company of those authors who describe their writings—often sequels, but sometimes also memoirs or works in other genres—as homages to Austen, personal effusions inspired by a beloved author. (In Chapter 5, I will consider how Hannon's depiction of Austen as a character compares to those of other contemporary writers.)

Unlike Hannon and Henderson, who invent scenarios in which advice from Austen's novels improves the lives of modern-day readers, William Deresiewicz's 2011 memoir *A Jane Austen Education* offers a sustained account of his own evolution, through reading Austen, from a selfish commitment-phobe into an enlightened, happily married man. Like Richardson, albeit in a much more literary mode, Deresiewicz stresses, and demonstrates, a form of interpretation that is essentially personal. Thinking about your own predicament while reading a novel, Deresiewicz maintains, can lead you to a fresh perspective on that work, as well as on yourself. "A process of mutual illumination began to unfold," he declares: "*Mansfield Park* taught me about my experiences, and my experiences taught me about *Mansfield Park*."[144] In particular, Deresiewicz claims that recognizing himself in Austen's heroines has helped him identify and overcome his own shortcomings. "Emma's cruelty, which I was so quick to criticize," he declares, "was nothing, I saw, but the mirror image of my own."[145]

Deresiewicz avails himself fully of the amateur's privilege to see himself in Austen's characters without regard to whether the "mirror image" he beholds distorts those characters somewhat. "Like Elizabeth [Bennet]," he observes on one occasion, "I thought I was just so damn smart that I couldn't stop myself from giving the rest of the world the benefit of my wisdom"[146]—a criticism that is more apt for Mary Bennet. Deresiewicz freely incorporates opinions, too, in his analysis of Austen's characters, as when he declares that Elizabeth Bennet's lack of concern about getting married betrays not that she "knew what she wanted from life" but that she "hadn't even started to figure it out."[147] This insight seems more applicable to the memoirist himself than to his subject. Overall, engaging as is Deresiewicz's narrative voice, a skeptical reader may well object that in *A Jane Austen Education* he is doing much the same thing for which he faults Elizabeth as well as his earlier self: giving the world the benefit of his wisdom by telling stories of his own transformation as a reader, and as a man, rather than providing tools that would allow his audience to pursue a comparable project for themselves.[148]

In contrast, Diane Wilkes's *Tarot of Jane Austen* (2006) places the power of interpretation squarely in the hands of readers. Complete and professionally usable, Wilkes's tarot deck features characters that she has selected from Austen's novels and mapped onto the traditional cards of the tarot. "Austen's books and the tarot," claims Wilkes in the full-length book of instruction and commentary that accompanies the cards, "contain one essentially identical message: the vital importance of balance in our everyday lives."[149] Wilkes declares that "if one reads Austen carefully, she provides a template for the way life should be lived."[150]

For each card, Wilkes provides a multi-part apparatus to assist with interpretation. She describes the scene or character shown in each card, situates that scene in terms of the novel's storyline, interprets the card in light of the source novel, and concludes with "Jane's Advice," which is addressed directly to the recipient of the reading and accompanied by a pertinent quotation from Austen's writings. Wilkes also suggests innovative ways of performing readings with the cards, including card combinations inspired by literary concepts (e.g. "The Bildungsroman Spread"[151]).

What distinguishes this tarot set from other advice literature based on Austen is first the manner in which it leaves the reader of the cards in charge of her or his own interpretation, and second the potential complexity of that interpretation. The characters Wilkes has chosen, including Austen herself as the "High Priestess," provide archetypes.[152] Yet interpreting the cards in the context of a tarot spread is neither simple nor straightforward. Indeed, as Wilkes describes it, tarot reading is both a critical and a creative act. "When a reader uses a tarot spread," she explains, "s/he tries to tell the 'story' of it to the querent," the recipient of the reading. Paying attention to "plot" as well as "theme or pattern or life-lesson," the reader "analyze[s] the composition of the spread," with the help of "observable details" in the card placement and the discernment of "patterns" that give the reading "resonance and cohesion."[153] A reader who is well acquainted with Austen can bring further depth to the interpretation. If two cards based on a single Austen novel appear in a spread, for example, readers who are familiar with that novel "can enhance the reading by thinking about how those two characters/situations interact with one another [in the original work] and weave that backstory into [their] reading."[154] *Tarot of Jane Austen* equips each reader—in both senses of that term—to achieve greater depth in both literary appreciation and personal insight, through an active, creative process.

Inspired by Austen to Create

In the phrase I have taken as the second epigraph to this book, Sheenagh Pugh asserts that "a good reader also creates."[155] That many readers of Austen, and viewers of Austen-based films, enjoy expressing their enthusiasm through writing creatively is evident from the proliferation of sequels to and spinoffs from Austen novels published since—and in many cases directly inspired by—the landmark 1995 BBC *Pride and Prejudice* miniseries.[156] Austen fan fiction has been studied from many vantage points.[157] Much attention has been given to how present-day writers have reworked Austen's originals, and efforts have been made to classify and categorize Austen-inspired fiction according to content and form.[158] Persuasive theories have been advanced as to why lovers of Austen would choose, and even feel empowered by Austen herself, to experiment with versions of her characters and settings.[159] In Chapter 6, I will examine these theories in more depth, and in relation to a range of fictional reworkings of Austen's novels. Here, I wish to attend briefly to an aspect of Austen sequels that has attracted little notice: the benefits their writers claim for interacting in this way with Austen's works.

Fiction inspired by Austen is both created by and intended for those who engage imaginatively rather than critically with what they read or view. The pseudonymous Rebecca Ann Collins, an Australian, explains that "the BBC's magnificent production" of *Pride and Prejudice* inspired her own book *The Pemberley Chronicles* (1997). Referring to herself in the third person, she informs her readers that if they

> watched spellbound as millions did as it [the 1995 miniseries] unfolded on your television screen and, seeing the two couples drive away as the closing credits and that magic music rolled, you wondered where life would have taken them, then Emily Gardiner's prologue, which opens the chronicles, will start you on that journey. It is for these readers, not for the J.A. Specialists or the literary establishment, that Rebecca Ann Collins has compiled *The Pemberley Chronicles*. It is to them, as much as to the beloved Miss Austen herself, that the book is dedicated.[160]

Collins could not be clearer in claiming her readership as composed of amateurs, those whose experience of Austen involves being "spellbound" and whose response to Austen is not to analyze but to "wonder."

Unlike academic writing, fan fiction aims to amuse, and—according to its creators—is often enjoyable to create as well (a claim more seldom made by scholars). That pleasure is fundamental to both the writing and the reading of an Austen sequel is asserted by Jane Dawkins in her introduction to *Letters from Pemberley: The First Year* (1998; 2007): "Although I have tried to be historically correct (or approximate), I am no expert on either the period or Miss Austen: this book's only purpose is to entertain. If the reader is as entertained in reading it as I have been in writing it, I shall be satisfied. The more I find out about Jane Austen, her works, and the society in which she lived, the more I want to know; it is a never-ending fascination."[161] United in a desire to be "entertained," the writer and reader of Austen-inspired fiction share as well a fundamental curiosity about Austen and her world.

Beyond diversion alone, Austen-based fiction has the potential, according to some writers, to deepen one's appreciation of Austen's art. While writing an *Emma* sequel titled *Perfect Happiness* (1996), Rachel Billington recalls that she "felt very close to Jane Austen and thought to [herself] that anyone wanting to understand her novels—literary critic, student or admiring reader—should try creating a chapter or two for themselves."[162] Indeed, fan fiction is often assigned as a creative writing exercise for schoolchildren. Pugh notes that many posters of online fan fiction identify their works' origins as a class assignment.[163] A similar idea to Billington's has been advanced by Diana Birchall, author of a *Pride and Prejudice* sequel as well as several novels featuring Mrs. Elton from *Emma*. Birchall asserts that "a new understanding of Austen's works can be gained by the unorthodox method of writing pastiche":

> To my surprise, examining the novel *Emma* with such a purpose in mind was most productive because it resulted in giving me new insights into Jane Austen's writing, and especially her subtle ways of framing a character.
>
> From thinking about a minor character in Emma, examining the story from her point of view, cutting away Austen's editorial perspective, we see that Mrs. Elton's behavior is open to a more sympathetic interpretation. Thus we are enabled to see the story afresh, and gain insight into Austen's methods of genius. Jane Austen purposely made Mrs. Elton obnoxious, to make Emma seem less obnoxious.[164]

According to Birchall, actively intervening into Austen's world by reworking a novel has the power to change both how we interpret and how we appreciate her writings.

Though Billington and Birchall focus on the advantages of attempting to write in Austen's style, a comparable claim could easily be made that *reading* pastiches of Austen brings fresh perspective on her writings as well—or at least serves as the spur to a fresh encounter with those writings. Hazel Holt, author of a novel, *My Dear Charlotte* (2009), based on Austen's letters, expresses just such a hope: "that anyone who reads *My Dear Charlotte* will be sent straight back to the letters themselves to discover again the delights they contain."[165] Similarly, the Welsh-born novelist Sarah Waters, who acted as judge for a contest for works "inspired by Jane Austen and Chawton House Library," remarks that the stories she selected as finalists "collectively lead us back to [Austen] with fresh eyes."[166]

Jane Dawkins's description of her "never-ending fascination" with Austen recalls the quotation from Michael Chabon with which I began this chapter. For many amateur readers today, the world of Austen's writings is indeed, as Chabon puts it, "endlessly inviting, endlessly inhabitable."[167] In the next chapter, we will see how places in the real world that hold associations with Austen invite readers to feel imaginatively at home.

Notes

1 Michael Chabon, "The Amateur Family," in *Manhood for Amateurs: The Pleasures and Regrets of a Husband, Father, and Son* (New York: Harper, 2010), 294. Elsewhere in his collection of essays, Chabon extends his conception of amateur enthusiasm beyond the popular realm per se: "Every work of art is one half of a secret handshake. ... Every great record or novel or comic book convenes the first meeting of a fan club whose membership stands forever at one but which maintains chapters in every city—in every cranium—in the world. Art, like fandom, asserts the possibility of fellowship in a world built entirely from the materials of solitude." "The Losers Club," in *Manhood for Amateurs*, 5.
2 Janice A. Radway, *Reading the Romance: Women, Patriarchy, and Popular Literature* (1984; repr., London: Verso, 1987), 88.
3 Ibid., 89, 101.
4 Janice A. Radway, *A Feeling for Books: The Book-of-the-Month Club, Literary Taste, and Middle-Class Desire* (Chapel Hill, NC: University of North Carolina Press, 1997), 114.
5 Ibid., 117.
6 Ibid., 116.
7 Ibid., 119.
8 Ibid., 117.
9 Harold Bloom, *How to Read and Why* (New York: Scribner, 2000), 21.
10 Ibid., 19.
11 Ibid., 22.
12 Ibid., 22–23.
13 Rita Felski, *Uses of Literature* (Malden, MA: Blackwell, 2008), 14.
14 Ibid., 13.
15 Ibid., 14.
16 Ibid., 135.
17 Ibid., 23.
18 Felski notes too that "novels yield up manifold descriptions of such moments of readjustment, as fictional readers are wrenched out of their circumstances by the force of written words." Ibid. Though Felski chooses supporting examples from other authors, those familiar with Austen's novels could easily supply relevant scenes; Elizabeth Bennet's re-reading of Darcy's letter in Volume 2, Chapter 13 of *Pride and Prejudice* is perhaps the most memorable.
19 Felski, *Uses of Literature* 54–55.
20 Kelley Penfield Lewis, "The Trouble with Happy Endings: Conflicting Narratives in Oprah's Book Club," in *The Oprah Affect: Critical Essays on Oprah's Book Club*, ed. Cecilia Konchar Farr and Jaime Harker (Albany: State University of New York Press, 2008), 216.
21 Quoted in Lewis, "The Trouble with Happy Endings," 221.
22 Ibid., 217.
23 Ibid.
24 Kate Douglas, "Your Book Changed My Life: Everyday Literary Criticism and Oprah's Book Club," in *The Oprah Affect*, ed. Farr and Harker, 239.
25 Ibid., 237.

26 Ibid.

27 Ibid., 236.

28 Elizabeth Long, *Book Clubs: Women and The Uses of Reading in Everyday Life* (Chicago: University of Chicago Press, 2003), 205–206.

29 Erin Blakemore, *The Heroine's Bookshelf: Life Lessons, from Jane Austen to Laura Ingalls Wilder* (New York: Harper, 2010), xi.

30 Ibid., xii.

31 Ibid., xvii, xiii.

32 Ibid., xv, xiv. In contrast with her paean to the power of reading, Blakemore's book discussions are not especially personal. Of *Pride and Prejudice*, for example, she remarks that she "find[s] Lizzy's spirit wherever authority is flouted, minds changed, or expectations challenged," without exploring any more specific links between Austen's heroine and her own life. *The Heroine's Bookshelf*, 16. See also Suzy Flory, *So Long, Status Quo: What I Learned from Women Who Changed the World* (Kansas City: Beacon Hill Press, 2009), which includes Austen as one of several inspirational female figures.

33 Blakemore, *The Heroine's Bookshelf*, xv.

34 Susannah Carson, introduction to *A Truth Universally Acknowledged: 33 Great Writers on Why We Read Jane Austen*, ed. Susannah Carson (New York: Random House, 2009), xi.

35 Ibid., xiv–xv.

36 My open-ended survey began by asking, "What does Jane Austen mean to you?" Because of the breadth of the question, not all responses focus exclusively on the experience of reading Austen's novels, but may include descriptions of the experience of watching Austen-based films. I will refer to "readers" throughout, recognizing how loosely I am using the term. I include identifying characteristics—country of residence, age range, and level of literary study—supplied by the survey participants, who remained anonymous. To allow comparison, I also identify the nationality of those whose published personal accounts I quote.

37 Jill Pitkeathley, *Cassandra & Jane: A Jane Austen Novel* (2004; repr., New York: Harper, 2008), 259.

38 "Your Jane Austen: What Do You Think?," interview with Angela Barlow, *Jane Austen's Regency World* 27 (2007): 45.

39 Long, *Book Clubs*, 179.

40 Hilary Mantel, "Jane Austen," in *Literary Genius: 25 Classic Writers Who Define English & American Literature*, ed. Joseph Epstein (Philadelphia: Paul Dry Books, 2007), 82.

41 Survey of visitors to Jane Austen's House Museum, July 13–23, 2009. All surveys were conducted in confidentiality and are transcribed exactly as written. Responses subsequently cited as JAHM survey.

42 Lori Smith, *A Walk with Jane Austen: A Journey into Adventure, Love & Faith* (Colorado Springs: WaterBrook Press, 2007), 3–4. I will discuss Smith's memoir in more depth in Chapters 4 and 6.

43 E-mail from Susanna Adams to Itta England, July 17, 2003. Accession records for Barbara Winn Adams Jane Austen Collection. Special Collections and Archives, Goucher College Library.

44 Frankie Brewer, quoted in Susannah Fullerton and Anne Harbers, eds, *Jane Austen: Antipodean Views* (Neutral Bay: Wellington Lane Press, 2001), 22.

45 JAHM survey.

46 Humphrey Carpenter, quoted in Maggie Lane and David Selwyn, eds, *Jane Austen: A Celebration* (Manchester: Fyfield Books, 2000), 18.

47 Elizabeth Shek, quoted in Fullerton and Harbers, eds, *Jane Austen: Antipodean Views*, 26.

48 Joe Bennett, quoted in Fullerton and Harbers, eds, *Jane Austen: Antipodean Views*, 162–63.

49 All quotations in this paragraph are from JAHM survey.

50 JAHM survey.

51 Ibid.

52 James Collins, "Fanny Was Right: Jane Austen as Moral Guide," in *A Truth Universally Acknowledged*, ed. Carson, 147. A version of Collins's essay reached a large audience thanks to its publication in the *Wall Street Journal*. "What Would Jane Do?: How a 19th-Century Spinster Serves as a Moral Compass in Today's World," *Wall Street Journal*, November 14, 2009.

53 William Deresiewicz, *A Jane Austen Education: How Six Novels Taught Me about Love, Friendship, and the Things that Really Matter* (New York: Penguin Press, 2011), 33. As a former Yale professor and the author of an acclaimed academic book on Austen and the Romantic poets, Deresiewicz occupies a very intriguing position on the scholar–amateur continuum, a position he does not explicitly address in his memoir itself.

54 Benjamin Nugent, "The Nerds of *Pride and Prejudice*," in *A Truth Universally Acknowledged*, ed. Carson, 94. Nugent identifies Mary Bennet of *Pride and Prejudice* as the portrait of a nerd before the term existed. Austen's detailed depictions of characters who experience social awkwardness and discomfort have been interpreted by Phyllis Ferguson Bottomer—an Austen lover who is by profession a speech-language pathologist—as depictions of behavior that we would now identify as being on the autistic spectrum. Bottomer stops short of recommending that present-day people with Asperger's read Austen, though she does assert that family members, clinicians, and the general public can benefit from examining Austen's novels with an awareness of the hallmarks of the condition. *So Odd a Mixture: Along the Autistic Spectrum in 'Pride and Prejudice'* (London: Jessica Kingsley, 2007). In my own teaching, I have been told by a student with Asperger's that he hopes that the study of nineteenth-century British novels, with their realistic psychological depictions of thoughts and their attention to nuances of dialogue and behavior, will help him better understand others' thoughts and feelings, as well as helping to educate him in conversing and behaving in a way that will be considered appropriate.

55 Smith, *A Walk with Jane Austen*, 10.

56 For instance, Elizabeth Long has argued that "it is in the representation of characters and their lives that 'classic' novels may be most influential in shaping modern sensibility." *Book Clubs*, 182.

57 Jenny Hartley, *Reading Groups* (Oxford: Oxford University Press, 2001), 138.

58 Long, *Book Clubs*, 130.

59 Ibid., 145–46.

60 Ibid., 177.

61 Ibid., 180.

62 Mary Ann O'Farrell has described the Republic of Pemberley as "self-consciously exclusive, even perhaps rebarbative." "Austenian Subcultures," in *A Companion to Jane Austen*, ed. Claudia L. Johnson and Clara Tuite (Oxford: Wiley-Blackwell, 2009), 483.

63 "General Group Read Guidelines," The Republic of Pemberley, accessed December 21, 2010, http://www.pemberley.com/pemb/adaptations/groupread/read.html#guidelines.

64 Ibid.

65 The ideas and questions raised by the "Group Read" participants are especially valuable because they appear in the readers' own words, rather than filtered through the voice of an instructor/writer as are the class discussions of Austen recounted by Rachel M. Brownstein in *Why Jane Austen?* (New York: Columbia University Press, 2011) or Azar Nafisi in *Reading Lolita in Tehran: A Memoir in Books* (New York: Random House, 2003).

66 "Is Wickham a Compulsive Liar?," posted by Kathleen Glancy, May 13, 2010, http://www.pemberley.com/bin/library/pandp2010.cgi?read=45720; "The Art and Nature of Lizzy and Darcy (Long)," posted by BarbaraB, May 20, 2010, http://www.pemberley.com/bin/library/pandp2010.cgi?read=46120.

67 The discussion of what would have happened had Fanny Price and Henry Crawford married begins with "If Fanny had married Henry this wouldn't have happened?," posted by Angela L, October 21, 2010, http://www.pemberley.com/bin/library/mp2010.cgi?read=48375.

68 "I'm finding myself having a little more sympathy for Darcy," posted by Karen G, April 13, 2010, http://www.pemberley.com/bin/library/pandp2010.cgi?read=43068.

69 "Thanks so much!," posted by Barb JA, October 27, 2010, http://www.pemberley.com/bin/library/mp2010.cgi?read=48608.

70 "Thank you Carol and thank you everybody," posted by Rachel G, October 27, 2010, http://www.pemberley.com/bin/library/mp2010.cgi?read=48591.

71 "I'm no Jane Austen expert.....yet............however........," posted by jeffrey, May 23, 2010, http://www.pemberley.com/bin/library/pandp2010.cgi?read=46408.

72 The conversion to Austen of the initially reluctant male reader is also the main plot

of Deresiewicz's memoir *A Jane Austen Education*. There, however, the similarities end. Deresiewicz is turned on to Austen while in graduate school, thanks to the inspiring example of a Columbia professor, Karl Kroeber. As a narrator, Deresiewicz recounts from a distance of more than a decade the encounters with Austen's novels that he credits with shaping him into an adult. Deresiewicz's interpretations of Austen's novels, while personally applied and clearly aimed at a broad audience, nevertheless demonstrate a range of reference, clarity of thought, and depth of development that indicate his scholarly training. Finally, of course, Deresiewicz's publisher, Penguin Press, is capable of marketing to a much larger audience than Chandler and Hill's tiny press.

73 Terry Hill, introduction to *Two Guys Read Moby-Dick*, by Steve Chandler and Terrence N. Hill (Bandon, OR: Robert D. Reed Publishers, 2006), 2. In spite of Hill's claims, his publisher designates *Two Guys Read Jane Austen* on the book's back cover as "Literary Criticism & Essays."

74 Steve Chandler and Terrence N. Hill, *Two Guys Read Jane Austen* (Bandon, OR: Robert D. Reed Publishers, 2008), v.

75 Ibid., vi.

76 Ibid., vii.

77 Ibid., 4–5.

78 Ibid., 6.

79 Ibid., 15.

80 Ibid., 15, 49. Karen Joy Fowler notes that her male friends who like Austen "say they first read her because some woman made them. When I ask what it is they like about her, they mostly say that she's funny." "Jane and Me," in *Flirting with Pride & Prejudice: Fresh Perspectives on the Original Chick-Lit Masterpiece*, ed. Jennifer Crusie (Dallas: BenBella Books, 2005), 225.

81 Hill and Chandler, *Two Guys Read Jane Austen*, 74.

82 Ibid., 123.

83 Ibid., 51.

84 Ibid., 73.

85 Ibid., 37.

86 Ibid., 45–46.

87 Felski, *Uses of Literature*, 54–55.

88 Ibid., 23.

89 Hill and Chandler, *Two Guys Read Jane Austen*, 68.

90 Ibid., 74.

91 Ibid., 88–89.

92 Ibid., 106.

93 Long, *Book Clubs*, 145–46.

94 Hill and Chandler, *Two Guys Read Jane Austen*, 79.

95 Ibid., 33.

96 Long, *Book Clubs*, 183.

97 Josephine Ross, *Jane Austen: A Companion* (2002; repr., New Brunswick, NJ: Rutgers University Press, 2007).

98 Jane Austen, *The Annotated Pride and Prejudice*, ed. David M. Shapard (2004; repr., New York: Anchor Books, 2007).

99 Joan Klingel Ray, *Jane Austen for Dummies®* (Hoboken, NJ: Wiley, 2006), 1. Worthy of note are two encyclopedic references—one a print source, one a pair of websites—designed to enlighten amateur readers of Austen. See Kirstin Olsen, *All Things Austen: An Encyclopedia of Austen's World*, two vols (Westport, CT: Greenwood Press, 2005), subsequently published in abbreviated form as *All Things Austen: A Concise Encyclopedia of Austen's World* (Westport, CT: Greenwood Press, 2008). Greenwood's "All Things" series also includes volumes on the Bible, Shakespeare, Chaucer, and Darwin. The anonymously created websites "Austenonly" and "A Jane Austen Gazetteer" focus, respectively, on topics and on places related to Austen's life and works; both sites are richly illustrated with reproductions from period books owned by the sites' creator. "Austenonly," http://austenonly.com/. "A Jane Austen Gazetteer," http://ajaneaustengazetteer.com/. Julie Wakefield identifies herself as the creator of these two websites in "Austenonly.com," *JASNA News: The Newsletter of the Jane Austen Society of America* 26.3 (2010), 18.

100 Ray, *Jane Austen for Dummies®*, 2.
101 Ibid., 270–75, 26.
102 Ross, *Jane Austen*, ix.
103 *The Annotated Pride and Prejudice*, ed. Shapard; Jane Austen, *The Annotated Persuasion*, ed. David M. Shapard (New York: Anchor Books, 2010).
104 "Annotated Yes, But With Scholarly Practice? No," posted by Joan Klingel Ray, March 23, 2007, http://www.amazon.com/review/R11IW3ZY6HE80V/ref=cm_cr_pr_ viewpnt#R11IW3ZY6HE80V.
105 John F. Peppel, posted October 27, 2007, ibid.
106 Jay Sax, posted November 2, 2010, ibid.
107 Patricia Meyer Spacks, introduction to *Pride and Prejudice: An Annotated Edition*, by Jane Austen, ed. Patricia Meyer Spacks (Cambridge, MA: The Belknap Press, 2010), 1.
108 7.
109 Ibid., 15.
110 Ibid., 14.
111 Ibid., 8.
112 Spacks, introduction to *Pride and Prejudice*, 24.
113 Jane Austen, *Pride and Prejudice: Insight Edition* (Minneapolis: Bethany House, 2007), 360; Jane Austen, *Sense and Sensibility: Insight Edition* (Minneapolis: Bethany House, 2010), 341. Neither of these editions credits editors on the title page; the dozen or so people who have contributed notes are identified on the copyright page.
114 Austen, *Pride and Prejudice: Insight Edition*, 7. A representative faith-focused annotation glosses as follows Marianne Dashwood's mention of her "desire to live, to have atonement for my God": "This is as close to a sermon as you'll get from Jane. She doesn't make many overt references to faith. That Marianne does shows the seriousness of her epiphany." Austen, *Sense and Sensibility: Insight Edition*, 308. As an example of an interpretation of one of Austen's characters in the light of contemporary evangelical Christianity, see the editors' praise of Jane Bennet as "a model of Christian living" who "extends grace and mercy to all around her." Austen, *Pride and Prejudice: Insight Edition*, 88.
115 Austen, *Pride and Prejudice: Insight Edition*, 7.
116 For example, readers of *Sense and Sensibility* are asked whether they believe "'true love' means loving only one person in a lifetime" and whether they would "prefer a marriage of fiery passion with great ups and downs or a steady marriage to a selfless husband." Austen, *Sense and Sensibility: Insight Edition*, 340–41.
117 Natalie Tyler, preface to *The Friendly Jane Austen: A Well-Mannered Introduction to a Lady of Sense & Sensibility* (1999; repr., New York: Penguin, 2001), xviii.
118 Ibid.
119 Similar in approach to *The Friendly Jane Austen* but with more comprehensive and up-to-date treatment of popular culture—as well as references to recent academic studies—is Carol Adams, Douglas Buchanan, and Kelly Gresch, *The Bedside, Bathtub & Armchair Companion to Jane Austen* (New York: Continuum, 2008), one of a series of accessible companions published by Continuum; other authors featured include Shakespeare, Dickens, Agatha Christie, and Virginia Woolf.
120 Margaret C. Sullivan, *The Jane Austen Handbook: A Sensible Yet Elegant Guide to Her World* (Philadelphia: Quirk Books, 2007), 12–13.
121 Josephine Ross, *Jane Austen's Guide to Good Manners: Compliments, Charades & Horrible Blunders*, illustrated by Henrietta Webb (New York: Bloomsbury, 2006), 14, vii.
122 Rebecca Dickson, *Jane Austen: An Illustrated Treasury* (New York: Metro Books, 2008).
123 The fantasy of touching Austen's manuscripts is evoked as well by a short film commissioned by the Morgan Library & Museum to accompany its 2009–2010 exhibition "A Woman's Wit: Jane Austen's Life and Legacy." The film depicts several prominent thinkers holding and reading the manuscripts included in that exhibition. "The Divine Jane: Reflections on Austen," directed by Francesco Carrozzini, 2009, http://www. themorgan.org/video/austen.asp.
124 To allow better comparison with other books that are aimed at the same audience or that take similar approaches to encountering Austen, I will postpone until subsequent

chapters discussion of the following works that model or prescribe self-help approaches to Austen. See Chapters 4 and 6 for fuller consideration of Smith, *A Walk with Jane Austen*, a memoir of how traveling in Austen's footsteps brought consolation to a young woman searching for answers to questions about love, faith, and literary ambition. See Chapter 6 for consideration of two advice books that derive explicitly Christian lessons from Austen's writings: Debra White Smith, *What Jane Austen Taught Me about Love and Romance* (Eugene, OR: Harvest House, 2007) and Sarah Arthur, *Dating Mr. Darcy: A Smart Girl's Guide to Sensible Romance* (Wheaton, IL: Tyndale House, 2005).

125 Lauren Henderson, *Jane Austen's Guide to Dating* (New York: Hyperion, 2005), 1.

126 Ibid.

127 Ibid., 3.

128 Ibid., 2.

129 Ibid.

130 Ibid., 283.

131 Ibid., 7, vii.

132 Ibid., 8.

133 *Sense & Sensibility*, directed by John Alexander, screenplay by Andrew Davies (2007; Burbank, CA: Warner Home Video, 2008). This miniseries version of *Sense and Sensibility* was a highlight of *Masterpiece*'s spring 2008 television presentation of "The Complete Jane Austen."

134 "Common Sense: A Life Coach on Austen," *Masterpiece*, accessed December 21, 2010, http://www.pbs.org/wgbh/masterpiece/senseandsensibility/coaching.html.

135 Cheryl Richardson, "Common Sense: A Life Coach on Austen," *Masterpiece*, last modified March 28, 2008, http://www.pbs.org/wgbh/masterpiece/senseandsensibility/coaching_pt1.html.

136 Cheryl Richardson, "Common Sense: A Life Coach on Austen," *Masterpiece*, last modified March 28, 2008, http://www.pbs.org/wgbh/masterpiece/senseandsensibility/coaching_pt2.html.

137 Douglas, "Your Book Changed My Life," 237.

138 In Marilyn Brant's novel *According to Jane* (New York: Kensington, 2009), Jane Austen directly and in her own voice advises a present-day young woman, albeit with a more narrow focus on romantic predicaments.

139 Patrice Hannon, *Dear Jane Austen: A Heroine's Guide to Life and Love* (2005; repr., New York: Plume, 2007), i.

140 Ibid., xiii–xiv.

141 Ibid., 59, 5.

142 Ibid., 29.

143 Ibid., ix.

144 Deresiewicz, *A Jane Austen Education*, 131.

145 Ibid., 12.

146 Ibid., 61.

147 Ibid., 50.

148 Like another memoir recently published by Penguin Press, Matthew B. Crawford's bestselling *Shop Class as Soulcraft: An Inquiry into the Value of Work* (2009), *A Jane Austen Education* offers a vicarious experience of transformation, as well as a tantalizing account of how one man found fulfillment (and, through publication, significant success) through exchanging one professional identity for another. Of course, the distance between think tank and motorcycle repair shop in Crawford's case is arguably larger than between professor and writer in Deresiewicz's.

149 Diane Wilkes, *Tarot of Jane Austen* (Turin: Lo Scarabeo, 2006), 7.

150 Ibid.

151 Ibid., 156.

152 Ibid., 15.

153 Ibid., 158.

154 Ibid.

155 Sheenagh Pugh, *The Democratic Genre: Fan Fiction in a Literary Context* (Bridgend, Wales: Seren, 2005), 218.

156 *Pride and Prejudice: The Special Edition*, directed by Simon Langton, screenplay by Andrew Davies (1995; New York: New Video, 2001), DVD.

157 Deidre Lynch has defended the study of Austen sequels on the grounds that they "might illuminate how Austen's works themselves link the pleasure of stories with the pleasures of stories' nostalgic repetition." "Sequels," in *Jane Austen in Context*, ed. Janet Todd (Cambridge: Cambridge University Press, 2005), 162.

158 See in particular Roberta Grandi, "Web Side Stories: Janeites, Fanfictions, and Never Ending Romances," in *Internet Fictions*, ed. Ingrid Hotz-Davies, Anton Kirchhofer, and Sirpa Leppänen (Cambridge: Cambridge Scholars Publishing, 2009), 23–42.

159 Lynch notes the "seal of authorial approval" conferred on Austen sequels by a family anecdote, included in James-Edward Austen-Leigh's *A Memoir of Jane Austen* (first published 1870; Oxford: Oxford University Press, 2002), concerning the futures Austen herself imagined for her characters. "Sequels," 162.

160 Rebecca Ann Collins, introduction to *The Pemberley Chronicles* (1997; repr., Naperville, IL: Sourcebooks Landmark, 2008), viii. Collins comments further that she intends her novel to return Austen's characters to "their original environment: nineteenth century England," in contrast to the tendency of other sequel-writers, as she puts it, to "turn the lives of the characters into a soap opera." Ibid., vii.

161 Jane Dawkins, *Letters from Pemberley: The First Year* (1998; repr., Naperville, IL: Sourcebooks Landmark, 2007), ix.

162 Rachel Billington, quoted in Lane and Selwyn, eds, *Jane Austen: A Celebration*, 15. Billington's *Perfect Happiness: A Sequel to Jane Austen's Emma* (London: Hodder and Stoughton, 1996) was republished as *Emma & Knightley: Perfect Happiness in Highbury: A Sequel to Jane Austen's Emma* (Naperville, IL: Sourcebooks Landmark, 2008).

163 Pugh, *Democratic Genre*, 158. For a discussion from a college teacher's perspective of the benefits of a collaborative assignment to write Austen fan fiction, see Amanda Gilroy, "Our Austen: Fan Fiction in the Classroom," *Persuasions On-Line* 31.1 (2010), http://www.jasna.org/persuasions/on-line/vol31no1/gilroy.html.

164 Diana Birchall, "Eyeing Mrs. Elton: Learning through Pastiche," *Persuasions On-Line* 30.2 (2010), http://www.jasna.org/persuasions/on-line/vol30no2/birchall.html.

165 Quoted in Jan Fergus, "Hazel Holt's *My Dear Charlotte*: A Novel Based on Jane Austen's Letters," *Persuasions On-Line* 30.1 (2009), www.jasna.org/persuasions/on-line/vol30no1/fergus.html. See also Hazel Holt, *My Dear Charlotte* (New York: Coffeetown Press, 2009).

166 Sarah Waters, foreword to *Dancing with Mr Darcy: Stories Inspired by Jane Austen and Chawton House* (Dinas Powys, Wales: Honno, 2009), 4.

167 Chabon, "The Amateur Family," in *Manhood for Amateurs*, 294.

Chapter 4

Getting Closer to Austen: Literary Tourism

Accessible guides to Austen's writings, life, and times aim to help amateur readers increase their understanding, as well as intensify their pleasure. Resources exist as well to aid enthusiasts who wish to combine an interest in Austen with another amateur pursuit, such as cooking or crafting. Such works as Maggie Black and Deirdre Le Faye's *The Jane Austen Cookbook* (1995) and Jennifer Forest's *Jane Austen's Sewing Box: Craft Projects & Stories from Jane Austen's Novels* (2009) encourage the reader to feel connected to the women of Austen's times, and to Austen herself, though participating in activities and experiencing sensations—the taste of a dish, the feel and look of embroidery—with which the author herself was familiar.[1] Austen lovers who prefer a more communal effort to feel as Austen felt can take part in English country dancing, the practice of which brings together steps and music—and sometimes costumes and interior architecture as well—that are common to, or at least beguilingly similar to, those of Austen's era.

Enjoyment and instruction mingle in all of these extra-literary activities, which offer participants the opportunity to cultivate a very personal, and often physical, appreciation of Austen's times. As Mike Crang, a specialist in geography and tourist studies, has argued, "engagement with Austen can be through non-textual practices, such as replica clothing, Regency dance events, and so forth. ... Even though participants are 'having fun,' making costumes can require considerable skills and personal research on clothing of the period. ... The knowledge gained by performance again creates different perspectives on Austen. For instance, wearing female costume can bring home what shifts in corsetry and design can mean in terms of freedom of movement and so forth, not just by representing femininity but in its lived practice."[2] The Austen scholar Celia A. Easton has attested to the pedagogical value of teaching undergraduate students basic English country dances and having them "use their bodies" to act out the structure of Austen's novels.[3]

Just as a work by or inspired by Austen may be enjoyed anywhere, by anyone, activities such as cooking, crafting, dressing up, or dancing are available to enthusiasts around the globe. Those with the means to travel to (or within) England can partake of another form of active engagement with Austen's world, which some visitors consider an especially potent way to feel closer to Austen: visits to places where the author lived.[4] Many readers feel that the desire to see the place where an author lived and wrote follows naturally from an interest in that person's life and works. In the words of Shannon McKenna Schmidt and Joni Rendon, authors of an international travel guide to literary places, "We realized that in our travels near and far, we've not only looked to novels to provide a new dimension to our travel experiences, but equally, we've sought out the literary places in our travels that will give us a deeper perspective on the books we cherish."[5] How exactly does that "deeper perspective" result from the experience of literary travel, and how do tourist sites work to bring about a sense of connection between a visitor and the long-dead author? Austen-inspired tourism has much to show us about what ordinary readers find meaningful about seeking out places and spaces associated with a beloved author, as well as the acts of imagination visitors must perform in order to feel a sense of closeness to that author.

As a subject of scholarly investigation, literary tourism lies at the crossroads of several disciplines, including geography and tourist studies, fan studies, and literary criticism. The different emphases and approaches of these disciplines have led to widely varied studies of literary tourism, from quantitative surveys, to highly theoretical analysis, to description of visits undertaken by scholars themselves. Yet to be considered, however, is how today's literary tourists make sense of their own experiences. In the next section, I will sum up the most thought-provoking and relevant ideas about literary tourism advanced by scholars, first outside and then within the discipline of literary criticism. After treating scholarship on literary tourism generally, I will consider prior studies of Austen-inspired travel by both non-literary and literary scholars. Finally, I will explain my own approach, which emphasizes the voices and views of ordinary visitors, as well as those of staff members whose efforts maintain the literary-tourism sites.

To understand what visitors and staff have to say about Austen-related places, we must first become acquainted with those places. In the second section of this chapter, I introduce the two main geographical sites on which Austen tourism centers, the village of Chawton in Hampshire and the city of Bath, and the very different buildings available for visit in each location. In Chawton, Jane Austen's House Museum—the seventeenth-century house where Austen lived from 1809–1817, the period during which she completed her six novels and published the first four—was opened to the public in 1949. In Bath, where Austen lived from 1801–1806, the Jane Austen Centre opened in 1999, offering tourists a place to gain greater acquaintance with Austen's time in the city and encouraging the activities of Austen fans. The Jane Austen Centre has yet to be studied as a site of Austen literary tourism, in spite of its prominence as a focal point for popular enthusiasm about Austen. More briefly, I will examine two other locations associated with Austen that are available—and in the case of the first, eager—for visitors: Winchester, the city where Austen lived her last few months, died, and was buried in 1817; and Steventon, the Hampshire village where Austen was born and lived her first twenty-five years (1775–1801).

The third and fourth sections of this chapter examine the present-day experience of Austen-oriented literary tourism, as recounted in published writings—including travel guides and memoirs—and as revealed in surveys of visitors and staff that I conducted at Jane Austen's House Museum.

Literary Tourism: Multidisciplinary Approaches

In Chapter 1, I asserted that the discipline of fan studies has much to offer literary scholars who wish to investigate the popularity of canonical authors. This is especially true in the case of travel inspired by the love of an author, which has a lot in common with travel inspired by the love of a television series or movie. The phenomenon of the fan pilgrimage, as such travel is called by scholars in fan studies, has been extensively studied and theorized; from that wide field, I will highlight claims that are especially pertinent to pilgrimages to sites with literary associations.

Roger C. Aden, a scholar of communication studies, has illuminated indirectly but valuably how immersion in a favorite text, of whatever medium, connects to the desire to visit places linked with the production of that text. Treating "symbolic pilgrimages" that take place fully within a fan's imagination through consumption of popular media, Aden explores the concept of escapism in a way that suggests a connection with actual travel: "Escapism ... is not necessarily a disavowal of interest in one's material situation. Instead, escapism through imagination is purposeful; it allows us to move from an unsatisfactory material place to a fulfilling place of the imagination, a promised land of our own creation. ... Escapism then can be envisioned as purposeful play in which we symbolically move from the material world to an imaginative world that is in many ways *a response to* the material."[6] For amateur readers who have exercised their imaginations through contact with their favorite Austen-oriented works, achieving a sense of greater closeness with Austen by literally traveling to a place that they expect will facilitate such an experience may demand an equally strong effort of the imagination. Aden's positive presentation of escapism as "purposeful play" offers us a useful perspective, too, on the testimonies of visitors who credit an Austen-related site with the power to take them back in time, or to make them feel at home. "The kind of escape popular stories promote," argues Aden, "is a ritualistic journey of the mind to spiritually powerful places where a vantage point that is anything but mundane affords us a reassuring view of an imagined promised land."[7] As we will see, some of those on both ends of the Austen tourist industry—visitors and staff members—do indeed associate Austen places with power both spiritual and emotional.

Examining actual pilgrimages undertaken by fans of what he terms "cult media," the fan studies scholar Matt Hills stresses the interrelationships of fans, their texts, and the geographical places associated with those texts (which are, in his study, chiefly television series and movies). "By seeking out the actual locations which underpin any given textual identity," argues Hills, "the cult fan is able to extend the productivity of his or her affective relationship with the original text, reinscribing this attachment within a different domain (that of physical space) which in turn allows for a radically different object-relationship, in terms of immediacy, embodiment and somatic sensation which can all operate to reinforce cult 'authenticity' and its more-or-less explicitly sacralised difference. The audience-text relationship is shifted towards the monumentality and groundedness of physical locations."[8] As we will see, literary fans too describe their impulse to travel as (to paraphrase Hills) the desire to extend their emotional connection with a beloved text into real-world places, which offer the opportunity to relate to an author and her world in a different—and potentially closer or more satisfying—way than through reading alone. "Cult geographies," contends Hill, "also sustain cult fans' fantasies of 'entering' into the cult text, as well as allowing the 'text' to leak out into spatial and cultural practices via fans' creative transpositions and 'genres of self.'"[9]

Hills argues that visitors' responses derive not only from their own mental and emotional investment—what he calls "an affective-interpretive process which spills into and redefines material space"—but from the "monumentality" of the physical location as well.[10] Tourist sites like Jane Austen's House Museum and the Jane Austen Centre cultivate, through forms of display and publicity, the sense of "monumentality" that visitors experience. Hills calls attention as well to the function of geographical sites as points of focus for ideas about a cultural figure: "Through Graceland, the significance of Elvis—something which would otherwise tend to be free-floating, and incidental to processes of signification—can be contained or 'anchored' in a visible, physical, and public fashion."[11] As we will see, in different ways Jane Austen's House Museum and the Jane Austen Centre each endeavors to occupy, in the public mind, the function of "anchor" for the significance of Jane Austen.

Bringing together the theories of Aden and Hills, the fan studies scholar Will Brooker stresses the inward process that necessarily accompanies fans' encounters with pilgrimage sites. "All geographical pilgrimage," contends Brooker, "in fact involves a degree of conceptual, inner, symbolic travel. ... Symbolic immersion and psychological leaps of faith are integral to many, perhaps the majority, of geographical media pilgrimages."[12] Examining sustained, narrative accounts of Austen-inspired tourism with an eye towards "psychological leaps of faith" yields insight into how travelers willingly intensify their own reactions to Austen-related places. As I analyze responses of visitors to Jane Austen's House Museum, too, I will attend to how traces of such "symbolic travel" emerge in visitors' own words.

In her groundbreaking monograph *The Literary Tourist* (2006), Nicola J. Watson explains the reluctance of her fellow literary scholars to consider the practice of tourism worthy of study. "Only the amateur, only the naïve reader," she sums up the resistant view, "could suppose that there was anything more, anything left, anything either originary or residual, let alone anything more legitimate or legitimating, to be found on the spot marked X."[13] Watson's edited collection *Literary Tourism and Nineteenth-Century Culture* (2009) further extends and applies her theories. "The embarrassment of literary tourism," Watson contends, "is encapsulated in the very phrase, which yokes 'literature'—with its long-standing claims to high, national culture, and its current aura of highbrow difficulty and professionalism—with 'tourism,' trailing its pejorative connotations of mass popular culture, mass travel, unthinking and unrefined consumption of debased consumables, amateurishness, and inauthenticity. As a practice that tries to make the emotional and virtual realities of reading accountable to the literal, material realities of destination, it is bound to make literary specialists uneasy."[14]

Watson persuasively makes the case that literary scholars should view literary tourism in the context of historical practices of reading. "Supplementing reading with travel," she asserts, is "a cultural practice [that] is historically specific and of relatively recent inception."[15] Rather than dismissing literary tourism as amateurish, she contends, we can view the practice as a vantage point onto the reading experiences of amateurs:

> If we wish to understand how readers read texts in the long nineteenth century we would do well to attend to the remaining traces of literary pilgrimage, because they are, however imperfect, indicators and records of that otherwise most elusive of things to pin down, how readers experience and live out their reading. To attend to the literary pilgrimage is to begin to construct a materialist history of amateur reading pleasures that continue to be available to this day … [including] how literature is consumed, experienced, and projected within the individual reader's life, and within a readership more generally.[16]

The "remaining traces of literary pilgrimage" include writings, such as travel guides and essays about journeys, that literary scholars have until recently not tended to take seriously in relation to the texts and authors that inspired the travel. The pilgrimage sites themselves are worthy of analysis too, according to Watson: "Most elaborate of these non-literary 'texts' is the writer's house," she contends, with "the house in which the writing has actually been done, the workshop of genius," serving as "the apogee of literary tourist sites."[17] On the whole, concludes Watson, literary tourism represents "a desire on the part of the tourist to construct a more intimate and exclusive relationship with the writer than is supposed to be available through mere reading."[18]

Watson and her contributors acknowledge the importance of gender, both of the author and of the visitor, to the experience of literary tourism.[19] Certainly the identity of Austen as a woman author matters greatly to tourists today, as we have seen in earlier chapters from visitors' comments about how inspirational they find her as a woman, or how they value her perspective as a woman. Austen tourist sites, exhibitions, and displays must necessarily invoke expectations of femininity; sometimes these expectations are challenged or overturned. Portrayals of Austen in visual media and in narrative forms, the subject of my next chapter, also grapple with assumptions related to femininity and beauty.

The contributors to Watson's *Literary Tourism* collection raise the question as well of the literary tourist's national identity. Paul Westover, writing of nineteenth-century American literary pilgrims to Britain, remarks that "Britain remained an imaginary possession for many nineteenth-century Americans because they felt they knew it through literature. ... To literate Americans, Britain *was* a book."[20] Ultimately, Westover concludes, "nationality [was] less important than shared cultural knowledge" in shaping the experience of the literary tourist.[21] Many present-day Austen-inspired tourists from outside England, too, attest to the sense of familiarity, even homecoming, that they experience at Chawton or Bath.

Like fan studies scholars, literary critics emphasize how crucially imagination and interpretation contribute to the experience of literary tourism. "Visitors," Watson asserts, "perform a variety of experiments in imagination."[22] Studying accounts by mid-nineteenth-century Americans of visits to Britain, Shirley Foster notes that

> actuality—the encountered reality—proved not always commensurate with expectation—the idealized preconceptions, built up from textual and anecdotal pre-knowledge. This discordance had to be negotiated so as to enable the tourist to come to terms with the disillusion it produced. One way of doing this was to ignore the deficiencies, continuing to offer unqualified veneration at hallowed sites. Another response, while acknowledging the constructed and codified nature of such cultural sanctification, sought to accommodate to its demands by using the imagination to create an alternative vision that enhanced reality with a degree of fictionalisation.[23]

In present-day accounts of visits to Austen sites, gaps between expectations and reality are indeed often visible, and efforts to bridge them discernible.

Four prior studies of Austen-related tourism demonstrate a variety of approaches to visitors' encounters with places and objects linked to Austen's life.[24] The tools and theories of the disciplines of tourist studies and geography have been applied by David Herbert and Mike Crang, while Claudia L. Johnson and Felicity James have brought to bear the perspective of literary scholars.

In a comparative study of tourism to Chawton and to Dylan Thomas's home in Laugharne, Wales, David Herbert undertook a survey of visitors to the Jane Austen House, as it was then known, in 1993 and 1994—just before the boom in Austen's popularity brought about by the wave of screen adaptations of her novels. Thus Herbert's findings represent the views of an earlier generation, as it were, of Austen appreciators. Herbert concentrates, understandably, on aspects of identity that are central to his discipline: for example, he differentiates among subjects according to their social class and assesses their "cultural competence" according to the number of Austen novels each has read.[25] While Herbert's quantitative analysis offers necessarily limited insight into visitors' individual reactions and responses, several of his synthesizing arguments are important to bear in mind. Herbert points out that the typical visitor to an author's house is not a literary pilgrim, intent on communing with a favorite figure, but rather a relatively casual visitor with modest expectations: "Some form of literary interest motivated most tourists, but the sample was not uniform. A significant minority viewed the visit to Chawton as a leisure, rather than a literary, experience. Spending a few hours in a relaxing, pleasant environment may have been as important as achieving some empathy with the author and her works."[26] Nevertheless, Herbert attributes to a literary site the capacity to inspire responses beyond those anticipated by a casual visitor: "Many people may arrive with ill-defined reasons, but the actual visit invokes and awakens a range of reactions that can include a sense of nostalgia or of longing for the particular kind of world they associate with the writer. Generalizations are valid but each visitor has some individual form of chemistry with the place, its presentation, and its associated characters and events, real-life or fictional."[27] It is that "individual form of chemistry" that I aim to discern from accounts, whether in narrative form or in short survey responses, of travel to Austen places.

In his essentially theoretical essay on Austen tourism, Mike Crang urges scholars to focus not on how displays present ideas about an author but instead on how visitors make their own meanings from what they experience.[28] "It is not about the accuracy of any of these representations," argues Crang; "rather, it is about interpreting reading and visiting as doing, as shaping real and imagined landscapes."[29] Like Nicola Watson, Crang makes the case for viewing literary travel as, in his words, "part of a disseminated practice of reading—where the action of reading is to connect disparate worlds from the text to home, to tourism, and so forth."[30] In Crang's view, objects on display at a literary site "suggest connection to an imagined place"; visitors perform the effort of "bringing together and articulating a range of imagined connections" among "their personal worlds," the place of their visit, and the author with whom that place is associated.[31] Crang acknowledges that these acts of connection may fail, or feel incomplete, yet he does not conclude that such efforts are misguided or fruitless: "All the readings and reenactments seem to try to make something concrete and present, but instead, they point to the absences and gaps. It gives us a twin sense of the instability of meaning and creative work of interpretation."[32] How literary tourists perform this "creative work" and grapple with the "instability of meaning" becomes apparent when we listen attentively to how, in their own words, they express their own experiences.

What Crang calls "the absences and gaps" that necessarily accompany visitors' efforts to connect with an absent author are the primary subject of Claudia Johnson's analysis of Jane Austen's House Museum as a tourist site, an analysis that she originally presented to the 2006 Annual General Meeting of the Jane Austen Society of North America. In Johnson's view, literary tourism represents an effort that is at best poignant, and at worst futile. To enter a building that is designated "Jane Austen's House," declares Johnson, is to "be charmed, but it is inevitable that we will be disappointed as well."[33] Describing items on display at the house as well as those donated in its decades of operation, Johnson argues that "we are being invited into a knowing make-believe that these things bring us into Austen's presence."[34] Johnson acknowledges the desire among Janeites to "connect with" Austen, and to be "move[d]" in particular by objects with a "connection to Austen's body."[35] Apparently sympathizing with such efforts—as evident in her insistent use of the first person plural—Johnson remarks "how desperate we are for any shreds ... we go to these lengths because there is so little of her left."[36] Ultimately, however, Johnson cautions visitors against fantasizing that objects and places can bring us closer to an author: "*treasures* cherished for their power to conjure Austen's presence also carry the risk of *bewildering* us into a too comfortable sense of the fullness of her being which, if we are to feel it at all, we will better find reading her novels."[37] Johnson's attention to what she calls "thwarted longing" and "disappointing gap[s]" is an important reminder of what we ignore if we, as Nicola Watson puts it, conceive of literary tourism solely as "a creative and transformative system of enhancing or extending reading activity."[38] Yet to focus, as does Johnson, only on thwarting and disappointment is to fail to acknowledge those many amateur readers who do find meaning in their journeys.

Johnson's approach to literary tourism demonstrates Watson's claim that the practice "is bound to make literary specialists uneasy."[39] In contrast, Felicity James's study of Chawton as a historical and present-day tourist destination demonstrates what can be gained by attending, without disciplinary prejudice, both to how visitors articulate their experiences and to how places of pilgrimage themselves represent the efforts of Austen lovers to pay tribute to her. Of especial value in James's analysis is her establishment of the continuity between nineteenth-century and twentieth- and twenty-first-century accounts of Austen-inspired travel. (James locates the latter primarily in blogs and websites.) For example, James quotes an 1880s tourist who cautions fellow Austen-lovers that they must be prepared, in visiting Chawton, to "do the rest for [themselves] and rehabilitate Jane Austen's house as it was during her living occupation of it"[40]—in other words, to transcend, through imagination, the distance and difference between the building as it presently stands and the one formerly known to Austen. James also astutely compares Jane Austen's House Museum with Chawton House Library, which was founded in 2003 by the American businesswoman and Austen lover Sandy Lerner as a center for the study of early English women writers.

In order to gain a wide perspective on what contributes to and results from encounters with literary sites, I have chosen in my own research on literary tourism to combine a variety of methodologies. I will describe, and use photographs to illustrate, what recent visitors would encounter at each Austen site.[41] Far from being static, museums, exhibits, and tourist sites evolve to meet the changing needs and expectations of the public, as well as to fulfill the educational, curatorial, and sometimes commercial aims of directors and staff. I have personally surveyed visitors, both quantitatively and qualitatively, at Jane Austen's House Museum, in order to ascertain what present-day tourists find interesting and moving about being present in the place where Austen wrote;

the comments of staff members and volunteers at the house museum also shed light on its meaning for people today. With respect to the Jane Austen Centre in Bath, I make use of an interview I conducted with its founder as well as documents, both public and archival, concerning Austen tourism in Bath. Other sources on which I draw include accounts of contemporary tourist experiences that scholars have not previously considered: visitors' comment books, which record exceptionally private responses; and published personal narratives and travelogues, which offer more depth of reflection (and thus material for analysis) than blog postings tend to. Publicity, promotional, and informational materials from Austen-related places shed additional light on how visitors are encouraged, by those in charge of or responsible for tourist sites, to think about the significance of traveling to those places.

Austen Places

Three kinds of locations hold associations with Austen. Those with most potency to spark the imagination are the places in which she lived and (to a lesser degree) those she visited. Through occupying temporarily a house where Austen lived (or stayed), or traversing a landscape well known to her, tourists—if they are so inclined—can cultivate feelings of a particular kind of closeness to Austen: seeing what she saw, inhabiting the space she inhabited, standing or walking where she stood or walked. Jane Austen's House Museum in Chawton is the preeminent example of such a site; the city of Bath, the village of Steventon, and the city of Winchester also fall into this category. The second kind of location is one that, while holding no direct connections to Austen's life, publicly displays objects once possessed by her. Of this type are two prominent London institutions: the British Library, which exhibits Austen's writing desk and a few of her manuscripts, and the National Portrait Gallery, which exhibits the only authentic portrait of Austen's face from her lifetime, a sketch by her sister Cassandra.[42] The third kind of place is one that holds neither connections to Austen's life nor Austen relics, but which functions in a different way to focus visitors' attention on Austen and her cultural significance. Such an institution is the Jane Austen Centre in Bath. Occupying a building with no historical link to the Austen family, the Jane Austen Centre emphasizes, through displays and sponsored activities, ideas about Austen rather than Austen-related objects.

London

The Austen sites accessible to the widest number of tourists are the British Library and the National Portrait Gallery, thanks to these institutions' central location in London and lack of entrance fee. Visitors to the British Library's

permanent exhibit titled "Treasures of the British Library" encounter Austen
material in the midst of a lineup of twenty literary-canonical all-stars, from
the manuscript of *Beowulf* to typescripts by Seamus Heaney.[43] Two items in the
exhibit case invite thoughts and feelings about Austen. The first, known as
"Volume the Third," is one of the manuscript books in which Austen recopied
short and medium-length pieces she wrote during her teenage years.[44] In
the playful dedications to her family members and friends that Austen wrote
to the pieces collected in "Volume the Third," visitors can see how she was
already thinking of herself as an author.[45] Musing about Austen's authorship
and writing process is encouraged as well by the presence of her writing desk,
which draws attention in the exhibit case as the only object that is not a book
or manuscript.[46] (The adjacent exhibit case, featuring highlights from the
Library's musical collection, does include Beethoven's tuning fork.) I will
consider in Chapter 5, in the context of other visual and verbal depictions
of Austen, how the portrait by Cassandra is exhibited at the National Portrait
Gallery.

Chawton

Located a few dozen miles from London, the village of Chawton is small,
quiet, and takes some effort to reach without a car.[47] For drivers, Jane Austen's
House Museum is signposted on the adjacent motorway, along with another
nearby attraction, the home of the naturalist Gilbert White. Everything about
the visitor's initial impressions of Jane Austen's House is modest and low-key. A
small parking lot across the street next to the local pub and teashop accommo-
dates cars and the occasional tour bus, while those walking from the bus stop
or from the nearby town of Alton (a stop on a local train line to London) make
their way down village sidewalks, past houses from various historical periods
that are home to local families. By advance appointment, visitors to Chawton
can arrange to take a tour of Chawton House Library, which is located in the
former Chawton Great House, a short walk away from the cottage in which the
Austen women lived.[48] St. Nicholas Church, on the grounds of Chawton House
Library, is available for visit by anyone; Cassandra Elizabeth Austen, Jane's
sister, and Cassandra Leigh Austen, her mother, are buried in the St. Nicholas
graveyard. Tourists with time, stamina, and a guidebook or map can set out
from Chawton on public footpaths to follow some of the walks that Austen is
known to have taken regularly for exercise or to visit friends.

Jane Austen's House Museum consists of the seventeenth-century cottage in
which the Austen women lived, together with a garden and period outbuildings.
(A newly built Learning Centre, underwritten by the Heritage Lottery Fund,
was added to the site in 2009, to accommodate school groups, educational
activities, and public lectures.) Throughout the museum, visitors encounter
items known to have been owned by the Austen family (though not necessarily

Figure 4.1: The side entrance to Jane Austen's House Museum, Chawton, Hampshire. Author photo.

during the years of the women's residence at Chawton); items believed to have been owned by the Austens; items authentic to the period but owned by others; replicas of items that the Austens owned; and non-period items present to shed light on the significance of Austen and her family. Such a mixed collection is typical of an author house museum that was equipped long after the author's death with furnishings and items variously donated, purchased, and loaned.[49] The earliest Annual Reports of the Jane Austen Society chronicle the acquisition of Austen "relics": in 1951, for example, the cottage gained among other items "a black and gold lacquered work table, once the property of Jane Austen, lent by Mrs. T. E. Carpenter" and "a cabinet of relics of the Austen family," including a scarf embroidered by Austen.[50]

Several of the house's ground floor and first floor rooms—particularly the dining room next to whose window Austen wrote and the bedroom she shared with Cassandra—are set up with displays that evoke those rooms' uses during the Austens' residence. Other rooms serve as exhibit spaces, and the top floor of the house contains staff offices that are off limits to visitors.[51] In the garden are flowers and herbs appropriate to a Regency country garden; the specific plantings and placement, however, do not reproduce what is known of the Austens' own garden.

Figure 4.2: The garden at the rear of Jane Austen's House Museum. Author photo.

As the name Jane Austen's House Museum indicates, the building and its grounds are at once a house and a museum, and the dual nature of the site makes it possible for visitors to concentrate on different aspects and pursue different goals. Those who wish to absorb atmosphere can hear the floorboards creak, play on the period square piano (doing so is allowed and even encouraged), look out the window next to Austen's small writing table, and inhale scents in the garden. Those who wish to imagine the presence of the Austens can focus on items of furniture and dress owned, and in some cases made, by them; the patchwork quilt, unusual in design, upon which mother and sisters collaborated is especially eye-catching. Those who wish to learn about Austen and her family can watch an introductory video, newly added with the Heritage Lottery redevelopment and narrated by Elizabeth Garvie, who played Elizabeth Bennet in the acclaimed 1980 BBC miniseries of *Pride and Prejudice*;[52] take in information on the recently redesigned exhibit placards; and browse in the open-access reference library. Those who are interested primarily in what Austen has meant to her readers can examine quotations from Austen lovers on display upstairs in the house; recognize photographs from Austen-related films hung in an outbuilding; and enjoy temporary exhibits, recent examples of which include costumes from film adaptations and objects created by practitioners of craft and design.[53] Return visits are encouraged by regularly scheduled programs including lectures, family activity days, musical performances, and creative writing workshops.

The name "Jane Austen's House Museum" was officially adopted on the advice of the museum's marketing manager, Madelaine Smith, in order to reinforce the site's identity, in her words, as Austen's "spiritual home," and to differentiate the building from its neighbor up the road, Chawton House Library.[54] Promotional brochures for Jane Austen's House Museum make as clear as possible the building's claim for significance as the "Home of Jane Austen, famous writer of *Pride and Prejudice*."[55] As of 2011, admission rates to Jane Austen's House Museum are £7 for adults, £6 for seniors and students. The total number of visitors in 2009 was 40,112, a moderate increase over recent years, though far below the total of 58,439 people who visited in 1996, the year after the enormously popular BBC adaptation of *Pride and Prejudice*.[56]

Bath

Bath's significance for Austen's readers is arguably as strong as Chawton's, though in a very different sense. During Austen's years living in Bath in the early 1800s, she did not, as far as we know, compose fiction; indeed, biographers and critics have long argued over whether to interpret that lack of literary productivity as evidence of Austen's unhappiness in the city. Yet, unlike Chawton and its environs, which do not figure as a setting in any of Austen's novels, Bath appears prominently—and very realistically—in two: *Northanger Abbey*, which Austen composed as a young woman, and *Persuasion*, which she worked on in the years before her death. Visiting Bath, even today, with these two novels in hand allows you to identify the streets and houses in which her characters lived, retrace the paths they walked, and imagine yourself among the crowds in the Assembly Rooms where her characters gathered to dance and gossip. Fans of the 1995 screen adaptation of *Persuasion*, directed by Roger Michell, can retrace as well the locations within Bath where key scenes were filmed.[57] Those immersed in the details of Austen's biography can add pilgrimages to the exteriors of the buildings (now privately owned) where members of her family lodged during visits to the city, especially 4 Sydney Place, the house where Austen lived the longest with her mother, father, and sister.

Unlike sleepy Chawton, Bath is a World Heritage City that is very well served by public transportation and attracts hundreds of thousands of national and international visitors a year. Given the city's strong appeal to tourists generally and its multidimensional interest to lovers of Austen, efforts to institutionalize Austen's presence in Bath are hardly surprising. In the early 1990s, when the house at 4 Sydney Place came up for sale, the location's suitability as a potential center for Austen studies or an Austen museum caught the attention of Maggie Lane, a noted author of popular-audience books about Austen and a dedicated member of the Jane Austen Society.[58] In a report titled "4 Sydney Place, Bath" that was circulated to fellow Society members in October 1992, Lane summed up as follows the rationale for founding an Austen tourist site in Bath, as well as concerns about potential competition with the existing museum in Chawton:

> Of all the houses she inhabited which survive to the present day, 4 Sydney Place is second only to Chawton Cottage in the length of her occupation. Certainly of all the houses in Bath with which she is connected, 4 Sydney Place is the most desirable and appropriate for the Jane Austen "world" to acquire. It is the house which has long borne a plaque to her name, the house which is pointed out from the tourist buses, and the house which admirers of the novels from all over the world stand outside and long to get in!
>
> ... Firstly, Bath needs a focus for the interest in Jane Austen which inspires many people to visit the city—or which is itself inspired *by* a visit to Bath. All lovers of Jane Austen go to Bath for her sake at some time; but there is nowhere in the city that they can visit to improve their knowledge of her association with Bath, nothing for them to do but walk the streets in her footsteps. Other people find an interest in Jane Austen is awakened by being in Bath, but similarly they are frustrated in their desire to find out more. A Jane Austen house open to the public in Bath would complement the main museum in Chawton by offering a second property in an entirely different location for established admirers to visit, as well as by introducing new people to the delights of Jane Austen—which must surely be one of the aims of the Society. Geographically and in every way Bath offers a contrast to Chawton, that fruitful contrast between town and country that so enriches the novels. It is right that both aspects of Jane Austen's life should be commemorated and made available to scholars and the general public.[59]

Not Lane and the Jane Austen Society, however, but an aspiring businessman named David Baldock was to succeed in establishing a very different kind of Jane Austen Centre, a site that would both capitalize on and aim to contribute to Austen's surging popularity.

"There was a huge gap in the market," recalls Baldock, looking back at the situation in Bath tourism when he first conceived the idea of developing a Jane Austen Centre that would, in the words of its promotional literature, "celebrat[e] Bath's most famous resident."[60] Much as Maggie Lane pointed out to the Jane Austen Society that Austen lovers had nowhere particular to visit in Bath, Baldock heard from the friend of a friend, an Austen fan, that she had visited Bath and felt disappointed that the city offered no focus for her enthusiasm. Baldock had personal reasons as well for the new venture, though not ones to do with an interest in Austen, whose books he had not read in school and about whom he frankly states he "didn't know anything." (He says, wryly, that he has read Austen's novels "*now*" and "can see the relevance" of them.) Disillusioned with his most recent job as a teacher, Baldock "wanted to deal with something people wanted, rather than education that the kids didn't want."

Baldock settled on what he now calls an "interpretive approach to Jane Austen's Bath," which relies on information and images rather than a building or objects with historical provenance. "It was out of the question for a number of reasons to get an actual Jane Austen house," he says; the Jane Austen Centre now occupies a period building that is down the street from one in which the Austen family did briefly live. As far as "Jane Austen memorabilia," says Baldock, "there wasn't any, and Chawton does that really well, and we couldn't afford it." Under no illusions about his own ability to develop strong content for an Austen site, Baldock turned to author Maggie Lane, who, as he recalls, agreed to become involved once he had secured a building. At the time of the Centre's opening in 1999, Lane described it to the Jane Austen Society of Australia as "complement[ing] Jane Austen's (Chawton) village home by demonstrating through displays what Regency Bath was like, and the importance of the city in her life and novels. It is also a source of information about Jane-Austen-related events and the starting point for guided tours of the city. It cannot and does not purport to be a museum."[61]

Visitors to the Jane Austen Centre now enter an inviting gift shop on the ground floor of 40 Gay Street before going upstairs to hear a staff guide introduce Austen's life and achievements in a colloquial, lively manner. According to Baldock, the guides receive "a minimal script" and are encouraged "to put their personality into it"; the personal touch, he says, is what the Centre has to offer, in the absence of priceless artifacts. A short video narrated by Amanda Root, who portrayed Anne Elliot in the 1995 screen version of *Persuasion*, plays as well, orienting visitors to Bath—and reminding film viewers of spots they might wish to revisit. The Centre's exhibit space, located on the building's basement level, includes further background information about the Austen family and Austen's writings, along with arrays of objects—such as costumes, tea sets, and decks of cards—that illustrate social customs of the Regency period. A final room calls visitors' attention to Austen's popularity today, through a montage of snapshots from Bath's Jane Austen Festival and the magazine *Jane Austen's Regency World*, both of which originated under the sponsorship of the Jane Austen Centre. Also on display, though without especial fanfare, is one of the Centre's comparatively few original possessions: a large portrait of Jane Austen that was commissioned by the Centre in 2002 and prepared by the forensic artist Melissa Dring. (In Chapter 5, I will return to the Dring portrait and compare it to other recent visual and verbal depictions of Austen.)

Visitors to Bath who seek a more sustained experience of feeling closer to Austen have several further options, all with ties to the Jane Austen Centre. On the Centre's third floor is a Regency Tea Room, open to the public, where you can sample the "Jane Austen blend" of tea or partake of baked goods named for Austen characters (e.g. "Crawford's crumpets"). Or you can buy a ticket to a ninety-minute "Walking Tour of Jane Austen's Bath" (£6 for adults, £5 for seniors and students) that passes by many Austen-related city locations and includes the reading, by your guide, of apposite quotations. If you'd like to dress up in the company of other enthusiasts, you can return in late September to the Jane Austen Festival, a ten-day set of events. To extend your encounter with Austen once you're back home, you can receive monthly e-mail newsletters from the Centre (in a mailing list, according to Baldock, of 30,000); make purchases from the Centre's extensive online gift shop (which Baldock says does "extremely well"[62]); or subscribe to the bimonthly glossy magazine *Jane Austen's Regency World*, at a rate of £33 for UK residents and £38.70 for those outside the UK.

Baldock says of the Jane Austen Centre that "we run it as a sharp business as much as we can." (As a tourist site without heritage significance, the Centre, he notes, is ineligible "for Arts Council or Lottery Funding, unlike many of our competitors.") That business sense is especially evident in Baldock's canny development of ancillary programs and activities that draw fresh press coverage, as well as visitors, to the site. The Jane Austen Festival, began, in his words, "as a way to get new press releases for the Jane Austen Centre"; ticketed Festival events now regularly sell out, according to Baldock, and recently introduced occasions such as a Costume Promenade through Bath have proved popular. The Festival has evolved, in Baldock's words, to emphasize "costume and involvement," which of course makes possible promotional photo ops; people "enjoy themselves immensely," he says, and then others see that enjoyment and want to take part as well. Other publicity-oriented endeavors include the "Jane Austen Regency World Awards," inaugurated in 2008, which recognize recent contributions to popular culture, and which, as Baldock puts it, represent "an attempt to put us at the center of everything Jane Austen."[63] Indeed, the Centre's website, at www.janeausten.co.uk, makes an implicit bid for its status as Austen central.[64]

Baldock stresses that the Centre's goal is not to appeal exclusively to what he calls "massive Austen fans." He points out that the gift shop sells "something like 20,000 Austen novels a year," to customers whose interest in Austen's writings is piqued by their visit. Yet the Centre clearly benefits from Austen's ongoing popularity: even years after the beloved 1995 adaptation of *Pride and Prejudice*, Baldock comments that "we wouldn't be successful without that BBC series." In its first year of operation, according to Baldock, the Jane Austen Centre welcomed 24,000 visitors; in 2009, he reports, the site met the goal of 60,000 that he had established for it at the outset.[65] As of 2011, ticket prices— £7.45 for adults, £5.95 for seniors and students—are nearly the same as those at Jane Austen's House Museum.[66]

Winchester

Most recently vying for prominence as an Austen tourist destination is the city of Winchester, and particularly Winchester Cathedral, the site of Austen's burial. Dedicated Austen pilgrims, of course, have long sought out Austen's grave in the north aisle of the Cathedral and the nearby memorial tablet, the texts of which offer views on the significance of her life from the perspective of two different generations of her family. (Famously, her gravestone makes no reference to her authorship, describing her only in terms of her personal characteristics and family ties. The wall tablet, placed in 1872, acknowledges that Austen "was known to many by her writings.") A short walk from the Cathedral, the house where Austen died is visible; a plaque commemorates the building's association with Austen. Now owned by Winchester College, the building is not open to ordinary tourists.[67]

In April 2010, Winchester Cathedral unveiled, with much publicity, an exhibit titled "The Jane Austen Story." "In celebration of England's favourite female novelist," according to the Cathedral's 2010 promotional brochure, "the exhibition will tell the story of Jane Austen's life in Hampshire; the countryside towns, villages, and characters that inspired her writing."[68] Temporarily installed displays of artifacts and manuscripts, in a separate case, accompany the permanent exhibit, which consists of four vertical display placards placed in the aisle leading to Austen's gravestone. The essentially factual, dry placards do not address why Austen remains "England's favourite female novelist." Instead, background information on Austen's life is chronologically presented according to the places where she lived, seemingly designed for those with no prior knowledge of Austen at all.

Steventon

There is comparatively little to see, but potentially much to feel, in Steventon, the village where Austen was born and grew up. The rectory where Austen lived until 1801 was demolished in 1823; only the land on which it stood is visible. However, the small parish church of which Austen's father was rector, and in which she regularly worshipped, has been maintained with dedication by local parishioners, with the aid of contributions from international lovers of Austen. St. Nicholas Church makes possible several experiences for the committed Austen traveler (who must come by car or van, since the village is not accessible by public transportation). The church's small size brings home just how circumscribed was the social world in which Austen spent her childhood and young adulthood. As you think about how much time the young Austen would have spent in the church's pews, depending on your own predilections you can imagine her steeping herself in Anglican liturgy and ritual, pondering human nature, or freeing her mind to work on her stories. More literally

Figure 4.3: The site of the rectory in Steventon, Hampshire, where Austen was born and lived with her family until 1801. The rectory building was demolished in 1823. Author photo.

than any other Austen-related location, St. Nicholas Church offers a shrine to Austen, in the form of a low, screened recess on one wall in which mementos from visitors and Austen societies are collected and displayed. Elsewhere in the building, plaques commemorate gifts towards restoration from Austen societies, reinforcing the church's identity as a point of pilgrimage for lovers of Austen.

Those who like to commune imaginatively with Austen will appreciate that St. Nicholas Church is the only building with strong associations to Austen that you can visit, on the inside as well as the outside, entirely on your own. As you walk up the wooded lane from the site of the rectory, stand in the church's aisle, or sit in a pew, you are alone with your ideas of Austen.

Seeking Austen through Travel

Promotional materials for Austen-themed travel entice visitors with promises of what can be experienced only through journeys to places known to Austen. "Thousands of visitors continue to flock to the landmarks of her life in Winchester and Hampshire's surrounding countryside to get closer to the

Figure 4.4: St. Nicholas Church, Steventon, of which Austen's father was rector until 1801. Author photo.

Figure 4.5: Recess in St. Nicholas Church, Steventon, containing mementos from Austen societies. Author photo.

'real' Jane Austen," declares a leaflet published by the Winchester City Council in order to promote a so-called "Austen Trail." "Find out why visiting the area is leaving so many Austen readers with a lasting sense of history, place and person."[69] The proprietors of a private tour company that offers Austen-oriented itineraries invite potential customers to "Follow in her footsteps, / And walk where she has walked / Stand where she must have stood, / And tread where she has trod. / Touch what she must have touched / And see what she has seen, / And just imagine ..."[70] Do actual travelers, as opposed to marketers, find that geographical closeness to the places Austen knew leads to a greater understanding of her, or stronger feelings about her? Or do Austen lovers find, in line with prevailing academic theories of literary tourism, that places associated with her disappoint as much as—or more than—they satisfy? Caroline Sanderson's travelogue *A Rambling Fancy: In the Footsteps of Jane Austen* (2006) and Lori Smith's memoir *A Walk with Jane Austen: A Journey into Adventure, Love & Faith* (2007) offer two perspectives on how a traveler's own goals, inclinations, and imaginative investment determine her response to visiting Austen places today.[71]

Published (and presumably commissioned) by the travel imprint Cadogan Guides, Sanderson's *A Rambling Fancy* is a first-person account of visiting what the author calls "the places most associated with Jane Austen."[72] Sanderson, an experienced guidebook writer who lives in England, explains her intention to "free-associate" with material from Austen's writings, as might anyone who embarks on a similar journey: "I made the decision not to try to provide a tourist guide and to restrict myself to places that could easily be visited by anyone. ... I solicited no insider knowledge, other than that which could be gleaned from books and tourist literature available to any visitor. As a result, my observations would largely be fresh and, however, fanciful, my own."[73] Sanderson's professed hope for her travels is modest: given how much "still eludes us" about Austen as a person, Sanderson decides to "focus on the places she knew," with the conviction that "each place has light to shed, in its own way."[74]

Sanderson emphasizes how vital it is that the Austen-seeking traveler be willing to look, think, and feel beyond what is actually physically present. Apropos of a description of Steventon, Sanderson apprises the reader that "if you wish to follow in Jane Austen's footsteps, you must use your imagination and you must use it above all now, at the beginning of the journey. Close your eyes and imagine that here in this field before you is a rectory."[75] For Sanderson herself, conjuring what is absent comes more easily than ignoring evidence of the modern world, including efforts to present Austen to contemporary tourists. Indeed, Sanderson's strongest sense of closeness to Austen arises in an undistinguished landscape "deep in the Hampshire countryside, about six miles from Chawton":

To see the place where Jane Austen had lived so contentedly and produced three of her world-famous novels had been fascinating. I had taken pleasure in treading the same floorboards and pavements, and seeing with my own eyes some of the objects mentioned in her letters: the china dinner service, the patchwork, the topaz crosses. Yet Jane herself had been curiously absent. Her presence had somehow evaporated with the careful orchestration of her heritage and Chawton itself, though beguiling, was nothing like the place she had known. ...

I stepped outside, looked around at the rutted lane and the mud, the ancient church, and the graveyard with its listing grey tombstones, and noticed the scent of wet grass on the wind. There were no cars, and hardly a sound could be heard. I took another lungful of damp air. Just for a fleeting moment, in another corner of Hampshire, I felt that at last I stood in that most elusive of Shangri-Las—the England of Jane Austen.[76]

For Sanderson, a feeling of intimacy with Austen's world comes most easily in places off the conventional Austen tourist trail: "It was the places that had made little or no attempt to pin down a 'heritage' Jane—Godmersham, Lyme Regis, and Steventon—where her words caught light, her characters lived on the page and I felt I knew her a little."[77] The few moments of excitement that Sanderson records take place at Godmersham, Edward Knight's estate in Kent, where she feels first a "thrill" when "standing in the very room where so many Austen reunions had taken place" and then "a completely unexpected sense of joy" when viewing the house from a nearby footpath.[78]

Throughout her journey, Sanderson seeks primarily to feel closer to Austen's sources of inspiration, rather than to the author herself. Sanderson does confess, apropos of what she describes as Cassandra's "rather unsatisfactory pencil sketch" of Austen's face, to wanting to look Austen "in the eye, in the hope of finding some clue to her genius."[79] In Chawton, however, Sanderson searches not for a feeling of Austen's presence but for signs of what might have kindled her authorial creativity: "An air of homely simplicity has been artfully preserved at Chawton Cottage: you search each austere corner in vain for anything that might have sent Jane's imagination soaring."[80] The "sense of joy" Sanderson experiences at Godmersham, too, results from feeling that now she fully understands Elizabeth Bennet's reactions when first beholding Darcy's estate at Pemberley.[81]

In spite of the moments of illumination she recounts, Sanderson concludes that on the whole her endeavor to pursue Austen geographically has actually yielded less insight than she has obtained through rereading Austen's writings. She faults Austen-themed tourist locations for "embroidering Jane Austen" in a way that "makes my sense of the real woman fade even further"; "her words," Sanderson decides, "are the only souvenirs from the journey really worth having."[82] In this respect, Sanderson aligns with the scholar Claudia Johnson, who points out the inadequacy of relics and rooms to conjure Austen's presence and recommends "reading her novels" as the only true way to cultivate a sense of closeness to her."[83]

In contrast to Sanderson, who sets out to "free-associate" about Austen places as a project for an "in the footsteps" guidebook series, American memoirist Lori Smith undertook her Austen journey with purely personal goals. A longtime, omnivorous fan of Austen, Smith presents her interest in visiting Austen-related locations as having emerged naturally and inevitably as her acquaintance with the author deepened. She states that she began to feel "after years of reading and rereading ... like I had nowhere left to go."[84] Having tried to sate herself with biographies and Austen's letters, she found that these materials only increased her desire "to see the Hampshire countryside," Bath, Chawton, and the other sites about which she had read.[85] The brevity of Smith's justification of her project suggests that she expects her readers will understand and perhaps even share her impulse to seek Austen via traveling to (or within) England. Like the authors of the guidebook *Novel Destinations*, Smith seems to take it for granted that a literary journey will result in "a deeper perspective on the books we cherish."[86] Smith is frank, too, about wanting to indulge her love of Austen adaptations by including film locations on her itinerary. Finally, Smith maintains a yet more private hope: that tracking Austen will transform her sense of herself, or in her words, that "somehow this proximity to Jane's life will help me understand my own."[87]

Smith, then, is the very model of an enthusiastic literary tourist, eager for feelings of intimacy and revelations that can only come from being "there," engaging her own senses with Austen places and artifacts. On few occasions, however, does Smith's experience live up to her expectations. Sometimes, as when she walks around Bath, little beyond basic recognition results from connecting actual places with the names she knows from her reading: "There are Austen remembrances around every corner. The center square contains the abbey and baths and Pump Room. ... Most of the spots I know from Austen—Laura Place, the Circus, the Royal Crescent, Queen Square, where Edward stayed when he came to town—are all just various shapes of town house assortments."[88] Sometimes, Smith recoils from an encounter that promises an uncomfortable sort of intimacy, as when she visits a descendant of Austen's brother Edward Knight and refuses his invitation to touch "an elegant dining-room chair that lifted up to reveal a chamber pot underneath," which he claims "Austen probably *did* use."[89] And sometimes, as at Jane Austen's House Museum, Smith admits to feeling let down: beholding the famed writing table associated with Austen, she notes that it is "tiny, small angles all around the top, on a little pedestal, not what I expected, and I thought she wrote in the drawing room and not the dining room."[90] Though Smith does not dwell on her disappointment on this or comparable occasions, she does confess to an overall sense of deflation about her journey: midway in her memoir, she states that her "adventure had become mundane; I was growing weary of stalking Jane."[91]

Only once does Smith describe herself as having been strongly affected by an encounter with actual Austen material. She visits the British Library in hopes of seeing "Jane's writing desk and a manuscript chapter from

Persuasion," and she leaves "hardly [able to] walk straight, all tingly and in awe."[92] Yet, significantly, it is not the sight of Austen's desk or her "small script with lines crossed through and words corrected" that elicits this strong reaction.[93] Rather, Smith is overwhelmed by the library's display of its literary and musical treasures: "I felt," she says, "as though I had walked into a sacred space, and everywhere I turned there was something new to inspire awe."[94] The sight of original manuscripts, Austen's among them, delivers at last the sense of intimacy and jolt of inspiration that Smith sought. Being "so close ... to these manuscripts that they actually touched, that they wrote," Smith muses that she too wants to "obey that calling" to create, though she herself is, she says, "not a genius" and "would be content simply to do some good work."[95]

It would hardly be prudent for the author of a memoir framed around an Austen pilgrimage to intimate, much less declare, that such travels do little to enhance one's perception of intimacy with Austen. Smith leaves it to the reader to notice that she responds not to Austen sites per se but to the personal meanings she ascribes to them. She notes, for instance, that at the end of *Persuasion,* "everything is sealed on a quiet walk on the gravel path behind the Circus. I would like to find that gravel path."[96] What Smith longs for is obviously not the path itself but the romantic resolution that takes place there. Similarly, when endeavoring with the assistance of a guidebook to trace a walking route through Hampshire thought to have been a favorite of Austen's, Smith remarks that she "doesn't think these are the paths Jane walked, of course. But I imagine this may be the way she felt walking them: gloriously alone, surrounded by the heat and health of nature, with friends waiting at the other end."[97] Again, it is not the actual path that matters to Smith but rather the feeling of connection with Austen that she cultivates while walking it, knowing all the while that she owes that sense of connection to the power of her own imagination.

Both Sanderson and Smith, then, suggest that the impulse to undertake a literary pilgrimage is understandable, even as they indicate that a satisfying journey requires effort—what the fan studies theorist Will Brooker called "psychological leaps of faith"[98]—in order to transform actual places and objects into ones that feel significant to the traveler. Sanderson and Smith felt most rewarded when they, like the nineteenth-century literary tourists studied by Shirley Foster, used their imaginations "to create an alternative vision that enhanced reality with a degree of fictionalisation."[99] Judging by the accounts of Sanderson and Smith alone, the experience of today's Austen-oriented literary tourists are little different, fundamentally, from those of earlier pilgrims, or fans of other media. But Sanderson and Smith, both published authors, are not necessarily representative of ordinary visitors to Austen sites. Let us now see what such regular visitors say about what motivated their journeys and what, if anything, they felt was significant about being in the place where Austen lived and wrote.

Visiting Jane Austen's House (When She Isn't There)

My title for this subsection comes from a comment my daughter, Lucy, who was then three years old, made about her own first visit to Jane Austen's House. As was our habit, Lucy and I reviewed the events of that day in her nighttime lullaby. "We visited Jane Austen's House," I sang, and Lucy added, "And she wasn't there." A place called "Jane Austen's House" encourages you, indeed, to think about someone who is not there. As Alison Booth has noted, "the very openness of an author's house to the public is proof of that author's absence."[100]

Like Lucy, not every visitor to Jane Austen's House arrives entirely of his or her own volition. One teenage boy from Australia who responded to my survey wrote that he was "dragged here by [his] parents," though he did also make clear that he was capable of being an enthusiastic literary tourist if he had input into the choice of authors: "J. R. R. Tolkien is awesome, far better. Have been to all the sites ... awesome."[101] Some visitors, while less reluctant than the Australian teenager, nevertheless declared that they were present chiefly for the sake of a companion with a stronger interest in Austen: "My wife loves Jane's work and it has always been a goal for her to come here," explained a man in his 30s from the US. Perhaps not surprisingly, male visitors—who comprised a quarter of my survey respondents overall—were more likely than female ones to identify themselves as supporters of the main Austen fan in the family.[102] "My wife's love & admiration of Jane Austen" brought an Englishman in his 60s, while another Englishman in his 60s mentioned that he was making "a repeat visit in view of [his] wife's fascination with Jane Austen."

Other men, however, claimed an interest of their own, though often one that began thanks to the influence of a female family member. "My wife is the fan, but I am also interested," a man in his 60s from Ireland told me. "She is a dreadful fan of Jane Austen. Is 'dreadful' the right word? She is pulling me in." An Englishman in his 70s gave this reason for his visit: "Because of my wife, I suppose. She adores Jane Austen's novels and we've got several videos. Because of her, I like Jane Austen's novels too." Less typical was an Englishman in his 80s, a resident of Winchester, who recalled fondly that "one is brought up with her and one is brought up with her novels. ... I read them first when I was 16 at school. *Northanger Abbey* was my set book, before the war. So I always had a great deal of affection and admiration for her. Can't say the same for Dryden, who was our set poet."

Many visitors explained that they considered their trip to Austen's house to be a natural extension of their interest in her writings or her life. "Because I enjoy reading her books and I wanted to get a feeling of where and how Jane Austen would have lived," stated a teenage girl from the UK. "As a fan of her novels, I was interested to see how her home could have influenced her magnificent books," said another teenage girl, this one from the US. An even more straightforward answer came from a UK woman in her 50s:

"Because I'm interested in Jane Austen." Pragmatic reasons accounted for many visits, as well: for each person who expressed a particular desire to visit, someone mentioned living or traveling nearby as the chief reason for stopping in.[103]

Judging from my survey, many visitors to Austen's house are already experienced literary tourists, whether to other Austen sites or to places associated with other authors. The city of Bath, Austen's grave in Winchester Cathedral, and the house in Winchester where she died were the sites to which visitors were most likely to have already traveled, followed by the Jane Austen Centre in Bath, Lyme Regis, the British Library, film locations, and Austen's birthplace in Steventon.[104] The most popular authors' houses already visited were those of Dickens, Shakespeare, the Brontës, Keats, Vita Sackville-West, Wordsworth, Hardy, and Milton.[105]

A more detailed view of what visitors hoped or expected to experience at Jane Austen's House emerges from their selection of phrases to describe their motives for visiting and their experience overall. "To gain a sense of what Jane Austen's life might have been like" was the most popular motive chosen, though each of the following motives was also considered important by visitors, on average: to gain knowledge about Austen's life and times, to appreciate the circumstances of her literary composition, to see what inspired her to write, to appreciate the historic building, to stand where Austen stood or walk in her footsteps, and to see items owned by her.[106] Less popular overall, though still of significance to some visitors, were phrases that suggested a more personal or emotional form of encounter: to feel closer to Austen, to feel her presence, to imagine myself in her place, or to thank her for the pleasure she has given me.[107] Similarly, fewer visitors chose to characterize their visit in personal or emotional terms—as a pilgrimage, dream come true, visit to a dear friend, or homecoming—than in terms of the activity's educational or enjoyable qualities. The most popular description of the visit was as a cultural experience comparable to an art gallery or museum, followed closely by a chance to step back in time, a pleasant day out, and an educational activity.[108]

That Jane Austen's House Museum proved both informative and enjoyable for visitors is evident from their responses, in their own words, when asked how they would describe the experience of their visit. Almost half of those who answered this question referred to their visit as "interesting," "informative," or "enlightening."[109] More than half either called their visit "enjoyable" or described it using adjectives that connote enjoyment, such as "pleasant," "beautiful," "lovely," and "peaceful."[110] Asked which particular exhibits or portions of Jane Austen's House they found most interesting, and which most emotionally moving, visitors singled out elements with strong connections to Austen's authorship: manuscript pages of her writing, first editions of her novels, and her writing table. Many also gave high marks to the letter Cassandra wrote shortly after being present at Jane's death, which is exhibited in facsimile, as well as to the gardens and "the overall atmosphere."[111] Austen's relics and possessions, such as her lock of hair and topaz cross necklace, were decidedly lower in the scale.[112]

A majority of respondents said the visit either exceeded or greatly exceeded their expectations; none stated that the visit fell short of their expectations.[113] Yet individual visitors did mention some elements of surprise or disappointment. One commented that the house was "a bit larger than expected," while another mentioned being "surprised as to her house being unimpressive from outside." The volume of visitors bothered a few people, including one who stated that "viewing in some rooms is difficult when there are a number of visitors especially because there is lots to *read*!" And some reported a mixture of satisfaction and disappointment, such as the woman who told me, "Takes you back in time, doesn't it? I have enjoyed looking round—didn't know what to expect but am a little disappointed—thought it would be bigger. It's not fully furnished. They could have a bit more. Too many people." On the whole, however, the high levels of visitors' self-reported satisfaction indicate that these ordinary tourists, unlike theorists of literary tourism or published travel writers, did not register a sense of insufficiency about the museum's effort, in Claudia Johnson's term, to "conjure" Austen.

Like Caroline Sanderson and Lori Smith, who stress the need for literary tourists to exert their imaginations, several of the most enthusiastic visitors to Jane Austen's House made it clear that their experience was affected not only by what they saw but also by what they imagined or felt while present.

It was amazing. I could completely imagine the Austens walking about the house in the various quarters. The atmosphere is incredibly serene and I'm not surprised at all that the majority of her work was written here.

Woman, 18–24, US

Quite moving for me because I frequently read and re-read her books. And very interesting just being able to walk around the house where she did her writing and see the little table.

Woman, 60s, UK

I enjoyed myself very much. The house had all kinds of interesting information that deepened my appreciation not only for Jane Austen but her family, world, and novels. Rather than being dry, as some museums are, Jane Austen's house felt lively and genuine.

Woman, 18–24, US

The writing desk, hair and other memorabilia made me feel closer to the actual woman—making her a presence beyond simply an abstract historical figure.

Woman, 25–29, US

I found the house very interesting also the lovely costumes and the beautiful peaceful garden. I could imagine Jane writing her books in the lovely surroundings.

Woman, 70s, UK

It was an extraordinary experience seeing for my own eyes the place in which Jane Austen lived, the items she used during day to day life and especially seeing the table on which she created such wonderful stories.

Woman, 18–24, UK

Brilliant. I felt as though I had stepped into one of her novels.

Woman, 50s, South Africa

These visitors welcomed, and cultivated, the feeling that being in Jane Austen's House brought them closer to Austen, her family, and the world depicted in her novels. Willingly and rewardingly, these visitors performed what Mike Crang calls the literary tourist's "creative work of interpretation."[114]

Still more intimate glimpses into the responses of ordinary tourists emerge from the museum's Visitors Comment Book, where, in more privacy even than an anonymously conducted survey, visitors attest to their love for Austen and their appreciation of the house. Here is a sample of comments from a single page of the comment book from the first week of April in 2009, a time when the site as a whole was in the busy and sometimes noisy throes of redevelopment:

> Great atmosphere, enjoyable.
> Exactly as I would have imagined their home—& thank you for the delightful flowers.
> Lovely—like the fact that the house hasn't been changed. Will come back!
> Finally I made it here. Lovely experience.
> The museum conveys the warmth and joy of JA's family & her sensitivity.
> Lovely—I could just move in.
> A wonderful day with a dear friend.
> Beautiful spring garden & inspirational house as ever.
> Lovely memoir of Jane.[115]

Arguably, a visitor who felt disappointed would be unlikely to record that reaction underneath a series of effusive entries. And a single line in a loose-leaf notebook does not accommodate a very nuanced response. Nevertheless, the degree of delight evident in these comments suggests that, for many, Jane Austen's House very effectively reinforces and intensifies their sense of affection for the author.

Visitors are not the only ones who enjoy the experience of being in Jane Austen's House. Many of the museum's staff members, both professional and volunteer, are lovers of Austen and take a special pleasure in working at the house where she wrote. "You have to have a love of Jane Austen," says Catherine Hogan, a volunteer steward, who describes herself as feeling "privileged" to work at the house. Hogan's own copies of Austen's novels, she says, "are dog-eared."[116] Louise West, the museum's Curator, calls the house "a place full of friends & happiness as a workplace! As the home of Jane Austen it instills in me feelings of awe, wonder, excitement and gratitude. Sometimes you take it all for granted & other times, e.g. when you're reading one of the novels in the garden & you look up and remember that it was written here you can hardly believe it."[117]

Like visitors, staff members comment appreciatively on the house's atmosphere—which, of course, they play a significant role in maintaining. Janet Johnstone, the museum's coordinator of volunteers, describes the house as "a place I love to be. It has a charm about it which we try very hard not to lose, at the same time as making sure we are providing what the general public expect of a museum."[118] "The house emits a special atmosphere which I feel every time I come," comments a woman volunteer after three months working at the museum. "There is a timeless sense to it."[119] Ian Dussek, a five-year volunteer, calls the museum "a breath of friendly fresh air."[120] According to Shirley Fitch, a volunteer, "the qualities in Jane Austen's characters and in Jane herself are reflected here—harmony, contentment, courage and liveliness."[121]

Some members of the staff credit the experience of sustained contact with Jane Austen's House with being restorative and healing, much as Austen's works can be. As Ann Channon, the longtime House Manager, puts it, "We love the house, and it loves us."[122] Olive Drakes tells the following very personal story of having found consolation through proximity to Austen and her family:

I came to live in Alton within walking distance of Jane Austen's House Museum, Chawton, four years ago. As my husband, who suffered from dementia, liked to sit peacefully in the Museum's garden, it was a walk we undertook regularly. Three months after his death I was pleased to be accepted as a volunteer at the House and found my work there really helpful as I adjusted to living alone.

Two hundred years have passed since this house became the Austen family home, but we tread the floorboards they trod and open and close the window shutters as they did. Scraps of their wallpaper still cling to the walls in hidden corners. We are surrounded by their possessions and by examples of their handwriting and needlework. The sensitivity with which this museum has been developed bridges the 200-year gap and brings the past to life.

A recent visitor to the house, a resident of Beijing, told me that the characters who populate Jane Austen's novels embody for him convincing human characteristics. Such statements make me marvel at creativity that spans two centuries and crosses cultural boundaries. As I spend time in Jane Austen's House, walk through her village and worship at her church (or the one that now stands on its site) I picture her in her family and village setting as daughter, sister, aunt and friend.[123]

Another volunteer characterizes the house as "an extension of a family—'Jane pulls you in.' I'm getting more hooked every time I come to the house."[124]

As all these remarks reveal, a shared interest in Jane Austen and an appreciation of the house in which she lived creates a sense of community among those who work at the museum. The building that was a family home in Austen's day has become home in another sense to another kind of family: a gathering place, with a powerful pull on the imagination, for those who care about Austen.[125]

The comments of visitors, staff members, and volunteers alike bear out the theory that literary tourism is fundamentally a journey of the imagination, albeit one that finds inspiration through contact with specific places known to be significant to the author in question. Each visitor creates her or his own encounter with Austen, with the assistance of—or, sometimes, in deliberate opposition to—elements of landscape and geography, museum exhibits, and objects that bear associations with the author and her family. Whether a visitor's ideas about Austen change or are reinforced through tourism depends, again, on the individual. While designers of displays and writers of informative placards can aim to increase knowledge or shift perceptions, ultimately each visitor makes personal decisions regarding how to interpret such material. Only by listening to literary tourists can we ascertain the variety of ways in which they encounter, and respond to, Austen places.

You don't need to travel to England, though, to imagine Austen. Thanks to the efforts of authors, visual artists, and filmmakers to evoke Austen today, images of her are available to you wherever you live. How, and with what effects, present-day creators represent Austen is the subject of the next chapter.

Notes

1 Jennifer Forest argues that "craftspeople then, as now, experienced the same creative impulse and sense of satisfaction or fulfilment when they turned a needle to a new piece of embroidery, sewed a novel trim to a bonnet or applied a brush to a blank canvas." *Jane Austen's Sewing Box: Craft Projects & Stories from Jane Austen's Novels* (London: Murdoch, 2009), 17.

2 Mike Crang, "Placing Jane Austen, Displacing England: Touring between Book, History, and Nation," in *Jane Austen and Co.: Remaking the Past in Contemporary Culture*, ed. Suzanne R. Pucci and James Thompson (Albany: State University of Albany Press, 2003), 123–24.

3 Celia A. Easton, "Dancing Through Austen's Plots: A Pedagogy of the Body," *Persuasions* 28 (2006): 252.

4 Lovers of Austen-based films, like fans of other forms of popular culture, can opt as well to visit locations familiar from their favorite adaptations. For an account of how historic houses have capitalized on their associations with Austen films, see Sarah Parry, "The Pemberley Effect: Austen's Legacy to the Historic House Industry," *Persuasions* 30 (2008): 113–22.

5 Shannon McKenna Schmidt and Joni Rendon, *Novel Destinations: Literary Landmarks from Jane Austen's Bath to Ernest Hemingway's Key West* (Washington, D.C.: National Geographic, 2008), ix.

6 Roger C. Aden, *Popular Stories and Promised Lands: Fan Cultures and Symbolic Pilgrimages* (Tuscaloosa: University of Alabama Press, 1999), 6; emphasis original.

7 Ibid., 8.

8 Matt Hills, *Fan Cultures* (New York: Routledge, 2002), 149.

9 Ibid., 150–51.

10 Ibid., 144, 149.

11 Ibid., 154.

12 Will Brooker, "A Sort of Homecoming: Fan Viewing and Symbolic Pilgrimage," in *Fandom: Identities and Communities in a Mediated World*, ed. Jonathan Gray, Cornel Sandvoss, and C. Lee Harrington (New York: New York University Press, 2007), 150, 163.

13 Nicola J. Watson, *The Literary Tourist* (Houndmills, Basingstoke: Palgrave Macmillan, 2006), 6.

14 Nicola J. Watson, introduction to *Literary Tourism and Nineteenth-Century Culture*, ed. Nicola J. Watson (Houndmills, Basingstoke: Palgrave Macmillan, 2009), 5.

15 Watson, *Literary Tourist*, 5.

16 Ibid., 8.

17 Ibid., 11, 90.

18 Ibid., 34. Alison Booth adds that literary tourism not only is something that amateur readers are inclined to undertake, but can be understood as a kind of reading itself: "In literary tourism the movements of readerly imagination and travel mimic each other, often entailing a visit to a real-world setting transformed by author and reader into the space-time of characters. Reading 'homes and haunts' narratives, visiting sites or participating in festivals share aspects of virtual reality or being 'lost in a book.'" "Time-Travel in Dickens' World," in *Literary Tourism and Nineteenth-Century Culture*, ed. Watson, 151.

19 The Brontës' house at Haworth is the only site associated with female authors that Watson considers in *The Literary Tourist*; she concludes that the Brontë Parsonage "offers itself to the reader-tourist as itself a historico-Gothic novel, a meta-text capacious enough to comprehend both the lives and works of the Brontës. They become the narrated rather than the narrators, as much characters as their own creations. Such, it seems, is the condition of female authorship; to be successful as a woman writer is only to be co-opted as a figure subjected to her own fictive landscapes." *The Literary Tourist*, 126. For an account of Elizabeth Gaskell's role as a subject of literary tourism and as a formative influence on Brontë tourism, see Pamela Corpron Parker, "Elizabeth Gaskell and Literary Tourism," in *Literary Tourism and Nineteenth-Century Culture*, ed. Watson, 128–38. Gail Marshall, in a study of nineteenth-century women tourists' response to Shakespeare-inspired tourism, contends that "the women find in Shakespeare a voice out of tune with their times, although not their own aspirations." "Women Re-Read Shakespeare Country," in *Literary Tourism and Nineteenth-Century Culture*, ed. Watson, 101. And Watson makes a broader claim for the "deeply rooted gendering of the literary tourist experience" throughout the nineteenth century, in "Rambles in Literary London," in *Literary Tourism and Nineteenth-Century Culture*, ed. Watson, 148.

20 Paul Westover, "How America 'Inherited' Literary Tourism," in *Literary Tourism and Nineteenth-Century Culture*, ed. Watson, 185.

21 Ibid., 186.

22 Watson, *Literary Tourist*, 4.

23 Shirley Foster, "Americans and Anti-Tourism," in *Literary Tourism and Nineteenth-Century Culture*, ed. Watson, 176.

24 See also Chieko Iwashita, "The Impact of Film, Television and Literature as Popular Culture on Tourism and the Postmodern Gaze" (master's thesis, University of Surrey, 1999). Iwashita compares visitors' reactions to Jane Austen's House Museum and to locations where scenes from the mid-1990s adaptations of *Pride and Prejudice* and *Sense and Sensibility* were filmed.

25 "At Chawton," concludes David Herbert, "60% of tourists could be classed as managerial, professional, or skilled white-collar." Out of the 223 respondents to his Chawton survey, "30 (13.5%) had read none of her novels. On the other hand, 28.2% had read six or

more, and over 60% had read three or more. Of the individual novels, *Pride and Prejudice* was the most widely read (80.3%), followed by *Sense and Sensibility* (58.3%) and *Emma* (56.5%). The question did ask about books read, but the frequent presentation of these stories on film and television undoubtedly raises awareness of them." "Literary Places, Tourism and the Heritage Experience," *Annals of Tourism Research* 28.2 (2001): 320, 322.

26 Ibid., 326.

27 Ibid., 328.

28 Barbara Hodgdon's investigation of Stratford-upon-Avon as a tourist site concentrates on analyzing the implications of exhibits. She frames her inquiry as follows: "I am primarily interested in reading Stratford as a virtual wonder cabinet for Shakespeare, as a collection of museum spaces that attempt to reconstruct and individuate him, assign him particular values, circulate and disseminate knowledges about him, and frame his histories with particular viewing agendas. ... My enquiry, which reads tours, individual site displays, artefacts, descriptive materials and catalogues, souvenirs and trinkets, is framed by a series of questions. What ideas, values, and symbols shape exhibition practices at Stratford's various properties and sites? What structures, rituals, and procedures determine the relations between material objects, bodies of knowledge, and the processes of ideological persuasion? What objects are displayed, and how are they reframed within a world of attention to encourage and play to particular habits of looking? ... What, in other words, are the strategies for (re)producing—and consuming, the subject called Shakespeare?" *The Shakespeare Trade: Performances and Appropriations* (Philadelphia: University of Pennsylvania Press, 1998), 194.

29 Crang, "Placing Jane Austen," 112.

30 Ibid., 111.

31 Ibid., 119, 125.

32 Ibid., 125.

33 Claudia L. Johnson, "Jane Austen's Relics and the Treasures of the East Room," *Persuasions* 28 (2006): 217–18.

34 Ibid., 218.

35 Ibid., 219.

36 Ibid., 229.

37 Ibid; emphasis original.

38 Ibid., 219. Watson contends that "depending on how the Author is valued in relation to the Reader, literary tourism will be condemned as derivative, parasitic, and decadent, or celebrated as a creative and transformative system of enhancing or extending reading activity." Introduction to *Literary Tourism*, 10.

39 Watson, introduction to *Literary Tourism*, 5.

40 Quoted in Felicity James, "At Home with Jane: Placing Austen in Contemporary Culture," in *Uses of Jane Austen: Twentieth-Century Afterlives*, ed. Gillian Dow and Clare Hanson (Houndmills, Basingstoke: Palgrave Macmillan, forthcoming). I am most grateful to Felicity James for sharing her essay with me before its publication.

41 My descriptions of Austen exhibits and tourist sites are current to my most recent visit to them in July 2010, with the exception of Steventon, which I last visited in July 2009. When recounting changes and developments at Jane Austen's House Museum, I draw on prior visits in 2009 and 2003; my presentation of the Jane Austen Centre is informed by a prior visit in 2007. All prices quoted are accurate as of August 2011.

42 For the duration of its exhibit "A Woman's Wit: Jane Austen's Life and Legacy," on view from November 2009 through March 2010, the Morgan Library & Museum in New York offered the most extensive exhibit available anywhere of Austen manuscripts, as well as copies of books owned by her.

43 A computer display near the exhibit case allows visitors to page through digital images of "Volume the Third," as well as items by other authors on display.

44 "Volume the Second" is also owned by the British Library; "Volume the First" is in the Bodleian Library, Oxford. The contents of all three volumes are included in "Jane Austen's Fiction Manuscripts," the digital project freely available at http//www.janeausten.ac.uk.

45 *Catharine, or The Bower*, for instance, is dedicated "To Miss Austen" (Cassandra), with references to works included in "Volume the First" and "Volume the Second":

"Encouraged by your warm patronage of The beautiful Cassandra, and The History of England, which through your generous support, have obtained a place in every library in the Kingdom, and run through threescore Editions, I take the liberty of begging the same Exertions in favour of the following Novel, which I humbly flatter myself, possesses Merit beyond any already published, or any that will ever in future appear, except such as may proceed from the pen of Your Most Grateful Humble Servt, THE AUTHOR." Jane Austen, *Juvenilia*, ed. Peter Sabor (Cambridge: Cambridge University Press, 2006), 241.

46 According to Freydis Jane Welland, an Austen descendant whose branch of the family owned the writing desk until 1999, its placement in the "care of the British Library" is intended to "provide pleasure and inspiration to future generations of writers and readers." Welland notes as well that "when the writing desk went back briefly to Chawton in 2003 for a meeting of Janeites, after an absence from the cottage of well over a century, some of the people there to witness the occasion found at that moment a felt sense of homecoming." "The History of Jane Austen's Writing Desk," *Persuasions* 30 (2008): 126, 128.

47 In her list of "Ten Best Austen Places to Visit," Joan Klingel Ray offers step-by-step instructions for reaching Chawton from London. *Jane Austen for Dummies®* (Hoboken, NJ: Wiley, 2006), 317. (It is also possible to reach Chawton by bus from Winchester, a cathedral city that draws visitors because of its beauty and history as the ancient capital of England.) Ray's list of Austen-related destinations includes many of the locations I treat in this chapter; without any explanation, however, Ray omits the Jane Austen Centre from her list of six "must-see sites" in Bath. Ibid., 320. For a reflective account of a visit by an Austen scholar to Chawton in 1997, see Rachel M. Brownstein, *Why Jane Austen?* (New York: Columbia University Press, 2011), Chapter 2.

48 Austen, her sister Cassandra, their mother, and a family friend named Martha Lloyd moved to Chawton on July 7, 1809. After the death of Rev. George Austen, Jane's father, in 1805, Mrs. Austen and her two unmarried daughters, who had little income of their own, changed residences frequently until they accepted the offer of Jane's wealthy brother, Edward Austen Knight, to move them into a cottage on his Chawton estate. Edward did not live at Chawton Great House but at another of his properties, Godmersham Park in Kent. Mrs. Austen and Cassandra remained at Chawton Cottage until their deaths in 1827 and 1845, respectively. Deirdre Le Faye, *A Chronology of Jane Austen and Her Family* (Cambridge: Cambridge University Press, 2006).

49 Alison Booth has commented of the Dickens Museum in particular that it, "like many house museums … is more collection than reconstruction: a curiosity shop of metonymies of the writing and reading experience and relics of the author and his associates." "Time-Travel," 154.

50 "Relics," in *The Jane Austen Society: Report for 1951* (Alton: C. Mills & Co., 1951), 4. As I explained in Chapter 2, although the Jane Austen Society was inaugurated in 1940 for the purpose of preserving Chawton Cottage, a separate Jane Austen Memorial Trust was eventually formed to administer the cottage, which was purchased by T. Edward Carpenter in 1947. Board members of the Jane Austen Memorial Trust have generally been members of the Jane Austen Society. Since 1994, the Senior Trustee, and de facto head of Jane Austen's House Museum, has been Tom Carpenter, a grandson of T. Edward Carpenter. Tom Carpenter recalls his early memories of Chawton Cottage and his adjustment to running the museum after what he calls "an active legal professional life, coupled with many hours spent as a Territorial Army soldier," in Maggie Lane and David Selwyn, eds, *Jane Austen: A Celebration* (Fyfield Books, 2001), 19.

51 In addition to a new building, the redevelopment made possible by the Heritage Lottery Fund included significant rearrangement of the house itself, most notably the opening of the kitchen, the refitting of a small room as a reference library available to visitors, and the relocation of the gift shop to an outbuilding.

52 *Pride and Prejudice*, directed by Cyril Coke, screenplay by Fay Weldon (1980; Burbank, CA: Warner Home Video, 2004), DVD. Elizabeth Garvie has recently been designated a patron of Jane Austen's House Museum, as has the scholar Kathryn Sutherland.

53 An installation titled "Under the Influence," "an exhibition of bold contemporary craft inspired by the museum and Jane Austen's life," was on view at Jane Austen's House Museum from June to September 2010. The artists, from the Farnham

University of Creative Arts, variously found inspiration in the materials of the museum's collections and in the activities that occurred in the house during Austen's lifetime, as well as those that take place now in the building's current incarnation as a tourist site. Given my own interest in visitors' responses to their experiences, I was particularly struck by Judy Dibiase's set of ceramic drawers, in which the artist included visitors' comments she had overheard while on her own visit to the house, such as a woman's remark that her "very old battered copy" of *Pride and Prejudice* "got [her] through [her] divorce." For a blog treating the development of the exhibition, see http://jahmexhibition.blogspot.com/2010/06/exhibition-opening. html.

54 Madelaine Smith, conversation with author, July 23, 2010. According to Smith, staff members at both Jane Austen's House Museum and Chawton House Library frequently confront confusion among visitors as to which building is which, as well as erroneous statements in the press about where Austen actually lived. Felicity James has called attention to ideas of family and home that are reinforced at Jane Austen's House Museum, as well as the significance of personal ties to Austen and Anglo-American partnerships in the founding of both Jane Austen's House Museum and Chawton House Library. "At Home with Jane."

55 "Jane Austen's House Museum," [2010], brochure.

56 I am grateful to Tom Carpenter for sharing with me these statistics, as well as his observation that visitor numbers usually rise after a new television broadcast or film release related to Austen. Conversations with author, July 13, 2009 and July 23, 2010.

57 *Jane Austen's Persuasion*, directed by Roger Michell, screenplay by Nick Dear (1995; Culver City, CA: Columbia TriStar Home Video, 1999), DVD.

58 Efforts to found a so-called "Jane Austen Centre" had been gathering momentum among Jane Austen Society members in the late 1980s, with attention focusing on the possibility of purchasing Chawton House from the Knight family descendants. As envisioned by Henry Rice, an Austen family descendant and chairman of the "Jane Austen Centre Trust," the "Centre will be for all those who admire the novelist and her works. There will be a major Library and Archive open to students and scholars and a permanent Exhibition in the public rooms. ... The Centre will contain the first Library as such to be devoted to Jane Austen and the Archive will hold significant family papers already promised for deposit there. ... It is hoped to return to the house some of its original furnishings. Altogether, we are seeking to restore Chawton House and its grounds to the character and condition they enjoyed in Jane Austen's lifetime." To Eileen Sutherland, May 9, 1989, Jane Austen Society of North America Records, 1975–2008, MS 0028, series I, subseries E, folder 11, Special Collections and Archives, Goucher College Library (hereafter cited as JASNA Archives).

59 Maggie Lane, "4 Sydney Place, Bath," circulated to the Jane Austen Society in advance of a meeting on October 14, 1992, JASNA Archives, series I, subseries E, folder 12. Referring to the proposal to locate an Austen Centre at Chawton House, Lane contends that "the last thing we want is to jeopardise the economic viability of Jane Austen's House Museum ('Chawton Cottage'): this is a real possibility if the sale of books and merchandise were reduced by competition from a second outlet in Chawton." Ibid.

60 David Baldock, interview with author, July 27, 2010. Unless cited separately, information regarding the founding and development of the Jane Austen Centre is taken from this interview. Recent Jane Austen Centre brochures feature cover images of contemporary young women in Regency dress, along with the tagline "Celebrating Bath's most famous resident."

61 "Jane Austen Centre in Bath," *JASA News*, December 1999, accessed January 24, 2011, http://www.jasa.net.au/newsdc99.htm#bathcntr.

62 With a wide selection of both books and merchandise, the Jane Austen Centre certainly serves as a center for Austen-inspired consumption. As Allison Thompson has argued, "the range of Austen artifacts available in the market today supports many different ways of interacting with the author, her characters and even her era. The romantic articles that evoke a Regency period 'as it should have been,' the crafts that pay homage to her

or that explore some aspect of her characters, the ironic items that express a counter-image of Austen—all of these are ways in which fans can actively shape the reception of their own particular Austen as well as put their own interests and personalities on display by reference to her." "Trinkets and Treasures: Consuming Jane Austen," *Persuasions On-Line* 28.2 (2008), http://www.jasna.org/persuasions/on-line/vol28no2/thompson.htm.

63 The Jane Austen Centre was also behind the well-publicized hoax in 2007 in which slightly rewritten first chapters of Austen's novels were submitted to, and rejected by, present-day publishers. See Louise Jury, "Pride or Prejudice?: Publishers Fail to Recognize Austen," *Evening Standard* (London), July 19, 2007, 3.

64 In contrast, Jane Austen's House Museum occupies the less streamlined web address www.jane-austens-house-museum.org.uk.

65 An analytical report of tourism in the Bath region in 2006, prepared by The Tourism Company, allows comparison between numbers of visitors at the Jane Austen Centre and other area attractions. With 40,000 visitors, the Jane Austen Centre was about as popular as No. 1 The Royal Crescent, a historical house museum, which received 41,000 visitors. In contrast, Bath Abbey received 350,000 visitors, and the major historical draw of the city, the Roman Baths, received 851,000. "B&NES Destination Management Plan, Final Report," October 2007, accessed January 10, 2011, http://www.bathnes.gov.uk/SiteCollectionDocuments/Environment%20and%20Planning/Bath%20and%20North%20East%20Somerset%20Destination%20Management%20Plan.pdf.

66 Directly inspired by the Jane Austen Festivals sponsored in Bath by the Jane Austen Centre, residents of Alton recently began highlighting that town's connections with the Austen family by holding a "Jane Austen Regency Week" in July. Adapting the Jane Austen Centre's tag line "Celebrating the life of Bath's most famous resident," Alton's organizers use the phrase "Celebrating the time Jane spent in Alton & Chawton"; the week's homepage is http://www.janeaustenalton.co.uk/index.php. A museum of local history, the Curtis Museum, maintains a permanent exhibit on Regency-era Alton that stresses links to the Austens. Two free walking tour maps, published by the Alton Chamber of Commerce and Industry, point out buildings known to Austen that are still visible in Alton and en route from Chawton. Alton-oriented Austen tourism is best described as nascent.

67 Participants in the 2011 tour of England sponsored by the Jane Austen Society of North America did, however, have the opportunity—for what the tour brochure discreetly termed "separate pricing"—to enter the house where Austen died. "Tour Itinerary: Jane Austen: Celebrating *Sense and Sensibility*," January 2011, http://www.jasna.org/tours/tour2011-itin.html.

68 "Winchester Cathedral: New for 2010, The Jane Austen Story," 2010, brochure.

69 "Austen: Landmarks of the Author's Life in Hampshire," Winchester: Winchester City Council, n.d., brochure.

70 "Jane Austen Country Tour: The Dancing Years," Hidden Britain Tours, [2010], brochure.

71 For an account of Austen-inspired travel by Janeites of a much earlier generation, see Constance Hill, *Jane Austen: Her Homes and Her Friends* (1901; repr., Philadelphia: Pavilion Press, 2003), which recounts the fervent efforts by sisters Constance and Ellen Hill to track down as many locations as possible known to Austen. Hill's account continues to be a touchstone for many Austen guidebook writers: see in particular Anne-Marie Edwards, *In the Steps of Jane Austen: Walking Tours of Austen's England* (1991; repr., Madison, WI: Jones Books, 2003). For a breezy account of travels and studies inspired by Austen, see Alice Steinbach, "Sense and Sensible Shoes," in *Educating Alice: Adventures of a Curious Woman* (New York: Random House, 2004). For a prettily illustrated guidebook that seems designed as much for armchair as for actual travel, see Katharine Reeve, *Jane Austen in Bath: Walking Tours of the Writer's City* (New York: The Little Bookroom, 2006).

72 Caroline Sanderson, *A Rambling Fancy: In the Footsteps of Jane Austen* (London: Cadogan Guides, 2006), 11. *A Rambling Fancy* is part of an "in the footsteps" series of travelogues published by Cadogan; other authors and locations featured include Rebecca West (the Balkans), Edward Lear (Italy), Thomas Hanbury (Mortola) and J. R. R. Tolkein.

Sanderson's previous travel title for Cadogan is the children's book *Pick Your Brains about Greece*.

73 Sanderson, *A Rambling Fancy*, 11, 12.
74 Ibid., 13.
75 Ibid., 15.
76 Ibid., 176–77.
77 Ibid., 218–19. Lyme Regis, a town on the English Channel coast visited by Austen, figures prominently in *Persuasion*.
78 Ibid., 118, 131.
79 Ibid., 181.
80 Ibid., 145.
81 Ibid., 131.
82 Ibid., 218–19.
83 Johnson, "Jane Austen's Relics," 219.
84 Lori Smith, *A Walk with Jane Austen: A Journey into Adventure, Love & Faith* (Colorado Springs, CO: WaterBrook Press, 2007), 4.
85 Ibid.
86 Schmidt and Rendon, *Novel Destinations*, ix.
87 Smith, *A Walk with Jane Austen*, 12.
88 Ibid., 164.
89 Ibid., 106; emphasis original.
90 Ibid., 96.
91 Ibid., 119.
92 Ibid., 121.
93 Ibid., 121–22.
94 Ibid., 122.
95 Ibid., 121, 122.
96 Ibid., 170.
97 Ibid., 95. Smith identifies this guidebook only in her endnotes as being Edwards' *In the Steps of Jane Austen*.
98 Brooker, "A Sort of Homecoming," 163.
99 Foster, "Americans and Anti-Tourism," 176.
100 Booth, "Time-Travel," 151. Novelist Michael Thomas Ford plays with this convention of literary tourism by having his version of Jane Austen—a vampire who is still alive, though incognito, as a romance novelist in our own time—hide in her house from rabid fans who have come to see where their favorite author lives. *Jane Goes Batty* (New York: Ballantine Books, 2011).
101 Survey of visitors to Jane Austen's House Museum, July 13–23, 2009. All surveys were conducted in confidentiality and are transcribed exactly as written. Subjects had a choice of two surveys: a short version, consisting of three open-ended questions that could be completed in writing or by oral interview, or a long multiple-choice version to be completed in writing. I collected a total of 120 short surveys and 50 long surveys. Unless otherwise noted, all subsequent quotations and data in this chapter are taken from these surveys.
102 Of my 170 total respondents, 25% were male and 75% female. 64% were from the UK, 15% from the US, and 20% from other countries, including 12 visitors from Australia. 9% of visitors were under 18; 9% 18–24; 6% 25–29; 5% 30–39; 12% 40–49; 19% 50–59; 19% 60–69; 13% 70–79; and 5% 80–89. 1% of respondents did not specify their nationality; 3% did not give their age.
103 Of the 120 respondents to the short survey, 19 mentioned a particular desire to visit (e.g. "I had to come" or "I always wanted to come"), while 23 mentioned proximity.
104 Of the 50 respondents to the long survey, 21 had visited Bath, 18 Austen's grave in Winchester Cathedral, 16 the house in Winchester where she died, 14 the Jane Austen Centre in Bath, 13 Lyme Regis, 11 the British Library, 9 film locations, and 5 her birthplace in Steventon. Of course, visitors to sites such as Bath and the British Library did not necessarily seek out those institutions for their Austen associations in particular.
105 Of the 50 respondents to the long survey, 7 had visited a Dickens house, 7 Shakespeare,

4 the Brontës, 4 Keats, 4 Vita Sackville-West, 4 Wordsworth, 3 Hardy, and 3 Milton. Other authors mentioned (by 2 visitors) were Beatrix Potter and (each by 1 visitor) Henry James, Mary Russell Mitford, William Morris, Gilbert White, Virginia Woolf, Winston Churchill, Roald Dahl, Dr. Johnson, Tennyson, Arthur Conan Doyle, and Lewis Carroll.

106 On a scale of 5 to 1, where 5 = very important and 1 = not at all important, these motives received the following average ratings from the 50 respondents to the long survey: to gain a sense of what Jane Austen's life might have been like (4.6), to gain knowledge about Austen's life and times (4.2), to appreciate the circumstances of her literary composition (4.2), to see what inspired her to write (4.1), to appreciate the historic building (4.0), to stand where Austen stood or walk in her footsteps (4.0), and to see items owned by her (4.0).

107 On a scale of 5 to 1, where 5 = very important and 1 = not at all important, average ratings were as follows: to feel closer to Austen (3.3), to feel her presence (3.1), to imagine myself in her place (3.1), or to thank her for the pleasure she has given me (2.9).

108 On a scale of 5 to 1, where 5 = exactly how I would describe my visit and 1 = not at all how I would describe my visit, average ratings were as follows: a cultural experience comparable to an art gallery or museum (4.4), a chance to step back in time (4.4), a pleasant day out (4.3), an educational activity (4.0), a tourist visit (3.7), pilgrimage (3.3), dream come true (3.0), visit to a dear friend (2.9), homecoming (2.5).

109 Of the 120 respondents to the short survey, 39 called their visit "interesting," 18 "informative," and 2 "enlightening."

110 Of the 120 respondents to the short survey, 23 described their visit as "enjoyable," 14 as "pleasant," 11 as "beautiful," 8 as "lovely," 7 as "peaceful," 5 as "charming," 2 as "tranquil," and 1 each as "restful" and "serene."

111 As I mentioned in Chapter 2, this letter by Cassandra was owned by Alberta H. Burke and bequeathed by her to the Morgan Library.

112 On a scale of 5 to 1, where 5 = very interesting/emotionally moving and 1 = not at all interesting/emotionally moving, these elements received the following average ratings from the 50 respondents to the long survey: manuscript pages of her writing (4.5 interesting, 4.3 moving), first editions of her novels (4.4 interesting, 3.9 moving), her writing table (4.3 interesting, 4.2 moving), Cassandra's letter after Jane's death (4.2 interesting, 4.2 moving), the gardens (4.4 interesting, 3.9 moving), the overall atmosphere (4.4 interesting, 3.9 moving), the lock of Austen's hair (3.8 interesting, 3.6 moving), Jane's and Cassandra's topaz crosses (3.7 interesting, 3.7 moving).

113 Of the 50 respondents to the long survey, 22 said the visit met their expectations, 15 said it exceeded their expectations, and 13 said it greatly exceeded their expectations. One respondent, who had visited several times, wrote that the visit met her expectations "because I knew what to expect! Had this been my first visit, I would have ticked box 1" (greatly exceeded).

114 Crang, "Placing Jane Austen," 125.

115 Jane Austen's House Museum, "Visitors' Comment Book," March 30, 2009 to April 3, 2009.

116 Conversation with author, July 13, 2009.

117 Survey of staff members at Jane Austen's House Museum, July 27, 2009. Any identifying details or names are included with the express permission of the respondents. Subsequently cited as JAHM Staff Survey.

118 JAHM Staff Survey.

119 Ibid.

120 Ibid.

121 Quoted in Louise West, "A Happy House," *Jane Austen's Regency World* 1 (2003), 11.

122 Conversation with author, July 20, 2009.

123 JAHM Staff Survey.

124 JAHM Staff Survey.

125 As Felicity James points out, Jane Austen's House Museum invites the visitor "to appreciate a family narrative on several levels. From the oak tree she planted in the garden (now re-planted from a seedling) to her patchwork quilt, her narrative is written into

a domestic English landscape, emphasised by the origins of the museum, which was established in memory not only of Austen but also of the founder's son, Lieutenant Philip John Carpenter, killed in action in 1944." James points out too the family ties of Tom Carpenter, the current Senior Trustee, to his grandfather, the museum's founder. "At Home with Jane."

Chapter 5

Envisioning Austen: Portraits, Fiction, Film

"Each of us has a private Austen." So begins Karen Joy Fowler's bestselling novel *The Jane Austen Book Club* (2004).[1] Our "private Austen" is our personal sense of Jane Austen as both woman and writer—an interpretation that, according to Fowler, necessarily reflects our sense of ourselves. Fowler's character Sylvia, for whom family is paramount, thinks of Austen as "a daughter, a sister, an aunt. Sylvia's Austen wrote her books in a busy sitting room, read them aloud to her family, yet remained an acute and nonpartisan observer of people. Sylvia's Austen could love and be loved, but it didn't cloud her vision, blunt her judgment."[2] In contrast, Sylvia's daughter Allegra thinks of Austen as an author who "wrote about the impact of financial need on the intimate lives of women" and whose books belong "in the horror section."[3] In her acknowledgments, Fowler states that her own private Austen is the one "who showed her work to her friends and family and took such obvious pleasure in their responses."[4]

Like generations of readers, the members of Fowler's Jane Austen Book Club have formed impressions of Austen from reading her writings and biographies of her. How Fowler's characters imagine Austen is influenced too by the sole surviving authentic portrait of her face, a watercolor by Cassandra Austen. Again like many Austen devotees, Fowler's characters feel less than satisfied with this image.[5] "Cassandra Austen's sketch of her sister," explains the novel's narrator, "wasn't a very attractive portrait; we were certain she had been prettier than this, but when you need a picture of Jane Austen you don't have a lot of choices."[6]

Many more choices exist today, in a variety of media, to gratify those with an appetite for depictions of Austen. Best known is the biographical feature film ("biopic") *Becoming Jane* (2007), which starred Anne Hathaway as a Jane whose exploits in both love and authorship departed significantly from the historical record.[7] (Throughout this chapter and the next, I will refer to characters and depictions of Austen as "Jane," and will continue to refer to the author herself by her surname.) Yet *Becoming Jane* is only one of a host of works that have reinvented Austen, creatively and sometimes daringly, to suit today's audiences. Popular novelists have granted their Janes opportunities for love, adventure, and self-expression that far exceed those known to have been available to the actual Austen.[8]

Austen scholars have tended to dismiss these fictional representations of Austen both because of the works' unapologetic inventiveness and because their authors work in genres—from detective fiction to romance to horror— that Austen herself did not choose in her mature novels.[9] Yet these recreations of Austen for a present-day popular audience have much to tell us about how amateur readers wish to imagine her, and why. So too does another group of Austen representations that have yet to be seriously considered by scholars: recent portraits.

All of these invented versions of Austen appeal to—and, in many cases, result from—amateur readers' curiosity about what Austen was "really" like: how she looked, what she thought, what she experienced as a woman and author. The creators of these portrayals use a variety of strategies to flesh out the historical record about Austen, which is notoriously limited. One tactic is to fill in the gaps of what is known for certain about Austen's life with material from her fiction; in an unfortunate side effect, Austen seems then like an uninspired writer who drew only on her own experience. Another is to invoke images from successful screen versions of Austen's novels, which are more likely to be familiar to a broad audience than are her writings or personal history. Other portrayals of Austen venture deep into fantasy, often integrating elements— such as vampires—that reflect contemporary popular taste.

Visual and verbal portrayals of Austen today participate in, and contribute to, a long tradition of reinventing her image and propagating wishful myths about her. Furthermore, each subsequent depiction of Austen takes advantage of the imaginative latitude established by earlier representations: detective Jane, in other words, paves the way for vampire Jane. In the next section, I first consider briefly how Austen's own family members inaugurated these reinventions and myths; then, I show how scholarly work on biographical approaches to Austen illuminates creative representations of her as well. The following section focuses on how Austen's physical appearance has recently been represented in portraits, on screen, and in fiction. How contemporary novelists envision Austen's life experiences is the subject of the following section. The final section investigates cinematic and fictional depictions of the relationship between the Austen sisters. I show how these portrayals offer fans the opportunity to imagine themselves in unique intimacy with Austen.

Austen Images and Austen Myths

As is well known, Austen published no autobiographical writings during her lifetime. Her identity as author was concealed from her first readers, who knew from the title page of *Sense and Sensibility* only that the novel was written "By a Lady."[10] Subsequent title pages of Austen's novels identified the author only in association with previous titles: the first edition of *Pride and Prejudice*, for example, appeared as "By the author of *Sense and Sensibility*."[11] No prefatory material or dedications in any of the novels Austen saw through to publication indicated who she might be.[12] In contrast, the dedications penned by the teenage Austen to her stories and sketches—collectively known now as her juvenilia—abound in personal and family detail, as well as comically overblown declarations of literary ambition.[13]

Myth-making about Jane Austen began with the "Biographical Notice" that her brother Henry Austen appended to the two novels, *Northanger Abbey* and *Persuasion*, that he published together in December 1817, following her death in July of the same year. (Austen's identity as author had already been noted in several obituaries.)[14] Henry contributed a capsule history of his sister's life and a sketch of her character, placing stress on her modesty, good temper, and religious devotion.[15] The feminine paragon portrayed by Henry is hard to square with the often acerbic narrator of Austen's novels, let alone the biting commentator Austen shows herself to be in her private letters. Of course, the original readers of the "Biographical Notice" did not have access to the latter documents.

Henry's description of his sister's appearance deserves especial notice. According to him, Austen's "features were separately good. Their assemblage produced an unrivalled expression of that cheerfulness, sensibility, and benevolence, which were her real characteristics. Her complexion was of the finest texture. It might with truth be said, that her eloquent blood spoke through her modest cheek."[16] Deliberately deflecting attention from his sister's surface to what he wishes to be known of her character, Henry frustrates any would-be portraitist, or any devotee of Austen who seeks to envision a particular face.

Offering more material for the imagination, Caroline Austen recalled fifty years after her aunt's death that Austen's

> was the first face that I can remember thinking pretty, not that I *used* that word to myself but I know I looked at her with admiration—Her face was rather round than long—she had a bright, but not a pink colour—a clear brown complexion and very good hazle eyes—She was not, I beleive, an absolute beauty, but before she left Steventon she was established as a very pretty girl, in the opinion of most of her neighbours—as I learned afterwards from those who still remained—Her hair, a darkish brown, curled naturally—it was in short curls round her face (for *then* ringlets were *not*.)[17]

While Caroline does provide more specifics about Austen's features, what she chiefly conveys is how admiringly she, as a young girl, viewed her aunt. As someone who literally "looked at [Austen] with admiration," Caroline thus invites readers to imagine that they, too, could have looked at Austen—and, perhaps equally thrillingly, could have been looked at by her.

Taken together, Henry's and Caroline's descriptions create the impression of a healthy, graceful woman who, while attractive, would not have been singled out for her beauty, as are the heroines she created. That Austen's relatives took such trouble to recall and describe her physical appearance furthermore indicates that curiosity about a woman author's looks is hardly unique to present-day readers.

The process, which Henry began, of recasting Austen's image in accordance with the biographer's own views of femininity—and/or those of his anticipated audience—continued with the publication in 1870 of the first full-length biography of Jane Austen, *A Memoir of Jane Austen* by her nephew James-Edward Austen-Leigh. As Kathryn Sutherland puts it, "here we have Jane Austen as remembered by the Steventon or Hampshire Austens, for whom she is nature loving, religious, dutifully domestic, and middle class."[18] A different version of Austen emerged in 1884 when Lord Brabourne, a great-nephew from the wealthier Knight branch of the family, edited and released a hitherto unpublished batch of her surviving letters, along with a substantial biographical preface. In Sutherland's words, Brabourne's Austen is "a more emotional figure, inward and passionate, and of course more gentrified."[19] Even Austen's own relations, in other words, held and propagated competing visions of her.

Sutherland persuasively traces these varying depictions of Austen back to Cassandra Austen. Cassandra not only kept many of her sister's private papers from view by destroying them, but also divided up the remainder among different branches of the family. According to Sutherland, Cassandra "decisively shaped, through stewardship of the archive, through its calculated division, and through conversation, what was available (and to whom) in the next generation. ... As the guardian of her sister's reputation and material effects, Cassandra is the key to what tangibly remains."[20] More than any other person, including Austen herself, Cassandra determined what can and cannot be known about Austen. Cassandra's role as gatekeeper to Austen's legacy invites two possible responses from devoted readers who are curious about Austen. Austen fans can resent Cassandra for limiting access to their beloved author. Or, as Sutherland has suggested, Cassandra can be celebrated for opening up so much space to imagine Austen. "Cassandra Austen," Sutherland writes, "did biographers a profound service when she censored or destroyed her sister's private papers and correspondence. Whatever her reasons and whatever was burned, Cassandra licensed the imagining of fact, the dream of history."[21]

As both Sutherland and John Wiltshire have argued, the comparative paucity of biographical sources concerning Austen encourages and even requires biographers to exercise their ingenuity. "Jane Austen lived two hundred years ago," writes Wiltshire, "and (if one thinks about it dispassionately) there can be very little new to be known about her own inner or personal life."[22] "The primary sources for a life of Jane Austen," as Sutherland puts it, "are challengingly thin: no private diaries to suggest the existence of an inner life, a self apart."[23] Thus each new biographer of Austen imagines her life anew, taking advantage of what Wiltshire calls the "hybrid form" of biography, which mixes "fact and make-believe" and is "involved as much with a figure of myth or collective fantasy as with a series of historical occurrences."[24] Sutherland too emphasizes the freedom of the biographer to interpret what remains: "In the hands of the skilful recorder, gaps and silences are even more eloquent than evidence."[25]

Not only must Austen's biographers invent and embroider, but the effect of their doing so, according to Wiltshire, is to offer a fantasy of direct access to their subject. The "impulse to know the author's innermost secrets," he contends, "is the keynote of all lives of Jane Austen."[26] Wiltshire identifies this wish as "a kind of love … the readers' desire to ferret out the smallest details of the loved one's life, to share the secrets of her heart, to participate in, or merge her world with their own."[27] Sutherland agrees, arguing that "even more than its close relation the novel, biography appeals to an urgent human need—to know fully and completely another person and to have access to their innermost thoughts." Biography, in Sutherland's words, "simultane-ously feeds and denies our fantasies of intimacy."[28] Mary Ann O'Farrell points out an especially explicit example of such a fantasy in Valerie Grosvenor Myer's popular biography *Jane Austen: Obstinate Heart* (1997): an opening chapter titled "What Was She Like?"[29] "To want to know what Jane Austen was like—to want to personify—is to want something in excess of what historicist contextualization or biographical detail might yield," contends O'Farrell. "Such knowing demands a relation that includes me, that ultimately is about me."[30]

Those who treat Austen's life in genres other than biography have even more liberty to personalize the encounter between fan and author, and to remake the author in the image of the fan. Indeed, Wiltshire's and Sutherland's arguments about Austen myths and biography apply well to imagined versions of her life that take forms other than conventional biography. Authors of biographical novels and creators of biopics, who are free from any disciplinary constraints of fidelity to the historical record, have greater latitude to purvey a fantasy of access to the "real" Austen, and to tailor their depiction of her for particular groups of present-day readers and viewers. Sutherland claims that "biography is the interface between high culture and the mass market";[31] so too, in their way, are novels and films about Austen's life that are designed for popular audiences. Sutherland observes that biographies of Austen "have so far tended to be national portraits, hemmed in by national cultural assump-tions"; she wonders how Austen's life would appear "from a non-English perspective."[32] In the popular realm, such depictions already exist: we will see in particular how American authors and actresses have interpreted Austen for international audiences.

Literary scholars may well agree with Wiltshire's rather tart declaration that "the critical enterprise has a better chance of putting us in touch with the essential Jane Austen, whatever that is, than the biographical," or the more creative.[33] Like biographies, many fictional and cinematic depictions of Austen tantalize readers and viewers with the possibility of unprecedented personal access to the essential, or the "real," Austen. Yet to fault popular recreations of Austen for delivering invented rather than true versions of her is to miss the opportunity to appreciate how these works both respond and contribute to her ongoing appeal. We must take these works on their own terms, as forms of entertainment that make no claim to adhere to—and indeed sometimes revel in their freedom from—scholarly standards. Crucial to bear in mind here is Douglas Lanier's argument, which I acknowledged in Chapter 1, regarding the importance of setting aside preconceptions about fidelity when examining popular representations of Shakespeare.[34] Scholars would also do well to recognize what Austen's writings, in spite of the literary-canonical status they have acquired, share with the popular works that reinvent her life today. As Barbara M. Benedict has influentially argued, Austen did not aim her own fiction exclusively at highbrow readers. Instead, Benedict declares, Austen's "intertextuality suggests that she conceived of her novels in the context of current fiction, as a part of popular literature, and designed her novels to reach the audiences who were reading contemporary novels."[35] Judy Simons too has called attention to the common ground in genre and technique that many present-day Austen-based works share with their sources of inspiration. "The dominant forms of the Austenian continuation—burlesque, pastiche, and excess—are identical to those which captivated Austen," Simons observes.[36] Though Simons is referring to sequels in particular, her observation is equally relevant to creative reworkings of Austen's life.

Sutherland has called portraiture a "near relation" of biography, a concept that is especially useful for approaching visual images, both artistic and cinematic, of Austen.[37] Again, Cassandra is our gatekeeper—or our enabler. Only two authentic images exist of Austen from her lifetime, both small watercolor sketches by Cassandra. One, which is signed and dated 1804, shows a bonneted woman viewed from the back—leaving ample room for imagination, indeed.[38] The other sketch is neither finished nor dated; it is believed to have been created circa 1810.[39] In this portrait, Cassandra depicts Jane from the front, with her face—the only fully finished part—in three-quarter view; her torso and folded arms are lightly drawn in pencil. Rather than circulate this unsmiling, rather uncompromising image of Austen, her biographer nephew J. E. Austen-Leigh commissioned a new, more appealing portrait to accompany his 1870 *Memoir*. Lord Brabourne chose yet a different picture for his 1884 collection of Austen's letters.[40] And, as both Sutherland and Emily Auerbach have separately shown, prettified images of Austen have flourished ever since.[41]

Like any popular depiction of Austen, a portrait appeals to a given viewer to the extent that it captures how that viewer believes or imagines Austen to have looked. As Sutherland puts it, the "truth" of a portrait "depends less on descriptive accuracy—did Jane Austen really look like this or like this—than on the coincidence of the perceptions shared by portraitist and viewer."[42] So too do cinematic and fictional portrayals of Austen ring true to the extent that they match, and gratify, the expectations of their audience.

Face to Face with Austen: Visual and Verbal Portraits

Nearly all the eminent figures featured in London's National Portrait Gallery are represented by professional artists, in formal portraits whose scale, pose, and finish unmistakably signal the subjects' cultural importance. Not so Austen. Cassandra's watercolor likeness of her sister's face is almost on the scale of a miniature, nearly as tiny as the "little bit (two Inches wide) of Ivory" to which Austen famously compared her own novels.[43] In this portrait, Jane looks off to the side rather than meeting the viewer's eyes, and her facial expression shows no effort to charm or engage. As Kathryn Sutherland puts it, "the sketch is resolutely private."[44] That the portrait has what Sutherland calls an "amateur lack of finish" is understandable, even inevitable.[45] Cassandra, as was typical of amateur female artists of the period, did not have the training to execute

Figure 5.1: Cassandra Austen, portrait of Jane Austen, pencil and watercolor, c. 1810, 11.4 cm x 8 cm. © National Portrait Gallery, London. The sole authentic likeness of Austen's face.

a more polished portrait. Furthermore, oils—the conventional medium of professional painting in every genre—were off limits at the time to English girls and women who learned drawing as a so-called feminine accomplishment.[46]

Exhibiting Cassandra's "private" sketch in a public gallery poses a challenge not only because of the work's diminutive size but because its medium, water-color, requires that it be displayed in a climate-controlled case. The National Portrait Gallery's curators have grouped the sketch with portraits of other English authors from the Romantic period: Austen has Scott on her left, Burns on her right, and Coleridge, Keats, and Southey above her.[47] Reminding the viewer that some contemporary women authors were portrayed more monumentally, two large-scale portraits of Mary Wollstonecraft and Mary Shelley face off from opposite walls of the same room. To see Cassandra's portrait, you have to lean in to the exhibit case and look closely. The colors are almost invisible; the contrast between the dark portions (hair and eyes) and pale portions (face, dress, and cap) is what catches your eye. It's up to you to interpret Austen's expression as determined, lost in thought, or peeved. Certainly she does not look witty or friendly, and nothing about the sketch conveys a sense of her genius—or even of her activity as a writer.

A glimpse into the reception history of Cassandra's portrait emerges from the correspondence of Alberta H. Burke, the Baltimore collector of Austen whom I profiled in Chapter 2. The National Portrait Gallery acquired this portrait at auction in 1948; Alberta opted not to bid on the sketch. Alberta's longtime dealer, Percy H. Muir, stated his approval of the portrait's new ownership and made plain his own reaction to the image: "I suppose it [the National Portrait Gallery] is the proper place for it as it is the only authentic record, but really it was so completely unattractive that I cannot think that it was worth the price paid for it."[48] Alberta replied that she agreed "that the portrait is really a hideous object, but as the only authentic likeness, it has a sentimental aura which makes it an interesting object. I am very glad that it is now a national possession, and I hope to see it if I ever come to England again."[49]

In 2002, the Jane Austen Centre in Bath, a tourist site that has no historical connection to the Austen family, unveiled a new portrait of Austen commis-sioned by that Centre's director, David Baldock and created by Melissa Dring.[50] Life size, the pastel portrait aims to show Austen as she would have looked during the years she lived in Bath (1801–1806). Dring, a British portraitist and police forensic artist by training, states that she consulted descriptions of Austen by her contemporaries as well as surviving portraits of other members of the Austen family. Her "speculative likeness," Dring declares, "is based almost entirely on solid fact"; "little guesswork was needed."[51] While she took Cassandra's sketch as her "natural starting point," Dring says she wanted "to bring out something of Jane's lively and humorous character, so evident in her novels and all contemporary accounts of her. Cassandra's drawing may have been quite like Jane physically, but has failed to catch her sparkle."[52] Dring describes the facial expression with which she endowed her Jane as "a complex

Figure 5.2: Melissa Dring, *Jane Austen*, 2002. Pastel, 90 cm x 56 cm. © The Jane Austen Centre, Bath. The Centre's director, David Baldock, commissioned the portrait to show Austen in her late 20s, her age when she and her family lived in Bath.

one, of delightful, private amusement. She is going to poke fun at some pomposity somewhere. ... She is still, but underneath that cap she is seething with ideas, although she has also a serene, dreamy, inward looking quality. Jane's was not a loud voice, and this is a quiet little picture, but it has strength, like hers, and is subtle and complex."[53]

When Dring's portrait is viewed in person, the highlights in Jane's eyes do seem to sparkle, and her smile, while not broad, can be read as amused, or even sly. The very high coloring with which Dring has rendered Jane's complexion, however, creates an unfortunate impression of overall redness from eyes to mouth, including the prominent nose. This depiction of Austen may capture the author's wit, but it—like Cassandra's original sketch—portrays a woman who is farther from the standard of beauty in her day than is suggested by family members' descriptions.

A significant contribution of Dring's portrait is to represent Austen with emblems of authorship. Dring's Jane leans on her writing desk, one hand supporting her chin; a small piece of paper is near her elbow, and her quill pen stands ready in its inkwell. Dring explains that she took great care with the accuracy of these visual details, mentioning that she "was able to make sketches and calculate measurements" of Austen's original writing desk.[54] (As I mentioned in Chapter 4, that desk is now on display in the British Library.) Thanks to these visual cues, we see a woman not merely sitting but ready to write. It is not hard to imagine this Jane as pausing in the midst of writing a letter, or a manuscript page of fiction.

Another compelling image of a Regency woman at a desk—seemingly Austen caught in the very act of composition—was featured by New York's Morgan Library & Museum in publicity for its 2009–2010 exhibit "A Woman's Wit: Jane Austen's Life and Legacy." The drawing, done in pen and black ink with gray wash, shows a slender woman in a Empire-waist dress seated at a table, bent over to look closely at pages that her foreground hand seems ready to turn. Her other arm is hidden from us; we might guess that it holds a pen. We see the subject's face in profile and shadows, with not enough detail to judge its beauty or resemblance to accounts of Austen's looks. Overall, the subject's figure conveys an impression of elegance, ease, and intent concentration.

Despite these tempting signs, the drawing, by the twentieth-century American illustrator Isabel Bishop, actually depicts one of Austen's characters, not the author herself. Titled "The examination of all the letters which Jane had written to her," the drawing shows Elizabeth Bennet re-reading her sister's letters in Volume 2, Chapter 11 of *Pride and Prejudice*. Prepared by Bishop as part of a set of illustrations for a 1945 edition of that novel that was never published, the drawing originally appeared in a 1976 Book-of-the-Month Club edition of *Pride and Prejudice*.[55] By evoking Austen through her heroine, the Morgan's curators cleverly bypassed questions of accuracy and authenticity—and added to a long tradition of wishfully associating the author with witty,

Figure 5.3: Isabel Bishop, *The examination of all the letters which Jane had written to her*, 1945. Pen and black ink, gray wash, over pencil, on paper, 22.7 cm x 17.7 cm. The Pierpont Morgan Library, New York. Gift of Mrs. Robert E. Blum in honor of Charles Ryskamp on his 10th anniversary as Director. 1979.32:15. Photographic credit: The Pierpont Morgan Library, New York. This illustration appeared in publicity for the Morgan's 2009–2010 exhibit "A Woman's Wit: Jane Austen's Life and Legacy."

endearing Elizabeth. (In 1996, for example, Martin Amis pithily remarked that Elizabeth is "Jane Austen with looks.")[56] As we look at Elizabeth's act of reading and attitude of sisterly care, we imagine being able to see Austen's act of writing and absorption in her creative work.

Visitors to Winchester Cathedral in the summer of 2010 had the opportunity to see two new, and quite contrasting, portrait busts of Austen created by members of the UK's Society for Portrait Sculptors.[57] Positioned near Austen's grave among other displays in the Cathedral's "Jane Austen Story" exhibit was Philip Nathan's "Jane Austen," a dun-colored plaster bust approximately life size.[58] Nathan's Jane is solemn and inward looking; her mouth is set, unsmilingly, and lines around her mouth and cheeks make her look at least 41 (Austen's age at the time of her death). The hair curling under her cap and the ruffle of her collar do not soften her overall affect of severity. Strikingly, and disturbingly, her eyes are nearly closed, giving the impression almost of a death mask. (This effect is somewhat muted when the sculpture is viewed in profile, as it appears in Figure 5.4.) In Nathan's description of the sculpture in the exhibition catalog, he mentions that he consulted Cassandra's portrait as well as other family likenesses, but he offers no explanation of why he decided to portray Austen in such a somber manner.[59]

Displayed in the eastern end of the Cathedral, not far from bishops' tombs and chantry chapels, Nigel Boonham's "Jane Austen in Heaven" depicted an Austen very different in aspect, not only from Nathan's version but also from the portraits I have already discussed. Twice life size, this head of Austen is majestic and monumental, and it conveys an overall impression of confidence, even triumph.[60] (A photograph of "Jane Austen in Heaven" appears as the frontispiece to *Everybody's Jane*.) Boonham's Jane looks upward, her chin raised; her eyes and eyebrows are broad and expressive, and her mouth, set in an even line, suggests certainty, and perhaps contentment. Boonham explains the genesis of the sculpture in his description for the exhibition catalogue: "I began modelling a small head of Austen at my kitchen table. ... I was forced to tip the head backwards to read the forms of the face in the light. It soon became apparent that the head was far too small and should be monumental."[61]

Boonham has richly textured the surface of his plaster, so that the skin of Jane's face, her cap, and especially her broad, strong-looking neck look sculptural rather than delicate. (The bottom of Jane's neck and the back of her head are the most roughly surfaced, bearing visible impressions of both tools and fingers.) The title "Jane Austen in Heaven" and the sculpture's placement in the Cathedral among representations of other Christian worthies encourage the viewer to imagine Austen as a secular saint.[62] According to Boonham, "the title came into being because somehow the tipping back reminded me of the title of a painting by Stanley Spencer called *John Donne Arriving in Heaven*. The thought of what Jane Austen, a perceptive observer, might see in Heaven was delicious."[63] Jane's confident expression, together with the very few cues to femininity included by Boonham, suggest an author who belongs in the

Figure 5.4: Philip Nathan, *Jane Austen*, 2010. Plaster, 0.46 m. Photograph courtesy Steve Russell Studios Ltd. Sculpture displayed at Winchester Cathedral June–August 2010 as part of "In This Sacred Place," an exhibition of works by the Society of Portrait Sculptors.

pantheon of literary greats—and who is aware of that status herself. Boonham remarks in the exhibition catalogue that "Jane Austen is a central figure in the literary psyche of the UK (and the English speaking world). It seems a gross omission that there is no official portrait statue or monument to Jane Austen in Britain."[64] Of course, in the absence of an official portrait, lovers of Austen can choose the one that comes closest to their own private conception of the author—or look beyond all of those depictions to envision her for themselves.

Through movement and speech, an actress portraying Austen can create a much richer impression than any portrait, whether in two or three dimensions. Austen's wit, so difficult to convey in a static medium, is easily communicated through mobile facial expressions, smiles, and laughter. (Of course, even the most able actress can only make her Jane seem witty and intelligent if the screenplay supplies her with suitable dialogue.) When an actress looks at the camera, furthermore, she seems to be making eye contact directly with the audience, which creates an effect of intimacy that goes well beyond the experience of viewing an artwork.

The image of Austen that has unquestionably reached the largest present-day audience is that of the American actress Anne Hathaway, who starred in the 2007 biopic *Becoming Jane*. As played by the beautiful Hathaway, Jane is an elegant, energetic young woman who outshines her sister Cassandra, portrayed by the pleasant-faced but hardly glamorous English actress Anna Maxwell Martin. While Hathaway is shown with dark, curly hair and hazel eyes—features to which Austen's niece Caroline attested—the actress's dazzling smile bears no resemblance to the tight mouth that appears in the real Cassandra's portrait of her sister. As befits the leading lady of a feature film, Hathaway's Jane is attractive and winning, as exceptional in her good looks as she is in her genius. *Becoming Jane*, which reached theaters only two years after the successful *Pride & Prejudice* film that starred Keira Knightley as Elizabeth Bennet, invited viewers to compare Hathaway's beauty favorably with that of Knightley.[65] Thus *Becoming Jane* fully satisfies the viewer's desire to imagine Austen as having equaled any of her heroines in loveliness, in spite of historical evidence to the contrary. Only in the final scene of *Becoming Jane*, in which Hathaway is aged by means of makeup and a frumpy Victorian hairstyle, does the audience see a version of Austen whose glow is dimmed.[66]

A more complex, yet still appealing, cinematic version of Austen appeared in the 2008 television biopic *Miss Austen Regrets*, the screenplay for which is based on Austen's letters.[67] The English actress Olivia Williams portrayed Austen in the last years of her life as a striking, vibrant woman still very much capable of charming potential suitors. Elegantly dressed—and, in a few bedroom scenes in the company of her young niece Fanny or her sister Cassandra, elegantly undressed—Williams's Jane has an enviable physique and complexion, even as a few faint facial lines make her age seem plausible. Arguably less absolutely gorgeous than Hathaway, Williams radiates intelligence as well as beauty. Cassandra, played here by the statuesque American actress Greta Scacchi,

Figure 5.5: Anne Hathaway as Jane Austen in *Becoming Jane,* 2007. Courtesy of Miramax. Hathaway's wide smile and dazzling beauty convey an impression of Austen very different from Cassandra's portrait.

Figure 5.6: Olivia Williams as Jane Austen in *Miss Austen Regrets,* 2008. © BBC Photo Library. Williams portrays Austen in the last few years of her life as a handsome, highly intelligent woman.

provides a visual contrast that has less to do with looks per se than with attitude and situation; we see Cassandra, apparently weary, taking care of domestic business while Jane travels and enjoys herself. The casting of both actresses tantalizes fans of Austen film adaptations, who will recognize Williams as having played Jane Fairfax in Diarmuid Lawrence's *Emma* (1996) and Scacchi as having played Mrs. Weston in Douglas McGrath's *Emma* (1996).[68] Williams's reappearance as Jane Austen is especially thought provoking for anyone who has pondered the similarities between the artistically gifted but reticent Jane Fairfax and her creator.

Verbal portraits of Austen in recent fiction vary considerably in the extent to which she is glamorized to appeal to popular audiences, and to meet the conventions of subgenres, such as romance, to which the novels adhere. (The examples I will treat in this section are all from novels by American authors.) Arguably closest in looks to the historical Austen is the heroine/ narrator of Stephanie Barron's ongoing series of detective novels, which has been published throughout the period of Austen's present-day popularity.[69] In Barron's novels, no one—not even Jane's beloved Cassandra or Lord Harold Trowbridge, the spy and adventurer to whom Jane is attracted—ever comments admiringly on Jane's face or figure, and she has no illusions about her own beauty. As her 30th birthday approaches, Jane offers us a visual image of herself that is the fullest in Barron's series:

> I wore a borrowed gown, made over in respect of the current season, that became me almost as much as it had graced Lizzy [her elegant sister-in-law] two summers before; my hair had been cut and dressed in curls all about my forehead, courtesy of the obliging Mr. Hall; and despite the closing of that decade beyond which a woman is commonly believed to cherish few hopes, I knew myself to be presently in good looks. I shall never again possess the bloom of eighteen; the bones of my face have sharpened of late, particularly about the nose, as tho' the flesh is stretched too tightly over it, and my complexion is coarser than it was ten years ago. But several months' trial of the air of Kent … *will* have their effect; and … my eyes were as bright as though I were embarked upon my very first ball.[70]

This passage evokes, of course, the return of Anne Elliot's "bloom" at age 27 in *Persuasion*.[71] Barron makes clear, however, that her own Jane, while bright-eyed, falls considerably short of Anne's loveliness. Barron's Jane seems well aware that others' interest in her does not depend on her looks; she neither regrets her level of beauty nor tries to remedy it. Like the sister and aunt remembered by Henry and Caroline Austen, respectively, Barron's Jane is a woman of substance who encourages admiration for more than her appearance alone. In other ways, of course, Barron's adventurous detective heroine is the antithesis of the quiet Christian whom Henry depicts in his "Biographical Notice."

In contrast to Barron's self-assured Jane, the narrator of Patrice Hannon's *Dear Jane Austen: A Heroine's Guide to Life and Love* (2005; 2007) is concerned with setting right the historical record regarding her looks. "Do not tell Cass," this Jane confides,

> but her sketch of me has given the world quite the wrong idea of my looks. … I was never conventionally pretty and yet those who knew me found my face quite attractive. I had a natural liveliness that brought colour into my cheeks, and my eyes sparkled with merriment more often than not. I believe my tall, thin figure—I was a pretty height—would quite fit your era's fashion. When I was not in a gay mood, I suppose I did not look so well—somewhat forbidding, perhaps—but as you shall see, that can be said of us all.[72]

Like Karen Joy Fowler, whose characters in *The Jane Austen Book Club* feel "certain [Austen] had been prettier than" Cassandra's portrait,[73] Hannon encourages readers to improve upon that less than satisfying sketch as they imagine Jane for themselves. Intensifying the message that love can render any face more attractive, Hannon's Jane then quotes and discusses passages from Austen's own novels that exemplify the relation between regard and perceived attraction.

Thoroughly reinvented to meet the tastes of romance readers is the heroine of Sally Smith O'Rourke's *The Man Who Loved Jane Austen* (2006).[74] In this novel, a twentieth-century Virginia gentleman actually named Fitzwilliam Darcy travels back in time and falls in love with Jane Austen. First striking Darcy as "slender and … somewhat pretty," Jane soon impresses him as being "much prettier than he had previously thought, with a firm but sensuous mouth, regular features framed by beautiful dark brown hair"—as well as eyes that "sparkle in the light and seem to contain infinite depths of intelligence and understanding."[75] Readers or viewers who remember the spell Elizabeth Bennet's "fine eyes" cast over Mr. Darcy in *Pride and Prejudice* will notice that O'Rourke has borrowed that attribute for her own heroine.[76] Darcy does not yet recognize this "pretty brunette" as being *the* Jane Austen; when he does, he thinks anew "how extraordinarily attractive she was, bearing not the slightest resemblance to the poorly done sketch of a frumpy sixteen-year-old that was the only known portrait of Jane Austen to have survived into his time."[77] (Darcy is apparently thinking of Cassandra's portrait of Jane's face, though the age is off by 20 years.) His impression of Jane's attractiveness only grows the more of her he sees. Having watched Jane undress behind a screen, he recalls with evident pleasure and erotic charge that she was "naked behind the thin dressing screen, her slender, full-breasted figure limned in the dancing firelight."[78] Through the eyes of O'Rourke's Darcy, readers can indulge in fancying a Jane who—like Anne Hathaway in *Becoming Jane*—is just as beautiful as she is talented.

Rather than simply improving Austen's looks, as does O'Rourke, Michael Thomas Ford has Jane herself welcome her transformation in *Jane Bites Back* (2010), a campy vampire-infused send-up of the Austen industry. Ford's Jane, who goes by the surname Fairfax, may be a vampire, but she is also a bookstore owner who has been "forty-one for the past two centuries" and has long given up on making the most of her appearance.[79] In a series of scenes, Jane undergoes a makeover, with results that both impress and move her. She "couldn't believe how she looked" after a new haircut and color; her new hairstyle seems "modern, natural-looking, and perfect, Jane thought."[80] Taught by a young friend how to apply makeup, Jane is "amazed at the transformation her face had undergone. It was still her, just a new and improved her. Best of all, she wasn't all tarted up like some courtesan. … 'I had no idea I could look like this,' she said. Then, to her immense surprise, she began to cry. 'I had no idea,' she said again."[81] Jane's appearance reaches yet another level when she is prepared for a television interview by a professional makeup artist (who, in one of Ford's characteristic gags, confesses to being an ardent admirer of *Mansfield Park*): "Tomboy had transformed her face. Instead of looking tired and stressed out, she looked fresh and alive. 'I can't believe that's me,' she said. 'Thank you.'"[82] In each of these scenes, Ford emphasizes that Jane Austen is still Jane Austen, just better-looking—"modern," "improved," "fresh." By having Jane herself react with gratitude to her updated image, Ford makes the boldest possible claim for his own re-envisioning of Austen. What greater fantasy could be conceived, than that Jane herself would appreciate your own private Austen?

Reinventing Austen

Depictions of Austen in fiction and film offer audiences a choice of ways to imagine not only her looks but also her life experiences. Because Cassandra suppressed the majority of her sister's letters, our knowledge of Austen's personal history is quite limited. We know that she received a proposal of marriage in 1802 from Harris Bigg-Wither, a wealthy family friend a few years her junior, and that she first accepted and then refused him.[83] Rumors and family stories about Austen's other suitors have long circulated, and, after her death, she inspired declarations of love from certain of her male devotees as well.[84] Yet popular interest in Austen as a woman capable of ardent love, and even of sexual desire, is a recent phenomenon.[85] Moving well beyond the historical record and into the realm of fantasy, some writers and filmmakers depict Austen's life as eventful, even adventurous. An Austen who chafes against social constraints and is eager for escapades appeals to present-day audiences who conceive of her as a woman ahead of her time. Finally, these depictions address readers' curiosity about what Austen's writing meant to her and why she decided to publish anonymously—views that, again, are not available in the historical record. Casting realism aside, writers deploy devices including time travel, prophecy, and immortality in order to acquaint Austen with her future success. All of these representations both depend on and gratify fans' wishes to conceive of their beloved author as having been personally satisfied and professionally rewarded.

Old myths of Austen as a prim, repressed spinster with a dull life and no desire for fame were decisively overturned in 1996 with the publication of Stephanie Barron's first "Jane Austen mystery."[86] Developed over eleven volumes (to date), Barron's treatment of Austen is the most extensive contemporary portrayal of the author as a character.[87] Adventurous, courageous, and passionate, this Jane refuses to resign herself to conventional expectations of women's behavior. "That she often felt frustrated by the limited experience and opportunity accorded women is evident in this manuscript and elsewhere," writes Barron in her foreword to the first mystery, in her persona as the supposed editor of Austen's rediscovered personal narratives.[88] Challenged by a Frenchwoman who asks what a woman can do "in a proceeding so determined by men," Jane replies, "I have never been willing to admit that inequality. ... I spend the better part of my life endeavouring to redress it."[89] As a detective must, Barron's Jane observes dead bodies, takes part in investigations, testifies at inquests, and even fires a gun (at a target, not a person). She comes into direct contact with unsavory characters of every description: spies and traitors, courtesans and adulterers, smugglers and actresses. (Barron returns repeatedly to the Napoleonic context that notoriously remains offstage in Austen's published novels.)

Anticipating criticism for her audacity in having Jane solve mysteries and foil crimes, Barron cannily justified her effort by appealing to her readers' knowledge of and devotion to Austen. The same skills that made Austen a fine novelist, Barron contends, suit her to solve mysteries: "Her genius for understanding the motives of others, her eye for detail, and her ear for self-expression—most of all her imaginative ability to see what *might* have been as well as what *was*—were her essential tools in exposing crime."[90] What's more, Barron asserts, Austen would have relished such work: "a woman of her intellectual powers and perception of human nature would enjoy grappling with the puzzle presented by a criminal mind."[91] Lest readers balk at the idea of Austen not only solving but narrating mysteries, Barron alludes on her proprietary website to *Northanger Abbey*'s famous passage defending the genre of the novel and celebrating women authors: Barron declares that "novel-writing, in Austen's day, was regarded as a frivolity, for the simple reason that it depicted life as it was actually lived—and because its primary readers were women. ... Had she lived, Jane would be writing detective novels today."[92]

Barron invents opportunities for her Jane to experience passion as well as adventure. Kissed "full upon the mouth" by a opportunistic man in the first mystery, Jane experiences first "shame" and "mortification" and then, as she states, "a want I cannot admit, even to myself."[93] Jane enjoys a "crushing embrace" and passionate kiss with the object of her affections, a smuggler, in the second mystery.[94] Most lastingly, Jane is attracted to Lord Harold Trowbridge, a spy and adventurer whom Barron calls the "Gentleman Rogue," who dies at the end of Barron's seventh mystery, *Jane and the Ghosts of Netley* (2003). The physical aspect of Jane's and Lord Harold's intimacy Barron develops with restraint, especially in contrast to the romance-novel rhetoric with which she renders Jane's experiences of being kissed in the first two mysteries. All that Jane and Lord Harold share are a few handclasps. During one, "the current in his fingertips was so strong that I trembled," reports Jane;[95] the other is a clutch just before Lord Harold's death. Daringly, Barron appropriates a well-known phrase from one of Austen's letters that refers to her authorship—"if I am a wild beast I cannot help it"—to refer to Jane's passion for Lord Harold.[96]

Unconventional as she is in love and detecting, Barron's Jane does not initially thirst for literary fame. Indeed, Barron depicts Jane as inconsistent and ambivalent in her ambitions for her writing. At the beginning of the mystery series, having just rejected Harris Bigg-Wither's proposal, Jane concentrates on the financial rewards possible through publication: "I must earn some independence," she writes to Cassandra; "better to commerce in literature than in matrimony."[97] Yet later, while composing *Lady Susan*, Jane claims that she "write[s] entirely for [her] own amusement." "My wit," she declares, "will sustain me—the secret sarcasms of my pen, that must subject even the greatest to my power, unbeknownst to themselves."[98] Still later, Jane informs Lord Harold that she "aspire[s] to a career as an authoress," though she also disparages her four completed novels as not "fit to be read beyond the fireside circle."[99] (While Lord Harold encourages Jane—his dying words are "Promise me ... you will *write*"[100]—he does not actually read any of her works.) And even when *Sense and Sensibility* is already in proof, Jane demurs when a friend characterizes her as "an artist"; "I had never considered of myself in such exalted terms," she declares.[101]

Once Barron's Jane has seen her first two novels published, she gains confidence. She enjoys hearing *Sense and Sensibility* and *Pride and Prejudice* praised—indeed, when visiting a circulating library in Brighton, she makes sure to ask "with affected carelessness" about the novels' popularity among subscribers.[102] To her brother Henry, who is eager to bask in her success, she makes a strong claim for the advantages of continuing to conceal her authorship: "Anonymity accords me freedom to speak as I find—and I cherish freedom above all else!"[103] In spite of her determination to express herself, however, Barron's Jane appears less than fully committed to continuing her steady output. In the midst of composing *Mansfield Park*, she welcomes a trip to Brighton that, she states, allows her to escape the company of that novel's heroine: "I cannot *like* my poor Fanny," she confesses, "tho' her scruples are such as must command respect."[104] At least as invested, if not more, in her detective work as her novel writing, Barron's Jane appeals chiefly to fans' desire to imagine that Austen, in spite of her decorous fiction, enjoyed an adventurous life.

In contrast to Barron's Jane, who relishes a secret life as a detective and passionate woman, the heroine of Sally Smith O'Rourke's *The Man Who Loved Jane Austen* (2006) is both sexually curious and inspired as a novelist by her "romantic adventures."[105] After the horse-riding accident that (thanks to a mysterious time travel element) causes Fitzwilliam Darcy's arrival in 1810 Chawton, Jane nurses the handsome, apparently comatose man in her own bed, while fantasizing about this close contact: "conjuring up a wicked vision of Darcy's lean body lying in her bed and imagining the words he might speak if they were lovers in fact."[106] Upon hearing from Darcy about the dating practices common in his (our) own day, Jane asks him, to his amazement, to kiss her as he would his own contemporary. Given one kiss, she asks for "another, if you please," and before long she is plotting, to Darcy's surprise and delight, to spend the night with him before he attempts to reverse his time travel: "a night during which," she thinks, "she would dare to become his lover in the flesh as well as in the spirit."[107] The night does not come to pass, but O'Rourke's Jane takes comfort in knowing that she has been loved—and rewrites *First Impressions* (the early version of *Pride and Prejudice*) to reflect her own recent romance, "impulsively scratching out entire passages, substituting new ones that had the unaffected ring of genuine experience to them, adding one name to the book, over and over again."[108] With the romance she concocts for Jane, O'Rourke answers the hoary question of how an inexperienced spinster could write persuasively about love.

O'Rourke's Jane does, however, retain in one respect the modesty associated with the mythic Austen. While hungry for amatory experience, this Jane shrinks from literary recognition. Nevertheless, O'Rourke gratifies readers' desire to imagine that Austen could somehow have known how significant she would become. Fitzwilliam Darcy desperately tries to convince Jane that he is from the twenty-first century by revealing to her, "one day your name will be known throughout the world and people will be reading your works 200 years from now. Scholars in great universities will devote entire careers to studying them, to studying *you*."[109] Far from being pleased to think about her upcoming success, this Jane is so agitated by Darcy's claim to know the future that she believes him to be "mad."[110] Not his knowledge of her literary career but his digital watch successfully convinces her that he is not from her era.

The biopic *Becoming Jane* (2007), which reached a much larger audience than O'Rourke's novel, also characterizes Austen as taking the sexual initiative and putting her experiences to literary use.[111] After kissing Tom Lefroy, Jane asks him, "Did I do that well? … I wanted, just once, to do it well." As her romance with Tom progresses, we see Jane feverishly composing *First Impressions*, apparently newly inspired by her own feelings and sensations. Overall, the film suggests, as does O'Rourke's novel, that only a woman who knew what it was like to be passionately in love could have created such appealing courtships for her characters.[112] We have Tom Lefroy to thank, *Becoming Jane* implies, for

Austen's development from a merely "accomplished" writer into one whose
works have enduring appeal.

Yet *Becoming Jane* does depict Austen as more ambitious and professionally
savvy, and hence more welcoming of recognition, than the heroines of
O'Rourke's or Barron's novels. The film's Jane ventures to believe, to the scorn
of her unsupportive mother, that she could live by her pen. Thrilled to meet
the successful author Mrs. Radcliffe, Jane evidently takes to heart the older
woman's cautions on the difficulty of balancing marriage with work. The film's
final scene shows Jane seated among her fans, foremost among them her young
namesake, Tom Lefroy's daughter. Appreciation from an enthusiastic reader of
the younger generation stands in here for wider literary, or popular, acclaim.
Evidently welcoming the girl's admiration, Jane agrees to read aloud from *Pride
and Prejudice* in spite of her brother Henry's effort to shield her identity by
declaring that she wishes to remain anonymous.

Like its recent predecessors on screen and in fiction, *Miss Austen Regrets*
(2008) depicts Jane as keenly interested in love, continuing to form crushes
even as she painfully confronts their lack of reciprocation. The love that chiefly
sustains Jane in this film, however, is not passionate but sisterly, as I will discuss
in the final section of this chapter. *Miss Austen Regrets* breaks significant new
ground in portraying Jane, attractions and attractiveness aside, as a dedicated
author who thirsts for recognition in a society that does not reward women's
ambition. Her brother Edward, while encouraging of her writing in general,
displays discomfort with her desire to change publishers for *Emma* in the hope
of greater profits. "Dear Lord, I do wish you wouldn't think of it as writing for
money," he tells her. "Try to imagine how it reflects on us, your brothers, to
have an unmarried sister seeking employment." In a later scene, Jane proudly
presents a newly published copy of *Emma* to her niece Anna, whose infant
daughter she has just met. "Reading?" responds Jane's mother. "You won't have
time for that sort of childishness now, Anna." Hurt by this lack of interest, Jane
is doubly insulted, after failing to soothe the baby, to hear her mother describe
her as "hardly like a woman at all."

Yet approbation does come to Jane in *Miss Austen Regrets*, from an unexpected
source. Madame Bigeon, the housekeeper of Henry Austen's London house,
tells Jane that *Sense and Sensibility* (in translation) has been well received in
France and that women readers in particular are finding it very meaningful.
"Every woman, spinster or wife, every woman has regrets. So we read about your
heroines and feel young again, and in love, and full of hope, as if we can make
that choice again," Mme Bigeon declares to Jane, with great intensity. "This
is the gift which God has given you. It is enough, I think."[113] Mme Bigeon's
proclamation comes as a welcome contrast to the tendency of Jane's own family
to discount her achievement. Furthermore, reference to the 1815 publication
of Isabelle de Montolieu's French translation of *Sense and Sensibility* allows the
film's screenwriter, Gwyneth Hughes, to suggest without recourse to time travel
or prophecy how Austen's success with readers is beginning to build.[114]

While all of these period novels and films stop short of depicting Jane as fully bent on achieving literary fame, the authors of two recent novels that transport versions of her to later centuries invite readers to consider the possibility that she was just as ambitious as present-day writers. The twenty-first-century vampire Jane of Michael Thomas Ford's gleeful romp *Jane Bites Back* (2010) burns with outrage that she hasn't "seen a royalty check in almost two hundred years" while, all around her, opportunistic writers seize a "piece of the Austen pie."[115] Thrilled to have published a new novel, titled *Constance*, after two centuries of rejection letters, Ford's Jane enjoys all the fruits of present-day literary success, including a #1 listing on the *New York Times* bestseller list and the profitable sale of film rights. Even as Ford entertains readers with an unapologetically ridiculous plot, his depiction of Austen as longing for proper recognition registers more seriously.

In a very different literary mode, the acclaimed English novelist Ian McEwan portrays an aspiring girl writer in *Atonement* (2001) whose efforts and attitudes resemble those of the young Austen. McEwan's choice of an epigraph from *Northanger Abbey* alerts readers to possible parallels with Austen's novels, and indeed his heroine Briony Tallis is recognizable in some ways as a reinvention of *Northanger Abbey*'s heroine Catherine Morland. On another level, however, McEwan's depiction of a young writer's precocious concern with literary achievement and the trappings of professionalism is decidedly reminiscent of Austen herself.[116]

Like the young Austen, who evidently took delight in imagining her future fame when creating the dedications to her juvenilia, Briony indulges fantasies of being admired one day as an author rivaling those in her family's library. "My younger sister, Briony Tallis the writer, you must surely have heard of her," she imagines her brother one day "boasting" to his friends.[117] Briony prepares for her future vocation and fame not only by writing and daydreaming but also by rendering her stories in a polished, publication-like form: she would "punch holes in the margins, bind the chapters with pieces of string, [and] paint or draw the cover" before taking each one "to show to her mother, or her father, when he was home."[118] Such care with imitating the appearance of published works recalls the efforts made by the young Austen in the manuscript volumes of her juvenilia, where she divided even short tales into chapters and included tables of contents as well as dedications.[119] (As I mentioned in Chapter 4, Austen's "Volume the Third" is on display at the British Library.)

An especially poignant appeal to lovers of Austen emerges at the end of McEwan's novel, when Briony—by now a renowned author of fiction who is celebrating her 77th birthday—watches her youngest family members present the play she wrote as a girl in Chapter 1 of *Atonement*. Sitting among her extended family, Briony enjoys receiving tribute for her successful career as a novelist and relishes as well the reminder of how much talent and determination she possessed in her early teens. Given the parallels McEwan has already implied between Briony and Austen as child writers, this final scene invites readers to cherish the fantasy that Austen, too, had had the opportunity for a long and productive life, and for satisfying public recognition. By creating a character reminiscent of Austen, yet distinct from her, McEwan allows readers the liberty to imagine for themselves what Austen might have thought, both in girlhood and maturity, about her writing.[120]

Relating to Austen

Curiosity about the person behind the author lies at the heart of an amateur reader's endeavor to forge a personal connection with Austen in spite of temporal, and often geographical, distance. While all fictional portrayals of Austen gratify this curiosity, some intensify a reader's sense of access to her by having Jane herself narrate, as in Barron's mysteries and Hannon's *Dear Jane Austen*.[121] Another method of increasing a reader's perception of intimacy with Austen is to depict a character who enjoys a special closeness with her, either as a dear friend or—most familiar of all—her sister. Mary Ann O'Farrell has argued that "to wonder what Jane Austen really was like is speculatively and tentatively to initiate the structure of identification and complementarity and difference that is friendship. Would she have liked me? Was she like me? Would she have challenged me or scared me? Shopped with me? Found me too much? Would I have liked those things? Is it possible she was writing to me?"[122] Fictional depictions of friendship or sisterhood with Austen directly address the questions that, according to O'Farrell, lie at the heart of an amateur reader's emotionally charged effort to feel closer to Austen.

The heroine of Amanda Elyot's novel *By A Lady: Being the Adventures of an Enlightened American in Jane Austen's England* (2006), for instance, is delighted to find that yes, in fact, Jane Austen *does* like her, *is* like her, and *will* shop with her. Having time-traveled to 1801 Bath, C. J. (short for Cassandra Jane) Welles meets Jane through a mutual acquaintance. Not only is Austen C. J.'s literary "idol," but, until her time travel, C. J. has been portraying the author in a play titled *By a Lady*.[123] Thrilled to meet Jane, C. J. enjoys gossip with her at a ball, promenades with her on a fine day, and chooses bonnets with her. Jane becomes, in essence, C. J.'s girlfriend—in the sense, of course, of a friend with whom one chats and goes shopping, not a lesbian partner. For C. J., spending time with Jane is "the fulfillment of one of her lifelong fantasies."[124]

In return for the pleasure of Jane's company, C. J. contributes to her friend's writing by offering both inspiration and practical help. Alone among the Bath characters, C. J. is aware "that Miss Austen's secret passion for 'scribbling' would one day place her in the pantheon of English novelists"—that is, if Jane can "overcome the writer's block that had plagued her since her family had been compelled to retrench."[125] In a rare dip into Jane's point of view, Elyot reveals that she "had found nothing to recommend Bath until she had made the acquaintance of Miss Welles. Perhaps now she might begin to regain her passion for storytelling."[126] C. J.'s friendship does indeed reignite Jane's creativity, and Elyot contrives as well a circumstance in which her time-traveling heroine has the opportunity actually to rescue Jane. When Jane is accused of shoplifting, C. J. bails her out not only because of friendship but out of concern for Jane's literary career: "if she were adjudged guilty," C. J. thinks, "the Jane Austen that the world would come to consider one of the greatest chroniclers of her age would never be born."[127] O'Farrell suggests that Austen fans wonder, "is it possible she was writing to me?"[128] Elyot purveys an even more potent fantasy: that Austen wrote *because* of you.

Likewise, films and novels that depict the relationship between the Austen sisters allow fans to imagine themselves in Cassandra's role, supporting Jane both personally and professionally. Both of the two recent Austen biopics highlight the emotional connection between Cassandra and Jane, who are in their 20s in *Becoming Jane* and late 30s/early 40s in *Miss Austen Regrets*.[129] These scenes of sisterly intimacy occupy comparatively little screen time, in contrast to each film's treatment of romantic episodes in Jane's life. Nevertheless, the actresses in both films portray with intensity the mutual devotion and reliance of the Austen sisters.

Becoming Jane stresses sisterly intimacy by depicting, on several occasions, Cassandra and Jane sharing a bed. Most poignantly, Jane (played by Anne Hathaway) holds the sleeping Cassandra (Anna Maxwell Martin) shortly after the scene in which Cassandra sobs out her grief at the death of her fiancé. After Jane rises to write, leaving her sister alone in bed, Cassandra, still lying down and looking very somber, asks Jane what she is writing. As Jane explains ("It is the tale of a young woman—two young women—better than their circumstances"), we see Cassandra beginning to smile, then to sit up. As she and Jane converse, evidently about *First Impressions*, they gaze intently at each other until Jane, in response to a question from Cassandra, declares that her fictional sisters will "both make triumphant happy endings. ... to very rich men."[130] At that point Cassandra laughs wryly, and Jane looks at her and then away. Both women are aware, evidently, of the gulf between their own recent experiences of love and those taking place in Jane's novel in progress. The scene conveys to viewers Cassandra's interest in Jane's writing, as well as the power of that writing to distract both women, at least temporarily, from their own disappointments and anguish.

In a later bedroom scene, we see Cassandra lying in bed, as before, while Jane, fully dressed, organizes her belongings for departure on her elopement with Tom Lefroy. Cassandra reproaches Jane: "You'll lose everything—family, place ... for what? A lifetime of drudgery on a pittance? [She pushes off the bedcovers, as if to stand up.] A child every year, no means to lighten the load. [She stands.] How will you write, Jane?"[131] Thanks to the force with which Anna Maxwell Martin delivers these lines, Cassandra's warning lingers, even though the scene ends with her giving Jane her own money and pearls to help with the intended marriage.

With one significant exception, which occurs close to the end of Jane's life, *Miss Austen Regrets* depicts the Austen sisters' closeness as emotional rather than corporeal. In contrast to *Becoming Jane*, Cassandra and Jane are separated for most of *Miss Austen Regrets*: while Cassandra remains at Chawton Cottage, often glimpsed taking care of domestic chores, Jane travels repeatedly to her brother Edward Knight's estate at Godmersham, in Kent, and also spends time in London. There, at Henry Austen's house, we see Jane chatting in bed with her niece Fanny Knight, who is portrayed by Imogen Poot as a starry-eyed, giddy young girl bent on love and marriage.

Though Cassandra and Jane share little screen time in *Miss Austen Regrets*, this film does establish that Cassandra not only appreciates Jane's writing, as in *Becoming Jane*, but actively facilitates it. Three brief scenes underline these acts of Cassandra's, as well as highlighting the two sisters' very different daily tasks. In the first, Jane reads a passage from *Persuasion* to Cassandra, who weeps over it while gutting a chicken. "I don't know how you can sit there with dry eyes," says Cassandra (played by Greta Scacchi). "I never weep over anything that might make me some money," replies Jane (Olivia Williams), with a glint in her eye.[132] In the second, Jane works on her manuscript of *Persuasion* while Cassandra comes in to set the table. Shortly after that, in the aftermath of an insult to Jane from Mrs. Austen (who calls her younger daughter "hardly a woman at all"), Cassandra assures Jane that she is "happy too." "Stuck here, looking after Mother, and me?" presses Jane. "Well, someone has to do it," Cassandra replies, apparently without any rancor.

Two more extended and emotionally intense scenes in *Miss Austen Regrets* explore Cassandra's role with respect to Jane's authorship. In the film's final scene, which takes place in 1820, Cassandra speaks the sentiments of grief from the real Cassandra Austen's letter about her sister's death—"She was the sun of my life, the gilder of every pleasure, the soother of every sorrow"[133]—while, to the outrage of the just-married Fanny Knight, pushing Jane's letters into the fire. "You still believe there's a secret love story to uncover?" Cassandra asks Fanny, with gentle but unmistakable mockery. Here, as throughout this film, Fanny's interest in the romantic episodes of her aunt Jane's life stands in for the curiosity of present-day audiences more generally. Accordingly, Scacchi's Cassandra rebukes any viewer whose thoughts, upon seeing Jane's letters destroyed, fly to the possibility of lost romantic secrets rather than lost insights into her creative process.

Miss Austen Regrets takes a more audacious step by indicating that Jane's writing career has been made possible, unintentionally, by Cassandra's influence upon the outcome of Harris Bigg-Wither's proposal of marriage to Jane in 1802.[134] This intervention of Cassandra's, which is wholly invented for the film, is briefly evident in the rushed opening sequence, when Cassandra, serious-faced, asks her sister "Are you sure?" while the Bigg sisters are visibly thrilled at Jane's initial acceptance. Just a few minutes before the film's conclusion, Cassandra returns, self-reproachfully, to this episode, while bathing the very ill Jane:

Cassandra: It's all my fault. If I'd stayed silent—if I hadn't persuaded you—if I hadn't nagged and nagged you to change your mind—I made you refuse him.

Jane: You made me see the choice for what it was.

Cassandra: Because of me, you chose loneliness and poverty.

Jane: Because of you, I chose freedom.

Cassandra: I didn't do it for you, Jane.

Jane: I know.

Cassandra [weeping]: I'm so ashamed.

Jane [reaching out]: Cassy.

[Fanny, who has been watching through the open door, turns away as the sisters embrace.]

Jane: Everything that I am, and everything that I have achieved, I owe to you, and to the life we have made here. To the love that we have together. This life I have? It's what I needed. It's what God intended for me. I'm *so* much happier than I thought I'd be. *So* much happier!—than I deserve to be.[135]

Throughout *Miss Austen Regrets*, Jane has flirted gleefully and sometimes also passionately with a range of men, commented appreciatively on their handsomeness, and reacted with disappointment and pain when her interest is not returned. On no other occasion in this film, however, does Jane give voice to sentiments remotely comparable to these. The primary relationship of Jane's life was with Cassandra, this film firmly declares, and it is she whom we have to thank for Jane's literary achievement.

Jill Pitkeathley's *Cassandra & Jane: A Jane Austen Novel* (2004) stands out among recent fictional depictions of the Austen sisters in the author's effort to convey Cassandra's distinct point of view and to invest her with a fully realized character.[136] Pitkeathley's psychological treatment of sisterhood was informed, as she explains in an appendix, by her own profession: "Trained as a counsellor myself, I am used to casting light on people's character through their relationships with others. For Jane Austen, there was no closer relationship than that with her elder sister, Cassandra."[137] Indeed, *Cassandra & Jane* explores new ground in two ways. First, Pitkeathley depicts the emotional relationship between the Austen sisters as fraught rather than idealized. Secondly, she explores Cassandra's role as the guardian of Jane's reputation and literary legacy.[138]

Pitkeathley's Cassandra candidly admits throughout her narration her own feelings and motives, even those that shame her. She has decided to burn many of Jane's letters for both their sakes, she explains, because "the world must see ours as the perfect sister relationship, always loving, always tranquil."[139] Cassandra tells the reader that the inscription on Jane's grave in Winchester Cathedral, which notoriously omits any reference to her authorship, represents "how I want her to be remembered."[140] Pitkeathley's Cassandra even wants to suppress the manuscript of *The Watsons* (a novel left unfinished by Austen) because she feels "afraid of what would be made of my feelings for Jane and hers for me if this part work were ever to be published."[141] By the end of Cassandra's narrative, she has worked through her feelings towards her sister to the extent that she can recognize that Jane "would have laughed at" their brother Henry's "Biographical Notice" of her, and that the idealized woman presented there "was not Jane, of course, but Henry understood that this was how she was to be remembered."[142]

Her insecurities and concern with propriety aside, Pitkeathley's Cassandra is exceptional too in the extent of her involvement in—not just support of—her sister's writing. Cassandra initially lacks confidence in her own literary opinions, although Jane assures her that "if you do not like what I write, I can be sure that no one else would judge it worthy, however clever I might think it."[143] Pitkeathley's Jane buoys Cassandra, too, by praising her own efforts: "She was always telling me what a brilliant artist I was," Cassandra recalls, "when in fact I have, and always had, a small talent."[144] Later, Cassandra assists more actively with Jane's composition, noting proudly that she "was able to help her [Jane] a good deal" with the revision of *Elinor and Marianne* (the first version of *Sense and Sensibility*) by thinking through structural changes as well as by copying out "the parts she was to keep."[145] The sisters' private time comes to include brainstorming sessions—"We talked about her writings, what she might include, characters she might draw ..."—and discussions of possible titles, including a conversation in which Cassandra helps Jane settle on "Persuasion."[146] In interactions like these, Pitkeathley takes to a new level the intimacy between the Austen sisters. Her characters do not proclaim their love for each other, as does Jane in *Miss Austen Regrets*. Nor do Pitkeathley's sisters demonstrate their physical intimacy, as do the bed-sharing sisters in *Becoming Jane*. Rather, this Cassandra and Jane enjoy a form of creative interconnection, by which Pitkeathley invites us to consider Cassandra as a direct contributor to, not just a facilitator or encourager of, Austen's great work.[147]

I noted earlier that the curious, romantically inclined young Fanny Knight portrayed in *Miss Austen Regrets* represents the twenty-first-century audience member who is more interested in Austen's loves than her novels. (Of course, *Miss Austen Regrets*, like all fictionalized treatments of Austen's life, indulges this interest even while reproving it.) In another sense, too, each imagined version of Cassandra serves as a stand-in for the present-day Austen fan. As Cassandra reassures Jane of her talent or of the rightness of her decision not to marry, fans comfort themselves with believing that Austen was pleased with her life. As Cassandra makes possible Jane's writing time or (at least in Pitkeathley's version) exchanges ideas with Jane, fans indulge in the fantasy that they could somehow have contributed to the production of her works. Finally, as Cassandra and Jane confirm their mutual affection, fans offer up their own devotion to Austen and dream that it is requited.

In each of these works, Jane's behavior also addresses the desires of Austen fans. When Pitkeathley's Jane praises her sister's smaller talent, the reader too feels approved of by Austen. At the end of *Miss Austen Regrets*, not only Cassandra but also the viewer is relieved to hear Jane proclaim that she is "*so much happier than I thought I'd be. So much happier!—than I deserve to be.*" When Jane thanks Cassandra—or in some cases forgives her—for her advice and intervention, so too do fans thank or forgive the historical Cassandra Austen for her role in curtailing access to her sister's life.

Each fictional or cinematic portrayal of Austen both takes for granted and assuages amateur readers' longing to feel personally connected to their beloved author. And, as has always been the case, popular depictions of Austen confirm readers' tendency to project onto her their own hopes and beliefs, however anachronistically. Portrayals of beautiful, adventurous, or ambitious Janes thoroughly reinvent the myths that persisted about Austen until the era of her current popularity. These efforts to conceive of a liberated Austen can be interpreted as a wish to reward her in the realm of imagination for her own ingenuity in creating, out of comparatively limited materials, fiction of enduring interest. As Austen's readership continues to broaden, we can expect to see yet more versions of her, each of which represents, in Karen Joy Fowler's words, someone's "private Austen"[148]—and which may succeed, too, in embodying at least some aspects of the "private Austen" cherished by the reader or viewer.

Like representations of Austen herself, reworkings of her novels also reflect the interests and wishes of contemporary fans. The next chapter examines reinventions of Austen's writings that aim to bring her world closer to the worlds inhabited, imaginatively or actually, by particular groups of present-day American readers.

Notes

1 Karen Joy Fowler, *The Jane Austen Book Club* (New York: G. P. Putnam's Sons, 2004), 1.
2 Ibid., 2.
3 Ibid., 4.
4 Ibid., 288.
5 Emily Auerbach sums up critical commentary on Cassandra's portrait and offers her own appreciative view of it in *Searching for Jane Austen* (Madison: University of Wisconsin Press, 2004), 19.
6 Fowler, *Jane Austen Book Club*, 233. What Fowler's characters find most rewarding to discuss—and what, thanks to her creativity, their own histories reflect and refract—is Austen's novels, not their own perceptions of her as a woman. An exception is the character Prudie's dream of an elegant present-day Jane—"blond, neat, modern. Her pants are silk and have wide legs"—who helps dispose, psychologically at least, of Prudie's own difficult mother. Ibid., 115.
7 *Becoming Jane*, directed by Julian Jarrold, screenplay by Sarah Williams and Kevin Hood (2007; Burbank, CA: Buena Vista Home Entertainment, 2008), DVD. This film was most directly influenced by Jon Spence's biography *Becoming Jane Austen* (London: Hambledon and London, 2003).
8 A recent American musical-theater version of *Pride and Prejudice* places Jane Austen onstage with her characters, where she comments on the composition of the novel; her first song is titled "The Creaking Door." Lindsay Warren Baker and Amanda Jacobs, *Jane*

Austen's Pride & Prejudice: A Musical, premiered 2006 at the Ohio Light Opera (Wooster, OH), workshop performance in New York City, February 26, 2007. Patricia Rozema's 1999 film adaptation of *Mansfield Park* notoriously assigns many of Austen's own observations—and indeed writings—to Fanny Price; in my view, this strategy has the effect of reinterpreting Fanny, not Austen. *Mansfield Park*, written and directed by Patricia Rozema (1999; Burbank, CA: Buena Vista Home Entertainment, 2000).

9 Rachel M. Brownstein in particular has criticized the tendency of today's popular authors to create fiction about Austen that Austen herself would never have written. *Why Jane Austen?* (New York: Columbia University Press, 2011). John Wiltshire reminds scholars that we too have been guilty of creating Austen in our own respective images, as "sassy, spunky, postcolonial, radical, transgressive, sexually complex and ambiguous." *Recreating Jane Austen* (Cambridge: Cambridge University Press, 2001), 8.

10 For a facsimile of the title page of the first edition of *Sense and Sensibility*, see David Gilson, *A Bibliography of Jane Austen*, new ed. (Winchester: St. Paul's, 1997), 13.

11 Ibid., 31.

12 *Emma* does contain a dedication, to the Prince Regent, but nothing is revealed about the novel's author except that she considers herself, in this context, to be "His Royal Highness's dutiful and obedient humble servant." Jane Austen, *Emma*, ed. Richard Cronin and Dorothy McMillan (Cambridge: Cambridge University Press, 2005), lxxx.

13 See Chapter 4, footnote 45. The difference between Austen's gleeful comments about authorship and fame in her juvenilia and her public reticence as an adult published novelist has been much commented upon by biographers and critics.

14 Gilson, *Bibliography*, 470–71.

15 Regarding Austen's attitudes towards authorship, Henry declared that "she became an authoress entirely from taste and inclination. Neither the hope of fame nor profit mixed with her early motives. ... So much did she shrink from notoriety, that no accumulation of fame would have induced her, had she lived, to affix her name to any productions of her pen." The "Notice" concludes with Henry's firm statement that his sister's "opinions accorded strictly with those of our Established Church." Henry Austen, "Biographical Notice of the Author" (1817), repr. in Jane Austen, *Persuasion*, ed. Janet Todd and Antje Blank (Cambridge: Cambridge University Press, 2006), 329, 331.

16 Ibid., 328.

17 Caroline Austen, *My Aunt Jane Austen: A Memoir* (1867), repr. in J. E. Austen-Leigh, *A Memoir of Jane Austen and Other Family Recollections*, ed. Kathryn Sutherland (Oxford: Oxford University Press, 2002), 169; emphasis original.

18 Kathryn Sutherland, *Jane Austen's Textual Lives: From Aeschylus to Bollywood* (Cambridge: Cambridge University Press, 2005), 79. Sutherland has fully investigated and persuasively asserted the importance to Austen's reception history of the writings of her nieces and nephews, including unpublished family memoirs.

19 Sutherland, *Jane Austen's Textual Lives*, 77.

20 Ibid., 78–79.

21 Ibid., 59. See also Terry Castle's observation that "it is impossible for the lover of Jane Austen—and lover is the operative word here—to have anything but mixed feelings about Austen's older sister, Cassandra." "Was Jane Austen Gay?," in *Boss Ladies, Watch Out!: Essays on Women, Sex, and Writing* (New York: Routledge, 2002), 125.

22 Wiltshire, *Recreating Jane Austen*, 15.

23 Sutherland, *Jane Austen's Textual Lives*, 62.

24 Wiltshire, *Recreating Jane Austen*, 17, 25.

25 Sutherland, *Jane Austen's Textual Lives*, 59.

26 Wiltshire, *Recreating Jane Austen*, 15.

27 Ibid., 16.

28 Sutherland, *Jane Austen's Textual Lives*, 58.

29 Valerie Grosvenor Myer, *Jane Austen: Obstinate Heart: A Biography* (New York: Arcade, 1997).

30 Mary Ann O'Farrell, "Jane Austen's Friendship," in *Janeites: Austen's Disciples and Devotees*, ed. Deidre Lynch (Princeton: Princeton University Press, 2000), 45.

31 Sutherland, *Jane Austen's Textual Lives*, 60.

32 Ibid., 109–110.

33 Wiltshire, *Recreating Jane Austen*, 27–28.

34 "One of the foundational axioms of the popular aesthetic is the continuity of biography and art. It is beside the point, then, to chastise popular representations of Shakespeare for their myriad and often willful factual inaccuracies, for they are less concerned with historical fidelity than with the ideological work of servicing, extending, reorienting, and at the same time drawing upon Shakespeare's inherited cultural authority, one of pop culture's most valuable resources." Douglas Lanier, "Shakespeare™: Myth and Biographical Fiction," in *The Cambridge Companion to Shakespeare and Popular Culture*, ed. Robert Shaughnessy (Cambridge: Cambridge University Press, 2007), 112.

35 Barbara M. Benedict, "Sensibility by the Numbers: Austen's Work as Regency Popular Fiction," in *Janeites*, ed. Lynch, 64.

36 Judy Simons, "Jane Austen and Popular Culture," in *A Companion to Jane Austen*, ed. Claudia L. Johnson and Clara Tuite (Oxford: Wiley-Blackwell, 2009), 472.

37 Sutherland, *Jane Austen's Textual Lives*, 110.

38 Margaret Kirkham, "Portraits," in *Jane Austen in Context*, ed. Janet Todd (Cambridge: Cambridge University Press, 2005), 68. Kirkham provides full descriptions and histories of all likenesses of Jane Austen and unauthenticated images associated with her, including the so-called "Rice Portrait" of a young girl and a profile silhouette titled "L'aimable Jane."

39 Ibid., 69.

40 The image selected by Brabourne is a rendering of the disputed "Rice portrait." Auerbach, *Searching*, 20–21.

41 Sutherland describes Cassandra's portrait as a "crude pencil and watercolour likeness" that is "sharp-faced, pursed-lipped, unsmiling, scornful even, and withdrawn." *Jane Austen's Textual Lives*, 112. Emily Auerbach points out that a process of "softening appears over and over again in the presentation of women writers"; she compares Austen's history in portraiture to that of Emily Dickinson in particular. *Searching*, 23.

42 Sutherland, *Jane Austen's Textual Lives*, 110–111.

43 Jane Austen to James Edward Austen, December 16–17, 1816, *Jane Austen's Letters*, ed. Deirdre Le Faye, new ed. (1995; repr., Oxford University Press, 1997), 323.

44 Sutherland, *Jane Austen's Textual Lives*, 115.

45 Ibid. Another striking example of an amateurish-looking likeness in the National Portrait Gallery is Branwell Brontë's group portrait of his three sisters.

46 On drawing as a feminine accomplishment in Austen's time, see Ann Bermingham, *Learning to Draw: Studies in the Cultural History of a Polite and Useful Art* (New Haven: Yale University Press, 2000).

47 For an account of how Cassandra's portrait was previously displayed by the National Portrait Gallery, see Rachel M. Brownstein, *Why Jane Austen?* (New York: Columbia University Press, 2011), Chapter 2.

48 Percy H. Muir to Alberta Burke, June 8, 1948, Alberta H. and Henry G. Burke Papers and Jane Austen Research Collection, MS 0020, container 8, folder 7, Special Collections and Archives, Goucher College Library (hereafter cited as Burke Collection).

49 Alberta Burke to Percy H. Muir, June 23, 1948, Burke Collection, container 8, folder 9. Nearly thirty years later, after Alberta's death, her husband Henry recalled in a letter to the Austen bibliographer David Gilson that Cassandra's sketch "did not fetch a very high price at Sotheby's and I doubt whether the National Portrait Gallery would have gone much higher if we had been bidding. I felt, however, that this was one item that we should not pursue." Henry Burke to David J. Gilson, December 17, 1975, Burke Collection, container 2, folder 8.

50 See Chapter 4 for a discussion of the Jane Austen Centre in the context of Austen-inspired literary tourism.

51 Melissa Dring, "A New Portrait of Jane Austen," *Jane Austen's Regency World* 1 (2003): 5. Sutherland points out that press coverage for the Dring portrait claimed it, misleadingly, as "*the* definitive portrait of Jane Austen." *Jane Austen's Textual Lives*, 117; emphasis original. Margaret Kirkham judges the Dring portrait "bizarre." "Portraits," 76.

52 Dring, "New Portrait," 6.

53 Ibid., 9.
54 Ibid., 8.
55 Isabel Bishop, "The examination of all the letters which Jane had written to her," The Pierpont Morgan Library Department of Drawings and Prints, 1979.32:15. Information on the original commission of the drawing is included in the Morgan's catalog entry for the drawing, accessible from http://corsair.themorgan.org/.
56 Martin Amis, "Jane's World," *New Yorker,* January 8, 1996, 31.
57 Nigel Boonham, who contributed an Austen sculpture to the exhibit and who edited the exhibit catalogue, notes that "the majority of people who visit Winchester Cathedral are there to see Jane's grave! So much so that when we were setting up the exhibition I tried to get a least 4 sculptors to make a portrait head of her, so there would be 4 different interpretations!" E-mail message to author, February 10, 2011.
58 See Chapter 4 for my discussion of the "Jane Austen Story" exhibit that opened in Winchester Cathedral in April 2010.
59 In the entry for Nathan's work in the Society of Portrait Sculptors' catalog for the exhibition, he states that "Jane's severe little mouth is a difficult and rather incongruous feature until one speculates that her father seems to have lost his upper front teeth and that Jane, portrayed by the sincere but less flattering efforts of her sister, could by that time have been suffering from a similar disadvantage. If that was so, it may suggest reluctance on Jane's part to sit for portraits and explain why a definitive likeness is not available to us." *In This Sacred Place* (n.p., 2010), 46. "I am aware that my portrait of Jane does look sombre," Nathan commented in response to reading my description of it. "I am afraid it was the result of having too little time to do as I had originally intended, which was to explore an acceptable structural base and try various permutations from which I would then develop a much lighter and more amusing image. ... I have it in mind to make further attempts at a Jane Austen portrayal." Letter to author, March 10, 2011.
60 Boonham identifies the sculpture as twice life size, .67 m, in his catalog entry. *In This Sacred Place*, 18. Boonham has since cast the first of an edition of the sculpture in bronze. E-mail message to author, February 10, 2011.
61 *In This Sacred Place*, 18.
62 Intensifying the association of Austen with sainthood, Boonham's three other works exhibited at the Cathedral at the same time depicted Christ (two versions) and Mary Magdalene.
63 *In This Sacred Place*, 18. Boonham describes himself as a "latecomer to the delights of the Austen books" who has since "unequivocally joined the horde of fans, made pilgrimage to Chawton and read biographies of Jane." Ibid. Boonham mentions too that an early mentor of his was the Austen bibliographer Geoffrey Keynes, who he thinks "would be thrilled that I had made a portrait of Jane, particularly because of the Stanley Spencer influence, whom he knew!" E-mail message to author, August 30, 2010. See Chapter 2 for discussion of Keynes's *Bibliography of Jane Austen* and its influence on the American collectors Alberta and Henry Burke.
64 *In This Sacred Place*, 18.
65 *Pride & Prejudice*, directed by Joe Wright, screenplay by Deborah Moggach (2005; Universal City, CA: Universal Studios, 2006), DVD.
66 In a very entertaining plenary talk for the Annual General Meeting of the Jane Austen Society of North America, the organization's former president, Joan Klingel Ray, pointed out the similarity in looks between the aged version of Hathaway and portraits of George Eliot. "Jane Austen for Smarties," Chicago, IL, October 2008.
67 *Miss Austen Regrets*, directed by Jeremy Lovering, screenplay by Gwyneth Hughes (Burbank, CA: Warner Home Video, 2008), DVD.
68 *Jane Austen's Emma*, directed by Diarmuid Lawrence, screenplay by Andrew Davies (1996; New York: New Video Group, 1999), DVD; *Emma,* written and directed by Douglas McGrath (1996; Burbank, CA: Buena Vista Home Entertainment, 1999), DVD.
69 Stephanie Barron's series began with *Jane and the Unpleasantness at Scargrave Manor: Being the First Jane Austen Mystery* (New York: Bantam, 1996).
70 Stephanie Barron, *Jane and the Genius of the Place: Being the Fourth Jane Austen Mystery* (New York: Bantam, 1999), 130–31; emphasis original. The cover images

chosen by Bantam vary considerably in their representations of Austen, as well as in their degree of accordance with Barron's verbal description of her heroine. Most congruent are Carol Inouye's profile portraits of Jane for the first and second volumes, which present a pleasant-looking, though hardly beautiful, woman—albeit one whose sharp features and exaggeratedly almond eyes bear little resemblance to the face sketched by Cassandra. Particularly egregious are Kinuko Y. Craft's depictions of Jane as a statuesque, curly haired blonde for the covers of Stephanie Barron, *Jane and the Ghosts of Netley: Being a Jane Austen Mystery* (New York: Bantam, 2003) and Stephanie Barron, *Jane and His Lordship's Legacy: Being a Jane Austen Mystery* (New York: Bantam, 2005).

71   "A few years before, Anne Elliot had been a very pretty girl, but her bloom had vanished early," reports the narrator in Volume 1, Chapter 1 of Austen's *Persuasion*. As Anne's happiness increases, so do her good looks: by Volume 2, Chapter 8, "her eyes were bright, and her cheeks glowed,—but she knew nothing about it." Austen, *Persuasion*, ed. Todd and Blank, 6, 201.

72   Patrice Hannon, *Dear Jane Austen: A Heroine's Guide to Life and Love* (2005; repr., New York: Plume, 2007), 115.

73   Fowler, *Jane Austen Book Club*, 233.

74   For a thorough consideration of the conventions of the romance novel, as well as that genre's debts to Austen, see Pamela Regis, *A Natural History of the Romance Novel* (Philadelphia: University of Pennsylvania Press, 2003). Examples of mass-market romance novels that respond to Austen's plots and her present-day popularity include Laurie Brown, *What Would Jane Austen Do?* (Naperville, IL: Sourcebooks Casablanca, 2009); Gwyn Cready, *Seducing Mr. Darcy* (New York: Pocket Books, 2008); and Chamein Canton, *Waiting for Mr. Darcy* (Columbus, MS: Genesis Press, 2009).

75   Sally Smith O'Rourke, *The Man Who Loved Jane Austen* (New York: Kensington, 2006), 124–25. For a more detailed treatment of this novel, see my article "Austen's Adventures in American Popular Fiction, 1996–2006," in "New Directions in Austen Studies," ed. Susan Allen Ford and Gillian Dow, special issue, *Persuasions On-Line* 30.2 (2010), http://www.jasna.org/persuasions/on-line/vol30no2/wells.html.

76   Mr. Darcy tells Caroline Bingley in Volume 1, Chapter 6 of *Pride and Prejudice* that he has been "meditating on the very great pleasure which a pair of fine eyes in the face of a pretty woman can bestow." Jane Austen, *Pride and Prejudice*, ed. Pat Rogers (Cambridge: Cambridge University Press, 2005), 30.

77   O'Rourke, *Man Who Loved*, 132, 163.

78   Ibid., 201.

79   Michael Thomas Ford, *Jane Bites Back* (New York: Ballantine Books, 2010), 17.

80   Ibid., 176, 177.

81   Ibid., 179.

82   Ibid., 201.

83   J. E. Austen-Leigh, *Memoir*, ed. Sutherland, 212.

84   See for instance Auerbach's acerbic commentary on Rudyard Kipling's 1926 poem "Jane's Marriage." *Searching*, 31.

85   The amorous side of Austen's life has been emphasized by biographers including John Halperin, "Jane Austen's Lovers," in *Jane Austen's Lovers and Other Studies in Fiction and History from Austen to Le Carré* (1985; repr., New York: St. Martin's, 1988) and Spence, *Becoming Jane Austen*.

86   For a comprehensive history of myths of the loveless Austen, see Auerbach, *Searching*, Chapter 1. Noteworthy pre-1995 depictions of Austen as a character include two plays—Joan Austen-Leigh's *Our Own Particular Jane* (Victoria: A Room of One's Own Press, 1975) and Howard Fast's *The Novelist: A Romantic Portrait of Jane Austen* (New York: Samuel French, 1992)—and Barbara Ker Wilson's novel *Antipodes Jane: A Novel of Jane Austen in Australia* (New York: Viking, 1985), reprinted as *The Lost Years of Jane Austen* (Berkeley: Ulysses Press, 2009).

87   The eleventh and most recent volume is Stephanie Barron, *Jane and the Canterbury Tale: Being a Jane Austen Mystery* (New York: Bantam, 2011). For a more detailed consideration of Barron's first nine mysteries, see Wells, "Austen's Adventures."

88   Barron, *Jane and the Unpleasantness*, x.

89   Stephanie Barron, *Jane and the Man of the Cloth: Being the Second Jane Austen Mystery* (New York: Bantam, 1997), 210.

90   Barron, *Jane and the Unpleasantness*, xi; emphasis original.

91   Ibid.

92   Stephanie Barron, "Detective Jane Austen," accessed April 28, 2011, http://stephanie-barron.com/books.php. Austen's defense of the novel appears at the end of Volume 1, Chapter 5 of *Northanger Abbey*. Jane Austen, *Northanger Abbey*, ed. Barbara M. Benedict and Deirdre Le Faye (Cambridge: Cambridge University Press, 2006), 30–31. As a contrast to assertions like Barron's that Austen would be just like us were she alive today—or would appreciate our efforts at paying tribute to her in our popular genres—see the comics of the Canadian artist Kate Beaton, who depicts Jane as distinctly irritated by her fans' selective interpretations and fanciful reworkings of her novels. Beaton's comics are archived and searchable at http://www.harkavagrant.com.

93   Barron, *Jane and the Unpleasantness*, 200–201.

94   Barron, *Jane and the Man*, 253.

95   Barron, *Jane and the Ghosts*, 221.

96   Ibid., 106. As transcribed by Deirdre Le Faye, Austen's sentence reads, "If I *am* a wild Beast, I cannot help it." To Cassandra Austen, May 24, 1813, *Jane Austen's Letters*, 212.

97   Barron, *Jane and the Unpleasantness*, 10–11.

98   Barron, *Jane and the Genius*, 196, 130. For a history of the writing and publication of the epistolary novella known as *Lady Susan*, see Jane Austen, *Later Manuscripts*, ed. Janet Todd and Linda Bree (Cambridge: Cambridge University Press, 2009), xlvii–lxiii.

99   Barron, *Jane and the Ghosts*, 87.

100 Ibid., 292; emphasis original.

101 Stephanie Barron, *Jane and the Barque of Frailty: Being a Jane Austen Mystery* (New York: Bantam, 2006), 31.

102 Stephanie Barron, *Jane and the Madness of Lord Byron: Being a Jane Austen Mystery* (New York: Bantam, 2010), 53.

103 Ibid., 62.

104 Ibid., 104; emphasis original.

105 O'Rourke, *Man Who Loved*, 197–98. As one of O'Rourke's present-day characters comments, "every schoolgirl who's ever gotten hooked on P&P secretly suspects that the character [of Darcy] must have been drawn from the author's personal experience." Ibid., 63.

106 Ibid., 198.

107 Ibid., 215, 252.

108 Ibid., 223.

109 Ibid., 202–203; emphasis original.

110 Ibid., 203.

111 All quotations from the screenplay of *Becoming Jane* appear by permission of Miramax and the film's screenwriters Sarah Williams and Kevin Hood. Though adventurous, the heroine of *Becoming Jane* is more a watcher than a doer. She attends a fair full of shocking activities, including a brutal fistfight in which her lover Tom Lefroy is injured. Only when Jane accepts Tom's marriage proposal does she embark on an escapade herself, running with him at dawn through the Hampshire woods to catch a stagecoach. The elopement (which has no basis in fact) comes to an abrupt end when Jane discovers that Tom's family relies on him for financial support and would be disadvantaged by his marriage to a woman without fortune.

112 In depicting Austen as inspired by her romances, both O'Rourke's novel and *Becoming Jane* demonstrate the influence of Spence's biography *Becoming Jane Austen*, which asserts that "Tom Lefroy did not dwindle to insignificance. He found his natural place in her imagination, and he remained there for the rest of her life" (117). Marina Cano López and Rosa María García-Periago point out the extent to which *Becoming Jane* is indebted to the successful biopic *Shakespeare in Love* (1998), which also depicts a canonical author inspired by his personal experience to write about love. "Becoming Shakespeare and Jane Austen in Love: An Intertextual Dialogue between Two Biopics," *Persuasions On-Line* 29.1 (2008), http://www.jasna.org/persuasions/on-line/vol29no1/cano-garcia.html.

113 All quotations from the screenplay of *Miss Austen Regrets* appear by permission of BBC Films and the film's screenwriter Gwyneth Hughes.

114 For discussion of Montolieu's translation, see Isabelle Bour, "The Reception of Jane Austen's Novels in France and Switzerland: The Early Years, 1813–1828," in *The Reception of Jane Austen in Europe*, ed. Anthony Mandal and Brian Southam (London: Continuum, 2007), 21–25. A striking example in recent fiction of a prophecy of Austen's future fame occurs in Syrie James, *The Lost Memoirs of Jane Austen* (New York: Avon, 2008), in which a gipsy palm reader announces that Jane "has a special gift" and "shall be *immortal*," and who urges her to "go work your magic, my lady!. ... Go! Share it with the world!" (270–71; emphasis original).

115 Ford, *Jane Bites Back*, 9.

116 For a fuller consideration of McEwan's response to Austen, see my article "Shades of Austen in Ian McEwan's *Atonement*," *Persuasions* 30 (2008): 101–11.

117 Ian McEwan, *Atonement* (New York: Doubleday, 2001), 4.

118 Ibid., 6.

119 Jan Fergus has argued that by "creating something very like a printed book, but for family circulation, Austen was typically having it both ways: treating her writing both privately, as a family entertainment, and yet seriously, 'publishing' her own collected works." *Jane Austen: A Literary Life* (Houndmills, Basingstoke: Macmillan, 1991), 52–53.

120 Another thought-provoking example of an indirect evocation of Austen, this one in a distinct literary subgenre, is John Kessel's description of Mary Bennet at the conclusion of a story in which that character encounters Victor Frankenstein: "But for a woman whose experience of the world was so slender, and whose soul it seemed had never been touched by any passion, she came at last to be respected for her understanding, her self-possession, and her wise counsel on matters of the heart." "Pride and Prometheus," in *The Baum Plan for Financial Independence and Other Stories* (Easthampton, MA: Small Beer Press, 2008), 315.

121 Jane also narrates in James's *Lost Memoirs of Jane Austen*.

122 O'Farrell, "Jane Austen's Friendship," 45.

123 Amanda Elyot, *By a Lady: Being the Adventures of an Enlightened American in Jane Austen's England* (New York: Three Rivers Press, 2006), 83. Elyot attributes her inspiration for *By a Lady* to the experience of performing (under the name Leslie Carroll) in a 1996 production of Fast's play *The Novelist*. Ibid., v. For a more detailed treatment of *By a Lady*, including attention to Elyot's device of crafting Jane's dialogue from Austen's actual writings, see Wells, "Austen's Adventures."

124 Elyot, *By a Lady*, 152.

125 Ibid., 93, 253.

126 Ibid., 253.

127 Ibid., 256. Readers familiar with the charge of shoplifting leveled in 1799 against Austen's aunt Jane Leigh-Perrot will recognize the source of this episode of Elyot's novel. See Claire Tomalin, *Jane Austen: A Life* (New York: Alfred A. Knopf, 1997), 149–51.

128 O'Farrell, "Jane Austen's Friendship," 45.

129 For analysis of how recent depictions of the Austen sisters have been influenced by portrayals of sisters in screen adaptations of Austen's novels, see my article "The Closeness of Sisters: Imagining Cassandra and Jane," *Persuasions On-Line* 30.1 (2009), http://www.jasna.org/persuasions/on-line/vol30no1/wells.html.

130 *Becoming Jane*.

131 Ibid.

132 *Miss Austen Regrets*.

133 Cassandra Austen to Fanny Knight, July 20, 1817, *Jane Austen's Letters*, 344. As I mentioned in Chapter 4, a facsimile of this letter is displayed at Jane Austen's House Museum in Chawton.

134 Not surprisingly, the Bigg-Wither proposal figures prominently in many biographical fictions. For a short story by an Austen devotee (and former president of the Jane Austen Society of North America) that focuses on this episode, see Elsa A. Solender, "Second Thoughts," in *Dancing with Mr Darcy: Stories Inspired by Jane Austen and Chawton House* (Dinas Powys, Wales: Honno, 2009), 21–29.

135 *Miss Austen Regrets*.

136 See Veronica Bennett, *Cassandra's Sister* (2006; Cambridge, MA: Candlewick, 2007), for a depiction of the relationship between the Austen sisters in their teenage years.

137 Jill Pitkeathley, *Cassandra & Jane: A Jane Austen Novel* (2004; repr., New York: Harper, 2008), 261.

138 For a more detailed treatment of *Cassandra & Jane*, see Wells, "Closeness of Sisters."

139 Pitkeathley, *Cassandra & Jane*, xii.

140 Ibid., xiv. See Chapter 4 for a discussion of Austen memorials at Winchester Cathedral.

141 Pitkeathley, *Cassandra & Jane*, 149.

142 Ibid., 236.

143 Ibid., 29.

144 Ibid., 24.

145 Ibid., 61.

146 Ibid., 83, 208–209. According to the editors of the Cambridge edition, the title *Persuasion* was "probably" chosen by Henry Austen. Austen, *Persuasion*, ed. Todd and Blank, lxxxiii.

147 Pitkeathley's follow-up novel *Dearest Cousin Jane: A Jane Austen Novel* (New York: Harper, 2010), places Eliza de Feuillide, Jane's cousin and eventual sister-in-law, in the role of promoter of Jane's writing.

148 Fowler, *Jane Austen Book Club*, 1.

Chapter 6

American Austen Hybrids:
Sex, Horror/Paranormal, Faith

In the first panel of a comic by Canadian-born artist Kate Beaton, Jane Austen looks horrified while an unseen character announces, "I saw this and I thought of you!". The next panel shows the cover of the book that so disturbs Jane: the title is "Sense and Sensibility and Mr Darcy and Sharks in Space Riding Motorcycles Plus There Is a Time Machine."[1] In another comic, Beaton attacks with comparable vehemence and humor the propensity of present-day audiences to go looking for sex in Austen. "Are you writing another story with Mister Darcy [?]" asks a somewhat vacant-looking fan, leaning over Jane's shoulder as she composes. "NO! This novel is a social commentary," Jane replies, looking angry. "Is it a social commentary about hunky dreamboats [?] ... Is there a makeout scene [?]" persists the fan, until Jane shouts "LEAVE ME ALONE [!]."[2]

With her characteristic wit, Beaton both spoofs and seriously criticizes the recent vogue for adding anachronistic elements to Austen's novels in order to satisfy present-day popular audiences. In the first comic I described, Beaton takes aim at the two bestselling Austen "mash-ups," *Pride and Prejudice and Zombies* (2009) and *Sense and Sensibility and Sea Monsters* (2009), which were "co-authored" by Seth Grahame-Smith and Ben H. Winters, respectively.[3] In the "hunky dreamboats" comic, Beaton's target is broader, encompassing both the tendency of some everyday readers to concentrate exclusively on Austen's love plots and also sexed-up modern versions of Austen's novels, including screen adaptations. The reactions of Beaton's Jane in both comics represent those of any devotee of Austen's writings who feels offended or affronted by contemporary treatments of and approaches to her and her works.

Unique to our era is the impulse to infiltrate Austen's novels with—or, depending on your point of view, open them up to—sex and erotica, as well as horror and paranormal content that is equally out of place in her realistic fictional worlds. On the other end of the cultural spectrum, too, and with significantly less publicity, present-day evangelical Christians have re-envisioned Austen's life and works in terms congruent with their own beliefs. These two efforts to recast Austen result in works that are poles apart, yet the process of creating these hybrids is the same in each case.[4] Elements absent in Austen's writings or kept to a minimum by her are made explicit and expanded to suit the taste of a particular group of present-day readers. Thus aficionados of erotica and the paranormal can enjoy a helping of Austen that incorporates elements of some of their favorite popular genres, while devout Christian readers can integrate their appreciation of Austen with their spiritual practice—and even adopt her as a faithful forebear. As much more extreme reinvents than period sequels to or updated versions of Austen's novels, such hybrid works are especially revealing of what certain present-day amateur readers are willing to do to, and with, Austen.[5]

Austen hybrids are unmistakably an American phenomenon, although individual works, notably *Pride and Prejudice and Zombies*, have reached an enthusiastic international audience. US writers are evidently much less affected than UK ones by reverence for Austen as a cultural figure. And US publishers, in a time of great uncertainty and change in the industry, have demonstrated a readiness to invest in ever more audacious reworkings of the Austen brand.[6]

Individual Austen hybrids differ in their degree of distance from her world and words, as well as in their authors' motives for creation and anticipated audience. Although some hybrids are written by self-professed Austen fans, on the whole these works do not qualify as fan fiction in the conventional sense, since they are not written to please other fans—and, indeed, may repel some who consider themselves devotees of Austen's writings. Nevertheless, theories of fan fiction are useful in helping us to move beyond visceral reactions to the content of these hybrids and to attend instead to the works' aims, effects, and reception. I will begin by singling out recent theories of fan fiction that are especially relevant to hybrid works. Next I will consider how, and with what justification, sex has been imported into Austen's world. The rise in horror and paranormal Austen hybrids, which often carry an erotic charge of their own, is the subject of the next section. I conclude by examining versions of and commentaries on Austen's novels that are directed at Christians and that, in a few cases, reach out to a broader audience as well.

Austen Hybrids and Theories of Fan Fiction

Definitions of fan fiction abound, and do not always coincide. In Chapter 1, I quoted Daria Pimenova's definition of fan fiction as "non-profitable, non-commercial texts based on other fictional texts (series, movies, and books) and written by their fans."[7] Pimenova offers an alternative, more capacious rule of thumb as well: "Fan fiction is what calls itself fan fiction."[8] Most applicable to Austen hybrids is Sheenagh Pugh's broad definition of fan fiction as "writing, whether official or unofficial, paid or unpaid, which makes use of an accepted canon of characters, settings and plots generated by another writer or writers."[9] The inclusiveness of Pugh's definition with respect to genre is also helpful, since not all fan writing inspired by Austen is fiction. Abigail Derecho points out that even creators themselves do not necessarily agree about what constitutes fan fiction; she takes as an example an online thread debating "whether a published book containing bawdy, sexually explicit parodies of Jane Austen's *Pride and Prejudice* can be called fan fiction or not."[10] (I will return to the book in question, *Pride and Promiscuity: The Lost Sex Scenes of Jane Austen* [2001], in the next section.)

Helpful as well for approaching Austen hybrids is Rebecca Tushnet's definition of fan texts from a legal perspective as "a third type of creation, neither pure copies of another author's work nor authorized additions to the original."[11] US courts, Tushnet explains, "find that a legitimate transformation exists when the new work makes overt that which was present in the original text covertly (at least as some readers saw it): transformative fair uses make subtext text. ... The fair use test asks whether the critic has found something in the original or has simply added unrelated content to it. As applied to fan creations, then, the test would find transformation if the new work was far enough from the original, but not too far."[12] Prospective readers of Austen fan fiction, including hybrids, perform their own informal version of a fair use test in order to decide whether or not to invest time and imagination in a certain work. Each reader has his or her own sense of what is "far enough from the original, or not too far" to give pleasure, and makes his or her own judgment of whether the foregrounding of a "covert" element is compelling or off-putting. Tushnet contends too that writers of fan fiction are invested in "making the characters they use recognizable as related to the official versions. ... Fans, like courts analyzing transformative fair uses, see their work as inextricably related to the source texts, bringing meaning out as much as they are putting meaning in."[13] Of course, a certain kind of entertainment can result as well from the juxtaposition of recognizable qualities (e.g. Elizabeth Bennet's outspokenness) with obviously invented ones (e.g. martial arts skills).

Of the subcategories into which scholars have divided fan fiction, the following apply to the Austen hybrids I will examine. The process Henry Jenkins terms "eroticization" governs the invention of sex scenes for Austen's characters.[14] Sex scenes between same-sex characters fall into the subcategory of "slash," which, as Kristina Busse and Karen Hellekson explain, "posit[s] a same-sex relationship, usually one imposed by the author and based on perceived homoerotic subtext."[15] The infusion of paranormal or horror elements is a version of a so-called "AU" or "alternative universe" scenario, in which, as Pugh broadly defines the term, a "fanfic story ... at some point deliberately departs from the canon on which it is based."[16] Jenkins's category of "genre shifting," in which a fan interprets an original text "through the filter of alternative generic traditions," can also apply to horror and paranormal hybrids.[17] How to categorize Christian reworkings of Austen's novels is less straightforward. Readers who are not believers themselves might consider such efforts "alternative universe," while evangelicals might well view such works as illuminating aspects of Austen's writings that secular readers have long overlooked.

Like writers of fan fiction generally, creators of Austen hybrids are inspired—and sometimes emboldened—by the example of others.[18] Daria Pimenova argues persuasively that existing fan fiction not only furnishes later writers with material for reworking but also can inspire new acts of creation. "The acquaintance with fandom and the wish to write in it," Pimenova claims, "as a rule happens through reading other fan fiction and thus through getting an alternative view on an established text. Fan fiction opens the reader's eyes to the possibility of treating the source text in an active way instead of remaining a passive consumer."[19] Similarly, Kate Bowles asserts that "fandom is not mere consumerism—it is the game of cultural production itself."[20] Bowles identifies in debates over the commercialization and quality of Austen fan fiction "a struggle … between fans and fans—literary fans, scholarly fans, television fans."[21] Such struggles are visible too in the often polarized reception of Austen hybrids.

Austen hybrids differ from traditional fan-authored fiction not only in content but also in creators' motives and the experience offered to readers. One of the reasons that Austen hybrids seem so shocking is that, until quite recently, Austen's writings have been treated much more respectfully than other popular works that attract creators of fan fiction.[22] Pugh, writing in 2005, emphasizes the tendency of Austen fan fiction writers to conceive of their productions as tributes to their beloved author and, as a result, to voluntarily limit themselves in reconceiving her works.[23] In contrast, recent creators demonstrate other intentions—to arouse, shock, or (in the case of Christian reworkings) spiritually edify—and as a result enjoy considerable freedom to play with Austen's texts.[24] Douglas Lanier has argued that Shakespeare fan fiction takes place "in a spirit of critique, anarchy, pleasure, recuperation, participation."[25] The same is certainly true of those Austen hybrids that drastically and cheerfully depart from her subject matter and style.

Lanier's analysis of Shakespeare fan fiction is helpful in particular for making sense of the unprecedented role of sex, violence, and the paranormal in recent reworkings of Austen's novels and depictions of her life. Objections are often made to popular adaptations of Shakespeare, Lanier declares, on the grounds that such works "focus on what is titillating, violent, anarchic, banal, or silly and thus undermine the very principles of aesthetic and moral cultivation for which Shakespeare is symbol and vehicle."[26] The very existence of such objections, Lanier implies, indicates the power of fan fiction to challenge cultural assumptions about what is valuable. "Shakespop's wilful violation of taste," he argues, functions "as popular resistance to official, class-coded canons of taste that Shakespeare has come to stand for."[27] Such resistance is certainly evident in the Austen realm, especially in works—most famously *Pride and Prejudice and Zombies* (2009)—that flaunt their creators' identity as anti-fans.[28] Hybrid approaches to Austen can demonstrate, too, fans' delight in bringing together their interest in Austen with their other enthusiasms, e.g. for zombie or vampire stories. As Lanier contends, "fan fiction thrives on popular transgressiveness, the inclusion of sex, romance, violence, humour, anarchy, and surrealism absent from favourite works, and it points to the impulse to force cultural 'master-texts' to address the issues, needs, and pleasures they don't engage."[29] Whether inventing scenes of sex, horror, or churchgoing for Austen and her characters, present-day creators exercise more ingenuity and audacity than ever before in reshaping Austen's works, and in some cases her life as well, to suit their own sensibilities.

Lanier's work on Shakespeare fan fiction also illuminates two very distinct phenomena in Austen hybrids: the rising profile of slash, an element long absent from online Austen fan fiction, and the increasing appeal of Austen to evangelical Christians.[30] "Reassignments of Shakespeare's identity" in terms of sexuality, race, and gender, Lanier contends, "marshal the considerable cultural authority associated with his works to lend legitimacy and dignity to groups historically denigrated. It is for that reason, for example, that the gay popular press has been concerned to claim Shakespeare as one of its own, even though Shakespeare's depictions of sexuality, unconventional though they may be, do not line up well with modern notions of homosexuality."[31] Unlike Shakespeare, Austen as a historical figure has not been claimed by gay authors as one of their own, and she has yet to be portrayed as a lesbian character. The possibility of same-sex desire within her fictional worlds, however, has recently begun to be explored. In a very different register, evangelical Christians' resolve to connect Austen's life and worlds with their own can also be understood as a bid, by members of a culturally marginalized group, for legitimacy and dignity.

Sex

The absence of physical passion in Austen's novels, which accords with her contemporaries' ideas of what lady novelists should represent, has long irritated those readers who yearn for a more inclusive, and arguably more realistic, depiction of human life. As Charlotte Brontë famously complained in an 1850 letter to her publisher, "the Passions are perfectly unknown to her [Austen] ... what sees keenly, speaks aptly, moves flexibly, it suits her to study, but what throbs fast and full, though hidden, what the blood rushes through, what is the unseen seat of Life and the sentient target of death—*this* Miss Austen ignores."[32] Not until our own era, however, have creators dared to infuse Austen's writings with sexual content. As recently as the early 1990s, a cartoon depicting "Jane Austen's Sex Boutique" derived its humor, according to Roger Sales, from the juxtaposition of "the subject of sex with a cultural icon that was universally acknowledged to be its complete antithesis."[33]

Several of the influential 1990s Austen film adaptations expanded the boundaries of Austen's treatment of bodies and desire. Most famously, the

1995 miniseries version of *Pride and Prejudice* depicted a fully physical Darcy, including views of him bathing, fencing, and—as no one needs reminding—arising from an impromptu swim at Pemberley to the astonishment of Elizabeth.[34] Helen Fielding impressed this scene yet more indelibly on the popular imagination by portraying single British women fetishizing the figure of the wet-shirted Darcy in her bestselling novel *Bridget Jones: The Edge of Reason* (1999).[35] Fans of the miniseries who sought out the companion volume *The Making of Pride and Prejudice* (1995) were not surprised to learn that the screenwriter, Andrew Davies, considers "the central motor which drives the story forward" to be "Darcy's sexual attraction to Elizabeth," and that he interprets Austen's emphasis on Elizabeth's physical fortitude—demonstrated in the novel through walking and running—as being "a coded way" of signaling that Elizabeth "has got lots of sexual energy."[36]

Not all introductions of sex to Austen's world were welcomed with equal enthusiasm in the 1990s. Patricia Rozema's film adaptation of *Mansfield Park* (1999) challenged viewers' sensibilities by including glimpses of heterosexual intercourse as well as lesbian flirtation.[37] Indeed, associations of Austen and her characters with lesbianism provoked a high level of public discomfort throughout this decade. *Emma in Love: Jane Austen's Emma Continued* (1996), a sequel by British author Emma Tennant, attracted disapprobation by showing Emma in love with and yearning for a woman.[38] "The voice of Elise now sounded in the whistling of the wind," Tennant writes, referring to the object of Emma's desire: "low, a foreign voice that brought storms to her [Emma's] neck and down her spine; and, wherever her hands might roam to hold it at bay, her very soul."[39] Terry Castle, an American professor of English parentage, was disparaged on both sides of the Atlantic after a 1995 essay in *The London Review of Books* in which she speculated on the "primitive adhesiveness—and underlying eros—of the sister-sister bond" between Jane and Cassandra Austen.[40] As Castle later summed up the attacks against her, "I was accused of 'outing' Jane Austen, I was obviously both depraved and insane."[41]

Given the ambivalence of turn-of-the-millennium audiences towards the idea of sex in Austen, the humor of *Pride and Promiscuity: The Lost Sex Scenes of Jane Austen* (2001) was far from assured a warm welcome. A back cover blurb seeks to reassure Austen fans who are nervous about the book's premise: "So wickedly funny, I could not resist," states Elsa A. Solender, the then-president of the Jane Austen Society of North America. Co-authors Arielle Eckstut and Dennis Ashton claimed to have discovered "Jane Austen's lost sex scenes. SEX SCENES. Along with letters to her editor arguing and anguishing over the extensive cuts she was asked to make in order for her novels to be seen as acceptable and decent to her publisher."[42] Twelve "lost" scenes make up the book, plus a letter from the publisher Richard Crosby declining Austen's novel *The Watsons* on the ground of its filth. Eckstut and Ashton carefully link each invented scene to a specific point in its host novel, offering clever explanations for how the "missing" material answers questions that have long puzzled Austen's readers.

Though Eckstut and Ashton avoid graphic language and descriptions, the sexual acts they depict run the gamut. Emma Woodhouse pleasures herself, while opportunities for intimacy are seized by Elizabeth Bennet and Mr. Darcy. The intimacy of the Crawford siblings edges into incest, and—more surprisingly—Elinor Dashwood confesses to a brush with bestiality. Charlotte dominates Mr. Collins, and Catherine Morland stumbles on Henry Tilney's dungeon. On the slash side, the Bingley sisters trick Jane Bennet into a lesbian ménage, praising her for her "stamina, [her] extreme pliability, and [her] eagerness to learn," while Frank Churchill compliments Mr. Knightley on his "rigid and erect" posture before propositioning him via a dirty charade.[43]

Eckstut and Ashton portray not only Austen's characters but the author herself as utterly free of shame and prudery. In an invented letter, Jane only reluctantly accedes to her publisher's demands that she clean up *Pride and Prejudice* and insists that her name not appear on the title page of the supposedly revised work. To Cassandra, in another invented letter, Jane confesses her "surprise & utter disappointment at these thoroughly unpleasant requests. Is he [Egerton, her publisher] so blind as not to see how very natural are the sorts of displays I detail? I am in desperate need of your counsel & yet I fear that I may have already drop'd all chances of publication."[44]

Pride and Promiscuity offended some readers and delighted others, sparking debates about plausibility, entertainment value, and exploitation. *Pride and Promiscuity*'s mixed reception among readers can be glimpsed in the book's forty reviews by Amazon customers, of which seventeen award the title only one star out of a possible five. "I felt duped," posted one Amazon.com customer. "Because it is a parody? No. I have a sense of humor (although I *really* wanted it to be real). But, as someone else has already mentioned, never in 200+ years could a true fan stretch the imagination far enough to believe that this was written by Jane Austen. … If you are truly a fan of Ms. Austen's, reread the real thing and use your erotic imagination instead."[45] Reissued in paperback in 2008, *Pride and Promiscuity* remains in print, able to reach new readers whose appreciation for cheeky, absurd takes on Austen has been honed by recent mash-ups. Unapologetically irreverent, yet still retaining some points of contact with Austen's characterization, word choice, and syntax, these "lost sex scenes" paved the way for still more audacious interventions into Austen's writings and life.

Readers' curiosity about the possible sex lives of Austen's characters was addressed in a different way by Linda Berdoll, a first-time author whose epic-length sequel to *Pride and Prejudice* focuses on the joyful eroticism of Darcy and Elizabeth's marital bond. Originally titled *The Bar Sinister* and published by a tiny press in 1999, Berdoll's novel reached a much larger audience following its 2004 release by Sourcebooks Landmark as *Mr. Darcy Takes a Wife: Pride and Prejudice Continues.*[46] Berdoll's success at landing a mainstream publishing contract offers hope to other Austen fan fiction writers, many of whom have joined her at the imprint Sourcebooks Landmark.[47]

In her preface, Berdoll quotes Charlotte Brontë's criticism of Austen for ignoring "the Passions" before offering her own rationale for engaging in what Henry Jenkins terms "eroticization":[48] "Jane Austen wrote of what she knew. ... As befitting a maiden's sensibilities, her novels all end with the wedding ceremony. What throbs fast and full, what the blood rushes through, is denied her unforgettable characters and, therefore, us. Dash it all! We endeavour to right this wrong by completing at least one of her stories, beginning whence hers leaves off. Our lovers have wed. But the throbbing that we first encounter is not the cry of a passionate heart. Another part of her anatomy is grieving Elizabeth Bennet Darcy."[49] Indeed, the reader discovers in the second paragraph of Berdoll's novel that Elizabeth suffers from "a sore nether-end" as a result of vigorous "conjugal congress."[50] Delighting in Darcy's smell on her body, she takes pleasure in imagining him "naked as God made him. And aroused."[51] Darcy matches and encourages Elizabeth's lust, beginning during their engagement period, when Elizabeth's "virtue was not compromised in deed ... [though] besmutted considerably by her own intentions."[52] Berdoll's interest in exploring the sex lives of Austen's characters extends beyond her central pair: she assures us, for instance, that "whatever were Wickham's drawbacks as a provider, he was a prolific and masterful lover."[53]

As the preceding quotations make clear, Berdoll is much less invested than the authors of *Pride and Promiscuity* in attempting a believable recreation of Austen's literary style. Indeed, Berdoll's author bio makes clear that her imagination was "piqued" not by Austen's novel but by the 1995 miniseries version of *Pride and Prejudice*.[54] *Mr. Darcy Takes a Wife* can thus be best understood as fan fiction that builds on, and literalizes, the "sexual energy" that screenwriter Andrew Davies sought to convey in that television adaptation.[55] As with *Pride and Promiscuity*, readers' reactions to Berdoll's brazenly erotic writing have diverged sharply. Out of 538 Amazon.com reviews, 154 customers awarded *Mr. Darcy Takes a Wife* five stars and 192 awarded one star.[56]

Both Berdoll's sequels and *Pride and Promiscuity* proceed from the assumption that everyone knows you can't find sex scenes in Austen.[57] By including Austen in *Literary Lust: The Sexiest Moments in Classic Fiction* (2006), Stella Hyde takes a different tack, encouraging readers to give Austen credit for what she did depict. Hyde's goal, as she states in her introduction, is to equip the sexually bored with "a much classier option" than sex manuals or toys: "a selection of the hotter scenes from classic literature ... with instructions on how to translate them from between the pages to between the sheets."[58] Featuring *Pride and Prejudice* and *Mansfield Park*, Hyde encourages her readers to adapt for their own purposes Austen's long country walks and flirtatious theatricals. Beyond Hyde's specific recommendations for how to apply what she calls Austen's "admirable restraint" to twenty-first-century love lives, Hyde offers a ringing defense of Austen's approach to desire. "Some people will tell you that there is no sex in Austen's oeuvre," she declares, "but that is because they are careless readers. ... Austen lust is all about restraint, pleasure postponed, the quivering deliciousness of unconsummated desire."[59]

The most daring presentation of "Austen lust" to date is Ann Herendeen's in *Pride / Prejudice: A Novel of Mr. Darcy, Elizabeth Bennet, and Their Forbidden Lovers* (2010). As the slash mark in Herendeen's title hints, the "forbidden lovers" on whom she concentrates are same-sex pairs: she matches Darcy with Bingley and Elizabeth with Charlotte Lucas. Herendeen steers clear of the campy approach to Austen slash taken by Eckstut and Ashton in *Pride and Promiscuity*. Instead, Herendeen delves deeply into her characters' emotional connections as well as their sexual activities, which are as frequent as those of Berdoll's characters in her erotic sequels to *Pride and Prejudice* but much more explicitly represented.

In an essay appended to *Pride / Prejudice,* Herendeen explains as following her motivation and approach:

> As I read and reread the novel, it seemed to me that ... in Darcy and Bingley Austen was showing readers what today we might call "bisexual" men. These are not "gay" men; their love exists not as an exclusive, self-contained pairing, but in the context of the society in which they lived, where marriage to a lady of good family was the objective of every gentleman of property, just as marriage to a 'gentleman in possession of a good fortune' was necessary for every young lady. ... *Pride / Prejudice* is a way of bringing to light the alternative universe that was invisible in Austen's time.[60]

Herendeen's use of the term "alternative universe" both explicitly associates her novel with fan fiction and reminds the reader that some alternative universes have more historical basis than others. Regarding her decision to depict not only same-sex desire but hard-core sex acts, Herendeen argues that "it's because we don't see sex as inherently sinful or disgusting that we can include it in adaptations of older works without regarding the new material as erotica or obscene."[61]

Given the new ground that Herendeen is breaking both in Austen erotica and in Austen slash, it is hardly surprising that many responses to *Pride / Prejudice* recorded on Amazon.com are vehemently unappreciative.[62] Herendeen's sheer originality, however, has been recognized by some readers. One recommends the book to "fans who want something radically different in their Austen diet," while a self-identified author of Austen sequels toasts Herendeen "for doing something no one else has done and I don't think anyone else would attempt to do."[63] Several reviewers defend Herendeen by comparing *Pride / Prejudice* favorably with other reworkings that shock without contributing a new perspective on Austen's world. One poster argued that "if Seth Grahame-Smith can introduce zombies to Jane Austen—adding novelty but offering no real insight on the original—why not?"[64] Other reviewers suggest that readers who find Herendeen's same-sex content offensive should examine their own assumptions about what is and is not all right to do with Austen's characters.

"Within P & P variations it seems to be easily accepted," writes one, that Darcy "might be a werewolf, a vampire, a dragon, a ghost or a zombie hunter—but love a man—oh my, how gross!"[65]

How it came to be "easily accepted"—if indeed it has been—to view Darcy as a vampire is the subject of the next section.

Horror and the Paranormal

Credit for the earliest idea to infuse Austen's world with violence and supernatural beings goes to the bestselling English fantasy novelist Terry Pratchett, who (according to Sheenagh Pugh) mentioned in a 2003 talk that he had "once written a *Lord of the Rings/Pride and Prejudice* crossover in which orcs attack Hunsford Parsonage."[66] Of course, Austen was no stranger to the Gothic fiction of her day, which she famously parodies in *Northanger Abbey*. In that novel, Catherine Morland learns that the thrilling terrors her reading has prepared her to discover around every corner actually imperil her less than do the real-world horrors of selfishness and greed. The first vampires to bear Austen associations, albeit distantly, appeared in Stephenie Meyer's phenomenal bestseller *Twilight* (2005), a novel that Meyer claims to have intended as an homage to *Pride and Prejudice*.[67] Scenes of cartoonish violence, especially towards unpopular minor characters (e.g. Mr. Collins), appear in Emma Campbell Webster's *Lost in Austen: Create Your Own Jane Austen Adventure* (2007), a version of *Pride and Prejudice* that places the reader in Elizabeth Bennet's shoes. The book that decisively introduced Austen to horror and vice versa, of course, is *Pride and Prejudice and Zombies* (2009), which was issued with the double by-line of Jane Austen and Seth Grahame-Smith, having initially been conceived by an editor at Quirk Books, Jason Rekulak.

As Rekulak tells the story, his admiration for outrageous mash-up videos on YouTube led him to muse on how a classic literary title, safely out of copyright, might be entertainingly combined with extremely unexpected genre content. "I began by making a list of classic works in the public domain—*Moby Dick*, *Great Expectations*, and so forth," Rekulak recollects. "Then I made a second list of elements we might use to enhance those classic works—ninjas, pirates, etc. Then I started to draw lines between the two columns. Once I drew a line between *Pride and Prejudice* and 'Zombies,' I knew I had a title, and I could easily imagine how the book would work."[68] Rekulak was hardly a lifelong Austen lover, as he explained to the audience of a panel discussion on Austen adaptation held in January 2010 at the Morgan Library & Museum:

> When I was sixteen years old and my English teacher assigned *Sense and Sensibility*, I just thought it was about the most boring book in the world. Later I read some remarks by Richard Price, the really famous New York writer, who was growing up in the Bronx, and his teachers were pushing Jane Austen on him. And he had the same reaction: "I don't understand ...

who are these people, I can't relate to this." And he didn't really get turned on to books until he read a book called *Last Exit to Brooklyn.* I was sort of the same way when I first encountered Jane Austen in south Jersey in the early 80s. ... I do remember writing a book report anyway on *Sense and Sensibility* even though I had only read about six chapters of it. And I remember the teacher handing back the assignments and telling us what everyone had decided to write about. When she got to me, she gave me back my paper, and she announced, "And Jason wrote *his* report on the first six chapters of *Sense and Sensibility.*"[69]

Seth Grahame-Smith, whom Rekulak commissioned to write the zombie content, similarly recalls being "bored to tears" by *Pride and Prejudice* in high school.[70] The distance from Austen's world to that of young American men, especially "in south Jersey in the early 80s," seemingly could not be greater.

As a grown man, however, Rekulak developed a greater appreciation for Austen's writing. "One of the great pleasures of this whole experience for me," he told the Morgan audience, "has been the opportunity to just sit in a room and get paid to read these books over and over and over. Obviously I'm not the same person at 38 that I was at 16, and I really did discover just how wonderful these books are. I remember the second time I read *Pride and Prejudice,* before we put the zombies in it, I remember running out to say to our receptionist, 'Oh my God, this book is like the template for every romantic comedy I've ever seen!' And she looks at me, and she's like, 'Of course.'"[71] By offering a gleefully gory reading experience that is entirely removed from the classroom, Rekulak and Grahame-Smith appeal in particular to readers who, like their own younger selves, would find Austen in the original to be hard going.[72]

The concept of *Pride and Prejudice and Zombies* evidently piqued the taste of book buyers, who made an international bestseller of the title.[73] The runaway success of *Zombies* took Rekulak and Grahame-Smith by surprise. As Grahame-Smith remarks in his introduction to the "deluxe heirloom edition" of the title, the project began with "no discussions of best-seller lists ... no dreams of movie adaptations, audiobooks, or Croatian translations. It just seemed like a lot of fun."[74] Rekulak attributes the frenzy over the book's publication to a perfect storm of web interest: "Sometime in February 2009 the book exploded onto the blogosphere, and within days there were hundreds of blogs and websites talking about the book. They did the marketing for us. It was phenomenal and I wish we knew how to replicate it."[75] Quirk Books followed up with *Sense and Sensibility and Sea Monsters,* for which Ben H. Winters joined Austen as co-author, as well as a prequel and sequel to *Pride and Prejudice and Zombies*—subtitled *Dawn of the Dreadfuls* (2010) and *Dreadfully Ever After* (2011), respectively—written (with no "co-author") by Steve Hockensmith.[76]

The entertainment value of both *Pride and Prejudice and Zombies* and *Sense and Sensibility and Sea Monsters* rests in large part, of course, on the shocking juxtaposition of Austen's supposedly well-mannered characters with scenes of gruesome carnage (in *Zombies*) and threatening monsters (*Sea Monsters*). Each title is a joke in itself, one that the books' cover images replicate in the visual realm. The cover of *Zombies* features a Regency woman with her lower face and neck eaten away, while *Sea Monsters* shows a somber-looking Regency woman embracing a man with multiple face tentacles, who turns out to be Colonel Brandon. On all the books, including Hockensmith's, soberly lettered white titles on a black ground further play with the conventional presentation of paperback literary classics.

For readers who are already familiar with Austen's novels, one of the potential pleasures of reading these two mash-ups lies in the scenes where the physical dimensions added by Grahame-Smith and Winters intensify the tension established by Austen. In *Zombies*, for instance, Grahame-Smith follows the climactic dialogue between Elizabeth and Lady Catherine de Bourgh, during the latter's visit to Longbourn, with a literal duel between the two outspoken opponents, who in this version are well matched martial artists.[77] In *Sea Monsters*, Winters accompanies the excruciating conversation between Elinor Dashwood and Lucy Steele that takes place at the end of Volume 1 of *Sense and Sensibility* with an attack by "the Devonshire Fang-Beast," whose ravages Elinor must fight off even as she parries Lucy's conversational thrusts.[78] Speaking of another intervention, his transformation of Col. Brandon into a "man-monster," Winters commented as follows to the Morgan Library audience on the choice between importing new content into Austen's novels and imaginatively reworking what is already present:

> What I tried to do throughout writing the book was, rather than make up new concepts and thrust them upon Austen, although I do some of that, was to take Austen's concepts, the things that she was already doing, and amplify them or accentuate them, using these ridiculous concepts that I brought to the book. So the idea of Brandon being a man-monster, it's like, we know, you all know, that Marianne doesn't love Brandon, finds herself resistant to him, because he's stiff, and wears the flannel waistcoats, and because he's so old. … So all that I've done, is make her challenge in finding him attractive a little more challenging, so that then we as the reader are all the happier when she manages to see his inner goodness, despite his preposterous appearance.[79]

Winters pointed out too that Marianne's dialogue has to change "just a little, little bit" to accommodate her new source of disgust.[80]

The influence of *Zombies* and *Sea Monsters* is evident in a host of imitations, none of which has achieved anything close to the success of the two titles originally conceived by Rekulak.[81] Beyond the Austen realm, the mash-up craze has extended into the works of other nineteenth-century authors, including the Brontës and (from Winters) Tolstoy.[82] Seizing the cultural moment, writers with experience in other forms of genre fiction, especially paranormal romance, have reworked both Austen's characters and Austen herself. In many cases, these creators—unlike Rekulak and Grahame-Smith—are self-professed Austen fans who take pleasure, they say, in bringing their love of Austen together with their particular interests as storytellers.

"Today, the combination of Austen and paranormal may seem an obvious one," writes Susan Krinard in her introduction to *Bespelling Jane Austen* (2010), a collection of four Austen-inspired paranormal novellas released by the romance publisher Harlequin.[83] Krinard, who describes herself as having written paranormal novels for fifteen years and having been "a Jane Austen fan for much longer than that," was excited by her idea of "retelling *Pride and Prejudice* as a contemporary vampire story."[84] She states that she conceives of *Bespelling Jane Austen* as a tribute to the appreciation of Austen she shares with her co-authors, declaring that "if Miss Austen knew how far our love for her works would take us, how much we would want to make her world our own, I don't think she would be displeased."[85] The brief introductions to the novellas offered by Krinard's co-authors, too, make clear their longstanding interest in Austen, as well as their sense of comfort in imaginatively recasting her fictional worlds. Colleen Gleason, who chose to rework *Northanger Abbey* with a vampire theme, explains that when she first read Austen's novel she knew she had "found a kindred spirit in not only Jane, through her tongue-in-cheek rendering of a Gothic novel, but also a heroine I could relate to in Catherine Morland. Like me, Catherine sees stories everywhere, making up histories and Gothic tales in her mind. As a writer, I do that every day."[86]

The imaginative license available to all Austen lovers in the wake of *Pride and Prejudice and Zombies* is most fully evident in the works of two authors who have envisioned Austen herself as a vampire: Janet Mullany's *Jane and the Damned* (2010) and Michael Thomas Ford's *Jane Bites Back* (2010) and *Jane Goes Batty* (2011).[87] Of course, Mullany and Ford take advantage as well of the latitude established by the fictional and cinematic depictions of Austen that I discussed in Chapter 5, especially Stephanie Barron's Austen mysteries (1996–2011 and continuing) and the biopic *Becoming Jane* (2007).[88] Yet Mullany and Ford move so far beyond their predecessors that their depictions of Austen seem to belong to another era entirely. Demolishing myths of Austen as innocent and modest, both Mullany and Ford portray her as confident, sexually experienced, and matter of fact in meeting her own needs, whether for blood, love, or literary recognition.

Mullany and Ford play in different ways with the concept of immortality, which is crucial to their novels' vampire content, their treatment of Austen's literary aspirations and, in Ford's case, her cultural legacy as well. Jane's ambitions as a writer are evident from the outset of *Jane and the Damned*, as her disappointment at receiving the manuscript of *First Impressions* "*Declined by Return of Post*" leads her to behave recklessly at the Basingstoke Assembly Rooms and become vulnerable to the depredations of a vampire.[89] Mullany does not portray Jane's introduction to blood-drinking as a quasi-sexual experience, as is typical in vampire fiction. Instead, Mullany depicts Jane's experience as freeing and reminiscent of the exhilaration of her literary composition: "Through a mouthful of blood she growled—yes, Jane Austen, the cultured and respectable daughter of the Austen family *growled*, and then laughed messily. And the taste—like lightning, like the way she felt once, in another life, when the words flowed and she laughed aloud at her own cleverness and the delicious interplay of her characters."[90] As this passage makes clear, Mullany's Jane revels in her freedom as both a creator of fiction and a drinker of blood.

Yet Mullany confronts Jane with the possibility that acceptance of life as a vampire might deprive her of her gifts as a writer, when Jane's vampire mentor comments that he has "never heard of any one of the Damned who distinguished himself in the arts of letters."[91] Mullany thus offers a new twist on the choice between marriage and literary composition faced by earlier fictional and cinematic versions of Austen. Jane's likely prospects of literary success, as her mentor points out, are poor: "You write a few books that entertain your family and you win a little fame, perhaps even some money, while you live. And after, what then? Your books languish forgotten on dusty bookshelves and you are but a name on a binding that disappears with decay and time. You think your books offer you a chance at immortality? Oh, Jane, do not delude yourself."[92] Mullany's Jane nevertheless chooses to leave the company of vampires, return to her family, and pursue her writing. A fanged cross-dressing murderer this Jane may be, but beneath her outrageous exterior she remains committed—for the time, at least—to her family and her pen.[93] In Mullany's forthcoming sequel, *Jane Austen: Blood Persuasion* (2011), the tension between Jane's vampire and literary selves will presumably arise again.[94]

For Ford, the vampire premise makes possible an extended fantasy that Jane Austen remains alive today, able to comment on her fame and exploitation even as she achieves bestseller status, under the name Jane Fairfax, with a new "Austenesque" romance. Fully conversant with contemporary popular culture, Ford's Jane throws out references to *Twilight*, Sookie Stackhouse, and *Abraham Lincoln: Vampire Hunter*. Though unimpressed by the novels of Charlotte Brontë (whom, in undead form, she battles), this Jane is decidedly broadminded regarding reworkings of her own novels: she confesses to finding "amusement" in *Pride and Prejudice and Zombies* and "rather lik[ing]" *Clueless*.[95] We might expect that vampirism would distance Jane from her present-day admirers, but in fact the opposite is the case. Ford presents Austen fans with a Jane who is (aside from the need to drink blood) just like them. Indeed, it is tempting, if gruesome, to think of Ford's vampire Jane as making literal my concept of the Austen omnivore.

Like the authors of *Bespelling Jane Austen*, then, Ford and Mullany claim the paranormal as a realm in which Austen fans, at least certain omnivorous ones, can feel at home. As long as Austen's plots and characters retain cultural currency, writers of genre fiction will doubtless continue to create new hybrids that infuse Austen's worlds with popular material of the moment.

Faith

Reworking Austen in a very different way, and for a very different purpose, than writers of erotic and horror/paranormal versions of her novels are evangelical Christian writers who earnestly endeavor to present Austen's works, and to a degree her life as well, as appropriate and rewarding material for faithful readers to contemplate. Far from trying to sex up Austen's novels, Christian audiences appreciate the restraint with which she depicts passion. These readers and viewers share, too, the cultural value of sexual purity before marriage that comes through unmistakably in her novels (and in all but the most risqué screen adaptations).[96] Yet virginity before marriage is far from the only element in Austen that attracts today's Christian audiences. The morality of Austen's fictional worlds holds strong appeal, as does Austen's own identity as the daughter of a clergyman and the author of prayers.[97] Rather than delighting in imagining a transgressive Austen, these readers cherish the image of a Jane who, as depicted by her brother Henry in his "Biographical Notice" (1817), was "thoroughly religious and devout," as they aspire to be themselves.[98]

Of course, significant differences exist between Austen's Anglicanism and the various forms of Christianity to which present-day readers adhere. As Laura Mooneyham White argues, "contemporary Christian readers may feel that they have an advantage over their more secular counterparts in terms of an enhanced awareness of Austen's worldview … but they are likely to be mistaken, at least in part. This is because, though the central doctrines of the Church remain unchanged, much of the foundational worldview of the Georgian Anglican Church and that of contemporary Christians differs considerably, and the presumptions each hold about the social and cultural role of the church are even farther apart."[99] Conceiving of Austen as an inspirational Christian forebear, then, takes a considerable effort of interpretation.

Austen's high profile among present-day Christian readers and writers results from her high profile in mainstream culture. The imaginations of secular and faithful audiences alike have been sparked by the same beloved screen adaptations of Austen's novels. Furthermore, Christian responses to Austen take the same forms as secular ones: guides to her writings aimed at amateur readers, popular biographies, advice manuals, biographical fiction, sequels, and updated versions of her novels in the genres of fiction and film. Unlike Austen-inspired books released by mainstream publishing houses, however, those written by Christians for Christians tend to be published by presses that specialize in religious content, and hence have received little recognition by the wider culture.[100]

Christian approaches to Austen, as to any major cultural figure, risk being faulted by secular audiences for bias or selectiveness. Beyond concerns about accuracy or agenda, those who do not themselves connect to Austen on the grounds of faith can feel uncomfortable seeing her novels adopted—some might say co-opted—by readers whose concerns are so different from their own. In this sense, secular readers are in the same position with respect to Christian Austen material as are scholarly readers with respect to popular treatments of Austen that do not hew to, or that openly subvert, academic standards. Like Austen-related popular materials more generally, Christian works that respond to Austen must be taken on their own terms and with an open mind. Only then will the variety among these approaches be visible, as well as their significance as one part of the landscape of popular present-day responses to Austen.[101]

The most comprehensive re-imagining of Austen for a contemporary Christian audience is Debra White Smith's "Austen Series" (2004–2006), published by the Christian press Harvest House, which recasts all six of Austen's published novels as present-day romances starring characters of faith.[102] For the most part, Smith weaves in relatively unobtrusively the evangelical content that her readers expect. Indeed, given the latitude Smith's contemporary setting offers to rework Austen as she sees fit, the degree of her fidelity to Austen's depiction of religious life is striking. With only a few exceptions, notably a pivotal encounter between her Elizabeth Bennet and Darcy characters at an altar rail, Smith depicts little more churchgoing or regular religious observance—including prayers or Bible reading—than does Austen.[103]

Establishing that her heroines and heroes are people of faith requires Smith to add less to Austen's characterizations than one might expect. Apart from her highly moral Fanny Price character and her version of Catherine Morland, portrayed as a religious seeker, Smith's heroines could all be described in the terms with which *First Impressions'* Dave Davidson (Darcy) thinks of Eddi Boswick (Elizabeth): as being "reverent, [but] not the most demonstrative church member."[104] Smith's most significant intervention is to weave explicit references to religious conversion into the transformative changes of heart experienced by certain of Austen's heroines, as when Anna Woods (Marianne) turns back to Bryan Brixby (Col. Brandon) after an extended, near-death vision of the "the Giver of Life."[105]

Sexual restraint, not surprisingly, is crucial to Smith's romances, for her heroes as well as her heroines. Unlike Austen, who remains discreetly silent on the subject of her heroes' sexual experience, Smith makes plain that the godliness of these characters extends as well to their stewardship of their bodies. Ethan Barrimore (Edmund Bertram), for example, has "determined to keep himself sexually pure and as far removed from temptation as possible. … allow[ing] the Lord to lead him to his mate when the time was right."[106] Yet Smith sanitizes neither the desires nor the behavior of those characters who, in

Austen's novels, sexually transgress or come close to doing so. Linda Boswick (Lydia Bennet) does actually sleep with her Wickham and get pregnant—although she redeems herself for that sin by remembering "the sanctity of human life" and choosing marriage over abortion.[107]

With these embellishments and interventions, Smith renders in a form recognizable to her own readers the Christian beliefs and practices that Austen left implicit. At the same time, Smith preserves those aspects of Austen's original texts, particularly the concern with feminine purity, that resonate with an evangelical audience. That Smith's "Austen Series" takes place in the present day frees her, of course, from having to grapple with what morals or faith meant in Austen's era, or to Austen herself.

In contrast, Sarah Arthur, author of *Dating Mr. Darcy: A Smart Girl's Guide to Sensible Romance* (2005), seeks to make not only *Pride and Prejudice* but also Austen's views on faith relevant to her own young readers. Published by Tyndale, a Christian press, *Dating Mr. Darcy* coaches young evangelical women through reflections on themselves and their potential marriage partners, using *Pride and Prejudice* as a touchstone.[108] Like authors of secular dating guides based on Austen's writings, Arthur encourages her readers to identify who among their own acquaintance behaves like Elizabeth Bennet and Darcy, or Wickham and Lydia. In our era as in Austen's, declares Arthur, "singles in the dating 'market' often have only brief, contrived opportunities to get to know each other," a situation that affects alike those who are "silly and selfish" and those who are "respectable."[109] To be "respectable" in Arthur's terms clearly means to be sexually chaste as well as generally virtuous, much as would have been true in Austen's time.

Arthur asserts, too, a more substantial correspondence between Austen's world and that of the readers of *Dating Mr. Darcy*. "Jane lived in a time," Arthur contends, "when the Christian faith was taken for granted" and when "'principles' and 'morals' and 'duty'" were terms used for "the standards that God has set for us in the Bible."[110] For Arthur, it is not sufficient to identify Austen as having lived in a pervasively Anglican world. Arthur aims also to characterize Jane as a believer in a sense that will be recognizable to her own young evangelical readers. This effort is evident in Arthur's interpretation of the three prayers attributed to Austen, a reading that is both carefully couched and creative. "It could be argued," writes Arthur, "that her [Jane's] prayers indicate that she felt a personal *experience* of God to be central to the life of faith, even if the language of having a personal *relationship* with God would have sounded foreign to her."[111] In her appended "Guide to Reflection," Arthur strives further to make Austen's prayers relevant to her own readers, by juxtaposing excerpts from those prayers with questions such as "in what ways have I sinned against my loved ones through the unkind things I've thought, said, or done?"[112] Arthur's insistent personalization of Austen's prayers is at odds with their rhetoric, which Bruce Stovel has described as "speak[ing] in a shared voice of a generic predicament."[113] Encouraging her own readers to reflect spiritually on prayers written by Austen, however, is crucial to Arthur's project of establishing Jane as an inspirational forebear for young women of faith.

The capacity of Austen's characters not only to inspire but also to empower young Christians is suggested by a 2003 feature film that updates *Pride and Prejudice* to present-day Provo, Utah, the location of Brigham Young University. Directed by Andrew Black, *Pride & Prejudice* depicts characters who, like Black himself, have chosen to embrace life as members of the Church of Jesus Christ of Latter-Day Saints in ways that suit their own personalities and aspirations. In an effort to appeal to broader audiences, the film avoids explicitly mentioning the terms "Mormon" and "Latter-Day Saints," even in scenes where characters attend church. As a result, *Pride & Prejudice* portrays Christian faith generally as an appealing, rewarding life path for young people.[114]

Like Austen's Elizabeth Bennet, who finds much to object to in the mores of her culture but who stops well short of transgressing those mores, the Elizabeth of Black's film is "frustrated by the society she lives in, but not rebellious."[115] Disenchanted with the flirtation-heavy, marriage-minded culture that surrounds her, Elizabeth is focused more on her vocation—to "be a great writer," as she puts it in her opening voiceover[116]—than on securing a husband. Her priorities place her at odds with her friends and fellow undergraduate students, especially her man-chasing housemate Lydia.

That thoughtful, ambitious Elizabeth feels at home in her church is established most plainly by a brief scene in which she addresses fellow church members. Elizabeth stands in front of a blackboard, dressed up and gesturing towards her listeners, all of whom seem to be women. Her face lit up with enthusiasm, she holds a thick book open in her hand—presumably a book of scripture, given the list of Bible references visible in the middle of the blackboard. The image of Elizabeth as a spiritual instructor is powerful and memorable, as is the indication that she finds satisfaction in exploring her ideas within the framework of devotions.

The sympathy conveyed by this film for a range of Christian believers comes across as well in one of its most notable departures from the plot of Austen's novel: the establishment of a romance between the Mr. Collins and Mary Bennet characters. The film's most devout characters, they are also initially its two most relentlessly satirized.[117] Awkward but eventually rather endearing, Collins and Mary ultimately find fulfillment in choosing and sharing their own approach to Christian belief.

Like his Elizabeth, the film's director, Andrew Black, recognizes the foibles of members of his church. His criticism does not extend to the church itself, however, and need not, since Mormonism, as he presents it, offers space for such very different characters as Collins, Mary, and Elizabeth to become the best and happiest versions of themselves. By reinventing Elizabeth as an aspiring writer who is in no hurry to marry, furthermore, Black encourages the viewer to see her as an updated incarnation of Austen herself.

A more nuanced meditation on the significance of Austen to one particular young Christian woman emerges from Lori Smith's *A Walk with Jane Austen: A Journey into Adventure, Love & Faith* (2007). Smith's narrative is a hybrid in a different sense: a blend of memoir, travelogue, and spiritual reflection.[118] Unlike other writers who have published on Austen with Christian presses, Smith openly acknowledges the difference between the beliefs depicted by Austen and those held by twenty-first-century evangelicals. "Jane's books are Christian," contends Smith, "in that there is a solid Christian moral foundation throughout her writing, but they are not Christian books per se by today's definition."[119] Indeed, Smith makes the case for only one explicitly Christian aspect of Austen's writing: "an awareness and remembrance ... of that other world that is a focus of Christianity."[120] And Smith locates this quality not in Austen's novels but in her letters.

Smith's tolerant approach to the religious and spiritual aspects of Austen's life and writings distinguishes her from writers such as Debra White Smith (no relation) and Sarah Arthur who have rewritten or reframed Austen to make her more palatable to present-day believers. That Smith searches in Austen's writings for personal insight rather than morals or guidelines for conduct separates her as well from those secular writers who have derived didactic guides to behavior from Austen's novels. Smith, the author of a guide for Christian singles, was to her dismay and disappointment not yet married at age thirty-three. She decided to travel in Austen's footsteps in order, she explains, to "sort out the possibilities of my life, working and dreaming to ensure that sans husband and children, I will still somehow be significant. ... somehow this proximity to Jane's life will help me understand my own."[121] Her memoir teases its readers with the possibility of a romantic conclusion for this very appealing-sounding young woman, who endearingly and with considerable humor confesses her enthusiasms, insecurities, and struggles with faith—as well as with an undiagnosed long-term illness.

Faith is a chief, if not the only, element that Smith feels she has in common with Austen's heroines, and even more so with Austen herself. Smith states early on that she is "curious about [Austen's] faith, which evinces itself in a gentle way in her writing"; she is herself, she explains both "struggling to believe" and to find a spiritual home "outside the stuffy, often sickly sweet, and sometimes nonintellectual spirituality of the evangelical Christian world" in which she grew up and attended college.[122] Smith is careful not to overstate the overlap between her own understanding of faith and that of Austen. She acknowledges that Austen's writings do not contain "anything that would hint at any spiritual angst, any struggle to believe or not believe, or even any deep spiritual emotion"[123]—qualities that are all present, often affectingly so, in Smith's memoir. Though she speculates that "in fundamentals of belief" she and Austen might be "much the same," Smith states that she "recognize[s] that Jane's religious experiences must have been far different" from her own, in part because Austen "didn't have to deal with the evangelical culture [Smith] was raised in—the one in which Christian things are separate from other normal (or as the church sometimes describes them, 'worldly') things."[124] Aside from those "fundamentals of belief," on which Smith does not elaborate, she claims common ground with Austen on the basis of their appreciation of "the ridiculousness that the church can bring out, if not encourage, in people."[125]

Smith's response to the prayers written by Austen also demonstrates her awareness and acceptance of the distance between Austen's apparent faith, and her language for expressing it, and Smith's own. Having quoted a portion of one of the prayers about the undeservedness of God's blessings, Smith comments that "I read that and felt terribly insecure. *Oh, dear God, you have given abundant blessings. I do not deserve them, and I cannot help but ask for more. I* am sure this is not what Jane intended, but at the moment I do not feel secure in the whims of God."[126] Returning to the same prayer later in her memoir, Smith senses "a desperation" in its portrayal of "a God who may be capricious at times, whose favor may not last."[127] Again, Smith offers her interpretation without any claim that it aligns with Austen's own beliefs, or any concern that it might not.

Smith achieves her own most transcendent moments of spiritual certainty not by reflecting on Austen's faith or the prayers written by her but instead through the experience of Anglican worship.[128] Smith does find solace, however, in recognizing a parallel between her experience and Austen's in an area closely related to religious belief: the practice of chastity. "My bed is always empty," Smith writes of her commitment for reasons of faith to sexual abstinence. "It is one of the things about my life that seems ridiculous in the twenty-first century that would not have seemed so to Jane."[129] Nor, accordingly, does Austen's own lack of sexual experience seem ridiculous or unfortunate to Smith—as it evidently has to those novelists and filmmakers who have provided their Janes with passionate kisses and even trysts. Given that Smith herself differentiates firmly between love and its physical expression, she has no difficulty in extending the same courtesy to Austen.

Smith finds comfort, too, in thinking of herself as having been blessed by the grace of God. Though Smith vows in the last line of her memoir that she "will try again" to find romantic love, she declares that she has discovered she does not need it. "I feel incredibly blessed to be in such a family," she writes, "with dear friends, with the prospect of work that I love, living a small life surrounded by small goodnesses with this tremendous grace."[130] Smith credits her reflection on Austen for this lesson in contentment with respect to both love and professional ambition. Austen, Smith declares,

> did not want to be famous. ... She enjoyed making money with her writing ... [but] never believed that being big was important. These are the things I want for myself. ... God does not love me because of anything I can do; this still astonishes me. He simply loves me. ... This life—this loving your family

and friends and doing good work and telling good stories life—may feel small, but it is far from ordinary. It is the best life, the extraordinary life. It was Jane's, and I hope it will be mine.[131]

Faith aside, Smith finds that envisioning Austen as satisfied with her life helps her feel satisfied with her own. What Smith offers, then, is a model for self-discovery, one that can be followed by readers regardless of their religious convictions. All amateur readers, Smith implies, can come to know themselves better through reflecting on their interest in and sense of connection to Austen—or indeed any author whose works they cherish. Smith demonstrates that by deepening acquaintance with an author, whether through reading or travel, we deepen our understanding of ourselves.

Smith's memoir is a rare example of an Austen hybrid that, in its style and subject matter, achieves broad audience appeal. On the whole, however, Austen hybrids reach out to audiences with quite specific tastes—e.g. for vampires—or beliefs. By linking Austen's worlds to unexpected material, hybrids do encourage omnivorousness of a particular sort. And each hybrid, like any work with an Austen tie, holds the potential to introduce a reader to Austen for the first time or to spur a formerly reluctant reader to a new encounter with her writings. The more distant a given hybrid is from Austen's writings, however, the less likely it becomes that a fan of the hybrid will be converted into a reader of Austen—or that a devotee of Austen will appreciate the hybrid in question. Even as hybrids pique the taste of certain audiences, these works run the risk of alienating those readers from others to whom Austen matters.

How contact with Austen, according to her fans, achieves the reverse effect—overcoming distance and differences, including between scholars and amateurs—is the subject of my final chapter.

Notes

1 Kate Beaton's comic, titled "Where This Is Going," is the third of a three-part series. In the opening strip, an Austen fan in Regency dress announces to Jane, "I found this today at the bookshop, I thought you would be most pleased with it," while presenting the surprised Jane with a copy of "Pride and Prejudice and Monster Trucks." Kate Beaton, "Austen Mania," accessed May 5, 2011, http://www.harkavagrant.com/index. php?id=263.
2 Kate Beaton, "Jane Austen Comics," accessed May 5, 2011, http://www.harkavagrant. com/index.php?id=4.
3 Jane Austen and Seth Grahame-Smith, *Pride and Prejudice and Zombies* (Philadelphia: Quirk Books, 2009); Jane Austen and Ben H. Winters, *Sense and Sensibility and Sea Monsters* (Philadelphia: Quirk Books, 2009).
4 I follow Julie Sanders's definition of hybridity as "in literature a term deployed to describe a blend, fusion or compound of influences at the level of both language and form." *Adaptation and Appropriation* (London: Routledge, 2006), 161. "Mash-ups" such as *Pride and Prejudice and Zombies* are one species of hybrid.
5 For an exploration of outrageous juxtapositions involving Austen that take place outside

the realm of fiction, see Mary Ann O'Farrell, "'Bin Laden a Huge Jane Austen Fan': Jane Austen in Contemporary Political Discourse," in *Uses of Jane Austen: Twentieth-Century Afterlives*, ed. Gillian Dow and Clare Hanson (Houndmills, Basingstoke: Palgrave Macmillan, forthcoming).

6 2010 was noteworthy in the US literary market for Austen-inspired works not only because of the surge in hybrids but also because of the success of two novels with ties to *Sense and Sensibility*, both by acclaimed literary authors: Allegra Goodman, *The Cookbook Collector* (New York: The Dial Press, 2010) and Cathleen Schine, *The Three Weissmans of Westport* (New York: Sarah Crichton Books / Farrar, Straus and Giroux, 2010). Yet to be adequately explored is the role of publishers, both large and small, in promoting Austen-inspired works, as, for example, Claire Squires has illuminated the role of marketing in the contemporary British publishing industry more generally. *Marketing Literature: The Making of Contemporary Writing in Britain* (Houndmills, Basingstoke: Palgrave Macmillan, 2009).

7 Daria Pimenova, "Fan Fiction: Between Text, Conversation, and Genre," in *Internet Fictions*, ed. Ingrid Hotz-Davies, Anton Kirchhofer, and Sirpa Leppänen (Cambridge: Cambridge Scholars Publishing, 2009), 48.

8 Ibid., 45.

9 Sheenagh Pugh, *The Democratic Genre: Fan Fiction in a Literary Context* (Bridgend, Wales: Seren, 2005), 25. Recent studies of Austen fan fiction have focused on non-commercial writing, in the form of postings to the websites The Republic of Pemberley, the Derbyshire Writers' Guild at Austen.com, and Fanfiction.net. Roberta Grandi contends that "the so-called 'pro-fic' writers have become a minority compared to the vast crowd of fanficcers." "Web Side Stories: Janeites, Fanfictions, and Never Ending Romances," in *Internet Fictions*, ed. Hotz-Davies, Kirchhofer, and Leppänen, 24. As evidence of the enthusiastic readership for Austen-inspired material on Fanfiction.net, Amanda Gilroy cites the hundreds of reviews posted to two particular stories. "Our Austen: Fan Fiction in the Classroom," *Persuasions On-Line* 31.1 (2010), http://www.jasna.org/persuasions/on-line/vol31no1/gilroy.html. I would argue, however, that the sheer quantity of online Austen fan fiction limits the influence any individual work is likely to have on the popular imagination.

10 Abigail Derecho, "Archontic Literature: A Definition, a History, and Several Theories of Fan Fiction," in *Fan Fiction and Fan Communities in the Age of the Internet*, ed. Karen Hellekson and Kristina Busse (Jefferson, NC: McFarland, 2006), 62.

11 Rebecca Tushnet, "Copyright Law, Fan Practices, and the Rights of the Author," in *Fandom: Identities and Communities in a Mediated World*, ed. Jonathan Gray, Cornel Sandvoss, and C. Lee Harrington (New York: New York University Press, 2007), 67.

12 Ibid., 68–69. Of course, as works in the public domain, Austen's writings are free for anyone to rework. See Emma Campbell Webster's declaration that she "would like to thank Jane Austen, very much, for being out of copyright." *Lost in Austen: Create Your Own Jane Austen Adventure* (New York: Riverhead Books, 2007), 347.

13 Tushnet, "Copyright Law," 69.

14 Henry Jenkins, *Textual Poachers: Television Fans & Participatory Culture* (New York: Routledge, 1992), 179. For an adaptation of Jenkins's ten categories of television-inspired fan fiction to the realm of Austen fan fiction, see Gilroy, "Our Austen."

15 Kristina Busse and Karen Hellekson, "Introduction: Work in Progress," in *Fan Fiction*, ed. Hellekson and Busse, 10.

16 Pugh, *Democratic Genre*, 242. Busse and Hellekson define "alternative universe" fan fiction somewhat differently, as a story in which "familiar characters are dropped into a new setting." "Introduction," 11.

17 Jenkins, *Textual Poaching*, 174. Julie Sanders argues that a generic shift is characteristic of, though not required by, an appropriation, which she distinguishes as follows from an adaptation: "An adaptation signals a relationship with an informing sourcetext or original. … On the other hand, appropriation frequently affects a more decisive journey away from the informing source into a wholly new cultural product and domain. This may or may not involve a generic shift, and it may still require the intellectual juxtaposition of (at least) one text against another that we have suggested is central to the reading and spectating

experience of adaptations. But the appropriated text or texts are not always as clearly signaled or acknowledged as in the adaptive process." *Adaptation and Appropriation,* 26.

18 Pugh points out that online Austen fan fiction "is a multimedia fandom; fiction is as likely to be based on the Ang Lee film of *Sense and Sensibility* (1995) or Andrew Davies's TV adaptation of *Pride and Prejudice* (1995)" as on the novels by Austen. *Democratic Genre,* 27. Grandi credits the biopic *Becoming Jane* with sparking an interest among writers of fan fiction in "experimenting with fictions dedicated to the author's existence and loves." "Web Side Stories," 35–36. Of course, as I showed in Chapter 5, fiction starring Austen as a character predates the release of *Becoming Jane.*

19 Pimenova, "Fan Fiction," 52–53.

20 Kate Bowles, "Commodifying Austen: The Janeite Culture of the Internet and Commercialization through Product and Television Series Spinoffs," in *Jane Austen on Screen,* ed. Gina Macdonald and Andrew F. Macdonald (Cambridge: Cambridge University Press, 2003), 21.

21 Ibid., 19.

22 The metafictional novelist Jasper Fforde plays on the idea of shielding Austen by placing the offices of Jurisfiction, the agency that polices the book world, "at Norland Park, the house of the Dashwoods in *Sense and Sensibility.* The family kindly lent the ballroom to Jurisfiction on the unspoken condition that Jane Austen books would be an area of special protection." *Thursday Next in The Well of Lost Plots* (New York: Viking, 2003), 99.

23 Pugh quotes extensively from the guidelines developed by the Republic of Pemberley for its "Bits of Ivory" fan fiction pages, rules that she describes as "more prescriptive, and restrictive, than most." An earlier version of the Pemberley guidelines, Pugh notes, excluded explicit sexual content, profanity, and violence on the grounds that "Jane wouldn't have done it." As Pugh puts it, the fan fiction sanctioned by the Republic of Pemberley "may be used as a way for fans to express their own creativity but is primarily there to celebrate *her.*" *Democratic Genre,* 37–38; emphasis original. The Republic of Pemberley website now identifies Bits of Ivory as an "archive" containing "fan fiction by Pemberleyans written from 1997 to 2008." The Republic of Pemberley homepage, accessed March 8, 2011, http://www.pemberley.com/.

24 For theories of play as applied to fan fiction and appropriations, respectively, see Pimenova, "Fan Fiction," 56 and Sanders, *Adaptation and Appropriation,* 25.

25 Douglas Lanier, *Shakespeare and Modern Popular Culture* (Oxford: Oxford University Press, 2002), 85. For an assertion that fan fiction constitutes an "ethical practice," see Derecho, "Archontic Literature," 77.

26 Lanier, *Shakespeare and Modern Popular Culture,* 100.

27 Ibid.

28 See the authors' note on the back cover of *Pride and Prejudice and Zombies,* which identifies Austen as the author of several "masterpieces of English literature" and describes her "co-author," Seth Grahame-Smith, as having "once [taken] a class in English literature." Austen and Grahame-Smith, *Pride and Prejudice and Zombies.*

29 Lanier, *Shakespeare and Modern Popular Culture,* 82.

30 For theories regarding the absence of slash from online Austen fan fiction, see Pugh, *Democratic Genre,* 104 and Grandi, "Web Side Stories," 31. Gilroy comments that her college students stayed away from writing slash for a fan fiction course assignment in spite of having been exposed to academic discussions of Austen and homosexuality. "Our Austen."

31 Douglas Lanier, "Shakespeare™: Myth and Biographical Fiction," in *The Cambridge Companion to Shakespeare and Popular Culture,* ed. Robert Shaughnessy (Cambridge: Cambridge University Press, 2007), 109.

32 Charlotte Brontë to W. S. Williams, April 12, 1850, reprinted in B. C. Southam, ed., *Jane Austen: The Critical Heritage,* 2 vols (London: Routledge & Kegan Paul, 1968, 1987), 1:128; emphasis original.

33 Roger Sales, *Jane Austen and Representations of Regency England,* new ed. (London: Routledge, 1996), 14. Sales describes as follows a cartoon that appeared in 1992 in Britain's *Sunday Telegraph* newspaper: "A twee, old-fashioned shopfront announces that it is 'Jane Austen's Sex Boutique' and the sign in the window says 'We're in the extremely

chaste sex shop guide.' The example is offensive," states Sales, "and yet it encapsulates the way in which Austen is often used to symbolise a lost innocence." Ibid.

34 *Pride and Prejudice: The Special Edition*, directed by Simon Langton, screenplay by Andrew Davies (1995; New York: New Video, 2001), DVD.

35 Helen Fielding, *Bridget Jones: The Edge of Reason* (New York: Viking, 1999), 35. In spite of her enthusiasm for the wet-shirted television Darcy, Bridget makes clear in Fielding's first novel that she does respect some limits to imagining Austen's characters. Drawing an analogy to men as football viewers, Bridget declares that Darcy and Elizabeth are her "chosen representatives in the field of shagging, or, rather, courtship. I do not, however, want to see any actual goals. I would hate to see Darcy and Elizabeth in bed, smoking a cigarette afterwards. That would be unnatural and wrong and I would quickly lose interest." Helen Fielding, *Bridget Jones's Diary* (New York: Viking, 1996), 215.

36 Sue Birtwistle and Susie Conklin, *The Making of Pride and Prejudice* (London: Penguin and BBC, 1995), 3, 4. Andrew Davies's screen adaptations of *Sense and Sensibility* and *Northanger Abbey*, first broadcast in 2008 and 2006 respectively, also raised some eyebrows for their depictions of sexuality. *Jane Austen's Sense & Sensibility*, directed by John Alexander, screenplay by Andrew Davies (Burbank, CA: Warner Home Video, 2008), DVD. *Jane Austen's Northanger Abbey*, directed by Jon Jones, screenplay by Andrew Davies (2006; Sherman Oaks, CA: Granada International Media, 2008), DVD.

37 *Mansfield Park*, written and directed by Patricia Rozema (1999; Burbank, CA: Buena Vista Home Entertainment, 2000), DVD. Stressing the colonial context of the Bertram family's wealth, Rozema portrays Sir Thomas Bertram as a depraved slaveholder who, as glimpsed in drawings done by his son Tom, has participated in torture, sodomy, and rape.

38 Rebecca Munford examines this and other aspects of the reception of Emma Tennant's Austen sequels in "'The Future of Pemberley': Emma Tennant, The 'Classic Progression' and Literary Trespassing," in *Uses of Jane Austen*, ed. Dow and Hanson.

39 Emma Tennant, *Emma in Love: Jane Austen's Emma Continued* (1996; London: Fourth Estate, 1997), 157.

40 Terry Castle, "Was Jane Austen Gay?," in *Boss Ladies, Watch Out!: Essays on Women, Sex, and Writing* (New York: Routledge, 2002), 128.

41 Ibid., 135.

42 Arielle Eckstut and Dennis Ashton, *Pride and Promiscuity: The Lost Sex Scenes of Jane Austen* (New York: Simon & Schuster, 2001), xi.

43 Ibid., 18, 101.

44 Ibid., 9.

45 "I was duped!," posted by Lunazen, June 4, 2001, http://www.amazon.com/Pride-Promiscuity-Lost-Scenes-Austen/product-reviews/1439140502/ref=cm_cr_pr_link_next_2?ie=UTF8&showViewpoints=0&pageNumber=2. The book's inventiveness did appeal to some readers, however, such as the Amazon.com customer who posted the following: "I think it's amazing that Jane Austen created characters that seem so alive that people are able to imagine them in new situations. Other Austen fans will enjoy reading these scenes, and even people who haven't read her books will laugh when they read these sex scenes described with such proper, old-fashioned style. It's a hilarious mix! So, loosen your corset and bust a chuckle!" "Loosen your corset!," posted by Steve Gillard, June 20, 2001, http://www.amazon.com/Pride-Promiscuity-Lost-Scenes-Austen/product-reviews/1439140502/ref=dp_top_cm_cr_acr_txt?ie=UTF8&showViewpoints=1.

46 Linda Berdoll effusively thanks the Sourcebooks editor Deb Werksman for "single-handedly rescuing [her] first book, *The Bar Sinister*, from the bowels of self-publishing purgatory." *Darcy & Elizabeth: Nights and Days at Pemberley* (Naperville, IL: Sourcebooks Landmark, 2006), 431.

47 On its homepage, Sourcebooks claims to be "the unquestioned worldwide leader in Austen continuations." "The Sourcebooks Story," accessed March 10, 2011, http://www.sourcebooks.com/the-sourcebooks-story.html. Sourcebooks also promotes its Austen-related titles on www.austenfans.com, a site that aggregates information about Austen and popular culture.

48 Jenkins, *Textual Poachers*, 179.

49 Linda Berdoll, preface to *Mr. Darcy Takes a Wife: Pride and Prejudice Continues* (Naperville, IL: Sourcebooks Landmark, 2004), vii.
50 Ibid., 2.
51 Ibid., 4.
52 Ibid., 19.
53 Ibid., 8.
54 "About the author," Berdoll, *Mr. Darcy Takes a Wife*, 469.
55 Birtwistle and Conklin, *Making of Pride and Prejudice*, 4.
56 For an appreciative account of Berdoll's *Mr. Darcy Takes a Wife* by an enthusiast whose initial interest in Austen sequels was piqued by that novel, see Laurel Obstgarten, "In defense of Linda Berdoll," *Austen Sequels* (blog), March 3, 2011, http://www.austensequels.com/2011/03/in-defense-of-linda-berdoll.html.
57 See also a recent version of *Pride and Prejudice* published, in the style of *Pride and Prejudice and Zombies*, with new content inserted into Austen's text: Annabella Bloom and Jane Austen, *Pride and Prejudice: The Wild and Wanton Edition* (Avon, MA: Adams Media, 2011).
58 Stella Hyde, introduction to *Literary Lust: The Sexiest Moments in Classic Fiction* (New York: Atria, 2006), 6.
59 Ibid., 68.
60 Ann Herendeen, "The Story Behind *Pride / Prejudice*," in *Pride / Prejudice: A Novel of Mr. Darcy, Elizabeth Bennet, and Their Forbidden Lovers* (New York: Harper, 2010), 410.
61 Ibid., 411.
62 Amazon.com customer reviewers who granted *Pride / Prejudice* one star described the book, variously, as "pictureless porn," "pure trash," "just ridiculous," and " a travesty." Frances K. Harville "bookgeek," "Eye-opener...or something!," October 11, 2010; J. Barrett "Crazy about Sequels," "Trash is the kindest word I can think of," January 27, 2010; Mandie Dietz "P&PFreak," "More like Plow and Pillager," January 30, 2010; and Marjorie M. Conder "big reader," February 27, 2010 "What a terrible book!!!!!!!," http://www.amazon.com/Pride-Prejudice-Elizabeth-Bennet-Forbidden/product-reviews/B004KAB8DY/ref=cm_cr_pr_hist_1?ie=UTF8&showViewpoints=0&filterBy=addOneStar.
63 Harriet Klausner, "Enjoyable erotic over the top of Big Ben," January 29, 2010, and DJ Clawson, "This book deserves at least ONE 5-star review for originality," January 30, 2010, http://www.amazon.com/Pride-Prejudice-Elizabeth-Bennet-Forbidden/product-reviews/B004KAB8DY/ref=dp_top_cm_cr_acr_txt?ie=UTF8&showViewpoints=1. In the realm of Austen and popular culture, no new idea remains original for long. Following Herendeen's lead is Mitzi Szereto's *Pride and Prejudice: Hidden Lusts* (Berkeley: Cleis Press, 2011).
64 Raisa, "Shameless and Sexed-up—So crazy it just might work?," August 27, 2010, http://www.amazon.com/Pride-Prejudice-Elizabeth-Bennet-Forbidden/product-reviews/B004KAB8DY/ref=dp_top_cm_cr_acr_txt?ie=UTF8&showViewpoints=1.
65 Beth Massey "enrage_femme," "Darcy and Bingley embrace change—and I loved every minute," September 11, 2010, ibid.
66 Pugh, *Democratic Genre*, 125.
67 The discussion guide to the movie tie-in paperback version of *Twilight* alerts readers to the intended homage and encourages them to ponder parallels with *Pride and Prejudice*. Stephenie Meyer, *Twilight* (2005; New York: Little, Brown, 2008), n.p. For an overview of Meyer's reworking of Austen, see Shirley Kinney and Wallis Kinney, "The Jane Austen-*Twilight* Zone," accessed March 10, 2011, http://www.jasna.org/film/twilight.html.
68 Dan Wagstaff, "Q & A with Jason Rekulak," September 2, 2009, http://undeathmatch.wordpress.com/2009/09/02/q-a-with-jason-rekulak/.
69 "From Gothic to Graphic: Adapting Jane Austen Novels," panel discussion moderated by Juliette Wells, Morgan Library & Museum, January 26, 2010.
70 Jennifer Schuessler, "I Was a Regency Zombie," *New York Times*, February 21, 2009, http://www.nytimes.com/2009/02/22/weekinreview/22schuessler.html.
71 "From Gothic to Graphic."
72 Engaging a new generation was the goal, explains Nancy Butler, of the graphic-novel version of *Pride and Prejudice* launched in 2009 by Marvel Comics. "Young readers

would now get a chance to meet the Bennets, the Bingleys, and Mr. Darcy—and maybe be tempted to visit the actual book." Introduction to Jane Austen, *Pride & Prejudice*, adapted by Nancy Butler and Hugo Petrus (New York: Marvel, 2009), iv. See also Jane Austen, *Sense & Sensibility*, adapted by Nancy Butler and Sonny Liew (New York: Marvel, 2010).

73 "Since its publication in April 2009, *Pride and Prejudice and Zombies* has been translated into French, German, Italian, Chinese, Japanese, Spanish, Polish, Portuguese, Hungarian, Serbian, and Croatian." "About the Authors and Illustrator," *Pride and Prejudice and Zombies: The Deluxe Heirloom Edition*, by Jane Austen and Seth Grahame-Smith (Philadelphia: Quirk Books, 2009), 360.

74 Seth Grahame-Smith, introduction to *Pride and Prejudice and Zombies: The Deluxe Heirloom Edition* (Philadelphia: Quirk Books, 2009), 10.

75 Wagstaff, "Q & A with Jason Rekulak."

76 Steve Hockensmith, *Pride and Prejudice and Zombies: Dawn of the Dreadfuls* (Philadelphia: Quirk Books, 2010) and *Pride and Prejudice and Zombies: Dreadfully Ever After* (Philadelphia: Quirk Books, 2011).

77 Austen and Grahame-Smith, *Pride and Prejudice and Zombies*, 284–93.

78 Jane Austen and Ben H. Winters, *Sense and Sensibility and Sea Monsters* (Philadelphia: Quirk Books, 2009), 125. Physical literalization of Austen's conversational tensions is evident in a different way in Herendeen's *Pride / Prejudice*: "Austen has brilliantly conveyed the more cerebral aspects of this perfect match in scenes that read like conversational sexual intercourse," states Herendeen, "and I have necessarily extended this form of lovemaking into the couple's engagement and married life." Herendeen, "The Story Behind *Pride / Prejudice*," 414.

79 "From Gothic to Graphic."

80 Ibid.

81 Sourcebooks Landmark, the imprint that specializes in Austen sequels, has published Jane Austen and Wayne Josephson, *Emma and the Vampires* (Naperville, IL: Sourcebooks Landmark, 2010).

82 Charlotte Brontë and Sherri Browning Erwin, *Jane Slayre* (New York: Gallery, 2010); Leo Tolstoy and Ben H. Winters, *Android Karenina* (Philadelphia: Quirk Books, 2010). Seth Grahame-Smith followed up his *Zombies* success with *Abraham Lincoln: Vampire Hunter* (New York: Grand Central Publishing, 2010).

83 Susan Krinard, introduction to *Bespelling Jane Austen*, by Mary Balogh et al. (Ontario: Harlequin, 2010), 6.

84 Ibid. For a theory of how paranormal fiction in general and vampire fiction in particular extend Austen's own treatment of masculinity, see Sarah S. G. Frantz, "Darcy's Vampiric Descendants: Austen's Perfect Romance Hero and J. R. Ward's Black Dagger Brotherhood," *Persuasions On-Line* 30.1 (2009), http://www.jasna.org/persuasions/on-line/vol30no1/frantz.html.

85 Krinard, introduction, 7.

86 Colleen Gleason, introduction to *Northanger Castle*, in *Bespelling Jane Austen*, by Balogh et al., 94. See also Amanda Grange's dedication to Catherine Morland of her novel *Mr. Darcy, Vampyre* (Naperville, IL: Sourcebooks, 2009).

87 Janet Mullany, *Jane and the Damned* (New York: Avon, 2010); Michael Thomas Ford, *Jane Bites Back* (New York: Ballantine, 2010); Michael Thomas Ford, *Jane Goes Batty* (New York: Ballantine, 2011).

88 *Becoming Jane*, directed by Julian Jarrold, screenplay by Sarah Williams and Kevin Hood (2007; Burbank, CA: Buena Vista Home Entertainment, 2008), DVD. Stephanie Barron's series began with *Jane and the Unpleasantness at Scargrave Manor: Being the First Jane Austen Mystery* (New York: Bantam, 1996) and has reached Stephanie Barron, *Jane and the Canterbury Tale: Being a Jane Austen Mystery* (New York: Bantam, 2011).

89 Mullany, *Jane and the Damned*, 1.

90 Ibid., 53; emphasis original.

91 Ibid., 150. Mullany does follow the lead of earlier depicters of Austen by presenting Jane as newly inspired by her experiences: "It was time for the creation of another character. Someone handsome and untrustworthy who would charm and entice for his

own amusement. A man who would prey upon innocence and generosity, yet provide pleasure and delight. Now she understood the significance of the touch of fingertips, the intimacy of a glance, a touch; how it was possible for the greatest propriety to mask passion and desire." Ibid., 268.

92 Ibid., 290.

93 An attachment to Cassandra is another important factor in the decision of Mullany's Jane to live among humans; Jane has earlier imagined "the grief her sister would inevitably experience as she waited all her life for Jane to return" from her new companions, whom Cassandra does not know to be vampires. Ibid., 217.

94 Janet Mullany, *Jane Austen: Blood Persuasion* (New York: Avon, 2011).

95 Ford, *Jane Bites Back*, 45; Ford, *Jane Goes Batty*, 29. By presenting Charlotte Brontë as a humorless vampire, of course, Ford allows his Jane to take revenge for the later author's unappreciative comment about the "Passions" being missing in Austen's work.

96 As a reminder that not all self-identified Christians consider Austen appropriate reading, see Kenneth R. Morefield's account of his past experience teaching in what he calls "a fundamentalist environment." Morefield points out the existence of readers "who can and do have moral objections to reading or assigning Jane Austen." "'Emma Could Not Resist': Complicity and the Christian Reader," *Persuasions* 25 (2003): 198.

97 The three prayers attributed to Austen appear as Appendix D in Jane Austen, *Later Manuscripts*, ed. Janet Todd and Linda Bree (Cambridge: Cambridge University Press, 2009), 573–76.

98 Henry Austen, "Biographical Notice of the Author" (1817), repr. in Jane Austen, *Persuasion*, ed. Janet Todd and Antje Blank (Cambridge: Cambridge University Press, 2006), 331. See Chapter 5 for further discussion of Henry's depiction of his sister.

99 Laura Mooneyham White, *Jane Austen's Anglicanism* (Aldershot, Hampshire: Ashgate, 2011), 4. See White's introduction for an overview of the divergent critical approaches to Austen taken by secular and religiously minded scholars.

100 One Austen adaptation with religious content that is not aimed exclusively at Christian readers is Carrie Bebris, *North by Northanger (Or, The Shades of Pemberley)* (New York: Forge, 2006), which imagines the Roman Catholic past of Northanger Abbey and grants Elizabeth Darcy a Mary relic, handed down from generations of women, for protection in childbirth.

101 Because a complete survey of all faith-based treatments of Austen is beyond my scope, let me point briefly to the following sources. For a Christian-inflected introduction for general readers to Austen's novels, comparable to several guides I discussed in Chapter 3, see Peter Leithart, *Miniatures and Morals: The Christian Novels of Jane Austen* (Moscow, ID: Canon Press, 2004). Leithart is also the author of a life of Austen aimed at Christian readers, *Jane Austen* (Nashville: Thomas Nelson, 2009), which stresses "the Christian humility, selfless charity, childlike joy and playfulness that [Leithart] believe[s] were central to Austen's character and to her best characters" (155). (Also published in Thomas Nelson's "Christian Encounters" series are lives of Anne Bradstreet, J. R. R. Tolkein, Johann Sebastian Bach, and Isaac Newton, among others.) A sequel to *Pride and Prejudice* that touches on the idea of God's plan for human lives is Eucharista Ward, *A Match for Mary Bennet: Can a Serious Young Lady Ever Find Her Way to Love?* (Naperville, IL: Sourcebooks Landmark, 2009). (Ward is a nun of the order of the Sisters of St. Francis and a retired high-school English teacher.) A biographical novel about Austen aimed at young-adult Christian readers is Nancy Moser, *Just Jane: A Novel of Jane Austen's Life* (Minneapolis: Bethany House, 2007), which proclaims the importance of developing one's God-given talents. As ever with popular Austen material, the self-publishing realm contains interpretations that range even further afield from mainstream tastes and conventions. See for instance Muriel Keller Evans, *Jane Austen, Her Golden Years: A Historical Novel Highlighting Her Family and Faith* (n.p.: Xulon Press, 2009), in which, among other invented and heavily re-imagined scenes, Jane converses with William Wilberforce and articulates her views on Evangelicalism.

102 Debra White Smith is also the author of *What Jane Austen Taught Me about Love and Romance* (Eugene, OR: Harvest House, 2007), an advice book that relates the moral

dilemmas of Austen's characters to those faced by contemporary evangelicals, including Smith herself. For an analysis of *What Jane Austen Taught Me*, as well as a more detailed treatment of Smith's "Austen Series" and Sarah Arthur's *Dating Mr. Darcy*, see my article "True Love Waits: Austen and the Christian Romance in the Contemporary U.S.," in "The Global Jane Austen," ed. Susan Allen Ford and Inger Sigrun Brody, special issue, *Persuasions On-Line* 28.2 (2008), http://www.jasna.org/persuasions/on-line/vol28no2/wells.htm.

103 Smith does change one of Austen's most ridiculous clergy characters, Mr. Collins of *Pride and Prejudice*, into the vice-president of an oil company. Apparently, Austen's satire of the clergy might offend some of Smith's more conservative readers. The unavailability of ordination to women in Austen's day allows Smith to steer clear of an issue that is highly controversial among some evangelical groups.

104 Debra White Smith, *First Impressions* (Eugene, OR: Harvest House, 2004), 269.

105 Debra White Smith, *Reason and Romance* (Eugene, OR: Harvest House, 2004), 293.

106 Debra White Smith, *Central Park* (Eugene, OR: Harvest House, 2005), 23.

107 Smith, *First Impressions*, 255.

108 Arthur has made a career of basing inspirational works on popular films: she is the author as well of guides dealing with J. R. R. Tolkein's *The Lord of the Rings* and C. S. Lewis's *The Lion, the Witch, and the Wardrobe*.

109 Sarah Arthur, *Dating Mr. Darcy: A Smart Girl's Guide to Sensible Romance* (Wheaton: Tyndale House, 2005), 5.

110 Ibid., 89, 87.

111 Ibid., 88; emphasis original.

112 Ibid., 155.

113 Bruce Stovel, "'The Sentient Target of Death': Jane Austen's Prayers," in *Jane Austen's Business: Her World and Her Profession*, ed. Juliet McMaster and Bruce Stovel (New York: St. Martin's, 1996), 194.

114 For a fuller account of Black's *Pride & Prejudice* that focuses on the film's effort to reach a broad audience, see my article "Jane Austen in Mollywood: Mainstreaming Mormonism in Andrew Black's *Pride & Prejudice* (2003)," in *Peculiar Portrayals: Mormons on the Page, Stage, and Screen*, ed. Mark T. Decker and Michael Austin (Utah State University Press, 2010), 163–82.

115 "Casting Notice," accessed March 14, 2011, http://www.ldsfilm.com/Pride/PrideAndPrejudice2.html.

116 *Pride & Prejudice*, directed by Andrew Black (Excel Entertainment Group, 2003), DVD.

117 Austen does indicate that the pedantic Mary considers Collins well suited to herself and "might have been prevailed on to accept him." *Pride and Prejudice*, ed. Pat Rogers (Cambridge: Cambridge University Press, 2006), 139.

118 In the UK, *A Walk with Jane Austen* was released by Lion Hudson with the somewhat more literal subtitle "A Modern Woman's Search for Happiness, Fulfilment, and Her Very Own Mr. Darcy."

119 Lori Smith, *A Walk with Jane Austen: A Journey into Adventure, Love & Faith* (Colorado Springs, CO: WaterBrook Press, 2007), 37.

120 Ibid., 144.

121 Ibid., 11–12.

122 Ibid., 11, 15.

123 Ibid., 25.

124 Ibid., 37.

125 Ibid., 38. Smith cites Mr. Collins as an example of ridiculousness; earlier, she remarks wryly that "it's a truth universally acknowledged among single Christian women that single Christian guys beyond a certain age are weird." Ibid., 31.

126 Ibid., 101.

127 Ibid., 176.

128 Ibid., 202. Smith mentions on the blog that preceded her book, though not in the memoir proper, that she has "recently found a home in the Anglican church." Lori Smith, "Kathleen Norris Meets Bridget Jones," November 8, 2005, http://www.followingausten.com/2005/11/kathleen-norris.html.

129 Smith, *A Walk with Jane Austen*, 181. Smith discusses her commitment to chastity more

fully in her earlier book, *The Single Truth*, where she also suggests that concentrating on Mr. Darcy, at least the version incarnated on screen by Colin Firth, aids in keeping her vow. Lori Smith, *The Single Truth: Challenging the Misconceptions of Singleness with God's Consuming Truth* (Shippensburg, PA: Treasure House, 2002), 144.

130 Smith, *A Walk with Jane Austen*, 217–18.

131 Ibid., 217. Characteristically, Smith separates the way she imagines Austen felt about fame from her sense that God loves her, Lori Smith, regardless of what she achieves. In contrast, Nancy Moser's young-adult Christian-audience novel *Just Jane* concludes with Cassandra Austen assuring Jane that her writing "is who you are. ... God has a plan for each of us, Jane, a unique purpose. ... Now you need to find your own contentment in being just Jane" (351).

Chapter 7

Coming Together Through Austen

Austen fans from the 1990s came into their own as material for fiction in Helen Fielding's enormously popular novels, *Bridget Jones's Diary* (1996) and *Bridget Jones: The Edge of Reason* (1999).[1] "Just nipped out for fags prior to getting changed ready for BBC *Pride and Prejudice*," Bridget records in Fielding's first novel, which takes place during 1995, the year that the BBC broadcast its new *Pride and Prejudice* miniseries. "Love the nation being so addicted. ... The basis of my own addiction, I know, is my simple human need for Darcy to get off with Elizabeth."[2] Bridget is no snob about television adaptations, unlike one of her more highbrow acquaintances who declares primly that "with the Classics people should be made to prove they've read the book before they're allowed to watch the television version."[3] Indeed, the viewing habits of Bridget and her friends are unashamedly self-indulgent, focused on visual pleasures rather than literary thoughts. In *Bridget Jones: The Edge of Reason*, Bridget's friend "Shaz fiddled with the *Pride and Prejudice* video to try to find the bit where Colin Firth dives into the lake. ... We all fell silent then, watching Colin Firth emerging from the lake dripping wet, in the see-through white shirt. Mmm. Mmmm."[4]

In the wake of *Bridget Jones's Diary*, British and American lovers of Austen have increasingly turned to fiction, as both writers and readers, in order to explore their own enthusiasm and compare themselves to other fans. Fictional characters, like their real-world counterparts, read Austen in book groups—most famously in Karen Joy Fowler's bestselling novel *The Jane Austen Book Club* (2004)—in academic classrooms, and, often obsessively, on their own.[5] As Marilyn Francus has noted, a subgenre of recent novels about Austen fans concentrates on the rehabilitation of the addicted reader/viewer whose imagination has become too thoroughly permeated with Austen's characters, particularly those of *Pride and Prejudice*.[6] For those whose love of Austen becomes too strong, another avenue of escape depicted in film and fiction is time travel into the Regency, or into the world of *Pride and Prejudice* itself.[7]

All of these representations of Austen fans meditate on the importance of Austen's novels to amateur readers today, particularly women. (Much fiction about Austen fans tends to reinforce the stereotype that Austen lovers, or addicts, are overwhelmingly female; Fowler's *Jane Austen Book Club*, for example, has only one male member.) Recently, novelists have explored further how people of different ages, genders, and nationalities connect with each other through devotion to Austen. Most potently, as imagined by some writers, a deep appreciation for Austen can bring together amateur and academic readers, across the great gulf of attitude and language that has long separated these two groups.[8]

The first section of this chapter focuses on three recent novels that depict the divide between amateur and professional approaches to Austen. Each novel's heroine experiences a version of a split between creative and analytic selves, which she re-integrates by reflecting on Austen's writings and by pursuing amateur reading practices such as literary tourism (involving many of the sites I discussed in Chapter 4). Important to each heroine, too, is contact with Austen devotees, including some who participate in an organization or society dedicated to Austen. I turn then to an actual author society, the Jane Austen Society of North America (JASNA), which since its inception in 1979 has offered a home to a broad spectrum of Austen lovers, from amateurs to academics. Drawing on JASNA's archives, I examine the motives of the organization's founders and trace efforts by them and their successors to make the new society both distinctive and welcoming to all of Austen's readers. I conclude by calling on everyone to whom Austen matters to come together to explore her works, her influence, and the importance of literature today.

Moving along the Scholar–Amateur Continuum in Fiction

Georgina Jackson, the heroine of Elizabeth Aston's novel *Writing Jane Austen* (2010), is initially extremely reluctant to allow herself to join the company of Austen fans. An American-born postdoctoral research fellow in history and the author of a critically acclaimed but bleak novel about the underside of Victorian life, Georgina prides herself on having never read an Austen novel. "I'm not good with romance," she declares to her friend Henry, a physicist, and his teenage sister Maud, an Austen enthusiast. "Her novels are all about young woman falling in love and getting husbands, aren't they? Not my thing at all."[9] Only because Georgina desperately needs employment does she accept the commission to complete a newly discovered fiction manuscript attributed to Austen. Georgina's editor calls the project the "chance of a lifetime";[10] to Georgina, the assignment feels like a curse, forcing her outside her comfort zone as both a reader and a creator. "I'm not that kind of novelist," she tells Henry. "Novelists come in two varieties, those who are basically reporters and those who do imagination. Austen's imagination, I'm reporter through and through. She's romantic. I go for realism."[11]

So invested is Georgina in her identity as an anti-fan that she tries every possible stratagem to prepare herself for her project short of actually opening an Austen novel, in spite of Maud's insistence that a "treat" lies in store for her when she finally reads Austen.[12] Confidently applying her training as a historian, Georgina heads to Oxford's Bodleian Library in order to tackle her research "in a rational manner. Get an idea of what Austen was about. Get a feel for the period. Background stuff. Historical, social, she'd be on firm ground there."[13] To her dismay, however, Georgina discovers that her scholarly background is of no avail at all in helping her make sense of a recent issue of *The Journal of Contemporary Austen Studies* (a title invented by Aston).[14] "Nothing in Literary Theory 101 had prepared her for this," the narrator reports, as Georgina peers at article titles including *"Astigmatic bio-cultural structuralism in Jane Austen's Juvenilia"* and *"Proto-synaptic supratexts versus intercolonial rations: social relapses in Mansfield Park."*[15] No academic neophyte, Georgina reminds herself sensibly that "each discipline had its own language, its jargon, its formulae for short-cutting to the substance of what the writer had to say. She could decode it for history. Eng Lit had its different vocabulary, that was all. Was there a dictionary? A glossary, explaining the meaning of arcane phrases? Of course not, no more than there was in her own field. Who would take the trouble to provide it? Those in the know didn't need it, and lay people wouldn't be interested."[16]

Not surprisingly, given Aston's build-up, when Georgina does eventually read Austen, she is smitten, "overwhelmed by great art" as she has been on few occasions in her life.[17] Abetted by Maud and Henry, she consumes all of Austen's novels in a marathon, sleep-deprived reading session. Even before her conversion to a passionate Austen devotee, however, Georgina has moved away from the academic identity that anchored her at the beginning of Aston's novel. As Georgina discovers that she doesn't care about the termination of her research fellowship on a trumped-up charge of plagiarism, "the titles of those articles on Jane Austen darted into her head. When had scholars become academics? When had a genuine thirst for knowledge become a relentless and jargon-ridden pursuit of publication? Before her time, and how much of a scholar was she?"[18]

Georgina's sympathy for amateur readers grows stronger as she takes part in an Austen fans' tour of Bath. Full of "incredulity" as she listens to visitors from Russia and Texas discuss Austen's characters "as if they were real people," Georgina thinks censoriously that

> people loved to personalize and emotionalize fictive and historical characters—a distortion that conflicted with reality and was simply an indulgence.
>
> *Prig*, said a voice in her head, startling her. What harm did it do for people to feel involved with characters from the past or historical figures? Academic rigour and clear-headedness had never belonged to more than a small percentage of even the literate population.
>
> *Twice prig*, said the voice. *Maybe the nonacademics have more fun*, it went on. *Maybe Jane Austen and Dickens would have laughed at all the serious papers and tomes pronouncing on their writing.*

Odd how a writer like Dickens made you laugh as well as cry, and those commenting on him with the full rigour of trained academic minds seemed mostly to have had humour bypasses.[19]

What good, Georgina begins to wonder, is scholarship that not only ignores but seems unable to grasp the experiences and responses of ordinary readers?

As Georgina begins work on completing the unfinished Austen novel, Aston calls attention in another way to the tendency of academics to miss the point with authors like Austen. Aiming to turn out "a passable manuscript, correctly written in the style of Jane Austen," Georgina has "used the novels as templates," borrowing aspects of character and plot, and taking care that her "sentence length, vocabulary, syntax and punctuation" match Austen's.[20] Georgina's careful effort to stay within Austen's parameters earns her praise from a "terrifying academic" who has been hired by her publishers to vet her manuscript for compliance with Austen's style.[21] Georgina's Austen-loving young friend Maud, however, has a very different reaction to the manuscript: "it's unreadable. ... The trouble is, it isn't Jane Austen, because what it is, is dull. Jane Austen is never dull. ... It's no more Jane Austen than the Highway Code. It's all there, the names and characters and situations and all that, but all the people in it are as dead as dodos. Lifeless. Unquick. It's like Henry said, your heart isn't in it."[22] From this point forward, *Writing Jane Austen* becomes a meditation on creating Austen-inspired fiction (a subject close to the heart of Aston, the Oxford-educated author of several well-received novels about the descendants of Elizabeth and Fitzwilliam Darcy). Having decisively left behind her preconceptions about Austen, as well as about what is critically valuable, Georgina follows her heart and writes a novel that isn't "remotely like Jane Austen," or like her own grim first novel.[23] She is doubly rewarded for her courage: she "discover[s] what a joy writing could be," and her new book becomes a bestseller.[24]

As Georgina evolves from Austen-avoider to Austen-lover to inspired creator, she gains perspective on the limitations of scholarly approaches and comes to be comfortable defining herself outside an academic identity. While her immersive reading experience of Austen is the most important factor in Georgina's development, contact with the world of Austen's popularity is influential too. In Bath, Georgina browses in a shop called Darcy's founded by an old school friend of hers, who explains that she sells "anything and everything that has to do with Jane Austen and her times . ... If it has anything to do with Jane Austen, or we can stretch it to have a connection, then we can provide it."[25] In the company of Maud and Henry, Georgina visits Winchester and Chawton, where she responds especially strongly to the sight of Austen's "tiny" writing table.[26] Georgina is less affected by one of her earliest dealings with the world of Austen fans: a gathering of the Jane Austen Society in Oxford, to which she is dragooned to speak before she has read any Austen at all. To her relief, Georgina is not outed as an Austen know-nothing; all in attendance are students, who prove much more keenly interested in Georgina's experience as a published writer than in her thoughts about Austen.

Georgina's acceptance of the importance of pleasure in both reading and writing represents Aston's primary challenge to academic orthodoxy. Aston also pays tribute to everyday readers in her depiction, relatively brief as it is, of the student Jane Austen Society. With the exception of one pedantic questioner named Mary—apparently a nod by Aston to Mary Bennet of *Pride and Prejudice*—the students are far from the English-lit blowhards Georgina fears. Coming from a range of disciplines, they are at ease talking about Austen without jargon. One "beautiful young man in a ski hat" who is pursuing Oriental Studies, for instance, describes himself as "a big Janeite, okay? I love her sexy heroines."[27] That the students are less interested in criticism than in their personal responses—and in their own creative work as writers—bodes well for the future, Aston suggests. *The Journal of Contemporary Austen Studies* may never address a broad audience, but Austen's ordinary readers will continue to discuss her works among themselves and pursue their own projects inspired, however loosely, by her.

Like Aston's *Writing Jane Austen,* the American novelist Beth Pattillo's *Jane Austen Ruined My Life* (2009) portrays a recovering academic who learns, through contact with Austen lovers, to embrace her creative side. For Pattillo's heroine Emma Grant, shedding her scholarly identity involves a return to an earlier self. Before she earned her PhD at the University of Texas, she was once an obsessive reader: "One sentence of *Pride and Prejudice,*" she recalls, "and I was hooked like a junkie who had to keep coming back for a fix."[28] Emma blames Austen, and her own mother, for leading her to expect a happy ending in marriage—this is how, she believes, Austen has "ruined" her life.[29] Having been betrayed both personally and professionally by her husband, also a literary critic, Emma is determined to salvage her academic reputation by undertaking a betrayal of her own: bringing to light hitherto unknown Jane Austen letters, in spite of having promised to keep their existence a secret.

The conceit of lost letters is, of course, a hoary one in literary thrillers, deployed with especial ingenuity by A. S. Byatt in her acclaimed novel *Possession* (1990).[30] As I pointed out in Chapters 5 and 6, a similar premise operates in a number of Austen-inspired works of fiction, most notably Stephanie Barron's series of "Jane Austen mysteries."[31] Pattillo's inventive twist is to make the letters' method of concealment as intriguing as their contents, if not more so. As Emma gains the trust of the woman, Mrs. Parrot, who lured her to England with the hint of an unknown stash of Austen letters, the history of that stash begins to emerge. Known among themselves as "The Formidables," a term initially applied by Austen to herself and Cassandra, this small band of women guards all of the letters Austen wrote, "almost three thousand," according to Mrs. Parrot.[32] "Cassandra deputized the first of the lot [of Formidables] before her death," Mrs. Parrot reveals to Emma. "Fanny Knatchbull [Austen's niece, born Fanny Knight] was one."[33] The society of Formidables remains a tight one, as Mrs. Parrot explains: "There are only a handful of us at any given time. Never more than five, certainly."[34]

Even before Mrs. Parrot allows Emma to glimpse any of the hidden letters, the young American woman's reaction to learning of the existence of the Formidables alerts the reader that Emma will have a hard time keeping her scholarly cool. "A secret society? Devoted to Jane Austen? It was too fantastical to be believed. As an academic, I knew better than to give it a moment's credit. But as a woman ... a romantic. As my mother's daughter. My heart leaped into my throat."[35] Emma continues to respond to Austen in a new way as she pursues the tasks, many involving literary tourism, that Mrs. Parrot has devised to determine the younger woman's trustworthiness. Visiting St. Nicholas Church in Steventon, Emma is taken aback by how moved she feels: "I'd spent the past ten years learning everything there was to know about Jane Austen, but nothing I had read in a book or scholarly journal could have prepared me for the wave of emotion that threatened to carry me away. ... I was supposed to be a seasoned academic, an impartial observer and analyst of the object of my study."[36] Later, at the British Library, Emma is even more overwhelmed by the sight of the literary treasures on display: "I'd seen my share of rare manuscripts, but somehow, these particular pieces lined up side by side, a breathtaking record of the language and literature I loved, caused my throat to tighten."[37] Looking at a manuscript page of Austen's juvenilia elicits a still stronger reaction, which Emma tries to conceal lest she seem unprofessional to her traveling companion, a Walter Scott scholar. "I bit the inside of my cheek so I wouldn't cry. I didn't want to look like a total sap. After all, I was a serious scholar, not a fan, but at the moment, I sure felt like one."[38] Pattillo has not left herself much room for her heroine to have a yet more profound response to Jane Austen's House, but she just manages it, having Emma feel, while touching Austen's writing table, "a warm glow ... a kind of peace ... a life force" that she later thinks of as a "near-mystical experience."[39]

Emma's scholarly attitudes recede further as she begins to wonder in a very personal way about how Austen felt about her life. "Did she, like me, grow up believing her father's assurance that there was a divine plan leading her somewhere special? Had she died contented with her single state, or did she still hope to find a man worthy of her vow of marriage? This question, once purely academic, now felt intensely private."[40] Emma's new curiosity affects how she reads Austen's writings as well. Though she has long "made a practice of rereading each of the major novels annually," under the influence of Mrs. Parrot she "read[s] Jane Austen as [she has] never read her before," pursuing her curiosity about Austen's private life.[41] Another Formidable, Hester Golightly, directs Emma to take part in activities that will further develop her insight into Austen's life. "You must dance with a handsome young man, just as Jane would have done," she tells her. "Then you will have an inkling as to how she felt when she was here in Bath."[42] In the Assembly Rooms, Emma gamely does her best, humming a tune and mimicking the dances she has seen "performed in movies, and even at the occasional academic conference where a dance instructor had been brought in to lighten the atmosphere."[43] Her strenuous efforts to channel Austen come to nothing until her love interest, the Scott scholar, arrives and instrumental music wafts from an adjoining room, when Emma finally realizes "no wonder Jane Austen had loved it [dancing] so much."[44]

When Mrs. Parrot eventually invites Emma to become a new member of the Formidables, she cites the younger woman's life experience as the main reason. "A woman who has lost love, and then found it again, is precisely the kind of person we're looking for," Mrs. Parrot tells Emma.[45] By this point, however, it is clear to both Emma and Pattillo's readers that members of the "Jane Austen Mafia," as Emma calls them, are united by a different aspect of shared identity as well.[46] Mrs. Parrot herself, despite an appearance that reminds Emma of the colorful television character Hyacinth Bucket, turns out to be, under a different surname, "one of the greatest living experts on nineteenth-century British women writers."[47] Scholarly members of the Formidables evidently must let down their professional guard and cultivate their enthusiasm for Austen, as Mrs. Parrot has encouraged Emma to do.

Behaving like an amateur reader affects more than Emma's sense of Austen. Several chapters into the novel, she reveals to a new acquaintance, and to the reader, that she aspired long ago "to be a world-famous author" but was persuaded out of the ambition, first by parents anxious about her job prospects and then by her scholar husband, who looked down on her "pipe dream."[48] As Emma immerses herself in the places associated with Austen and allows herself to feel moved by contact with Austen relics, her desire to write surges up again. Most powerfully, Cassandra's portrait sketch of her sister, displayed in the National Portrait Gallery, inspires Emma first to meditate on Austen's achievement as a writer and then to sit right down on the gallery floor and put pen to paper herself, letting out words that had "been stored up for so long that there were oceans of them, pouring onto the page as quickly as my pen would allow."[49] "I had given in to that deep-seated, almost primeval impulse I'd ignored for years," she reflects joyfully. "I'd allowed myself to write. Not academic papers or abstracts or book reviews but real, original, personal writing. It felt glorious."[50] By the novel's end, Emma has made the acquaintance of an editor who expresses interest in her writing, which gives her "the chance to begin again."[51] (For reasons that Pattillo leaves somewhat underdeveloped, Emma has decided to turn down Mrs. Parrot's invitation to join the Formidables and to place her literary ambitions ahead of love, at least for the time being.)

In addition to inventing a heroine who, thanks to Austen, finds the courage to write, Pattillo contributes to Austen-inspired fiction by addressing in a new way Cassandra's role with respect to Austen's legacy.[52] As I explored in Chapter 5, Cassandra's destruction of the majority of her sister's letters has put her in a complicated position for today's fans, who on the one hand can revere and identify with her as Austen's closest friend, and on the other hand can resent her for concealing so much about her sister. Pattillo's imaginative solution of having Cassandra secretly preserve all the letters not only redeems Cassandra but extends the fantasy that the surviving letters would offer a coterie of dedicated and right-thinking Austen fans unparalleled access to their favorite author. What's more, in *Jane Austen Ruined My Life* not Cassandra but Jane herself makes the decision to keep her most personal letters from the public eye. "*Take the scissors to all the letters that might be used against me,*" Jane instructs Cassandra in 1817. "*If that task proves too onerous, burn them or contrive to conceal them however you see fit. Whatever you do, protect my children from the coarse and vulgar speculations of others. The world may know my words, but it has no such privileges with my heart.*"[53] By putting Jane in charge of her own archive, Pattillo transforms Cassandra from gatekeeper to sympathetic protector. By enlisting in the maintenance of the preserved papers women who are not Austen family descendants, Pattillo widens the circle of Austen's intimates, allowing all female fans—even Americans—to imagine that they might be worthy of access to Austen's secrets.

In Pattillo's follow-up novel *Mr. Darcy Broke My Heart* (2010), the Formidables return, this time protecting the early draft of *Pride and Prejudice* known as *First Impressions,* and two characters reach out to each other across the amateur/academic divide. Pattillo's heroine, Claire Prescott, is no Austen aficionado: speaking of Mr. Darcy, she declares, "My sister thinks he's the ultimate romantic hero, but I just don't get it."[54] Claire reluctantly takes the place of that Austen-loving sister in a summer seminar on *Pride and Prejudice* held at Oxford. Painfully conscious of her own lack of higher education, she is relieved to see her sister's name and occupation (teacher) on the list of course participants, rather than her own, "Claire Prescott, Unemployed Pediatrics Office Manager with No College Degree."[55]

Claire's inexperience with Austen actually serves as an advantage when an apparently dotty Oxford woman who identifies herself as an Austen family descendant shows Claire pages she claims are from the lost manuscript of *First Impressions.* Little acquainted with the finished novel, or with Austen's career, Claire reads the manuscript with fresh eyes. Indeed, Claire is not certain, at first, whether the handwriting is even Austen's: "I had no way of knowing," she thinks. "I was the wrong person, the worst person possible, really, to be sitting here trying to decide if this pile of pages was for real."[56] Unlike another ambitious seminar participant, a publisher who has heard rumors of the existence of *First Impressions,* Claire has no professional reasons of her own to exploit her discovery. Nor does Claire develop a flair for academic inquiry during her time at Oxford, though she enjoys the seminar discussions. When she heads to the Bodleian Library to try to discover "the truth about what might have changed between Austen's first version of *Pride and Prejudice* and the final one," she quickly becomes overwhelmed: "an hour and several Jane Austen biographies later, I wasn't sure I was cut out for scholarly efforts. My head swam with dates and descriptions and differing accounts."[57]

Claire does discover, however, that she needs no specialized tools to appreciate why Austen would have suppressed *First Impressions*. Claire's hard-won insight into herself allows her to understand the motives of another woman, even one who lived so long ago and achieved so much. "I may never be a true scholar," Claire tells the Formidable Mrs. Parrot. "But I think I've learned enough to know the most important thing about her."[58] Saying this, Claire feels "the strangest sense of connection with Jane Austen" and reflects on how her own history, while so different in its particulars from Austen's, has led her to have "more in common with Jane Austen than [she] would have ever guessed."[59]

The trust Claire learns to place in her own convictions derives in large part from the encouragement of a fellow seminar participant, Martin Blakely. Claire initially takes the knowledgeable, elderly Martin for a British "Austen fan," a judgment that he doesn't contradict.[60] To her chagrin, she later learns that he is "one of the world's leading Austen scholars," though she remains mystified by his presence in the course.[61] Both in conversations with Claire and when presenting to the seminar, Martin demonstrates a style of literary inquiry that is personal and deceptively simple. Speculating on why Austen would have urged Cassandra to keep *First Impressions* from the public eye, Martin declares, "We all choose what of ourselves we want to present to the world. ... Why would Jane Austen be any different?"[62] To the seminar, he makes a short, accessible speech focusing on Austen's choice to write about "ordinary people" who demonstrate "the most difficult kind of courage ... the kind we must find to know and understand our own hearts."[63] In response to Claire's question about why he would want to "hang out with a bunch of amateurs," Martin reminds her of the term's literal meaning—"*one who loves*"—and reveals that he "came here to be with people who read Jane Austen simply for the love of it. Not for academic reasons. Not for profit. Merely for the joy of her stories and language." "So you came here for the fun of it?" Claire asks, and he says, "Precisely."[64]

Hospitable to novices and experts of a range of ages, genders, and nationalities, the seminar Claire attends in Oxford might seem like a fantastic invention by Pattillo, a forum with no counterpart in the real world. Of course, Austen summer seminars do certainly exist in England, as elsewhere, and have inspired and informed many participants.[65] It is hard to imagine, however, a scholar of Martin Blakely's supposed caliber feeling at home in, and even rewarded by, participation in one of these courses.

Yet one organization has long brought together amateurs and scholars alike for fun and edification: the Jane Austen Society of North America (JASNA).

A New Kind of Fellowship: The Jane Austen Society of North America

The original, UK Jane Austen Society (JAS), founded in 1940, had American members from early on. Alberta H. Burke, the Baltimore lover of Austen whom

I profiled in Chapter 2, joined the JAS as a life member in 1947 and frequently attended its annual meetings, which were and continue to be held each July in Chawton to commemorate the date of Austen's death. As I pointed out in Chapter 2, the general attitude of British JAS members towards Americans in the mid-twentieth century seems to have been rather chilly.[66] By the mid-1970s, North American representation in the JAS had grown so extensive that a few members began discussing the possibility of forming an additional society on their own continent. One, J. David "Jack" Grey of New York City, a public school administrator, described his dedication to Austen as "approach[ing] fanaticism."[67] Another, Joan Mason Hurley, née Joan Austen-Leigh, of Victoria, British Columbia, was an author and Austen family descendant; her husband Denis Mason Hurley also played an important encouraging role.[68] A third, Lorraine Hanaway of Philadelphia, took part in planning the new organization and, according to Joan Mason Hurley, "could just as well" have joined herself and Grey as co-founders in 1979 had the two of them not jointly decided to invite Henry Burke instead (Alberta having died in 1975).[69]

According to Joan Mason Hurley, the impetus to form JASNA resulted from her own realization that American lovers of Austen were simply different from English ones and would feel more comfortable in their own company. She identifies three pivotal events that occurred at the 1975 JAS meeting, which commemorated the bicentennial of Austen's birth. First, Joan's husband Denis was "refused the use of a washroom" by the JAS chair, Sir Hugh Smiley. Next, while the Hurleys were waiting "in the famous tent where the committee was always re-elected 'en bloc,'" one of their neighbors "actually spoke" to them, and proved to be "a charming American woman" who was passionate about Austen. And finally, at a "bicentennial costume ball" held at Oakley Hall, near Steventon, "a tall handsome man in a blue coat like Mr. Bingley's" made Joan's acquaintance; he proved to be Jack Grey, who impressed Joan as "also a keen devotee."[70] "In my whole life I had almost never met anyone who cared about Jane Austen as I did," Joan recalls, "and now I was finding two such individuals in as many days!"[71] In a pub after the costume ball, in the company of two Steventon residents, Joseph and Joyce Bown, and their houseguest, Lorraine Hanaway, Denis "put forward the idea, which no one took seriously, it was a mere joke among ourselves, that we should found our own Jane Austen Society. We laughed. What an idea! But Denis was serious: if *we* founded a society, said he, people would speak to each other, the committee would be democratically elected, and compassion would be shown for those who needed a washroom."[72]

The idea of an Austen society that would be democratic in more senses than voting alone germinated over several years, as Grey, the Hurleys, Hanaway, and Burke met at various Austen-related events. In spite of their collective dissatisfaction with the JAS, they were at first loath to appear to challenge that society. As Joan puts it, "there was, at that time, in the entire world only the one society: the Jane Austen Society which met for one afternoon, once a year, in July, in a tent at Chawton, to hear a speech, drink tea and go home again."[73] In a 1978 letter to Henry Burke, Grey describes himself as having "great qualms over setting up a rival establishment."[74] Grey carefully approached Sir Hugh Smiley, the JAS chair, to express the American group's intentions: "Many people, some of whom belong to The Jane Austen Society, have asked me if an American counterpart existed. ... Now we envision the possibility of an annual, or biennial, conference on this side of the Atlantic, hopefully accompanied by a newsletter. We feel that this would give 'American' aficionados of Jane Austen the chance to meet and share their ideas, a chance for which they might have no other occasion to satisfy."[75] "Sir Hugh was very co-operative," recalls Joan, and "compiled a list with his own hand. The people were contacted. Would they be interested in joining a new society? One based over here? Three hundred and thirty-five replied that they would."[76]

From the outset, JASNA's co-founders planned to include scholarly content as well as opportunities for the kind of free discussion that they had found so limited at the JAS meetings. In a formal letter of invitation to Henry Burke, Grey and Joan Mason Hurley declared their intention for "an annual or biennial meeting" to which they would "invite scholarly speakers, dine and have the pleasure of meeting together to exchange ideas and 'talk Jane.'"[77] Grey secured the consent of distinguished American academics as patrons for the fledgling organization; according to Joan Mason Hurley, he "felt that their names, thus displayed [on stationery], would lend an air of credibility to what seemed to us both at the time an extremely shaky enterprise."[78] JASNA's initial constitution, too, emphasized the organization's dual function as, first, a "meeting place for persons of literary and cultural interests" pertaining to "the Jane Austen period," and, second, a promoter of "interest in the field of Jane Austen studies" that would "publish informative, bulletins, or journals for distribution among its membership."[79] In contrast, the original constitution of the JAS focused on the goal of founding and maintaining "the residence of Jane Austen, at Chawton in Hampshire, as a national memorial to the novelist."[80]

Balancing the expectations of academics and devotees proved somewhat challenging in JASNA's early years. Grey, who served as the organization's first president, was taken aback when scholars whom he invited to address a JASNA annual meeting requested payment for their services. The University of Pennsylvania professor Nina Auerbach, for example, replied to Grey, "I assume I'll hear from you later on regarding accommodations, remuneration, and so on, but this letter is to assure you that I accept with pleasure." Grey forwarded her letter to Henry Burke with the handwritten note, "I hope Goucher can furnish accommodations? Remuneration? As a 'first' I should think she'd be willing to do it 'gratis.' I suppose we have no choice."[81] Grey's own ideas for annual meetings were wide-ranging, as a November 1979 letter to Henry Burke shows: "George Tucker has a slide show that might interest some people. Someone else took film of the Oakley Ball in '75 which I, for one, would like to see. I thought that those two presentations might take place on Saturday afternoon, before the dinner. ... I have a dramatization of *MP* [*Mansfield Park*], not too bad and done by a friend of mine in England. Would a Goucher group be enticed into putting it on over the weekend?"[82] As planning proceeded for the 1980 annual meeting in Baltimore, Grey wrote to Henry Burke, "I *am* a bit concerned, however, that we are becoming too academic."[83]

In spite of Grey's qualms, early JASNA annual meetings succeeded in striking a tone that seemed, at least to the bibliographer and longtime JAS member David Gilson, to be quite distinct from that of a typical JAS July gathering. Responding to Henry Burke's report of the annual meeting held by JASNA in Baltimore in October 1980, Gilson remarked that "no contrast with the Chawton meeting of course can be justifiably made; your society began as a literary society with a high proportion of academics among its founder members, so that meetings of an academic cast are natural, whereas our society is basically not literary and the form of the meeting is something of an accidental growth."[84] In a 1984 essay on the origins of JASNA that was published in the society's journal, *Persuasions*, Joan Mason Hurley praised JASNA for sponsoring conferences that "are both convivial and scholarly." As evidence of the organization's distinctive appeal, she cited a letter from an invited speaker: "The conference made for one of the happiest meetings I have attended in many years. I keep telling my colleagues here—perhaps to their discomfort—that the conferences of our various academic organizations can't hold a candle to JASNA's for sheer delight and fellowship."[85]

Of course, providing a forum for Austen scholars to share new work while not alienating devotees was not easy. On the one hand, Lorraine Hanaway expressed to Henry Burke her pleasure at having invited for the 1983 annual meeting "a very bright young woman from the English dept at Swarthmore": Mary Poovey, who was soon to publish her influential monograph *The Proper Lady and the Woman Writer: Ideology as Style in the Works of Mary Wollstonecraft, Mary Shelley, and Jane Austen* (1984).[86] And one JASNA member, Jo Modert, envisioned the organization wielding authority regarding editions of Austen's novels: she proposed a "JASNA 'seal-of-approval,'" an idea that was not implemented.[87] On the other hand, George Tucker—he of the "slide show that might interest some people," as Grey put it in 1979—distributed an anti-academic poem at that same 1983 annual meeting at which Mary Poovey spoke. Titled "Meditation," Tucker's poem imagined Jane Austen herself addressing JASNA, and it ran, in part, "many self-styled Janeites have no right to read my books ... / Let's take our tea, Cassandra dear, beneath Celestial trees—/ In that special part of Heaven that's off bounds for PHDs!"[88] Also demonstrating the enthusiasm of non-academic Austen fans, one JASNA member, Steve Sikora, sent a letter seeking correspondence with those who, as he put it, "want and maybe even need to write letters about their experience with Jane Austen."[89]

Now as then, members of varying levels of devotion and academic interests feel at home, and in the company of friends, in JASNA. In the words of Iris Lutz, who began her term as JASNA's president in 2010, the organization is "a haven for anyone who has a true interest in Jane Austen—no matter what your background, how you were introduced to her novels, or how long you have been reading and studying her work. Despite our diversity, everyone in JASNA is on the same path, sharing the same goal: to deepen our understanding and appreciation of Austen's writing, her life, and her genius."[90] JASNA's deliberate, even proud, inclusivity is evident in the organization's mission statement as well: "to foster among the widest number of readers the study, appreciation, and understanding of Jane Austen's works, her life, and her genius."[91] In keeping with that aim, JASNA's two peer-reviewed journals, *Persuasions* and *Persuasions On-Line*, publish articles that, in the words of their editor, feature "clear and expressive writing appropriate for both academic and informed general readers" and "consider issues and concepts that open up the writings on a variety of levels, leading toward our common goal of becoming better readers and interpreters of Austen's works."[92] Writing in 1996, the British literary critic Roger Sales praised the *Persuasions* of that era for "show[ing] a healthy interplay between the pleasures of the fan club and a concern to promote historically informed critical readings. The English one [the journal of the JAS], by contrast, has always been deeply suspicious of most forms of literary and historical criticism."[93]

Newcomers to JASNA from both the fan and academic worlds must adjust to the organization's lively, participatory tone as well as to the range of activities at its annual meetings, which include dance workshops and balls as well as lectures. Novelist Laurie Viera Rigler captures the anxiety of a new JASNA member who is reluctant to attend an meeting lest she be sneered at for the origins of her interest: "I am too afraid of exposing myself to such a literary group, who would no doubt think me unworthy because my entrée to Austen was via Colin Firth prancing around in tight pants for the BBC. So what if I ran out and bought all the novels and read every single one before I saw another film adaptation. A woman with a Jane Austen action figure, still in the box no less (because the box is the best part), would surely be shunned by such scholarly folk."[94] From the scholarly side, Claudia L. Johnson—a frequent and popular invited speaker at JASNA events—comments of annual meetings that

> most academics I know take a rather dim view of these galas, where enjoyment rather than hermeneutic mastery is assumed to be the reward of reading, where reading is sociable rather than solitary, and where the stuff of erudition itself seems so different. On quizzes—a staple of JASNA meetings—academics fare quite poorly: having been taught to regard only certain relationships, scenes and (typically, closural) structures as significant, we rarely recollect the colour of this character's dress or that servant's name. We sometimes suffer the additional mortification of discovering our own papers becoming yet another relatively undifferentiated, unhierarchicalized item in the great repository of Austeniana assiduously collected by Janeites

and compiled in newsletters and reports, printed somewhere between recipes for white soup and the latest word jumble.[95]

Having myself presented at several JASNA annual and regional meetings beginning in 2001, when I was still a graduate student, I can attest that the cultural differences between the academic world and JASNA are profound. In particular, seeing fans and even some scholars attired in Regency dress takes some getting used to. So too do comments like one I received from an audience member after my first JASNA presentation: "I feel sure," announced an elderly man, "that Jane Austen knew she was a genius!" Doctoral-level literary study does not prepare you to follow up on such a remark.

Among canonical British authors, Austen is exceptional, perhaps unique, in having inspired more than one central society located in the UK.[96] Following the lead of JASNA, which maintains a membership of approximately 4000, Austen aficionados in other parts of the globe have begun their own national societies.[97] The Jane Austen Society of Australia, founded in 1989, includes "scholars, enthusiasts, amateurs and professionals, gathering on equal terms to study and celebrate the genius of Jane Austen."[98] Launched more recently are societies in Argentina, Japan, and Brazil. All of these groups encourage the reading and discussion of Austen's writings, as well as less serious activities such as viewing new film adaptations. Many members of national Austen societies also visit and support English places associated with Austen's life, as I mentioned in Chapter 4. Through annual meetings, regional events, and newsletters, members learn about new publications, both academic and popular, that concern Austen. Many creators of Austen-inspired works have found encouragement from, and an audience among, fellow society members.

Yet the majority of Austen amateurs do not belong to a society. JASNA member Jeanne Kiefer discovered in her survey of 4501 "Janeites"—defined by her as people who had read all six of Austen's novels—that only a quarter of them belonged to their national Austen society.[99] An even smaller percentage of visitors I surveyed at Jane Austen's House Museum in 2009 identified themselves as members of an Austen society.[100] Many factors inhibit lovers of Austen from attending meetings of, or joining, an Austen society. Perceptions of stuffiness, and of silliness, remain. Young readers may well feel that author societies are for older people. (In my own JASNA region, New York, a "Juvenilia" group of younger aficionados has a cutoff, tellingly, of age 45.) While many JASNA regional gatherings are offered free of charge, attending a multi-day JASNA annual meeting, typically held at a high-end city hotel, is not cheap. Thus many an Austen fan remains at home, alone or (like Bridget Jones) in the company of a few friends, finding solace and inspiration in Austen's writings and in works derived from them. Accessible guides to Austen's writings and world, as well as online blogs by and forums for Austen fans, allow every reader, if she or he chooses, to attain new insight into Austen and join—virtually, at least—the company of fellow aficionados.

The Popular Austen, at 200 and Counting

At regular intervals since 1995, claims have been made that Austen's pull on the popular imagination is waning, and another author has been designated "the next Jane Austen." In March 2011, the release of a new feature film version of *Jane Eyre* caused *Washington Post* film critic Monica Hesse to opine, "for two decades, Austen's Janeites have held the public hostage in an infinite Regency-era loop. ... The Charlottans have waited."[101] Hesse contends more seriously that "there might be some latent, dismissive misogyny involved in the concept that there is only enough cultural love for one female literary figure at any given time."[102] Indeed, no one wonders when "the next Shakespeare" will appeal to popular audiences; he and his works are always in style, and apparently infinitely capable of reinvention. Perhaps the same will prove true of Austen.

Austen enjoys an exceptional degree of momentum in our popular culture. Even if her influence begins to wane—which seems unlikely in the short term—it will take several years for all the projects and productions already in development to reach release. And we can expect considerable public attention to Austen's authorship in the decade of the 2010s, thanks to the series of bicentennial anniversaries of publication from October 30, 2011 (commemorating *Sense and Sensibility*) through December 2017 (commemorating *Northanger Abbey* and *Persuasion*). July 18, 2017, the 200th anniversary of Austen's death, will doubtless be recognized internationally too. These dates will resonate strongly for her existing fans, certainly, and media attention to the occasions may pique the curiosity of new readers as well.

As I noted in Chapters 5 and 6, we can also expect to see further imaginative versions of both Austen and her novels, as inspired by recent reworkings and in their turn inspiring still others. Judging by recent hybrids, whatever is uppermost in the popular imagination will join Austen material, with the effect of delighting some audiences and disgusting others. Originality will be ever more challenging to achieve in a crowded field, yet some bold new approaches to Austen are sure to emerge from perspectives we cannot yet guess. It remains to be seen where imaginative creators will take Austen next.

Regardless of what the future holds for Austen's prominence in popular culture, her writings will continue to engage everyday readers and spark their imaginations, as has been the case for more than 200 years. And, of course, scholars will continue to extend the professional arena of Austen studies established close to a century ago. Austen interests and delights us all. If we let down our guard, we can take the opportunity to come together, amateurs and scholars alike, and share what we love and have learned about this exceptional author—and indeed about other writers with whose works we connect. Austen inspires us. Let's inspire each other with the passionate reading practices, scholarly knowledge, and critical tools that we collectively have to share.

Through conversation, we can rediscover and proclaim why literary reading, and the study of literature, matter today.

What does Jane Austen mean to you?

Notes

1 In his short story "The Janeites," which was first published in 1924, Rudyard Kipling depicts an all-male group whose devotion to Austen helped them cope with the Great War. For commentary on "The Janeites" and its importance to Austen reception history, see Claudia L. Johnson, "Austen Cults and Cultures," in *The Cambridge Companion to Jane Austen*, ed. Edward Copeland and Juliet McMaster (Cambridge: Cambridge University Press, 1997), 214–17 and Kathryn Sutherland, *Jane Austen's Textual Lives: From Aeschylus to Bollywood* (Cambridge: Cambridge University Press, 2005), 16–23.

2 Helen Fielding, *Bridget Jones's Diary* (New York: Viking, 1996), 215. Bridget first appeared in Fielding's anonymously written newspaper columns in *The Independent* in 1995.

3 Fielding, *Bridget Jones's Diary*, 88.

4 Helen Fielding, *Bridget Jones: The Edge of Reason* (New York: Viking, 1999), 35.

5 In *Jane Austen in Boca* (New York: St. Martin's Press, 2002), Paula Marantz Cohen both updates the plot of *Pride and Prejudice* and depicts discussions of that novel by amateur readers, residents of a Jewish retirement community in Florida. For a cheerfully bawdy portrayal of a young New York woman, obsessed with Austen, who tries to live as she believes her favorite author would want her to, see Rosemarie Santini, *Sex & Sensibility: The Adventures of a Jane Austen Addict* (New York: Saint Books, 2005). Polly Shulman depicts a teenage Austen devotee in *Enthusiasm* (New York: G. P. Putnam's Sons, 2006), while in *Academy X* (New York: Bloomsbury, 2006) Andrew Trees portrays a high-school English teacher who contrasts his world to Austen's. See also the film version of Fowler's novel: *The Jane Austen Book Club*, written and directed by Robin Swicord (2007; Culver City, CA: Sony Pictures Home Entertainment, 2008), DVD.

6 Marilyn Francus, "Austen Therapy: *Pride and Prejudice* and Popular Culture," *Persuasions On-Line* 30.2 (2010), http://www.jasna.org/persuasions/on-line/vol30no2/francus.html. Francus concentrates on Shannon Hale's *Austenland* (New York: Bloomsbury, 2007) and Alexandra Potter's *Me and Mr. Darcy* (New York: Ballantine Books, 2007), a bestseller in the UK.

7 In the television miniseries *Lost in Austen*, which was broadcast to acclaim in the UK in 2008, the twenty-first-century heroine Amanda Price is so devoted to *Pride and Prejudice* that, when time travel places her among that novel's characters, she feels at home and eventually decides to stay there and marry Darcy herself. Time travel also figures in Laurie Viera Rigler's *Confessions of a Jane Austen Addict* (New York: Dutton, 2007), which follows the adventures of a dedicated Austen lover who must shift for herself in the Regency. Rigler's *Rude Awakenings of a Jane Austen Addict* (New York: Dutton, 2009) traces the adjustment of a woman displaced from Austen's era to present-day Los Angeles, where she ultimately becomes a consultant to film adapters.

8 For a lighthearted depiction of an amateur reader and Austen scholar coming to appreciate each other's points of view—and each other—see Adam Roberts, "Jane Austen and the Masturbating Critic," in *Flirting with Pride & Prejudice: Fresh Perspectives on the Original Chick-Lit Masterpiece*, ed. Jennifer Crusie (Dallas: BenBella Books, 2005). It is worth bearing in mind, too, that some very significant contributions to Austen scholarship have been made by authors without academic affiliations: David Gilson, Deirdre Le Faye, and Brian Southam are prime examples. Southam recounts his early days as an Austen scholar, before he turned to publishing, in "A Life Among the Manuscripts: Following in the Steps of Dr. Chapman," in *A Truth Universally Acknowledged: 33 Great Writers on Why We Read Jane Austen*, ed. Susannah Carson (New York: Random House, 2009), 26–35.

9 Elizabeth Aston, *Writing Jane Austen* (New York: Touchstone, 2010), 19.

10 Ibid., 11.

11 Ibid., 17.

12 Ibid., 18.
13 Ibid., 30.
14 Ibid.
15 Ibid., 31.
16 Ibid., 32.
17 Ibid., 143.
18 Ibid., 54.
19 Ibid., 79, 81.
20 Ibid., 222.
21 Ibid., 63.
22 Ibid., 269.
23 Ibid., 289.
24 Ibid., 295.
25 Ibid., 102, 105.
26 Ibid., 190.
27 Ibid., 42–43.
28 Beth Pattillo, *Jane Austen Ruined My Life* (New York: Guideposts, 2009), 2.
29 Ibid., xi.
30 A. S. Byatt, *Possession: A Romance* (New York: Random House, 1990).
31 Outside the Austen realm, a recent work of popular fiction that turns on the discovery of lost letters by a canonical English woman writer is Jennifer Vandever's *The Brontë Project: A Novel of Passion, Desire, and Good PR* (New York: Shaye Areheart Books, 2005).
32 Pattillo, *Jane Austen Ruined*, 25.
33 Ibid., 28.
34 Ibid., 256.
35 Ibid., 28.
36 Ibid., 57.
37 Ibid., 114.
38 Ibid., 115.
39 Ibid., 230, 231.
40 Ibid., 62. Emma's reference to her father's faith in God's plan is one of few indications in *Jane Austen Ruined My Life* that it is published by a Christian press. Guideposts apparently did not object to Emma thinking of the British Library's holdings as being "the holiest of relics" or of herself, in their presence, as "a worshipper who has stepped too close to the divine." Ibid., 114, 115.
41 Ibid., 91, 97.
42 Ibid., 135.
43 Ibid., 141.
44 Ibid., 144.
45 Ibid., 257.
46 Ibid., 200.
47 Ibid., 21, 250.
48 Ibid., 84, 85.
49 Ibid., 163–64. Emma interprets the face in Cassandra's sketch as looking "a little annoyed but not unpleasant, as if someone had interrupted her work, but since she loved that someone, she would tolerate the interruption. ... I believed, judging from her expression in this authenticated picture, that she'd hated having her image taken with as much ferocity as she adored painting verbal pictures of her characters." Ibid., 162. Pattillo also calls attention to the small size of the Austen portrait "compared with the other great figures of her day, whose images were captured on enormous canvases that dominated the high-ceilinged rooms." Ibid., 163.
50 Ibid., 165.
51 Ibid., 270.
52 Pattillo follows in the footsteps of earlier creators by inventing for the young Austen a new romance, which ends in bereavement much as did Cassandra's engagement to Tom Fowle. Pattillo explores Cassandra's life more fully in *The Dashwood Sisters Tell All* (New York: Guideposts, 2011), which features a "lost" diary of Cassandra's.
53 Like the Jane of the film *Miss Austen Regrets*, who reassures her sister that she has been

happy, Pattillo's Jane expresses her gratitude to Cassandra in a letter written not long before her death: "*I have been very happy to have had you as my life's companion . … My life has been my own, and I would not have lived it otherwise.*" Ibid., 259.

54 Beth Pattillo, *Mr. Darcy Broke My Heart* (New York: Guideposts, 2010), 14.
55 Ibid., 5.
56 Ibid., 48.
57 Ibid., 231.
58 Ibid., 253.
59 Ibid., 254.
60 Ibid., 54.
61 Ibid., 79.
62 Ibid., 131.
63 Ibid., 224, 225.
64 Ibid., 256.
65 In "Sense and Sensible Shoes," Alice Steinbach writes admiringly about the Exeter University summer Austen course she took with Hazel Jones. In *Educating Alice: Adventures of a Curious Woman* (New York: Random House, 2004).
66 "We hope that you will not think of yourselves as American strangers, but as one of us, if you will," Dorothy Darnell, the founder of the JAS, urged Alberta Burke following the latter's public donation of the lock of Austen's hair in her possession. Dorothy Darnell to Alberta Burke, July 26, 1949, Alberta H. and Henry G. Burke Papers and Jane Austen Research Collection, MS 0020, container 8, folder 9, Special Collections and Archives, Goucher College Library (hereafter cited as Burke Collection).
67 J. David Grey to Henry Burke, November 15, 1975, Burke Collection, container 2, folder 12.
68 Both Grey and Joan Mason Hurley were quoted and profiled briefly in the Talk of the Town piece that appeared in the *New Yorker* following JASNA's first meeting, in October 1979, at the Gramercy Park Hotel. "Homage," *New Yorker*, November 5, 1979, 42–43.
69 Joan Austen-Leigh, "The Founding of JASNA," *Persuasions* 15 (1993), http://www.jasna.org/persuasions/printed/number15/austen-leigh.htm. Joan Mason Hurley usually published under the name Austen-Leigh.
70 Austen-Leigh, "The Founding"; Joan Austen-Leigh, "Editorial," *Persuasions* 6 (1984), http://www.jasna.org/persuasions/printed/number6/austen-leigh.htm.
71 Austen-Leigh, "Editorial."
72 Austen-Leigh, "The Founding"; emphasis original.
73 Ibid. JAS annual meetings still follow this essential schedule, although meetings of regional subgroups may vary in content and approach.
74 J. David Grey to Henry Burke, October 21, 1978, Burke Collection, container 2, folder 12.
75 J. David Grey to Sir Hugh Smiley, November 26, 1978, Jane Austen Society of North America Records, 1978–2008, MS 0028, series II, subseries B, folder 1, Special Collections and Archives, Goucher College Library (hereafter cited as JASNA Archives).
76 Austen-Leigh, "The Founding."
77 J. David Grey and Joan Mason Hurley to Henry Burke, January [12?], 1979, Burke Collection, container 2, folder 12.
78 Austen-Leigh, "The Founding."
79 "The Jane Austen Society of North America Constitution and By-Laws," signed by Henry G. Burke, Secretary, May 21, 1979, JASNA Archives, series I, subseries A, folder 1.
80 "The Constitution of the Jane Austen Society," approved July 8, 1950, in *The Jane Austen Society: Report for the Period 1 October, 1949 – 31 December, 1950* (Alton: C. Mills & Co., 1950), 6. The JAS's current aims are broader, including "foster[ing] the appreciation and study of the life, work and times of Jane Austen and the Austen family"; "continu[ing] a programme of scholarly publications concerning Jane Austen and the Austen family"; securing Austen manuscripts and possessions; and "support[ing] the work of the Jane Austen Memorial Trust in maintaining the Museum at Jane Austen's House, Chawton." "Aims of the Society," accessed March 21, 2011, http://www.janeaustensoci.freeuk.com/.

81 Nina Auerbach to J. David Grey, October 31, 1979, Burke Collection, container 2, folder 12.

82 J. David Grey to Henry Burke, November 4, 1979, Burke Collection, container 2, folder 12.

83 J. David Grey, quoted in Austen-Leigh, "The Founding of JASNA"; emphasis original.

84 David J. Gilson to Henry Burke, November 17, 1980, Burke Collection, container 2, folder 8.

85 Austen-Leigh, "Editorial."

86 Lorraine Hanaway to Henry Burke, November 17, 1982, Burke Collection, container 3, folder 17.

87 Jo Modert to JASNA members, September 14, 1981, Burke Collection, container 3, folder 17. Modert is herself an example of a contributor to Austen scholarship from outside the academy: her edition *Jane Austen's Manuscript Letters in Facsimile* (Carbondale, IL: Southern Illinois University Press, 1990), was a labor of love funded by minimal grant support and prepared from home, where she was the primary caregiver of an ailing spouse.

88 George H. Tucker, "Meditation," October 10, 1983, Burke Collection, container 3, folder 18. Tucker is best known among Austen fans for his book *Jane Austen: The Woman: Some Biographical Insights* (New York: St. Martin's Press, 1994).

89 Steve Sikora to JASNA members, October 12, 1981, Burke Collection, container 3, folder 17.

90 Iris Lutz, "Message from the President," *JASNA News: The Newsletter of the Jane Austen Society of America* 26.3 (2010): 3. To date, JASNA has had only one president who is a scholar by profession: Joan Klingel Ray.

91 "About JASNA," accessed March 22, 2011, http://www.jasna.org/info/about.html.

92 "Submissions for *Persuasions* and *Persuasions On-Line*," accessed March 23, 2011, http://www.jasna.org/info/about.html.

93 Roger Sales, *Jane Austen and Representations of Regency England*, new ed. (London: Routledge, 1996), 15.

94 Rigler, *Confessions*, 64.

95 Johnson, "Austen Cults and Cultures," 223.

96 For a description of the culture and activities of the Lewis Carroll Society, see Will Brooker, *Alice's Adventures: Lewis Carroll in Popular Culture* (London: Continuum, 2004). For a recent account of a meeting of the George Eliot/George Henry Lewes Fellowship, see Rebecca Mead, "*Middlemarch* and Me," *New Yorker*, February 14, 2011.

97 "About JASNA."

98 "About JASA," accessed March 23, 2011, http://www.jasa.net.au/jaabout.htm.

99 Jeanne Kiefer, "Anatomy of a Janeite: Results from *The Jane Austen Survey 2008*," *Persuasions On-Line* 29.1 (2008), http://www.jasna.org/persuasions/on-line/vol29no1/kiefer.html.

100 Of the 50 visitors to Jane Austen's House Museum who completed the long version of my survey, only four were members of an Austen society. Survey of visitors to Jane Austen's House Museum, July 13–23, 2009.

101 Monica Hesse, "'Jane Eyre' Movie Rekindles Austen vs. Brontë, the Battle of the Bonnets," *Washington Post*, March 17, 2011, http://www.washingtonpost.com/lifestyle/style/jane-eyre-movie-rekindles-austen-vs-bronte-the-battle-of-the-bonnets/2011/03/08/ABTZY5k_story.html.

102 Ibid.

Bibliography

Adams, Carol, Douglas Buchanan, and Kelly Gresch. *The Bedside, Bathtub &* *Armchair Companion to Jane Austen.* New York: Continuum, 2008.

Aden, Roger C. *Popular Stories and Promised Lands: Fan Cultures and Symbolic Pilgrimages.* Tuscaloosa: University of Alabama Press, 1999.

Alberta H. and Henry G. Burke Papers and Jane Austen Research Collection. Special Collections and Archives. Goucher College Library, Baltimore.

Amis, Martin. "Jane's World." *New Yorker,* January 8, 1996.

Arthur, Sarah. *Dating Mr. Darcy: A Smart Girl's Guide to Sensible Romance.* Wheaton, IL: Tyndale House, 2005.

Aston, Elizabeth. *Writing Jane Austen.* New York: Touchstone, 2010.

Auerbach, Emily. *Searching for Jane Austen.* Madison: University of Wisconsin Press, 2004.

Austen, Henry. "Biographical Notice of the Author." 1817. In Jane Austen, *Persuasion,* edited by Janet Todd and Antje Blank, 326–32. Cambridge: Cambridge University Press, 2006.

Austen, Jane. *The Annotated Persuasion.* Edited by David M. Shapard. New York: Anchor Books, 2010.

—. *The Annotated Pride and Prejudice.* Edited by David M. Shapard. 2004. New York: Anchor Books, 2007.

—. *Emma.* Edited by Richard Cronin and Dorothy McMillan. Cambridge: Cambridge University Press, 2005.

—. *Jane Austen's Letters.* Edited by Deirdre Le Faye. New edn. 1995. Oxford: Oxford University Press, 1997.

—. *Jane Austen's Manuscript Letters in Facsimile.* Edited by Jo Modert. Carbondale, IL: Southern Illinois University Press, 1990.

—. *Juvenilia.* Edited by Peter Sabor. Cambridge: Cambridge University Press, 2006.

—. *Later Manuscripts.* Edited by Janet Todd and Linda Bree. Cambridge: Cambridge University Press, 2009.

—. *Northanger Abbey.* Edited by Barbara M. Benedict and Deirdre Le Faye. Cambridge: Cambridge University Press, 2006.

—. *Persuasion.* Edited by Janet Todd and Antje Blank. Cambridge: Cambridge University Press, 2006.

—. *The Poetry of Jane Austen and the Austen Family.* Edited by David Selwyn. Iowa City: University of Iowa Press, 1996.

—. *Pride & Prejudice.* Adapted by Nancy Butler and Hugo Petrus. New York: Marvel, 2009.

—. *Pride and Prejudice.* Edited by Pat Rogers. Cambridge: Cambridge University Press, 2006.

—. *Pride and Prejudice: An Annotated Edition.* Edited by Patricia Meyer Spacks. Cambridge, MA: The Belknap Press, 2010.

—. *Pride and Prejudice: Insight Edition.* Minneapolis: Bethany House, 2007.

—. *Sense & Sensibility.* Adapted by Nancy Butler and Sonny Liew. New York: Marvel, 2010.

—. *Sense and Sensibility: Insight Edition.* Minneapolis: Bethany House, 2010.

—. *The Works of Jane Austen: Minor Works.* Edited by R. W. Chapman. Rev. ed. Oxford: Oxford University Press, 1988.

Austen, Jane, and Ben H. Winters. *Sense and Sensibility and Sea Monsters.* Philadelphia: Quirk Books, 2009.

Austen, Jane, and Seth Grahame-Smith. *Pride and Prejudice and Zombies.* Philadelphia: Quirk Books, 2009.

—. *Pride and Prejudice and Zombies: The Deluxe Heirloom Edition.* Philadelphia: Quirk Books, 2009.

Austen, Jane, and Wayne Josephson. *Emma and the Vampires.* Naperville, IL: Sourcebooks Landmark, 2010.

Austen-Leigh, J. E. *A Memoir of Jane Austen and Other Family Recollections.* Edited by Kathryn Sutherland. Oxford: Oxford University Press, 2002.

Austen-Leigh, Joan. "Editorial." *Persuasions* 6 (1984): 2–3. http://www.jasna.org/persuasions/printed/number6/austen-leigh.htm.

—. "The Founding of JASNA." *Persuasions* 15 (1993): 7–13. http://www.jasna.org/persuasions/printed/number15/austen-leigh.htm.

—. *Our Own Particular Jane.* Victoria: A Room of One's Own Press, 1975.

Baker, Lindsay Warren, and Amanda Jacobs. *Jane Austen's Pride & Prejudice: A Musical.* Premiered 2006 at the Ohio Light Opera (Wooster, OH). Workshop performance in New York City, February 26, 2007.

Barbara Winn Adams Jane Austen Collection. Special Collections and Archives. Goucher College Library, Baltimore.

Barron, Stephanie. *Jane and the Barque of Frailty: Being a Jane Austen Mystery.* New York: Bantam, 2006.

—. *Jane and the Canterbury Tale: Being a Jane Austen Mystery.* New York: Bantam, 2011.

—. *Jane and the Genius of the Place: Being the Fourth Jane Austen Mystery.* New York: Bantam, 1999.

—. *Jane and the Ghosts of Netley: Being a Jane Austen Mystery.* New York: Bantam, 2003.

—. *Jane and His Lordship's Legacy: Being a Jane Austen Mystery.* New York: Bantam, 2005.

—. *Jane and the Madness of Lord Byron: Being a Jane Austen Mystery.* New York: Bantam, 2010.

—. *Jane and the Man of the Cloth: Being the Second Jane Austen Mystery.* New York: Bantam, 1997.

—. *Jane and the Unpleasantness at Scargrave Manor: Being the First Jane Austen Mystery.* New York: Bantam, 1996.

—. *Jane and the Wandering Eye: Being the Third Jane Austen Mystery.* New York: Bantam, 1998.

Bebris, Carrie. *North by Northanger (Or, The Shades of Pemberley).* New York: Forge, 2006.

Becoming Jane. Directed by Julian Jarrold. Screenplay by Sarah Williams and Kevin Hood. 2007. Burbank, CA: Buena Vista Home Entertainment, 2008. DVD.

Benedict, Barbara M. "Sensibility by the Numbers: Austen's Work as Regency Popular Fiction." In *Janeites: Austen's Disciples and Devotees*, edited by Deidre Lynch, 63–86. Princeton: Princeton University Press, 2000.

Bennett, Veronica. *Cassandra's Sister*. 2006. Cambridge, MA: Candlewick, 2007.

Berdoll, Linda. *Darcy & Elizabeth: Nights and Days at Pemberley*. 1999. Naperville, IL: Sourcebooks Landmark, 2006.

—. *Mr. Darcy Takes a Wife: Pride and Prejudice Continues*. Naperville, IL: Sourcebooks Landmark, 2004.

Berggren, Anne G. "Reading like a Woman." In *Reading Sites: Social Difference and Reader Response*, edited by Patrocinio P. Schweickart and Elizabeth A. Flynn, 166–88. New York: Modern Language Association of America, 2004.

Bermingham, Ann. *Learning to Draw: Studies in the Cultural History of a Polite and Useful Art*. New Haven: Yale University Press, 2000.

Billington, Rachel. *Emma & Knightley: Perfect Happiness in Highbury: A Sequel to Jane Austen's Emma*. Naperville, IL: Sourcebooks Landmark, 2008.

—. *Perfect Happiness: A Sequel to Jane Austen's Emma*. London: Hodder and Stoughton, 1996.

Birchall, Diana. "Eyeing Mrs. Elton: Learning through Pastiche." *Persuasions On-Line* 30.2. (2010). http://www.jasna.org/persuasions/on-line/vol30no2/birchall.html.

Birtwistle, Sue, and Susie Conklin. *The Making of Pride and Prejudice*. London: Penguin and BBC, 1995.

Black, Maggie, and Deirdre Le Faye. *The Jane Austen Cookbook*. London: British Museum Press, 1995.

Blakemore, Erin. *The Heroine's Bookshelf: Life Lessons, from Jane Austen to Laura Ingalls Wilder*. New York: Harper, 2010.

Bloom, Annabella, and Jane Austen. *Pride and Prejudice: The Wild and Wanton Edition*. Avon, MA: Adams Media, 2011.

Bloom, Harold. *How to Read and Why*. New York: Scribner, 2000.

Booth, Alison. "Time-Travel in Dickens' World." In *Literary Tourism and Nineteenth-Century Culture*, edited by Nicola J. Watson, 150–63. Houndmills, Basingstoke: Palgrave Macmillan, 2009.

Bottomer, Phyllis Ferguson. *So Odd a Mixture: Along the Autistic Spectrum in "Pride and Prejudice"*. London: Jessica Kingsley, 2007.

Bour, Isabelle. "The Reception of Jane Austen's Novels in France and Switzerland: The Early Years, 1813–1828." In *The Reception of Jane Austen in Europe*, edited by Anthony Mandal and Brian Southam, 12–33. London: Continuum, 2007.

Bowles, Kate. "Commodifying Austen: The Janeite Culture of the Internet and Commercialization through Product and Television Series Spinoffs." In *Jane Austen on Screen*, edited by Gina Macdonald and Andrew F. Macdonald, 15–21. Cambridge: Cambridge University Press, 2003.

Brant, Marilyn. *According to Jane*. New York: Kensington, 2009.

Bride & Prejudice. Directed by Gurinder Chadha. 2004. Burbank, CA: Buena Vista Home Entertainment, 2005. DVD.

Brinton, Sybil G. *Old Friends and New Fancies: An Imaginary Sequel to the Novels of Jane Austen*. 1914. Naperville, IL: Sourcebooks Landmark, 2007.

Brodie, Laura Fairchild. "Jane Austen and the Common Reader: 'Opinions of *Mansfield Park*,' 'Opinions of *Emma*,' and the Janeite Phenomenon." *Texas Studies in Literature and Language* 37.1 (1995): 54–71.

Brontë, Charlotte, and Sherri Browning Erwin. *Jane Slayre*. New York: Gallery, 2010.

Brooker, Will. *Alice's Adventures: Lewis Carroll in Popular Culture*. London: Continuum, 2004.

—. "A Sort of Homecoming: Fan Viewing and Symbolic Pilgrimage." In *Fandom: Identities and Communities in a Mediated World*, edited by Jonathan Gray, Cornel Sandvoss, and C. Lee Harrington, 149–64. New York: New York University Press, 2007.

Brown, Laurie. *What Would Jane Austen Do?* Naperville, IL: Sourcebooks Casablanca, 2009.

Brownstein, Rachel M. *Why Jane Austen?* New York: Columbia University Press, 2011.

Burt, Richard. "To E- or Not to E-?: Disposing of Schlockspeare in the Age of Digital Media." In *Shakespeare after Mass Media*, edited by Richard Burt, 1–32. New York: Palgrave Macmillan, 2002.

Busse, Kristina, and Karen Hellekson. "Introduction: Work in Progress." In *Fan Fiction and Fan Communities in the Age of the Internet*, edited by Karen Hellekson and Kristina Busse, 5–32. Jefferson, NC: McFarland, 2006.

Byatt, A. S. *Possession: A Romance*. New York: Random House, 1990.

Camden, Jen, and Susan Allen Ford, eds. "Joe Wright's *Pride & Prejudice* (2005)." Special issue, *Persuasions On-Line* 27.2 (2007). http://www.jasna.org/persuasions/on-line/vol27no2/index.html.

Cano López, Marina, and Rosa María García-Periago. "Becoming Shakespeare and Jane Austen in Love: An Intertextual Dialogue between Two Biopics." *Persuasions On-Line* 29.1 (2008). http://www.jasna.org/persuasions/on-line/vol29no1/cano-garcia.html.

Canton, Chamein. *Waiting for Mr. Darcy*. Columbus, MS: Genesis Press, 2009.

Carson, Susannah. Introduction to *A Truth Universally Acknowledged: 33 Great Writers on Why We Read Jane Austen*, edited by Susannah Carson, xi–xx. New York: Random House, 2009.

Castle, Terry. "Was Jane Austen Gay?" In *Boss Ladies, Watch Out!: Essays on Women, Sex, and Writing*, 125–36. New York: Routledge, 2002.

Chabon, Michael. *Manhood for Amateurs: The Pleasures and Regrets of a Husband, Father, and Son*. New York: Harper, 2010.

Chandler, Steve, and Terrence N. Hill. *Two Guys Read Jane Austen*. Bandon, OR: Robert D. Reed Publishers, 2008.

—. *Two Guys Read Moby-Dick*. Bandon, OR: Robert D. Reed Publishers, 2006.

Clueless. Written and directed by Amy Heckerling. 1995. Hollywood: Paramount Pictures, 2005. DVD.

Cohen, Paula Marantz. *Jane Austen in Boca*. New York: St. Martin's Press, 2002.

Collins, James. "Fanny Was Right: Jane Austen as Moral Guide." In *A Truth Universally Acknowledged: 33 Great Writers on Why We Read Jane Austen*, edited by Susannah Carson, 147–55. New York: Random House, 2009.

—. "What Would Jane Do?: How a 19th-Century Spinster Serves as a Moral Compass in Today's World." *Wall Street Journal*, November 14, 2009.

Collins, Rebecca Ann. *The Pemberley Chronicles*. 1997. Naperville, IL: Sourcebooks Landmark, 2008.

"The Constitution of the Jane Austen Society." In *The Jane Austen Society: Report for the Period 1 October, 1949 – 31 December, 1950*, 6. Alton: C. Mills & Co., 1950.

Crang, Mike. "Placing Jane Austen, Displacing England: Touring between Book, History, and Nation." In *Jane Austen and Co.: Remaking the Past in Contemporary Culture*, edited by Suzanne R. Pucci and James Thompson, 111–30. Albany: State University of Albany Press, 2003.

Crawford, Matthew B. *Shop Class as Soulcraft: An Inquiry into the Value of Work.* New York: Penguin Press, 2009.

Cready, Gwyn. *Seducing Mr. Darcy.* New York: Pocket Books, 2008.

Dawkins, Jane. *Letters from Pemberley: The First Year.* 1998. Naperville, IL: Sourcebooks Landmark, 2007.

Derecho, Abigail. "Archontic Literature: A Definition, a History, and Several Theories of Fan Fiction." In *Fan Fiction and Fan Communities in the Age of the Internet*, edited by Karen Hellekson and Kristina Busse, 61–78. Jefferson, NC: McFarland, 2006.

Deresiewicz, William. *A Jane Austen Education: How Six Novels Taught Me about Love, Friendship, and the Things that Really Matter.* New York: Penguin Press, 2011.

Dickson, Rebecca. *Jane Austen: An Illustrated Treasury.* New York: Metro Books, 2008.

"The Divine Jane: Reflections on Austen." Directed by Francesco Carrozzini. 2009. http://www.themorgan.org/video/austen.asp.

Dolby, Sandra K. *Self-Help Books: Why Americans Keep Reading Them.* Urbana: University of Illinois Press, 2005.

Douglas, Kate. "Your Book Changed My Life: Everyday Literary Criticism and Oprah's Book Club." In *The Oprah Affect: Critical Essays on Oprah's Book Club*, edited by Cecilia Konchar Farr and Jaime Harker, 235–52. Albany: State University of Albany Press, 2008.

Dow, Gillian, and Clare Hanson, eds. *Uses of Jane Austen: Twentieth-Century Afterlives.* Houndmills, Basingstoke: Palgrave Macmillan, forthcoming.

Dring, Melissa. "A New Portrait of Jane Austen." *Jane Austen's Regency World* 1 (2003): 5.

Eagleton, Terry. "Afterword." In *The Shakespeare Myth*, edited by Graham Holderness, 203–208. Manchester: Manchester University Press, 1988.

Easton, Celia A. "Dancing Through Austen's Plots: A Pedagogy of the Body." *Persuasions* 28 (2006): 252.

Eckstut, Arielle, and Dennis Ashton. *Pride and Promiscuity: The Lost Sex Scenes of Jane Austen.* New York: Simon & Schuster, 2001.

Edwards, Anne-Marie. *In the Steps of Jane Austen: Walking Tours of Austen's England.* 1991. Madison, WI: Jones Books, 2003.

Elyot, Amanda. *By a Lady: Being the Adventures of an Enlightened American in Jane Austen's England.* New York: Three Rivers Press, 2006.

Emma. Directed by Jim O'Hanlon. Screenplay by Sandy Welch. 2009. Burbank, CA: Warner Home Video, 2010. DVD.

Emma. Written and directed by Douglas McGrath. 1996. Burbank, CA: Buena Vista Home Entertainment, 1999. DVD.

Evans, Muriel Keller. *Jane Austen, Her Golden Years: A Historical Novel Highlighting Her Family and Faith.* N.p.: Xulon Press, 2009.

Fast, Howard. *The Novelist: A Romantic Portrait of Jane Austen.* New York: Samuel French, 1992.

Favret, Mary A. "Free and Happy: Jane Austen in America." In *Janeites: Austen's*

Disciples and Devotees, edited by Deidre Lynch, 166–87. Princeton: Princeton University Press, 2000.

Felski, Rita. *Uses of Literature*. Malden, MA: Blackwell, 2008.

Fergus, Jan. "Hazel Holt's *My Dear Charlotte*: A Novel Based on Jane Austen's *Letters*." *Persuasions On-Line* 30.1 (2009). www.jasna.org/persuasions/on-line/vol30no1/fergus.html.

—. *Jane Austen: A Literary Life*. Houndmills, Basingstoke: Macmillan, 1991.

Fforde, Jasper. *Thursday Next in The Well of Lost Plots*. New York: Viking, 2003.

Fielding, Helen. *Bridget Jones: The Edge of Reason*. New York: Viking, 1999.

—. *Bridget Jones's Diary*. New York: Viking, 1996.

Fish, Stanley. *Is There a Text in This Class?: The Authority of Interpretive Communities*. Cambridge, MA: Harvard University Press, 1982.

Fiske, John. *Understanding Popular Culture*. 2nd ed. London: Routledge, 2010.

Flory, Suzy. *So Long, Status Quo: What I Learned from Women Who Changed the World*. Kansas City: Beacon Hill Press, 2009.

Ford, Michael Thomas. *Jane Bites Back*. New York: Ballantine Books, 2010.

—. *Jane Goes Batty*. New York: Ballantine Books, 2011.

Ford, Susan Allen, and Inger Sigrun Brodey, eds. "The Global Jane Austen." Special issue, *Persuasions On-Line* 28.2 (2008). http://www.jasna.org/persuasions/on-line/vol28no2/index.html.

Ford, Susan Allen, and Gillian Dow, eds. "New Directions in Austen Studies." Special issue, *Persuasions On-Line* 30.2 (2010). http://www.jasna.org/persuasions/on-line/vol30no2/index.html.

Forest, Jennifer. *Jane Austen's Sewing Box: Craft Projects & Stories from Jane Austen's Novels*. London: Murdoch, 2009.

Foster, Shirley. "Americans and Anti-Tourism." In *Literary Tourism and Nineteenth-Century Culture*, edited by Nicola J. Watson, 175–83. Houndmills, Basingstoke: Palgrave Macmillan, 2009.

Fowler, Karen Joy. "Jane and Me." In *Flirting with Pride & Prejudice: Fresh Perspectives on the Original Chick-Lit Masterpiece*, edited by Jennifer Crusie, 219–30. Dallas: BenBella Books, 2005.

—. *The Jane Austen Book Club*. New York: G. P. Putnam's Sons, 2004.

Francus, Marilyn. "Austen Therapy: *Pride and Prejudice* and Popular Culture." *Persuasions On-Line* 30.2 (2010). http://www.jasna.org/persuasions/on-line/vol30no2/francus.html.

Frantz, Sarah S. G. "Darcy's Vampiric Descendants: Austen's Perfect Romance Hero and J. R. Ward's Black Dagger Brotherhood." *Persuasions On-Line* 30.1 (2009). http://www.jasna.org/persuasions/on-line/vol30no1/frantz.html.

Fullerton, Susannah, and Anne Harbers, eds. *Jane Austen: Antipodean Views*. Neutral Bay: Wellington Lane Press, 2001.

Garber, Marjorie. *Quotation Marks*. New York: Routledge, 2002.

—. *Shakespeare and Modern Culture*. New York: Pantheon, 2008.

Gilroy, Amanda. "Our Austen: Fan Fiction in the Classroom." *Persuasions On-Line* 31.1 (2010). http://www.jasna.org/persuasions/on-line/vol31no1/gilroy.html.

Gilson, David. *A Bibliography of Jane Austen*. New edn. Winchester: St. Paul's, 1997.

Gleason, Colleen. Introduction to *Northanger Castle*. In *Bespelling Jane Austen*, by Mary Balogh, Colleen Gleason, Susan Krinard, and Janet Mullany, 94. Ontario: Harlequin, 2010.

Goodman, Allegra. *The Cookbook Collector.* New York: The Dial Press, 2010.

Grahame-Smith, Seth. *Abraham Lincoln: Vampire Hunter.* New York: Grand Central Publishing, 2010.

Grandi, Roberta. "Web Side Stories: Janeites, Fanfictions, and Never Ending Romances." In *Internet Fictions,* edited by Ingrid Hotz-Davies, Anton Kirchhofer, and Sirpa Leppänen, 23–42. Cambridge: Cambridge Scholars Publishing, 2009.

Grange, Amanda. *Mr. Darcy, Vampyre.* Naperville, IL: Sourcebooks, 2009.

Gray, Jonathan, Cornel Sandvoss, and C. Lee Harrington. "Introduction: Why Study Fans?" In *Fandom: Identities and Communities in a Mediated World,* edited by Jonathan Gray, Cornel Sandvoss, and C. Lee Harrington, 1–16. New York: New York University Press, 2007.

Hale, Shannon. *Austenland.* New York: Bloomsbury, 2007.

Halperin, John. *Jane Austen's Lovers and Other Studies in Fiction and History from Austen to Le Carré.* New York: St. Martin's, 1988.

Halsey, Katie. *Jane Austen and Her Readers, 1786–1945.* London: Anthem, 2011.

Hannon, Patrice. *101 Things You Didn't Know about Jane Austen: The Truth about the World's Most Intriguing Romantic Literary Heroine.* New York: Adams Media, 2007.

—. "Austen Novels and Austen Films: Incompatible Worlds?" *Persuasions* 18 (1996): 24–32.

—. *Dear Jane Austen: A Heroine's Guide to Life and Love.* 2005. New York: Plume, 2007.

Harman, Claire. *Jane's Fame: How Jane Austen Conquered the World.* Edinburgh: Canongate, 2009.

Hartley, Jenny. *Reading Groups.* Oxford: Oxford University Press, 2001.

Henderson, Diana. "Shakespeare: The Theme Park." In *Shakespeare after Mass Media,* edited by Richard Burt, 107–26. New York: Palgrave Macmillan, 2002.

Henderson, Lauren. *Jane Austen's Guide to Dating.* New York: Hyperion, 2005.

Herbert, David. "Literary Places, Tourism and the Heritage Experience." *Annals of Tourism Research* 28.2 (2001): 312–33.

Herendeen, Ann. *Pride / Prejudice: A Novel of Mr. Darcy, Elizabeth Bennet, and Their Forbidden Lovers.* New York: Harper, 2010.

Hill, Constance. *Jane Austen: Her Homes and Her Friends.* 1901. Philadelphia: Pavilion Press, 2003.

Hill, Terry. Introduction to *Two Guys Read Moby-Dick.* By Steve Chandler and Terrence N. Hill. Bandon, OR: Robert D. Reed Publishers, 2006.

Hills, Matt. *Fan Cultures.* New York: Routledge, 2002.

—. "Media Academics as Media Audiences: Aesthetic Judgments in Media and Cultural Studies." In *Fandom: Identities and Communities in a Mediated World,* edited by Jonathan Gray, Cornel Sandvoss, and C. Lee Harrington, 33–47. New York: New York University Press, 2007.

Hockensmith, Steve. *Pride and Prejudice and Zombies: Dawn of the Dreadfuls.* Philadelphia: Quirk Books, 2010.

—. *Pride and Prejudice and Zombies: Dreadfully Ever After.* Philadelphia: Quirk Books, 2011.

Hodgdon, Barbara. *The Shakespeare Trade: Performances and Appropriations.* Philadelphia: University of Pennsylvania Press, 1998.

Holderness, Graham. *Cultural Shakespeare: Essays in the Shakespeare Myth.* Hatfield, Hertfordshire: University of Hertfordshire Press, 2001.

Holub, Robert C. *Reception Theory: A Critical Introduction.* London: Routledge, 2002.

Holt, Hazel. *My Dear Charlotte.* New York: Coffeetown Press, 2009.

"Homage," *New Yorker,* November 5, 1979.

Hutcheon, Linda. *A Poetics of Postmodernism: History, Theory, Fiction.* London: Routledge, 1988.

Hyde, Stella. *Literary Lust: The Sexiest Moments in Classic Fiction.* New York: Atria, 2006.

In This Sacred Place. N.p., 2010. Published by the Society of Portrait Sculptors in conjunction with the exhibition of the same name, shown at Winchester Cathedral.

Iser, Wolfgang. *The Act of Reading: A Theory of Aesthetic Response.* Baltimore: Johns Hopkins University Press, 1978.

Iwashita, Chieko. "The Impact of Film, Television and Literature as Popular Culture on Tourism and the Postmodern Gaze." Master's thesis, University of Surrey, 1999.

James, Felicity. "At Home with Jane: Placing Austen in Contemporary Culture." In *Uses of Jane Austen: Twentieth-Century Afterlives,* edited by Gillian Dow and Clare Hanson. Houndmills, Basingstoke: Palgrave Macmillan, forthcoming.

James, Syrie. *The Lost Memoirs of Jane Austen.* New York: Avon, 2008.

The Jane Austen Book Club. Written and directed by Robin Swicord. 2007. Culver City, CA: Sony Pictures Home Entertainment, 2008. DVD.

The Jane Austen Society: Report for the Period October, 1946 – September, 1949. Alton: C. Mills & Co., 1949.

Jane Austen's Emma. Directed by Diarmuid Lawrence. Screenplay by Andrew Davies. 1996. New York: New Video Group, 1999. DVD.

Jane Austen's Northanger Abbey. Directed by Jon Jones. Screenplay by Andrew Davies. 2006. Sherman Oaks, CA: Granada International Media, 2008. DVD.

Jane Austen's Persuasion. Directed by Roger Michell. Screenplay by Nick Dear. 1995. Culver City, CA: Columbia TriStar Home Video, 1999. DVD.

Jane Austen's Sense & Sensibility. Directed by John Alexander. Screenplay by Andrew Davies. Burbank, CA: Warner Home Video, 2008. DVD.

Jane Austen Society of North America Records, 1975–2008. Special Collections and Archives. Goucher College Library, Baltimore.

Jenkins, Henry. *Textual Poachers: Television Fans & Participatory Culture.* New York: Routledge, 1992.

Johnson, Claudia L. "Austen Cults and Cultures." In *The Cambridge Companion to Jane Austen,* edited by Edward Copeland and Juliet McMaster, 211–26. Cambridge: Cambridge University Press, 1997.

—. "The Divine Miss Jane: Jane Austen, Janeites, and the Discipline of Novel Studies." In *Janeites: Austen's Disciples and Devotees,* edited by Deidre Lynch, 25–44. Princeton: Princeton University Press, 2000. Previously published as "The Divine Miss Jane: Jane Austen, Janeites, and the Discipline of Novel Studies." *boundary 2* 23.3 (1996): 143–63.

—. *Jane Austen Cults and Cultures.* Chicago: University of Chicago Press, forthcoming.

—. "Jane Austen's Relics and the Treasures of the East Room." *Persuasions* 28 (2006): 217–29.

Johnson, Claudia L., and Clara Tuite, eds. *A Companion to Jane Austen.* Oxford: Wiley-Blackwell, 2009.

Kaplan, Laurie, ed. "*Emma* on Film." "Occasional Papers No. 3," *Persuasions On-Line,* 1999. http://www.jasna.org/persuasions/on-line/opno3/index.html.

Kaplan, Laurie, Nancy Magnuson, Sydney Roby, and Barbara Simons. *"Such a lovely display of what imagination does": A Guide to the Jane Austen Collection of the Julia Rogers Library, Goucher College.* 4th edn. Baltimore: Goucher College Library, 1996.

Kaufman, Rona. "'That, My Dear, Is Called Reading': Oprah's Book Club and the Construction of a Readership." In *Reading Sites: Social Difference and Reader Response*, edited by Patrocinio P. Schweickart and Elizabeth A. Flynn, 221–55. New York: Modern Language Association of America, 2004.

Keen, Andrew. *The Cult of the Amateur: How Blogs, MySpace, YouTube, and the Rest of Today's User-Generated Media Are Destroying Our Economy, Our Culture, and Our Values.* New York: Doubleday, 2008.

Kessel, John. "Pride and Prometheus." In *The Baum Plan for Financial Independence and Other Stories*, 279–315. Easthampton, MA: Small Beer Press, 2008.

Keynes, Geoffrey. *A Bibliography of Jane Austen.* London: Nonesuch Press, 1929.

Kieffer, Jeanne. "Anatomy of a Janeite: Results from *The Jane Austen Survey 2008.*" *Persuasions On-Line* 29.1 (2008). http://www.jasna.org/persuasions/on-line/vol29no1/kiefer.html.

Kipling, Rudyard. "The Janeites." In *Debits and Credits*, 124–49. Garden City, NJ: Doubleday, Page & Company, 1926.

Kirkham, Margaret. "Portraits." In *Jane Austen in Context*, edited by Janet Todd, 68–79. Cambridge: Cambridge University Press, 2005.

Krinard, Susan. Introduction to *Bespelling Jane Austen*, by Mary Balogh, Colleen Gleason, Susan Krinard, and Janet Mullany, 6–7. Ontario: Harlequin, 2010.

Lane, Maggie, and David Selwyn, eds. *Jane Austen: A Celebration.* Manchester: Fyfield Books, 2001.

Lanier, Douglas. "Shakespeare™: Myth and Biographical Fiction." In *The Cambridge Companion to Shakespeare and Popular Culture*, edited by Robert Shaughnessy, 93–113. Cambridge: Cambridge University Press, 2007.

—. *Shakespeare and Modern Popular Culture.* Oxford: Oxford University Press, 2002.

Le Faye, Deirdre. *A Chronology of Jane Austen and Her Family.* Cambridge: Cambridge University Press, 2006.

Leithart, Peter. *Jane Austen.* Nashville: Thomas Nelson, 2009.

—. *Miniatures and Morals: The Christian Novels of Jane Austen.* Moscow, ID: Canon Press, 2004.

Lewis, Kelley Penfield. "The Trouble with Happy Endings: Conflicting Narratives in Oprah's Book Club." In *The Oprah Affect: Critical Essays on Oprah's Book Club*, edited by Cecilia Konchar Farr and Jaime Harker, 211–34. Albany: State University of New York Press, 2008.

Long, Elizabeth. *Book Clubs: Women and the Uses of Reading in Everyday Life.* Chicago: University of Chicago Press, 2003.

Lost in Austen. Directed by Dan Zeff. Screenplay by Guy Andrews. 2008. Chatworth, CA: Image Entertainment, 2009. DVD.

Lutz, Iris. "Message from the President." *JASNA News: The Newsletter of the Jane Austen Society of America* 26.3 (2010): 3.

Lynch, Deidre. *At Home in English: A Cultural History of the Love of Literature.* Chicago: University of Chicago Press, forthcoming.

—. "At Home with Jane Austen." In *Cultural Institutions of the Novel*, edited by Deidre Lynch and William B. Warner, 159–92. Durham, NC: Duke University Press, 1996.

—. "Introduction: Sharing with Our Neighbors." In *Janeites: Austen's Disciples and Devotees*, edited by Deidre Lynch, 3–24. Princeton: Princeton University Press, 2000.

—, ed. *Janeites: Austen's Disciples and Devotees*. Princeton: Princeton University Press, 2000.

Lynch, Deidre Shauna. "Cult of Jane Austen." In *Jane Austen in Context*, edited by Janet Todd, 111–120. Cambridge: Cambridge University Press, 2005.

—. "Sequels." In *Jane Austen in Context*, edited by Janet Todd, 160–68. Cambridge: Cambridge University Press, 2005.

Macdonald, Gina, and Andrew F. Macdonald, eds. *Jane Austen on Screen*. Cambridge: Cambridge University Press, 2003.

Machor, James L., and Philip Goldstein, eds. *Reception Study: From Literary Theory to Cultural Studies*. London: Routledge, 2000.

Magnuson, Nancy. "A Collectors' Love Story: The Henry and Alberta Burke Collection at Goucher College." Podcast audio. December 13, 2008. http://www.omahapubliclibrary.org/whats-hot/podcasts.

Mandal, Anthony, and Brian Southam, eds. *The Reception of Jane Austen in Europe*. London: Continuum, 2007.

Mantel, Hilary. "Jane Austen." In *Literary Genius: 25 Classic Writers Who Define English & American Literature*, edited by Joseph Epstein, 75–82. Philadelphia: Paul Dry Books, 2007.

Margolis, Harriet. "Janeite Culture: What Does the Name 'Jane Austen' Authorize?" In *Jane Austen on Screen*, edited by Gina Macdonald and Andrew F. Macdonald, 22–43. Cambridge: Cambridge University Press, 2003.

Marshall, Gail. "Women Re-Read Shakespeare Country." In *Literary Tourism and Nineteenth-Century Culture*, edited by Nicola J. Watson, 95–105. Houndmills, Basingstoke: Palgrave Macmillan, 2009.

McEwan, Ian. *Atonement*. New York: Doubleday, 2001.

McGee, Micki. *Self-Help, Inc.: Makeover Culture in American Life*. Oxford: Oxford University Press, 2005.

Mead, Rebecca. "*Middlemarch* and Me." *New Yorker*, February 14, 2011.

Meyer, Stephenie. *Twilight*. 2005. New York: Little, Brown, 2008.

Miller, D. A. *Jane Austen: Or The Secret of Style*. Princeton: Princeton University Press, 2003.

Miss Austen Regrets. Directed by Jeremy Lovering. Screenplay by Gwyneth Hughes. Burbank, CA: Warner Home Video, 2008. DVD.

Monaghan, David, Ariane Hudelet, and John Wiltshire. *The Cinematic Jane Austen: Essays on the Filmic Sensibility of the Novels*. Jefferson, NC: McFarland, 2009.

Morefield, Kenneth R. "'Emma Could Not Resist': Complicity and the Christian Reader." *Persuasions* 25 (2003): 197–204.

Moser, Nancy. *Just Jane: A Novel of Jane Austen's Life*. Minneapolis: Bethany House, 2007.

Mukerjee, Ankhi. "'What is a Classic?': International Literary Criticism and the Classic Question." *PMLA* 125.4 (2010): 1026–42.

Mullany, Janet. *Jane and the Damned*. New York: Avon, 2010.

—. *Jane Austen: Blood Persuasion*. New York: Avon, 2011.

Munford, Rebecca. "'The Future of Pemberley': Emma Tennant, The 'Classic Progression' and Literary Trespassing." In *Uses of Jane Austen: Twentieth-Century*

Afterlives, edited by Gillian Dow and Clare Hanson. Houndmills, Basingstoke: Palgrave Macmillan, forthcoming.

Myer, Valerie Grosvenor. *Jane Austen: Obstinate Heart: A Biography*. New York: Arcade, 1997.

Nafisi, Azar. *Reading Lolita in Tehran: A Memoir in Books*. New York: Random House, 2003.

Nugent, Benjamin. "The Nerds of *Pride and Prejudice*." In *A Truth Universally Acknowledged: 33 Great Writers on Why We Read Jane Austen*, edited by Susannah Carson, 90–94. New York: Random House, 2009.

O'Farrell, Mary Ann. "Austenian Subcultures." In *A Companion to Jane Austen*, edited by Claudia L. Johnson and Clara Tuite, 478–87. Oxford: Wiley-Blackwell, 2009.

—. "'Bin Laden a Huge Jane Austen Fan': Jane Austen in Contemporary Political Discourse." In *Uses of Jane Austen: Twentieth-Century Afterlives*, edited by Gillian Dow and Clare Hanson. Houndmills, Basingstoke: Palgrave Macmillan, forthcoming.

—. "Jane Austen's Friendship." In *Janeites: Austen's Disciples and Devotees*, edited by Deidre Lynch, 45–62. Princeton: Princeton University Press, 2000.

Olsen, Kirstin. *All Things Austen: A Concise Encyclopedia of Austen's World*. Westport, CT: Greenwood Press, 2008.

—. *All Things Austen: An Encyclopedia of Austen's World*. 2 vols. Westport, CT: Greenwood Press, 2005.

O'Rourke, Sally Smith. *The Man Who Loved Jane Austen*. New York: Kensington, 2006.

Osborne, Laurie. "Harlequin Presents: That '70s Shakespeare and Beyond." In *Shakespeare after Mass Media*, edited by Richard Burt, 127–49. New York: Palgrave Macmillan, 2002.

Park, You-me, and Rajeswari Sunder Rajan, eds. *The Postcolonial Jane Austen*. London: Routledge, 2000.

Parker, Pamela Corpron. "Elizabeth Gaskell and Literary Tourism." In *Literary Tourism and Nineteenth-Century Culture*, edited by Nicola J. Watson, 128–38. Houndmills, Basingstoke: Palgrave Macmillan, 2009.

Parrill, Sue. *Jane Austen on Film and Television: A Critical Study of the Adaptations*. Jefferson, NC: McFarland, 2002.

Parry, Sarah. "The Pemberley Effect: Austen's Legacy to the Historic House Industry." *Persuasions* 30 (2008): 113–22.

Pattillo, Beth. *The Dashwood Sisters Tell All*. New York: Guideposts, 2011.

—. *Jane Austen Ruined My Life*. New York: Guideposts, 2009.

—. *Mr. Darcy Broke My Heart*. New York: Guideposts, 2010.

Pearson, Roberta. "Bachies, Bardies, Trekkies, and Sherlockians." In *Fandom: Identities and Communities in a Mediated World*, edited by Jonathan Gray, Cornel Sandvoss, and C. Lee Harrington, 98–109. New York: New York University Press, 2007.

Pimenova, Daria. "Fan Fiction: Between Text, Conversation, and Genre." In *Internet Fictions*, edited by Ingrid Hotz-Davies, Anton Kirchhofer, and Sirpa Leppänen, 44–61. Cambridge: Cambridge Scholars Publishing, 2009.

Pitkeathley, Jill. *Cassandra & Jane: A Jane Austen Novel*. 2004. New York: Harper, 2008.

—. *Dearest Cousin Jane: A Jane Austen Novel*. New York: Harper, 2010.

Poovey, Mary. *The Proper Lady and the Woman Writer: Ideology as Style in the Works of*

Mary Wollstonecraft, Mary Shelley, and Jane Austen. Chicago: University of Chicago Press, 1984.

Potter, Alexandra. *Me and Mr. Darcy*. New York: Ballantine Books, 2007.

Pride & Prejudice. Directed by Joe Wright. Screenplay by Deborah Moggach. 2005. Universal City, CA: Universal Studios, 2006. DVD.

Pride and Prejudice. Directed by Andrew Black. Excel Entertainment Group, 2003. DVD.

Pride and Prejudice. Directed by Cyril Coke. Screenplay by Fay Weldon. 1980. Burbank, CA: Warner Home Video, 2004. DVD.

Pride and Prejudice. Directed by Robert Z. Leonard. 1940. Burbank, CA: Warner Home Video, 2006. DVD.

Pride and Prejudice: The Special Edition. Directed by Simon Langton. Screenplay by Andrew Davies. 1995. New York: New Video, 2001. DVD.

Pucci, Suzanne R., and James Thompson, eds. *Jane Austen and Co.: Remaking the Past in Contemporary Culture*. Albany: State University of Albany Press, 2003.

Pugh, Sheenagh. *The Democratic Genre: Fan Fiction in a Literary Context*. Bridgend, Wales: Seren, 2005.

Radway, Janice A. *A Feeling for Books: The Book-of-the-Month Club, Literary Taste, and Middle-Class Desire*. Chapel Hill, NC: University of North Carolina Press, 1997.

—. *Reading the Romance: Women, Patriarchy, and Popular Literature*. 1984. London: Verso, 1987.

Ray, Joan Klingel. *Jane Austen for Dummies®*. Hoboken, NJ: Wiley, 2006.

—. "Jane Austen for Smarties." Plenary talk at the Annual General Meeting of the Jane Austen Society of North America, Chicago, IL, October 2008.

Reeve, Katharine. *Jane Austen in Bath: Walking Tours of the Writer's City*. New York: The Little Bookroom, 2006.

Regis, Pamela. *A Natural History of the Romance Novel*. Philadelphia: University of Pennsylvania Press, 2003.

"Relics." In *The Jane Austen Society: Report for 1951*, 4–5. Alton: C. Mills & Co., 1951.

Richardson, Cheryl. "Common Sense: A Life Coach on Austen." *Masterpiece*. Last modified March 28, 2008. http://www.pbs.org/wgbh/masterpiece/senseand-sensibility/coaching_pt1.html.

Rigler, Laurie Viera. *Confessions of a Jane Austen Addict*. New York: Dutton, 2007.

—. *Rude Awakenings of a Jane Austen Addict*. New York: Dutton, 2009.

Roberts, Adam. "Jane Austen and the Masturbating Critic." In *Flirting with Pride & Prejudice: Fresh Perspectives on the Original Chick-Lit Masterpiece*, edited by Jennifer Crusie, 51–62. Dallas: BenBella Books, 2005.

Ross, Josephine. *Jane Austen: A Companion*. 2002. New Brunswick, NJ: Rutgers University Press, 2007.

—. *Jane Austen's Guide to Good Manners: Compliments, Charades & Horrible Blunders*. Illustrated by Henrietta Webb. New York: Bloomsbury, 2006.

Mansfield Park. Written and directed by Patricia Rozema. 1999. Burbank, CA: Buena Vista Home Entertainment, 2000. DVD.

Ryskamp, Charles. Preface to *Jane Austen: Letters & Manuscripts in the Pierpont Morgan Library*, 7–11. New York: Stinehour Press, 1975.

Sachs, Marilyn. "Sequels to Jane Austen." In *The Jane Austen Handbook*, ed. J. David Grey with Brian Southam and A. Walton Litz, 374–76. London: Athlone Press, 1986.

Sales, Roger. *Jane Austen and Representations of Regency England.* New edn. London: Routledge, 1996.

Sanders, Julie. *Adaptation and Appropriation.* London: Routledge, 2006.

—. *Novel Shakespeares: Twentieth-Century Women Novelists and Appropriation.* Manchester: Manchester University Press, 2001.

Sanderson, Caroline. *A Rambling Fancy: In the Footsteps of Jane Austen.* London: Cadogan Guides, 2006.

Sandvoss, Cornel. "The Death of the Reader?: Literary Theory and the Study of Texts in Popular Culture." In *Fandom: Identities and Communities in a Mediated World,* edited by Jonathan Gray, Cornel Sandvoss, and C. Lee Harrington, 19–32. New York: New York University Press, 2007.

Santini, Rosemarie. *Sex & Sensibility: The Adventures of a Jane Austen Addict.* New York: Saint Books, 2005.

Schine, Cathleen. *The Three Weissmans of Westport.* New York: Sarah Crichton Books / Farrar, Straus and Giroux, 2010.

Schmidt, Shannon McKenna, and Joni Rendon. *Novel Destinations: Literary Landmarks from Jane Austen's Bath to Ernest Hemingway's Key West.* Washington, D.C.: National Geographic, 2008.

Schofer, Yvonne. "Percival H(orace) Muir." In *Twentieth-Century British Book Collectors and Bibliographers: First Series,* edited by William Baker and Kenneth Womack. Detroit: Gale Research, 1999. http://go.galegroup.com.librda.mville.edu:2048/.

Schweickart, Patrocinio P., and Elizabeth A. Flynn. Introduction to *Reading Sites: Social Difference and Reader Response,* edited by Patrocinio P. Schweickart and Elizabeth A. Flynn, 1–38. New York: Modern Language Association of America, 2004.

Sense & Sensibility. Directed by John Alexander. Screenplay by Andrew Davies. 2007. Burbank, CA: Warner Home Video, 2008. DVD.

Sense and Sensibility. Directed by Ang Lee. Screenplay by Emma Thompson. 1995. Culver City, CA: Columbia TriStar Home Video, 1999. DVD.

Shulman, Polly. *Enthusiasm.* New York: G. P. Putnam's Sons, 2006.

Simons, Judy. "Classics and Trash: Reading Austen in the 1990s." *Women's Writing* 5 (1998): 27–39.

—. "Jane Austen and Popular Culture." In *A Companion to Jane Austen,* edited by Claudia L. Johnson and Clara Tuite, 467–77. Oxford: Wiley-Blackwell, 2009.

Smith, Debra White. *Central Park.* Eugene, OR: Harvest House, 2005.

—. *First Impressions.* Eugene, OR: Harvest House, 2004.

—. *Reason and Romance.* Eugene, OR: Harvest House, 2004.

—. *What Jane Austen Taught Me about Love and Romance.* Eugene, OR: Harvest House, 2007.

Smith, Lori. *A Walk with Jane Austen: A Journey into Adventure, Love & Faith.* Colorado Springs: WaterBrook, 2007.

—. *The Single Truth: Challenging the Misconceptions of Singleness with God's Consuming Truth.* Shippensburg, PA: Treasure House, 2002.

Solender, Elsa A. "Second Thoughts." In *Dancing with Mr Darcy: Stories Inspired by Jane Austen and Chawton House,* 21–29. Dinas Powys, Wales: Honno, 2009.

Southam, B. C. "A Life Among the Manuscripts: Following in the Steps of Dr. Chapman." In *A Truth Universally Acknowledged: 33 Great Writers on Why We Read Jane Austen,* edited by Susannah Carson, 26–35. New York: Random House, 2009.

—, ed. *Jane Austen: The Critical Heritage.* 2 vols. London: Routledge & Kegan Paul, 1968, 1987.

Spence, Jon. *Becoming Jane Austen.* London: Hambledon and London, 2003.

Squires, Claire. *Marketing Literature: The Making of Contemporary Writing in Britain.* Houndmills, Basingstoke: Palgrave Macmillan, 2009.

Steinbach, Alice. *Educating Alice: Adventures of a Curious Woman.* New York: Random House, 2004.

Stovel, Bruce. "'The Sentient Target of Death': Jane Austen's Prayers." In *Jane Austen's Business: Her World and Her Profession,* edited by Juliet McMaster and Bruce Stovel, 192–205. New York: St. Martin's, 1996.

Sullivan, Margaret C. *The Jane Austen Handbook: A Sensible Yet Elegant Guide to Her World.* Philadelphia: Quirk Books, 2007.

Sutherland, Kathryn. *Jane Austen's Textual Lives: From Aeschylus to Bollywood.* Cambridge: Cambridge University Press, 2005.

Szereto, Mitzi. *Pride and Prejudice: Hidden Lusts.* Berkeley: Cleis Press, 2011.

Tabor, Stephen. "Sir Geoffrey Langdon Keynes." In *Twentieth-Century British Book Collectors and Bibliographers: First Series,* edited by William Baker and Kenneth Womack. Detroit: Gale Research, 1999. http://go.galegroup.com.librda.mville. edu:2048/.

Taylor, Gary. "Afterword: The Incredible Shrinking Bard." In *Shakespeare and Appropriation,* edited by Christy Desmet and Robert Sawyer, 197–205. London: Routledge, 1999.

Tennant, Emma. *Emma in Love: Jane Austen's Emma Continued.* 1996. London: Fourth Estate, 1997.

Thompson, Allison. "Trinkets and Treasures: Consuming Jane Austen." *Persuasions On-Line* 28.2 (2008). http://www.jasna.org/persuasions/on-line/vol28no2/ thompson.htm.

Tolstoy, Leo, and Ben H. Winters. *Android Karenina.* Philadelphia: Quirk Books, 2010.

Tomalin, Claire. *Jane Austen: A Life.* New York: Alfred A. Knopf, 1997.

Trollope, Joanna. "Homecoming." *Persuasions* 25 (2003): 21–25.

Trees, Andrew. *Academy X.* New York: Bloomsbury, 2006.

Troost, Linda, and Sayre Greenfield. "Introduction: Watching Ourselves Watching." In *Jane Austen in Hollywood,* edited by Linda Troost and Sayre Greenfield, 2nd ed., 1–12. Lexington: University Press of Kentucky, 2001.

—, eds. *Jane Austen in Hollywood.* 2nd ed. Lexington: University Press of Kentucky, 2001.

Tucker, George H. *Jane Austen: The Woman: Some Biographical Insights.* New York: St. Martin's Press, 1994.

Tulloch, John. "Fans of Chekhov: Re-Approaching 'High Culture.'" In *Fandom: Identities and Communities in a Mediated World,* edited by Jonathan Gray, Cornel Sandvoss, and C. Lee Harrington, 110–22. New York: New York University Press, 2007.

Tushnet, Rebecca. "Copyright Law, Fan Practices, and the Rights of the Author." In *Fandom: Identities and Communities in a Mediated World,* edited by Jonathan Gray, Cornel Sandvoss, and C. Lee Harrington, 60–71. New York: New York University Press, 2007.

Tyler, Natalie. *The Friendly Jane Austen: A Well-Mannered Introduction to a Lady of Sense & Sensibility.* 1999. New York: Penguin, 2001.

Vandever, Jennifer. *The Brontë Project: A Novel of Passion, Desire, and Good PR.* New York: Shaye Areheart Books, 2005.

Villaseñor, Alice Marie. "Women Readers and the Victorian Jane Austen." PhD diss., University of Southern California, 2009. *Dissertations & Theses: Full Text* (AAT 3389576).

Voights-Virckow, Eckhart, ed. *Janespotting and Beyond: English Heritage Retrovisions Since the Mid-1990s.* Tübingen: GunterNarrVerlag, 2004.

Wakefield, Julie. "Austenonly.com." *JASNA News: The Newsletter of the Jane Austen Society of America* 26.3 (2010): 18.

Ward, Eucharista. *A Match for Mary Bennet: Can a Serious Young Lady Ever Find Her Way to Love?* Naperville, IL: Sourcebooks Landmark, 2009.

Waters, Sarah. Foreword to *Dancing with Mr Darcy: Stories Inspired by Jane Austen and Chawton House*, 1–4. Dinas Powys, Wales: Honno, 2009.

Watson, Nicola J. Introduction to *Literary Tourism and Nineteenth-Century Culture*, edited by Nicola J. Watson, 1–12. Houndmills, Basingstoke: Palgrave Macmillan, 2009.

—. "Rambles in Literary London." In *Literary Tourism and Nineteenth-Century Culture*, edited by Nicola J. Watson, 139–49. Houndmills, Basingstoke: Palgrave Macmillan, 2009.

—. *The Literary Tourist.* Houndmills, Basingstoke: Palgrave Macmillan, 2006.

Webster, Emma Campbell. *Lost in Austen: Create Your Own Jane Austen Adventure.* New York: Riverhead Books, 2007.

Welland, Freydis Jane. "The History of Jane Austen's Writing Desk." *Persuasions* 30 (2008): 125–28.

Wells, Juliette. "Austen's Adventures in American Popular Fiction, 1996–2006." In "New Directions in Austen Studies," edited by Susan Allen Ford and Gillian Dow, special issue, *Persuasions On-Line* 30.2 (2010). http://www.jasna.org/persuasions/on-line/vol30no2/wells.html.

—. "The Closeness of Sisters: Imagining Cassandra and Jane." *Persuasions On-Line* 30.1 (2009). http://www.jasna.org/persuasions/on-line/vol30no1/wells.html.

—. "From Schlockspeare to Austenpop." In "Shakespeare and Austen," edited by Lisa Hopkins, special issue, *Shakespeare* 6:4 (2010): 446–62.

—. "Jane Austen in Mollywood: Mainstreaming Mormonism in Andrew Black's *Pride & Prejudice* (2003)." In *Peculiar Portrayals: Mormons on the Page, Stage, and Screen*, edited by Mark T. Decker and Michael Austin, 163–82. Utah State University Press, 2010.

—. "Mothers of Chick Lit?: Women Writers, Readers, and Literary History." In *Chick Lit: The New Woman's Fiction*, edited by Suzanne Ferriss and Mallory Young, 47–70. New York: Routledge, 2006.

—. "Seeking Austen, from Abroad: Lori Smith's Memoir *A Walk with Jane Austen* (2007)." In "Austen Abroad," special issue, *Transnational Literature* 1.2 (2009). http://dspace.flinders.edu.au/dspace/bitstream/2328/3412/1/Seeking%20Austen.pdf

—. "Shades of Austen in Ian McEwan's *Atonement.*" *Persuasions* 30 (2008): 101–11.

—. "True Love Waits: Austen and the Christian Romance in the Contemporary U.S." In "The Global Jane Austen," edited by Susan Allen Ford and Inger Sigrun Brody, special issue, *Persuasions On-Line* 28.2 (2008). http://www.jasna.org/persuasions/on-line/vol28no2/wells.htm.

West, Louise. "A Happy House." *Jane Austen's Regency World* 1 (2003): 11.

Westover, Paul. "How America 'Inherited' Literary Tourism." In *Literary Tourism and Nineteenth-Century Culture*, edited by Nicola J. Watson, 184–95. Houndmills, Basingstoke: Palgrave Macmillan, 2009.

White, Laura Mooneyham. *Jane Austen's Anglicanism*. Aldershot, Hampshire: Ashgate, 2011.

Wilkes, Diane. *Tarot of Jane Austen*. Turin: Lo Scarabeo, 2006.

Wilson, Barbara Ker. *The Lost Years of Jane Austen*. Berkeley: Ulysses Press, 2009. Previously published as *Antipodes Jane: A Novel of Jane Austen in Australia*. New York: Viking, 1985.

Wiltshire, John. "Afterword: On Fidelity." In *The Cinematic Jane Austen: Essays on the Filmic Sensibility of the Novels*, by David Monaghan, Ariane Hudelet, and John Wiltshire, 160–70. Jefferson, NC: McFarland, 2009.

—. "Jane Austen's England, Jane Austen's World." In *Jane Austen: Introductions and Interventions*, 108–20. London: Palgrave Macmillan, 2006.

—. *Recreating Jane Austen*. Cambridge: Cambridge University Press, 2001.

—. "Why Do We *Read* Jane Austen?" In *A Truth Universally Acknowledged: 33 Great Writers on Why We Read Jane Austen*, edited by Susannah Carson, 163–74. New York: Random House, 2009.

Woolf, Virginia. *The Common Reader*. 1925. New York: Harcourt, 1984.

Wright, Andrew. "Jane Austen Adapted." *Nineteenth-Century Fiction* 30.3 (1975): 421–53.

"Your Jane Austen: What Do You Think?" Interview with Angela Barlow. *Jane Austen's Regency World* 27 (2007): 45.

Index